HELL GATE

from Bonnie VS

HELL GATE

The Story of the Family That Settled Harlem
As Part of the Dutch Colony
That Became New York

Dorothy Hayden Truscott

MORGAN HALL

PUBLICATIONS

Cover: One of the earliest views of the Manhattan skyline, credited to Augustine Hermann, surveyor and cartographer (Courtesy of W. C. Snedeker)

Copyright © 2002, 2004

Printed in the U.S.A.

Project management/design/composition by MorganHall Publications, P.O. Box 216, Harvard, Massachusetts 01451

ISBN: 0-971-97561-2

To my husband, Alan, and my daughter, Catherine,
for their unstinting help at every stage of the earlier
edition and this paperback edition

—

Also to Banning Replier and Arthur Pogran,
who have made many constructive
and helpful suggestions

Table of Contents

MAPS

PART ONE

Letters from Rachel   1

PART TWO

Jan's Story   123

APPENDICES

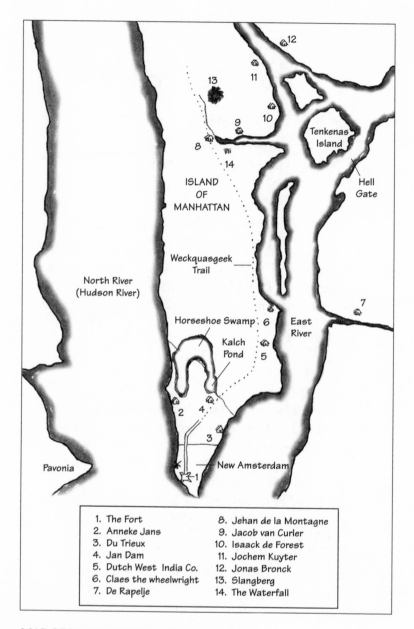

1. The Fort
2. Anneke Jans
3. Du Trieux
4. Jan Dam
5. Dutch West India Co.
6. Claes the wheelwright
7. De Rapelje
8. Jehan de la Montagne
9. Jacob van Curler
10. Isaack de Forest
11. Jochem Kuyter
12. Jonas Bronck
13. Slangberg
14. The Waterfall

MAP OF MANHATTAN, 1639

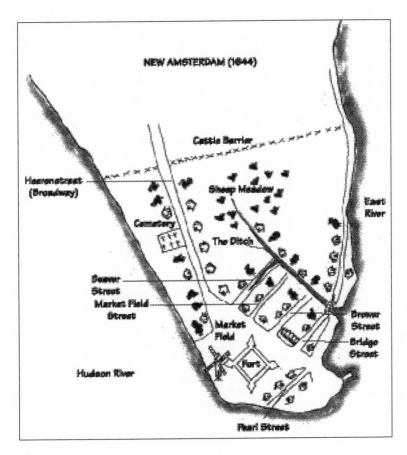

MAP OF NEW AMSTERDAM, 1644

PART ONE

—

Letters from Rachel

Zuider Zee

This 26th day of September
In the Year of Our Lord 1636
On board the *Rensselaerswyck*

Dearest Margariet,

It was so kind of you and Crispin to see us off from Amsterdam. Long after the crowd on the pier had faded into the distance, I could still recognize your bright orange scarf waving.

So far the children have behaved well, much better than on the canal journey from Leyden to Amsterdam. As I write I am sitting on one of the large wooden chests lashed to the main deck. You will scarcely believe it but there are three cows nearby, munching away on a pile of fodder and quite oblivious to their unconventional surroundings. An over-sized cat surveys the milk-supply through slitted eyes as she weighs the odds of being kicked against the pleasure of a pull at the cream. Little Rachel is fascinated.

Today the Zuider Zee is so calm that Jesse is able to walk about with only his small cane. Jehan does not like him to use a crutch.

"We live in a cruel world, my dear. Its face is set against the deformed. Let the boy stand erect and walk slowly with a cane if he must, but not a crutch."

And Jesse does. In fact his deliberate, almost dignified pace makes him seem older and wiser than his seven years. Only when he is hurried or agitated does his bad leg drag pathetically. His thin pinched face is not a little boy's face either. How I wish I could get some meat on that child.

At the moment the two boys are sitting on the deck playing with their father's chess set. Jesse is hunched awkwardly over the board, concentrating, but Jan does not have the patience. He is sprawled on his back waving his legs in the air as he waits for his turn. Did I tell you that Jehan gives the boys two hours of instruction every day? Jesse is coming along well with his Latin. Jan has not started Latin yet but he is very good with his numbers.

Another odd thing. The ship's small boat is covered with netting and serves to house chickens! Suppose the *Rensselaerswyck* sinks. Will all that poultry float away to safety while the rest of us go down with the ship?

Anyway, this morning Jan managed to crawl inside with the chickens. After he was washed and spanked I asked him why he did it.

"I had to count 'em Mama. Chickens don't stand still y'know."

The *Rensselaerswyck* has 38 passengers including 6 women, and a crew of 12. About half the passengers sleep in the great cabin where our family has four berths, two lower and two upper. Jehan and I sleep in one lower and Jesse and Little Rachel share the other. My brother Isaack and Jan each have one of the uppers which are slightly narrower. There is a curtain that I can draw for privacy but rarely do. You know how I hate the feeling of being shut in.

The less fortunate passengers sleep below deck where there are no portholes and you cannot even stand up straight without hitting your head. I have not been down and do not intend to go.

I promised to write about all our adventures but so far we have had none. This will get posted from the Island of Texel at the north end of the Zuider Zee.

Continued September 28th

This morning we had a scare. Jan disappeared. One minute he was playing chess with Jesse and the next minute he had vanished and Jesse was playing both sides of the board himself. He said Jan quit.

Of course I looked in the ship's boat first. Nothing but chickens. I checked the latrines, smelly wooden boxes slung over the rails. We keep a chamber pot under our bunk but Jan likes to use a latrine like a sailor. (He has to stand on a keg to reach.) I inspected the ship's cannon. Still no Jan.

Jehan was part of an important-looking group of men gathered by the mainmast. (At 43 my husband is the oldest on board—also the most dignified.) All were smoking their long clay pipes and discussing the virtues of tobacco. They were taking themselves so seriously that I hated to interrupt.

Instead I dragged Little Rachel over to the rail where Annetje, the Norwegian girl, sat on a crate knitting. Big around as a church she is nine months gone if she's a day and her face has that angelic glow that God sometimes grants to women near their time. She was happy to keep an eye on Little Rachel while I tracked down the missing Jan.

I tried the great cabin next. It was empty and I decided the boy must have gone below. I know I said I was never going down but this was an emergency. I was halfway down the after-ladder when the terror hit me. Sometimes it feels like a black bag dropping over my head so I can't breathe. Do you remember that little room without a window in our home in Leyden? I was always frightened of that room. One day, when I was about five, my brother, Hendrick, locked me inside in the dark with nothing but a stub of candle burning. I tried to scream but no sound came. All I could do was gasp for air as though I were drowning. Then the candle sputtered and went out. I can still remember that tiny flame dying and being sure I was going to die the same way. Mother found me unconscious on the floor and I learned later that Hendrick burst into tears because he thought he had killed me.

I know it is irrational. Everyone, especially Hendrick, has told me a hundred times over that it is irrational. But after all these years I am still afraid of being shut up in a closed space.

When you have three children of your own and a fourth on the way, you have to conquer irrational behavior. I forced myself to go down another rung. Thank God we don't have to sleep here with no portholes and no bunks.

Pale strips of light from the scuttle grating swayed back and forth across straw pallets piled in the shape of a fort. I recognized Jan's handiwork.

When I called out, my voice was barely a squeak. Holding the ladder tightly with one hand I kicked at the fort until it collapsed. Jan was not there. I hurried back up the companionway and paused at the top until my heart stopped pounding.

At that moment a commotion broke out on deck. Someone shouted that Jan had been caught climbing on the bowsprit and was being thrashed by order of Captain Schellinger. Dear God! How am I ever going to get three children safely across the Atlantic?

By the time I had retrieved Little Rachel and returned to the cabin, Jehan was already there rubbing salve on Jan's back.

"Your son has been in trouble with the authorities, my dear."

Jan is always *my* son when he is in trouble. Tears came to my eyes at the sight of the red welts on his back. Still I knew in my heart that the boy needed more discipline. Jehan is too lenient with both his sons. In the case of Jesse it doesn't matter for he is always a sensible and obedient child. But Jan was born wild. He pulled himself up on his elbows now and grinned at me.

"I'm gonna be a sailor when I grow up, Mama. Uncle Hendrick's gonna start learning me tomorrow."

Hendrick is ship's mate and I got the whole story from him soon enough. It seems the boy was discovered on the bowsprit by Stam, the cargo officer. At first shout Jan scrambled back and explained that he was practicing to be a sailor. The Skipper was understandably furious and ordered Stam to give the boy a good thrashing.

At this point Hendrick leaped forward and requested permission as the boy's uncle to administer the punishment himself.

"The lad is only six, Cap'n."

Permission was granted and Hendrick proceeded to give Jan such a sound thrashing as to melt the coldest heart. Even Stam was mollified.

"That's enough!" barked the Skipper.

The men were clearly impressed by Jan's pluck as well as his obvious ability to climb like a cat.

"Now tell me, lad," continued the Skipper. "Do you still want to be a sailor when you grow up?"

Jan held himself as straight as he could considering the condition of his backside, and managed a strangled "Yes, sir."

"Very well. We can use a cabin-boy. Report to your Uncle Hendrick in the morning. He will put you to work and teach you what you are capable of learning. But stay off that bowsprit or you'll spend the rest of the voyage in irons!"

Continued October 1st

This morning we reached Texel where we joined a dozen other ships, all waiting for the wind to turn. A crooked old gypsy came on board to read fortunes. She told Jehan he was destined to be a very important person, respected far and wide, with snow-white hair and lots of grandchildren. I could make up a better story than that myself but Jehan was pleased and gave her a whole guilder.

She said I would have a healthy baby girl, born in the middle of the Atlantic. I thanked her but I certainly hope she is wrong about the date. We expect to be at Manhattan by early December and I am not due until February.

Then she looked me straight in the eye and said the child would be named Marie. This really startled me because I have been anxious to name a girl Marie after my mother. But it is a common name.

Next it was Annetje's turn and the gypsy really fell on her face this time. She said Annetje would soon have a baby boy and he would be named "Stam." (Maybe she thought Annetje was married to our cargo officer whose name is Stam.) Anyhow Annetje burst into laughter and said if she gave birth to a boy he would be named Albert after his father. The gypsy was insulted and refused to admit she was wrong.

Captain Schellinger has just arranged with an incoming vessel to carry our letters back to Amsterdam so I must close. Give my regards to La Belle Gertrude. She could at least have come to see Hendrick off!

Your affectionate cousin,

Rachel

Storm

This 13th day of October
In the Year of Our Lord 1636
On board the *Rensselaerswyck*

Dearest Margariet,

We remained eight days at Texel until we were finally blessed with an east wind. By this time there were 22 ships waiting and we agreed to sail together as far as Plymouth, on the English coast.

At the last minute the gypsy came hobbling along the pier shaking her stick and screaming a warning. The *Rensselaerswyck* was the closest and we heard every dreadful word.

"Save yourselves, good men. Satan is brewing a tempest the like never seen by living soul!"

Stam and Hendrick were on the pier at the time and literally carried the woman away. Before they managed to gag her she pointed a bony finger at me. "For you a watery grave, my pretty vrouw!"

I don't mind telling you that I was truly upset even though I realized that the woman would say anything to avoid losing a whole fleetful of paying customers. However my fears were soon forgotten in the excitement of 22 ships setting sail together. Anchors were hauled up on tarred cables as officers bellowed out a hundred commands and seamen rushed to obey.

"Make fast the halyards!"

"Set the tops'ls!"

"Veer the braces!"

"Hoist the mizzen!"

"Hold her steady as you go!"

I cheered with the others as each white sail billowed. Then with seagulls circling overhead, we glided majestically out into open water.

By morning the easterly breeze had become a stiff wind driving us down the Flemish coast. At sunset we passed Dunkirk, the worst pirates' nest in Europe. Thank heavens we were not sailing alone.

After Plymouth the convoy began breaking up. We joined an Irish trader as far as Land's End and the Scilly Isles. At noon Sunday, October 13th, the trader left us heading north. We set our course southwest, all alone now, with sky overcast and a raw wind to chill the bone. A handful of passengers wrapped in woolens stood at the rail, watching in silence as our last link with civilization disappeared over the horizon.

When I get depressed like this I cheer myself up by thinking about the new home we are going to build on the island of Manhattan. Did you know that Hendrick stopped there in 1632 when he was a seaman for the Dutch West India Company?

"That island, Rachel, is the closest thing to paradise that exists on this earth. The fresh scent of flowers wafts across the water to approaching ships a mile away. In strawberry season one can lie down on the sweet earth and eat one's fill of the juicy berries without ever moving from that one spot. The rivers teem with fish, and a little child, wading along the shore, will quickly gather all the oysters a family can eat. The air is alive with the music of songbirds, and deer walk up to the very door of the cottage."

Did you meet Willem and Tobias? They are the two men that Uncle Gerard engaged to work for Hendrick for three years in exchange for their passage and a small wage. Willem is only 16 and has two fingers missing on his left hand, having been apprenticed to a butcher. He is strong enough but not much help so far. Tobias, however, is a widower and has taken over the task of cooking our daily meal. The poor man has a large, wine-colored birthmark covering half his face. At first I was embarrassed even to look at him. Of course nobody has mentioned it except Jan.

"Why's your face purple?" were the first words out of the boy's mouth.

I was mortified but Tobias took it in his stride.

"Born that way, Son," he said.

For purposes of sharing the fire-box, the passengers are divided into three groups. Our group includes the three Norwegians, Annetje, Albert, and Albert's younger brother, an overly-tall fellow known as Lanky.

Jan is now ship's cabin boy but he still eats with us and is always brimming over with nautical tidbits. Today, at the first whiff of Tobias's cooking, Jan scrambled down from the poop to announce that the *Rensselaerswyck*'s mainmast used to be a tall tree.

"Of course dear. All masts used to be tall trees."

"And they buried a dead baby under the roots!" he finished triumphantly.

"Who's been telling you dreadful tales like that?" I asked sharply. Annetje is fairly bursting with child now and I do not want her upset by any stories about dead babies.

"It's not a tale, Mama. It's true. Uncle Hendrick told me. Do you know why?"

Of course everyone wanted to know why. Far from being upset, Annetje was the most enthusiastic.

It seems they buried an unbaptized infant under the roots. Naturally an unbaptized soul cannot go to heaven so the little cherub has to spend eternity hovering above the top branches. When the tall tree was converted into our mast he supposedly remained up there watching over his new-found sailor friends below.

"Blasphemous superstition," growled the blacksmith, a hairy, muscular man with heavy black eyebrows that grow together with no break at the nose. He is given to quoting the Old Testament and appears ready to smite any who disagree with either him or the Almighty. I have seen him strike Hans, his pimply-faced apprentice and I suspect that he strikes "The Muis" as we nicknamed his timid little vrouw. Needless to say he is rarely contradicted.

"Not at all," retorted Annetje, doubly protected by her sex and condition. "I'm happy to have the cherub up there." She craned her neck to peer at the very top of the mainmast. "Besides, if the gypsy was right about the coming storm, we may need that cherub before we're done."

"Mock not the Lord, Madame," warned the blacksmith, as he strode from the deck, closely followed by the timorous Muis.

No sooner were they out of sight than the younger men gathered in a circle around Lanky who had already collected a guilder apiece from 15 persons eager to wager on the date that his sister-in-law would give birth. He was now holding the draw in front of witnesses, to determine who got which day.

The lottery was supposed to be secret because the blacksmith disapproved of betting, but even the pimply-faced Hans put up his guilder, although it is hard to imagine where he found one. Albert was barred for the rather crude reason that as Annetje's bedfellow he was in a position to influence the date. Jehan refused to wager on a medical matter, but Isaack put up his guilder optimistically only to be bitterly disappointed in the draw. He was assigned the last date, October 28th. If the baby did not arrive by then there would be a new draw, but by Annetje's count she was two weeks late already and Isaack's chances of collecting the 15 guilders were slim.

Lanky drew tomorrow's date. There were whispers that he had a tip from his sister-in-law and the draw was rigged. However when tomorrow came and went with no sign of labor pains, spirits revived. Isaack carries a copy of the list, and sailors and passengers continually sidle up to him to have a furtive glimpse. As each day passes he crosses off the top name with growing enthusiasm. Yesterday he was sufficiently encouraged to construct a chair with a proper back for Annetje's personal use. Needless to say, if she attempts to pick up so much as a blanket, two or three interested parties jump forward to help. If nothing else, the lottery adds a definite touch of excitement to the otherwise monotonous routine of shipboard life.

Jehan keeps a daily journal of the voyage and insists that Jesse do the same. "When you are a grown man, Son, you will cherish this record of your first great adventure."

Please God let Jesse live to be a grown man.

Each morning Jan brings a report of the ship's position. Then Jehan unrolls his map, spreads it out on the chest between the bunks and enters another tiny dot to mark our progress. Already the dotted line crawls a quarter of an inch down the coast from Texel, then an inch westward through the English Channel, and now another half inch south into the Bay of Biscay.

"Show your mother the route we are taking, Son."

With an air of importance Jan carefully traced our prospective course south to the Canary Islands off the coast of Africa, then west with the trade winds across the Atlantic, and up the coast of North America to the mouth of the Hudson in the territory labelled "Nova Belgica."

"Boys, all this land between the Virginias and New England belongs to the Netherlands. This was the dream of your famous grandfather, Jesse de Forest, leader of the Walloons. If he had lived he would have been the Colony's first Governor."

Continued October 21st

Today the main deck is a beehive of activity as a few of the handier passengers, including Willem, are constructing gun carriages. The sawdust makes Isaack sneeze which is no surprise. He has spent most of his 20 years sneezing. Mother used to say it was because he breathed through his mouth instead of his nose. But even sawdust could not dampen his enthusiasm for Willem's work.

"Blikskaters, Rachel! The lad's a born carpenter, even with two fingers missing!" He glanced at Annetje who sat comfortably on the new chair with her knitting perched on her swollen belly.

"Fifteen guilders is a lot of money," he whispered. "Do you think if she just sits there, without moving, . . . Gotchoo! Gotchoo! . . . she could hold out until the 28th?" He pulled out a large handkerchief and held it ready for the next sneeze.

I laughed and Annetje flashed him a smile, then staggered to her feet announcing that she was going to take advantage of the sunshine to do a big load of wash. There is a mischievous sense of humor behind that angelic face but Isaack gasped in horror. I quickly offered to do the laundry if he would play a game of chess with Jesse. He agreed, good-naturedly, but he was not much of a player and it is not easy for a grown man to risk losing in public to a seven-year-old. In no time there were more spectators watching the game than watching the carpentry.

So Annetje went back to her knitting and with the Muis to help me we got three heavy loads of wash under way. In spite of her tiny size the Muis is a strong worker, and rails and rigging were soon festooned with dripping drawers and stockings.

Somehow the satisfaction of a heavy chore well done, combined with the homey smell of clean clothes drying in the bright sun, erased my fear of drowning. For days I had been trying to ward off disaster by bribing the fates with extravagant promises. Now for the first time since that gypsy, I relaxed. What fools we mortals be.

Jesse eventually checkmated his uncle. Isaack was the only adult he had ever beaten except me, and I hardly mattered because I always hoped to lose. It annoyed me that Jehan never let the boy win. He gave him a handicap of a rook, then lay in his bunk reading while Jesse huddled over the board.

"This way, when the boy beats me he'll appreciate it, my dear. He would beat me now if I gave him a queen."

About four o'clock our invisible breeze died. The sails gulped and banged about trying in vain to catch a breath of wind, then with a final shudder they gave up the effort and we lay motionless on a sea of green glass.

There is something very frustrating about being becalmed. The Muis and I quickly removed the last of the drawers from the rigging before anyone could say it was our fault. Then the sailors began to whistle loudly for a wind. I took Little Rachel by the hand and walked over to the rail where Hendrick joined me.

"That son of yours is going to make a fine sailor," he said, nodding toward Jan who was whistling his heart out with the crew. "He's a quick learner and all the men like him, even the Skipper. Best of all he knows when to help and when to stay out of the way."

The whistling died as the men pointed with excitement to some birds flying high in formation. I wondered how they could exist so far from land.

"Those are stormy petrels, Sis. They spend their whole lives traveling back and forth over the Atlantic."

"Why have the men stopped whistling?" I asked.

"Stormy petrels can smell a gale miles away. Sailors say they circle to warn the ship. It's just a superstition."

We watched as the birds approached and deliberately wheeled round and round the *Rensselaerswyck*. Then, as if on signal, they sped away to the east and disappeared. I knew in my heart that it was no superstition. The gypsy had been right all the time.

Hendrick left, but I just stood there gripping Little Rachel.

"You hurted me, Mama."

I picked her up and together we stared at the sea. The air grew ominously heavy. Still there was no wind. Slowly the dark water began to swell and boil as though some evil force were thrashing about in the depths. Gray clouds, then angry black ones, began to pile up on the western horizon. Lightning zigzagged across the sky, followed by the rumble of distant thunder.

Now there was much shouting of orders as the crew struggled to take in the canvas and clear the deck of cows and gun carriages. Passengers scurried about collecting belongings and helping with obstinate cattle. Jehan took me by the arm. The wind struck as we reached the cabin. God in Heaven help us all!

For three days we were driven before the storm without sail. Sky and sea were one. The waves were as high as mountains. One minute a giant hand would lift us up to the very peak, then we would stagger and plunge headlong down the other side. It was difficult to tell night from day. The danger of fire was much too great to light the lantern that swung from the deckhead. For the most part we were in total darkness and the whole cabin smelled of vomit and urine.

I had Little Rachel pinned under me in the bunk and when the ship pitched I hung on to the sides for dear life to keep us both from falling. I had long ago thrown up everything in my stomach, but I could not stop. Jehan and Jesse were retching in the next berth. Isaack groaned above me.

The only person in that cabin who was not sick was Jan. Not only was he not sick, he kept getting hungry and munching on apples and hard biscuit.

"Don't worry, Mama. The cherub on the mainmast is watching over us."

The noise was deafening. Waves crashed and the wind howled. Even more terrifying was the shrieking and creaking of the ship's timbers. Above it all I could hear a woman screaming. Was it Annetje? Please don't let it be Annetje.

Every once in a while there is an hour or so of relative calm and I write a few words. Excuse the dreadful scrawl but there is almost no light. At first I believed that God would bring us safely though this. Now I realize that it is hopeless because the ship is falling apart piece by piece. Oh Margariet! If I had only listened to you. Why I continue writing I do not know.

I seem to have forgotten about Jehan and the boys. My whole world has narrowed down to this bunk and Little Rachel. She was weaned a year ago yet I still have milk to give, which is a miracle. We are tied in now but I do not let go of her. She gets sick in my arms and wets herself and cries. Mostly, thank God, she sleeps.

I was unconscious when the lightning struck. The simultaneous blast of thunder staggered the ship and for one insane moment I had a lopsided view of Hell in a flash of blinding light. I was looking down at two bodies tied in an open coffin. Another coffin was hurtling through the air like a missile. Then the world plunged back into darkness but the hideous image lingered on inside my eyes.

It took a while to realize that I was not dead. With the *Rensselaerswyck* at an angle I had been looking down at Jehan and Jesse tied in the next bunk. The other coffin must have been a box hurled by the lunging ship. Sweet Jesus, save us from this horror. I try to pray but I cannot remember the words.

My mind keeps wandering to ridiculous details. For one thing I worry about my great-grandmother's cradle which is stored in the ship's hold. It is over a hundred years old, and made of oak with bible scenes carved on the side. When my father fled from the Spanish he carried it on his back all the way from Avesnes to Leyden. At least I picture him carrying it on his back. Hendrick and Isaack and I were all rocked in that cradle. So were Jesse and Jan and Little Rachel. How ironic that it must spend eternity rocking shellfish on the floor of the Atlantic.

Then I worry about the sketch of Papa stored in our chest. It was done years ago by a fellow-student of Jehan's at the University of Leyden, a four-teen-year-old boy with green paint in his hair. Jehan says the boy is a genius and the sketch is very valuable but I doubt it. However it is a wonderful likeness of Papa. It is packed flat in the bottom of the chest, protected from wrinkling but not from water.

And I worry about the tulip bulbs which I was hoping to plant by our new home. Last year the price of bulbs soared as Holland went tulip-mad. Speculators bought and sold next year's crop at outrageous prices. Unusual varieties naturally brought the most. Of course my bulbs are only the ordinary red and yellow kind but they were expensive enough. When the water hits, they will begin to sprout like onions and be ruined.

It was during a particularly rough patch in the third night that I realized Jan was missing. I was certain that he had gone out onto the main deck and been washed overboard. By now the *Rensselaerswyck* is so badly damaged that even if she does not capsize it can only be a short time before she breaks up and everyone drowns. Does it matter so much that Jan goes first?

Trunks, boxes and bodies slid in one direction then the other. Suddenly the ship lurched so far over that she passed the vertical point and we seemed to be hanging upside-down. There was no way back from here. The *Rensselaerswyck* shuddered like a mortally-wounded animal that had given up the struggle. Then by some incredible miracle she began to right herself, creaking and groaning in protest. Above the noise I heard Jan's voice.

"I saw the cherub on the mainmast!" he yelled. "He's got a halo like the baby Jesus!"

I don't know if it was lightning that Jan saw, or just his imagination, or if there really was an angel on our mainmast. But the passengers in that cabin accepted Jan's statement without question and he was made to tell the story over and over again. Each time the description of the cherub grew more and more like the picture of the Christ Child in Jan's catechism from the Walloon Church in Leyden. Still, it always brought renewed hope.

On October 26th the wind was less violent. Jan reported that the crew tried to raise some sail but the mizzen ripped and blew away. During the night of the 28th there was a terrible crash. In the morning we learned that the prow had been knocked in.

Annetje still had not given birth. The pool dates had run out but there was no talk of another draw. The blacksmith had found out about the lottery and angrily ordered Lanky to return the money because the Almighty did not approve of betting. Lanky had no desire to oblige the blacksmith but he did not dare risk offending God at this particular time. So he gave each man back his guilder and in the process tripped over his own long legs and fell down the after-ladder.

"God's justice!" announced the blacksmith.

Still the gale continued. On the 30th, rations were distributed again, the cabin-deck was swabbed for the first time since the storm began, and vinegar sprinkled everywhere to disguise the other odors. I will never be able to smell vinegar again without feeling nauseous.

On November 2nd, the storm raged harder than ever. In the morning there was a loud crack as the overhang above the rudder gave way. It was then that Annetje went into labor.

For twelve hours she was very brave and did not cry out. When the pains were about five minutes apart I gave Little Rachel to Jehan and arranged for Annetje's husband, Albert, and their two youngsters to take my berth while I sat by Annetje, grasping the bottom of the upper bunk to keep my balance. Above me was Lanky, who was much too tall for an upper berth. An arm or a leg was always hanging down one side or the other.

I was not nauseous but I was cold and my arms ached. I had a pile of clean cloth ready, and thread and a sharp knife in my pocket. There was really not much I could do for Annetje so I kept telling her she was doing fine and everyone thought I was helping. If things started to go wrong I could always get Jehan, but everyone knows there is little hope left when you have to call in a doctor for a birth.

It was late afternoon when Annetje started to scream. Once she started she could not stop.

"It won't be long now," I told her.

Of course I didn't know any more than the man in the moon how long it would be, but Lanky heard me and called out to Albert.

"It won't be long now!"

Then a dozen voices throughout the cabin echoed my words of wisdom.

"It won't be long now!"

It is a strange thing that before Annetje went into labor, the cabin had been filled with groaning, wretched, despairing passengers. Now her piercing screams were the only sounds that could be heard above the howling of the elements. It was as though some twenty persons, welded together by her agony, were collectively straining in the dark to bring forth a new soul.

Jan came over easily as if he were born to swing from bunk posts like a monkey.

"Papa wants to know if you need him, Mama."

"Tell him there's no room and he'll only break a leg getting here."

He left and I could hear him pause at each berth on his way back with words of reassurance. "Don't worry. My Mama knows how to get good babies."

It was almost completely dark now and Annetje had been screaming steadily for an hour. Then with one final scream the baby came in a rush and a flood. I let go the upper berth and grabbed for it. God seemed to hold the ship steady as I caught the slippery head and shoulders. "Dear Lord, don't let it be dead." Now I had the feet in one hand. With the other hand I tried desperately to get the mucous out of the mouth and nose.

Then the ship lurched and I fell forward on top of the helpless creature. If it was not dead already I had surely killed it now. Somehow I managed to grab the feet again and slap its little bottom as hard as I could. Miraculously there came a lusty yell of protest. Thank you, dear God.

"Albert!" shouted Lanky. "You're a father!" He leaned down to ask if it was a boy.

I checked. "Yes, it's a boy, and he's alive!"

"Albert!" he yelled above the noise of the storm. "It's a boy!"

Then everyone began to shout and laugh and cry all at once. For a few brief moments there was genuine joy in that wretched cabin. But I was fighting against time. This little naked creature would surely freeze to death if I didn't hurry. It was completely dark now and I could have used six hands. Somehow I managed to knot the thread tightly around the cord in two places and cut between them. I wiped the infant and wrapped him in a fresh cloth and blanket. Then I handed him to his mother while I set about the impossible task of cleaning up.

"Lest anyone ever forget this miracle of God," shouted Albert, "We will name the child, Storm."

We were now slightly north of the dangerous Cape Finisterre which juts out from the coast of Spain. We had at one point passed the Cape at great peril, beating our way as far south as the coast of Portugal. Then we had been driven north again and were now in danger of being swept back into the Bay of Biscay. It was decided to run north with the wind and try to get back into the English Channel where we might be able to find shelter at Falmouth or Plymouth.

During the night of November 13th we saw land, which according to reckoning was the Scilly Isles again. The weather was very heavy with lightning and thunder. At daybreak a dangerous group of rocks called the Seven Stones appeared a league to starboard. For ten hours we tried to fight our way around Land's End as huge waves threatened to dash us against the rocks. Then at twilight, with a horrible splintering crash, we ran aground. For the hundredth time I clutched Little Rachel and commended my soul to the Lord.

Miraculously the *Rensselaerswyck* was not finished yet. By setting all possible sail, the Skipper dragged her off the rocks but the cost was heavy. The foresail blew away, the main sheet broke and we began to ship water at an alarming rate.

It was now impossible to get into the English Channel and we were being driven northeast along the coast of Cornwall. In vain we tried to get in to the ports of Padstow or Stratton by daylight. In vain we tried to run out to sea by night. On we plunged, helpless before the storm.

In the dark I used to keep the terror at bay by staring in the direction of the porthole opposite my berth and imagining a window. Always I have liked windows. I try to picture bright clean panes of glass with blue sky outside. Sometimes I add lace curtains or a bowl of tulips on the sill.

Now all the portholes were boarded over except for a very tiny one, high up at the other end of the cabin. This made it much harder to imagine my window.

Then in the middle of the night the terror struck. I tried to picture my window but it would not come. I began to have trouble breathing. I knew I had to reach that little porthole high up at the other end of the cabin. My heart raced as I untied myself in the dark and retied Little Rachel. Gasping for air I crawled uphill toward the foot of the bed. Suddenly, what had been uphill became downhill, and I was thrown into black space.

I landed on my shoulder. Somehow the pain was almost welcome and the warm blood soaking my sleeve seemed to relax my breathing. Far from bringing me to my senses however, it made me more determined than ever to see God's sky one last time.

I was now completely disoriented. The noise was deafening and it was pitch black. But I was sure I could see that one high-up porthole and began struggling toward it. By climbing on to a box and hanging to the side of a berth I eventually found my head close to the tiny uncovered port. Another head was there before me.

"There's a ship out there, Mama!" shouted a voice in my ear. "A ship without a mast!"

It was Jan's head although his body seemed to be missing. In my right mind I would have told him that he was crazy and there was nothing out there but ocean. As it was I just stood staring out at blackness, fully prepared to see a whole fleet if Jan said so. Then the ocean was lit by lightning. On the crest of the wave and falling toward us was a ship without a mast.

"We're gonna crash!" shouted Jan in my ear as the world went black again.

We waited for the blow that never came. Dimly I wondered if there were living souls inside that hull. At the next flash of lightning the ship without a mast had disappeared forever.

It was the child stirring in my womb that finally brought me to my senses. Somehow I made my way back to the bunk and Little Rachel without breaking any bones. If it were not for the pain in my shoulder the whole episode could have been a dream.

My father used to say that as a boy he had once touched the finger of Saint Nicholas which is preserved at the great church in Avesnes.

"If you are ever in danger on the high seas, my child, ask the patron saint of mariners to protect you."

"Blessed Saint Nicholas," I prayed. "Guide us to shelter before it is too late!"

By morning the *Rensselaerswyck* was shipping so much water that we might have to beach her regardless of cost. We were now running with reefed foresail along the fog-bound cliffs of Devon. If we were driven on to the rocks the ship would break into a thousand pieces. Even so, lives could be saved. All passengers were told to prepare for impact and to be ready for the order to abandon ship.

There was nothing one could do to prepare except pray. With the pain in my arm and the loss of blood I was only half-conscious anyway. Jehan checked to be sure that I was properly tied and kissed my forehead.

"Au revoir, sweet Jehan." I could not hear my own voice.

Vaguely it occurred to me that Jan was not tied, but it did not matter. If anyone survived this wreck it would be that agile monkey. I pictured my plucky little orphan wandering homeless through England. Then my mind drifted off into blessed unconsciousness.

The next thing I knew, Jehan was binding up my shoulder. The cabin lantern was lit, swaying gently back and forth on its chain, and the horrible pounding was gone.

"Thank you, Blessed Saint Nicholas, for this miracle."

At the last minute the fog had lifted and the Skipper sighted what looked like a huge oblong rock a few leagues off the coast. He recognized the Island of Lundy and for the first time in days we raised the topmast. Setting both topsails we headed for the island like a runaway horse pursued by a thousand raging devils.

"I thought we were going to capsize," Jehan told me, "or at the very least lose all our sails. But here we are in the lee of the island, safely anchored in twenty fathoms. What in the world did you do to this shoulder?"

I told him about my obsession to see the sky and how I imagined a ship without a mast.

"It was not your imagination, Sis," said Hendrick, who had come down to check on our condition. "I was on the bridge when we nearly collided with that ship without a mast. God rest the poor souls within her. Come with me and I'll show you your sky."

When Jehan finished with my shoulder, which was only a flesh wound, I followed my brother out on to the main deck. Sailors furiously manned the pumps as Lundy Island loomed above us like an enormous black wall against a dark gray sky. The storm still vented its wrath on the other side of this rock which Hendrick said must be 400 feet high and several miles long.

"She's shipping a lot of water, Sis, but we're going to make it. In the morning, with God's help and the wind behind us, we will reach that harbor." He pointed toward the English coast.

"What harbor?"

"Here. Look through this." He handed me the telescope. "Do you see a tiny light twinkling on the cliffs? It's on the charts, Rachel. There is a harbor beneath that light."

And so, by the grace of God, on Sunday the 16th of November, 1636, we have come to rest in a little harbor called Ilfracombe.

May the Lord be praised for his mercy.

> Your affectionate cousin,
>
> Rachel

Ilfracombe

Tuesday, November 18th
In the Year of Our Lord 1636
At Ilfracombe on the west coast of England

Dearest Margariet,

It is surely a miracle, but we are all still alive. The *Rensselaerswyck,* however, is in a sad state and will require several weeks to repair. In the meantime, Jehan arranged for us to take a room at the Golden Lion Tavern.

Beyond the cliffs the sea still raged as two sailors rowed us across the choppy harbor. Jesse was so weak that his father had to carry him in a blanket while I held Little Rachel. Rain beat down upon us as we huddled over our burdens like Biblical refugees. Only Jan was his usual lively self, standing poised in the bow, rope in hand, ready to leap on to the long stone pier.

We passed two other Dutch vessels that had been driven off course to find refuge in this remote harbor. Battered and dismal, they rocked beneath bare poles waiting for the weather to change. Lifeless fishing-boats lined the shore, where a few gray weatherbeaten houses offered little promise of welcome.

After a month of hell I was prepared to be grateful for anything with a floor that did not rock. To my surprise the Golden Lion proved to be a paradise. The innkeeper, a gaunt, taciturn man by the name of White, greeted us with a few amiable grunts. I was impressed with how fluently Jehan addressed him in English. I used to think English was a very low form of Dutch such as they speak in Friesland, but Jehan says it is a proper language.

Our room has a big feather-bed and a fireplace which the innkeeper proceeded to lay for us. Then Mistress White bustled in with candles and a flow of sympathetic, if incomprehensible, conversation, interspersed with exclamations of horror over the condition of the children. Jan was just dirty like any other boy who has not bathed or changed his clothes in a month. The other two were literally caked with filth. Little Rachel's hair was matted with foul-smelling grime.

The good woman ordered a large tub set by the fire and a cheerful, but simple-minded, young serving-girl brought soap and quantities of hot water. Every so often she would reappear with another steaming pitcher and vigorously toss the used slops out of the window with a simultaneous warning shout. Then she would hopefully inspect the street below to see if she had succeeded in dousing some unwary passer-by.

At last the children lay well-fed and sweet-smelling in the big feather-bed. Little Rachel looked like a sleeping angel with a halo of blond ringlets. Then Jehan, freshly scrubbed and shaven, went downstairs to the tavern. Now it was my turn. As long as I walk upon this earth I shall never forget the blessed feeling of easing my aching self into that wonderful hot water. Of such precious moments is heaven surely knit.

Stam left this morning to travel overland to Plymouth on the South coast. By the time he gets there the storm should be spent and he will find an Amsterdam-bound vessel to carry our mail (including my second letter to you.)

There are only two places to go in Ilfracombe: church and tavern. Most of our passengers sleep on board to save money but spend the day here at the Golden Lion. The one exception is the blacksmith whose temper has not been improved by our miraculous escape. If anything he is angrier than ever with the world in general, and in particular with his splotchy-faced apprentice, whom he calls a Jonah. Apparently he believes that God sent the tempest to punish Hans for wagering a guilder in the ship's pool. At one point Captain Schellinger had to intervene to save the lad from being hammered like a horseshoe on the anvil. Needless to say, Hans stays as far away from his grim employer as possible.

The Muis is less fortunate. According to the blacksmith, taverns are "cradles of the devil." After one brief sojourn ashore he spends his time aboard, reading his bible and keeping a careful eye on his timid vrouw. The man is clearly deranged and the girl hardly dares move or utter a word for fear of rousing his wrath.

Annetje tells me that she invited the Muis to come ashore with them. The poor thing never even raised her eyes as the smith gruffly refused. There is much talk at the tavern of rescuing her, at least for a few hours, but of course nothing is ever done about it. When the weather finally changed I saw my chance.

Jehan was worried that water had possibly got into our large chest. He sent two men out to the ship to collect it and I went along with Jesse and

Little Rachel in tow. Jan was already on board helping Hendrick. As expected, he was not pleased with my proposal to visit the Ilfracombe church.

"Potverdikki, Mama! Me and Uncle Hendrick got work to do."

So I dragged him. With the other arm I dragged his sister. I made Jesse hang on to my belt and I dragged him too. Inwardly I had to chuckle at the absurd picture we made staggering across the main deck. Outwardly, of course, I maintained the harried expression of a pregnant housewife being tortured by unruly offspring. We wobbled to a halt near the forward bulkhead where the Muis sat knitting by her glowering yoke-mate.

"Anna," I gasped. "I'm taking the children to the Ilfracombe Church to give thanks for our salvation. I would be very grateful if you could come along to help with Little Rachel."

She neither raised her eyes nor uttered a word, but if it were possible to read knitting-needles, I would swear I heard a flicker of hope in the faltering clicks.

The smith glanced beneath bushy brows at my protruding waistline.

"Why don't you answer Madame Montagne?" he growled at the girl. "A little work will do you good." Then he turned to me. "Take her. She is much stronger than she pretends."

The Muis slowly folded her knitting and stood up like someone moving in a trance. There was no expression on her face as she took Little Rachel from me and I began to wonder if she were possibly as deranged as her husband. We were halfway across the harbor before the girl relaxed. She looked over her shoulder toward the *Rensselaerswyck,* now blocked from view by other vessels. When she turned back, the lifeless mask had been replaced by her normal friendly, but shy expression.

The Muis was a different person away from her forbidding helpmate. She laughed and ran with the children and I was surprised to find what good company she was. Only once did she refer to the smith.

"Cornelis has not been himself recently," was all she said.

When our chest had been safely delivered to the Golden Lion, the Muis and I and the children set out for the Church of the Holy Trinity. It was further than I thought and slow going what with Jesse's leg and the cane, but we were in no hurry and it was pleasant to look about in the November sunshine.

Ilfracombe is, for the most part, a cluster of tiny fishermen's cottages near the harbor. One scraggly street leads from the pier gradually inland and uphill to the ancient stone church, surprisingly large and completely empty. In its dim, musty interior there was an air of timeless sanctity, diminished somewhat by Jan announcing in a loud whisper, "I can smell God in here."

After giving thanks for our miraculous salvation we wandered about for a while. Sunshine, streaming through stained glass windows, made colorful patterns on the gravestones in the floor. Jesse meticulously read out Latin inscriptions and warned the others where not to step. Little Rachel walked daintily around the graves. Jan leaped over them.

Then in the middle of that huge empty church, a black-robed vicar materialized out of nowhere and addressed Jesse in Latin. The boy proudly stammered a few words in reply.

Fortunately the good man spoke French as well, and we had a long conversation about our escape from the storm. He was particularly gratified that we had been able to see the lantern which shines every night from the high point this side of the harbor.

"That ancient stone building you see on top of the hill is the Chapel of Saint Nicholas, Madame. For three hundred years a lantern has stood in the oriel window facing the sea."

"How strange, mon Père, that the chapel should belong to Saint Nicholas," I said. "My father escaped from Avesnes long before I was born. He often spoke of seeing the finger of Saint Nicholas which is preserved at the great church there. During the storm I prayed to Saint Nicholas and your light was like his finger beckoning us to safety."

"The Lord works in mysterious ways, Madame. But it was Lundy Island, not the light, that saved the *Rensselaerswyck.*"

The vicar questioned us about life in the Netherlands and seemed surprised that we planned to continue our journey to the New World. When I said we were impressed by the hospitality at the Golden Lion, he told me that the tavern has been here since the fourteenth century, when Ilfracombe was a prominent port and not just a fishing village.

"Today, Madame, I have hardly any parishioners who can read and write, much less any students of Latin like your son."

He showed us the massive church-tower, originally a Saxon stronghold, which explains why the church stands so far from the village.

"Hundreds of years ago Vikings used to raid these shores, boys. Then the people fled into this tower, and pulled the ladder up after themselves."

"Can I go up?" asked Jan eagerly.

"You could if there were a ladder but . . ."

It was too late. Jan was already scrambling up the bare stone to the entrance above.

"It stinks up here, Mama, like someone forgot to use the potty!"

I was mortified but the vicar was not offended.

"Remarkable agility," he said, staring at the bare stone. "Most remarkable."

Jan descended less elegantly, but without hurting himself, and I decided it was time to go. The vicar suggested that we take the path along the clifftop overlooking the ocean.

"It's so clear today, Madame, that you will be able to see Lundy Island in the distance, rising like a stone fortress from the sea. In any case, the view is magnificent."

When I told him that Jesse was not strong enough for such a long walk, the vicar said he was shortly going to the village himself, and would be glad of the boy's company as far as the Golden Lion.

So the Muis and I and Little Rachel, with Jan racing ahead, set out for the path along the cliffs. The vicar was right. When we reached the top the view was spectacular. On the horizon, Lundy Island rose from the ocean like a man-made fort. A hundred feet below us, instead of a beach, stood huge razor-sharp slabs of rock. Today they were covered with seagulls. I shudder to think what they would do to a ship in a storm.

By now Jan was some distance ahead. Suddenly, without warning, he disappeared over the edge. Terrified, I hurried to the spot and peered down the vertical rock face. There, far below, the boy was already scrambling after seagulls. How he got down without killing himself was impossible to imagine. We shouted and waved but he could not hear over the roar of the ocean. I think the Muis was more frightened than I was.

"How will he ever get up again?" she cried as he disappeared around a curve in the shoreline.

There was nothing to do but follow the path along the cliff-top. My mind flew back to the time when Jan, who must have climbed every tree in Leyden, finally stepped on a dead branch and tumbled 30 feet to the ground without breaking a bone. Instead of thrashing the boy, Jehan gave him a lecture on how to distinguish dead wood from live.

"There's no use trying to teach a cat not to climb, my dear."

Dear God, please grant my little wild one nine lives.

After what seemed an eternity, but was probably only ten minutes, Jan came racing back along the cliff-top. I still don't know how he got down or how he got up again. He was anxious to demonstrate but I had no intention of running any more risks.

"We are all going straight back to the tavern for something to eat," I announced firmly. The Muis looked dubious but she was too shaken by Jan's escapade to object.

The Golden Lion is a far cry from the "cradle of vice" pictured by the blacksmith. There is a large homey fireplace with patrons sitting around at small tables, some drinking but many just warming themselves or gossiping. Today Annetje was there nursing baby Storm, with her husband and his brother sitting proudly on either side. Jesse had returned and was watching a game of darts together with my brother, Hendrick, and Stieffy, a tongue-tied hog dealer from the *Rensselaerswyck*. Jehan, looking very distinguished, sat with Captain Schellinger and some local merchants. My husband is in great demand nowadays, being the only one of us who can really speak English. He promptly rose and joined us, carrying a familiar square of paper.

"Good news, my dear. I have removed every item from our chest and there's not a speck of damp. Mirabile dictu! Even the picture of your father is in perfect condition." He placed the charcoal sketch on the table as the Muis looked on curiously.

"That's my Grandpa," Jan told her. "And her is Remember." He pointed to the water-soaked little girl in my father's arms. "She drownded but Grandpa saved her."

"Ooh! Can I see?" Annetje danced over, quite a feat with Storm still suckling. She sat down next to Jesse who had abandoned the darts game. "So this is your grandfather, the famous Jesse de Forest. My what a marvelous face."

"It was sixteen years ago," said Jehan, "the day the English Puritans left Leyden to join the Mayflower. Their barges were lined up along the Rapenburg Canal, right under the windows of the University.

"I was one of a crowd of students watching from that bridge." He pointed to the three stone arches of the Nun's Bridge in the background. "On the last barge, two little girls in sunbonnets were perched high up on a pile of boxes. The younger peeked shyly at the well-wishers from under her bonnet. The older one, she could only have been five or six, danced about on the topmost box, smiling and waving as the students cheered. Someone said her name was Remember Allerton. I was just thinking to myself what an extraordinary name when the child fell and disappeared with barely a ripple beneath the green water. Only her bonnet remained on the surface." Jehan pointed to the plucky little bonnet sailing in the foreground.

"I can still hear the mother shrieking 'Remember! Remember!'" he continued. "Then this giant of a man plunged from the bridge and reached the scene in seconds. With a mighty splash he dove below. I learned later that it was Jesse de Forest, leader of the Walloons. We held our breath as the sun sparkled on an ever-widening circle of empty green water."

Jehan did tell a story well. Of course he was really telling it for the benefit of the boys. They had heard it many times but loved every word.

"Then, from the very center of the circle, the big man burst from the water with the dripping Remember in his arms. And that's how I first saw your famous grandfather."

In the picture the girl's face was hidden by her wet hair but my father's expression of triumph was remarkable.

"Turn the paper over, Papa," said Jan with a mischievous grin. "I wanna see Remember's face."

"Don't be silly, Son." Jehan left to put the sketch away.

"What extraordinary eyes your father had, Rachel," said Annetje. "They say the Walloons were devoted to him."

"Yes. Everyone loved him. Jehan is not even a Walloon. Yet from that first day he worshipped Papa. When the Dutch West India Company asked my father to take a few men to the Amazon to select a site for a colony, Jehan was one of the first to volunteer." I did not tell her that all but one had eventually returned safely. Only my father lies buried forever near the mouth of the Oyapok, on the wild coast of South America.

"Do you know who made that sketch?" asked Annetje.

"A 14-year-old boy with green hair," I told her. "Rembrandt, the miller's son, they call him. He and Jehan were students together except Jehan was much older. He thinks the boy is a genius."

At this point the darts game finished and we were joined by Hendrick and his friend Stieffy, the hog dealer.

"Well, if it isn't the shy little Muis," announced Hendrick jovially as he ordered ale and mutton pies all round.

The Muis blushed and took Little Rachel onto her lap to cover her embarrassment. I used to think she had a rather plain face. Now, away from that dreadful blacksmith, she looked actually pretty.

Stieffy is a big kindly man with a bushy red beard and a booming laugh that compensates somewhat for his almost total lack of conversation. He sleeps in the berth above the blacksmith and the Muis, but spent most of the storm below deck with his six piglets. All six survived and are even now penned out back of the Golden Lion, growing fat on the remains of Mistress

White's mutton pies. If you don't mind a certain earthy smell he is quite good company.

"Stieffy," I said, "I think you have more friends than anyone on the ship."

"How can he make any enemies," laughed Hendrick, "when he never opens his mouth except to make that noise like a foghorn."

"Harumph!" roared Stieffy.

It was impossible not to laugh along with him. Even the Muis chuckled. As for Jan, he rolled on the floor like a clown holding his stomach.

Stieffy is under contract to van Rensselaer, the patroon, who owns the *Rensselaerswyck*. So are the Norwegians and the blacksmith.

"Uncle Hendrick," said Jesse, "when you get your tobacco plantation on Manhattan, will you be a patroon too?"

"Blikskaters, boy! I will have 200 acres. Van Rensselaer has 2000 square miles!"

"Then how do you become a patroon?" persisted Jesse.

"Very difficult. In the first place you have to be one of the original share-holders of the Dutch West India Company. Then the Company allows you to buy land from the Wilden and gives you the title of patroon providing you send over and maintain at least fifty men there. Several have tried. Van Rensselaer is the only one to succeed. He has agents out over half of Europe looking for colonists. Even so he has barely enough men and it's cost him an arm and a leg."

"Why doesn't the patroon conscript some English," asked Lanky wrapping those long legs round and round his stool. "It ought to be easy to persuade people to leave this God-forsaken place."

"Do you think van Rensselaer will ever visit his own Colony?" asked Annetje.

"No. He is too old and too rich. For him the patroonship is just an investment," said Hendrick, rising to his feet. "Now I must get back to supervise the rummaging. I'll take Jan with me, Rachel. When it comes to crawling into small stinky holes, nobody can beat this lad."

I shuddered at the thought of all that sewage seeping down into the ballast, but Jan beamed with pride, wolfed down the last of his pie, and jumped up eager to be off.

The Muis was also anxious to get back. I did not want her to arrive in company with my handsome, fun-loving brother, so I persuaded Jehan to escort her separately. In his dignified manner he thanked the blacksmith with such diplomacy that the brawny curmudgeon agreed to let his vrouw come ashore every morning to take care of Little Rachel. Nothing was said about our room being over the tavern. What the smith does not know will not hurt him.

On Sunday we all trooped up to the Church of the Holy Trinity to witness the baptism. True to his word, Albert had the baby christened Storm. Annetje now believes that the gypsy predicted they would call him "Storm" and that she, Annetje, misheard and thought the old woman said "Stam."

When the repairs and rummaging were almost finished, Captain Schellinger went to Barnstaple, twelve miles south of here, where he arranged for us to sail in company with two English ships about to cross the Atlantic. Stam returned from his overland journey to Plymouth bringing with him more hair-raising accounts of shipwrecks and disasters in the wake of the storm.

The cargo officer's return meant Hendrick was able to spend more time at the tavern. He also began to pay more attention to the Muis. The fact that he's married to Gertrude never stops my brother from appreciating a dainty ankle. All perfectly harmless, but it makes me uneasy because the smith is clearly deranged and you never know what he might do. Then, on Monday, the eighth of December, the blacksmith made his first and last appearance at the Golden Lion. Even when I shut my eyes I cannot wipe out that dreadful scene.

Half a dozen men, including both my brothers, were playing a card-game called "bone-ace." Hendrick asked the Muis to sit beside him for luck and had already collected a large pile of coins. He gave a handful of copper farthings to Little Rachel who was squatting on the floor contentedly dropping them one by one into a pewter bowl. I sat behind Isaack who was losing. However the stakes were not high and there was much drinking and joking going on.

I remember noticing Hans, the blacksmith's helper, standing behind Hendrick's chair. Suddenly the outside door flew open. Laughter died as that insane bull of a smith charged toward us. Hendrick rose. Only Little Rachel and Hans were between them. I grabbed the child and the smith flung his puny apprentice to the floor. A woman screamed. Wooden stools overturned as men sprang to their feet. Then I saw the flash of a knife in Hans's hand and I started to scream.

The next thing I knew Hans had fled and the blacksmith was on the floor with the little Muis desperately trying to quench the flow of blood from his neck. Jehan quickly pushed her aside and used a tablecloth to stem the bleeding. Under his supervision, four sailors carried the wounded man upstairs and laid him on our feather-bed. Jehan worked through the night but it was useless. Cornelis Thomasz, blacksmith, died at dawn in the tavern he despised.

That afternoon I stood beside the little Muis as they buried her husband in the wintry churchyard. She wept. But I knew she wept for the strong handsome man she had married far away in Rotterdam, not the wrathful tyrant he had become.

Captain Schellinger offered to arrange for the widow to return to the Fatherland but she refused. She said she had no family any more and would rather come with us to the New World and help me with the children. I was only too glad to have her.

What to do about Hans was more of a problem. That he had murdered his employer was indisputable but the Skipper felt sorry for the boy. Besides, if he reported a murder there was bound to be a long delay. So he informed the authorities that the death was an accident and we made preparations to sail on the first favorable wind.

Unfortunately the innkeeper's report did not tally with the Skipper's. The sheriff issued summonses to all concerned and removed the *Rensselaerswyck*'s rudder just to make sure. Two weeks after his death, the blacksmith's body was dug up and examined by the coroner. Young Hans confessed his guilt and was led away "in the name of the King."

I must close now. Stam is leaving for Barnstaple where an Amsterdam-bound ship will take our mail. (There's a big fat envelope to Gertrude from Hendrick.)

I pray that my next letter will be posted from Manhattan.

Your devoted cousin,

Rachel

Pirates

Off the coast of Africa

This 25th day of January
In the Year of Our Lord 1637
Off the coast of Africa

Dearest Margariet,

We had a near disaster yesterday. About noon a tiny sail was spotted on the western horizon and the passengers immediately began laying wagers as to whether she was Dutch or not. (Did you know that nine out of ten ships that sail the Atlantic are Dutch?) Then Jan scrambled down from the poop deck with a message from the Skipper.

"She's a Frenchman!" he yelled, "and the Skipper wants to speak to Papa."

Jehan departed muttering something about the Frenchman not following the regular trade routes, but I wasn't listening. I was concentrating on my insides. Yes, there was another twinge. Soon those twinges would become labor pains. I decided not to tell anyone yet, not even the Muis. What a Godsend the tiny widow has become. She and Little Rachel were in the cabin now, making a rag doll together.

I was roused from my daydreams by the shouting of orders above and the sudden activity of the crew. Jehan returned to announce that the Frenchman was on a course which would directly intercept us. This might be a coincidence but the Skipper suspected she was up to no good. To test her intentions we were changing course and adding every available inch of canvas.

For the first time I realized the danger. You hear so many tales of privateers who zig-zag the trade routes looking for a ship sailing alone. Do you remember that young couple that lived near Pieterskerk and decided to go to the West Indies? In a month the widow was back in Leyden with nothing but the clothes she stood up in. They had been overtaken by pirates near Dunkirk. The couple had a thousand guilders hidden under the mattress, but when a sword-waving rogue demanded his purse, the husband

31

claimed that he had no money. The villain didn't argue. He simply ran him through with the blade.

Of course the hysterical wife promptly handed over the purse, and the rest of the terrified passengers did likewise. Only two others were killed, a luckless fellow who really had no money, and a fool who tried to resist. The outlaws methodically transferred all the cargo, chests and livestock to their own ship, leaving the victims with barely enough rations to limp home.

I looked again at the tiny sail in the distance. Yes, she was definitely closer. Worse still, she had changed course to correspond with our new direction. An hour passed. In spite of our best efforts the gap between the ships was narrowing and it was becoming obvious that we could not out-run the Frenchman.

Captain Schellinger summoned Jehan and a few others to a council of war. One option was to change course tonight and try to escape under cover of darkness. Our chances were slim. In the end we would almost certainly be forced to fight or surrender. The *Rensselaerswyck* with only four cannon was no match for a privateer.

Instead the Skipper recommended that we grab the offensive immediately and pretend to be a privateer ourselves. Arms were issued to the crew and all able-bodied men, with the less fit given duty between decks. Jehan dug out his grandfather's sword from the bottom of our chest.

"I hadn't expected to need this," he said calmly but I could see the pulse thumping in his neck. Whenever Jehan is nervous you can see that pulse pounding away.

The main deck was quickly cleared with sailors' chests piled into the cabin, blocking all but the innermost berths. Women and children and two ailing male passengers were ordered into these. Jesse was already in my berth. I squeezed into his, and the two invalids climbed up above us. The one over me was so heavy that the bulge sagging down almost met the rise of my protruding stomach. The others, including the Muis and Little Rachel, were across the aisle.

Then hay was tossed into the cabin and three protesting cows were pushed in with us. Both bedridden men had miraculous recoveries at the sight of the cattle. They escaped just before the cabin door slammed shut. My heart sank as I heard the key turn in the lock. You know I cannot bear to be locked in anywhere.

"Don't let me hear a sound in there," shouted Stam. "If them young'uns so much as chirp, smother 'em."

One side of my bunk was completely blocked off with boxes and trunks. When I tried to rise up onto my elbows, my head hit the berth above. I was confined in a space the size of a coffin. I prayed that the terror would not hit.

If I could just stand up I was sure I would be all right, but a cow had wedged her rear end into the tiny open space at the end of our chest. I prodded her with my foot. She had no place to go and only rewarded me with a pile of moist dung.

It was no use looking for help. Jesse was asleep, and even awake he was as weak as a kitten. God knows where Jan was, and I was separated from the rest of the women by an insurmountable mountain range of undulating cattle. Now I was having trouble breathing. My stomach was so swollen that I could not turn over. I felt like a turtle stranded on its back.

At last by rocking from side to side I managed to get on to my stomach and drag myself sidewise to the chest. As I inched along I shoved books, biscuits and other displaced oddments onto the bed. Then with a tremendous effort I pulled myself to my feet on top of the chest. It was impossible to stand upright without hitting the deckhead, but I could lean my elbows on the upper berths. Slowly the terror disappeared.

From here I could see over the aisle-full of complaining cows. The Muis, who was holding Little Rachel, motioned for me to lie down but I had no intention of getting back into that coffin. If we were boarded by pirates they would find me on my feet. Oh Lord, I had forgotten the warning twinges. This was no time to go into labor.

Jan was the only one not isolated on one side of the aisle. To him the cows were a challenge. He swung back and forth over their heads, occasionally producing a moo of displeasure as he rested one foot on a broad bovine back.

Then we heard shouting. The portholes were blocked with piled-up chests but by hanging upside-down from the topmost, Jan could see out. He reported that the crew were taking in sail and we felt the *Rensselaerswyck* swing about. Now Jan could see the Frenchman. He said she was carrying six guns, three on a side.

"Potverdikki!" he whispered hoarsely. "We got wood logs in the starboard ports."

"Don't be silly," I whispered back. "Those are iron cannon."

No, he insisted they were wood and looked like four neatly-cut sections of bowsprit. He said the four real cannon, on their proper gun carriages, were mounted on the port side. Of course! From a distance the *Rensselaerswyck* would appear to be bristling with eight cannon. We gave the Frenchman only a minute to digest this profile. Then we swung 90 degrees and held our genuine broadside to the enemy.

Jan said that two men were assigned to each gun. Isaack and Stieffy, both in red stocking caps, were stationed by one of the fake cannon. Just as well, as I'm sure neither knows a thing about firing a real cannon.

"Gotchoo! Gotchoo!" Through the bolted door I could hear Isaack sneezing from imaginary gunpowder.

And so, with sails furled, we awaited the enemy. Jan, as usual, was hungry and crawled around under me searching for biscuits and apples. Jesse woke up and asked for water. Jan held it for him.

Then I had my first labor pain. I shifted my weight from one foot to the other and held tightly to the edge of the upper berth. It lasted only a minute. How could I pick such a dreadful time to give birth?

Across the aisle Annetje was searching for something in her trunk. She pulled out her purse and hid it under the mattress. Useless of course, but I could not help thinking about our own purse. Were we really going to hand over everything without a struggle? What choice did we have? Then I had an even more frightening thought. Jehan was so distinguished looking that the villains would expect him to have more and would assume we had hidden the rest. Then what would they do to us?

Still I must try to save a few guilders. Was there no place to hide anything except under the mattress? I tried to imagine this cabin without the boxes, trunks and cattle. Then I had an inspiration.

The first step was to get our purse from the chest. Even with Jan's help this was no easy task because I was standing firmly on the lid. If my stomach were not so big I could have stood on the edge of the bed. As it was I could not balance that way at all. Finally I put one foot on each lower berth and one hand on each upper. This meant Jan could open the chest only a few inches, but he found the purse and also a child's sock that I asked for. With my back to the aisle I quietly transferred a handful of gold coins to the sock and knotted it. I must not be too greedy. Then I deliberately hid the purse under the mattress while the others nodded their approval from across the aisle.

Jan alone was aware of the sock. I asked if he thought he could slip it inside the cabin lantern when no one was looking. He agreed eagerly and stuffed it into his pocket. Then he stuck an apple jauntily between his teeth and scrambled over the top bunks.

Jan is a born performer as well as a natural conspirator. First he went into his usual swinging act, leaping back and forth across the aisle. At one point the apple fell. He dove after it, wriggling under cow-bellies until he emerged with straw in his hair and a filthy apple in one hand. After a quick swipe with his shirt he restored the apple to his teeth, a position he clearly felt appropriate for his current assignment. I was sure the sock was now being trampled under bovine hoofs, but the next swing across the aisle there was a tiny clink as Jan passed behind the lantern. Thank heaven! The coins were safe at least until dark.

Suddenly there was a commotion outside and Jan leaped for his station at the porthole. Captain Schellinger was hailing the Frenchman through a speaking-trumpet and I strained my ears for the distant reply which was not long coming. The privateer claimed to be out of La Rochelle and looking for booty. They were planning to board us.

Then another bellow from Schellinger. He said we were out of Amsterdam and looking for good booty ourselves. This time he thundered so loudly that baby Storm began to howl and Annetje plopped a plump breast into his mouth to stifle him. The Muis hugged Little Rachel to keep her quiet and at the same time I felt another labor pain coming on. Sweet Jesus! It was not ten minutes since the last one. I tried walking up and down the length of the chest with an arm resting on each upper berth. I wished I could stand upright but at least it was better than lying down.

For one hour the two ships faced each other, just out of firing range. On deck our men glared at the enemy. I pictured Isaack and Stieffy scowling fiercely beneath red stocking caps as they manned their fake cannon. Thank God the pirates could not see inside the cabin where insanity reigned. Children whimpered, cows groaned. Jan flew through the air with an apple in his teeth and I paced up and down on top of a box having labor pains.

Finally the pirates decided there were easier pickings to be had elsewhere. They fired a parting salute and set out to the west. We fired one shot in response and speedily set all sail for the south. God be praised for our narrow escape.

Just after midnight, on a calm sea near the Island of Madeira, our baby girl was born. We named her Marie after my mother. There has never been a more beautiful, perfectly-formed child. God be doubly praised for this miracle.

It is now four months to the day since we left Amsterdam. I remember how I used to dread the thought of giving birth at sea among strangers, but there are no strangers anymore. Everyone from the Skipper down to the most lowly seaman considers himself an uncle to the two babies, Storm and Marie.

The dear little Muis has become like a sister to me. She takes complete charge of Little Rachel who adores her. For days on end I just sit on deck with the baby, watching the blue-green water roll endlessly by and dreaming of the beautiful home we will build on Manhattan with my red and yellow tulips by the door and bright shiny windows in every room. Hendrick says grapevines run wild on Manhattan, covering every tree-trunk. They do not get enough sun so the grapes are sour, but we will build arbors.

Papa always claimed that the Hudson Valley was the ideal place for a settlement. It was the Company Directors who would not listen. They sent him and Jehan to South America to select a site. Only then did they change their minds and dispatch thirty of Papa's followers to the Hudson. That was thirteen years ago.

One of those thirty was Papa's good friend, Philippe du Trieux. I wonder if he will be on hand to meet us when we arrive. Uncle Gerard wrote to say we were coming but there was no reply.

Near the Canary Islands we changed course and are now heading directly for the New World. A flying fish landed on deck splattering my skirt and the baby's blanket. Hendrick says it is a good omen.

Now we are in the Sargasso Sea, the calm center of the Atlantic about which the ocean currents circle. Golden weeds full of tiny crabs and seahorses lie on all sides. Willem told a harrowing tale of a ship that became trapped in these weeds and was swallowed by monsters. He used the hand with the fingers missing to grab at his neck like a claw, at the same time making horrible gargling noises in his throat. The children screamed with fright but Hendrick says the whole story is so much hogwash.

After seventeen days we emerged from the weeds into a heavy rainstorm. At noon there was a great uproar on deck and Willem rushed into the cabin shouting, "Make ready to abandon ship!"

Pandemonium broke out as passengers shoved and pushed their way out. I grabbed the baby. Behind me Jehan carried Little Rachel in one arm and helped Jesse with the other. God knows where Jan was.

On deck we were greeted by a terrifying spectacle. A huge column of water, a hundred feet high, was coming directly toward us. Above the panic I heard the Skipper shout a command to take in all sail. As the crew struggled desperately against time, the crowd pushed me toward the ship's boat. Dimly I wondered what had happened to the chickens. What good would a small boat be anyway? Now our sails were down and we lay helpless as the whirling tower of angry water was almost upon us.

"All passengers below!" bellowed the Skipper but it was too late.

The ship rocked violently and spray was everywhere. Instinctively I threw myself down on deck on top of the bundle that was Marie. Blessed Saint Nicholas, help us!

There was a terrible pounding noise, then more shouting, but this time for joy. Miraculously the spiraling water had passed behind us. We were safe and none the worse for the encounter except for a good soaking.

I have known men who do not believe in God, but they are not men who have sailed the oceans of this world.

Later Jehan told me privately that he thought Captain Schellinger's decision to take in the sail was a dangerous mistake. Hendrick, however, said it was our very sails that were drawing the waterspout toward us and the Skipper's decision had averted certain disaster. I do not know which is the truth.

Now we are headed northwest and the days grow colder. One dark, rainy Wednesday, we huddled miserably in the cabin. I was too discouraged even to knit. It was February 25th, exactly five months since we set sail from Amsterdam. I think most of us had given up hope of ever arriving anywhere.

Jehan unpacked Rembrandt's sketch and sat staring at it. Usually the expression of triumph on Papa's face is enough to lift his spirit. Today nothing could sweep away the gloom. Slowly he repacked the sketch.

At that moment Jan burst into the cabin.

"They found bottom!" he shouted.

"Where?" ... "What?" ... "How deep?" ... Everyone spoke at once.

"Fifty fathoms," he said, proudly. "Black stones and red stones and a whole buncha sand."

"Deo gratias," said Jehan.

That night the crew took soundings every hour as the depth gradually decreased. Jehan could not sleep. I felt him turning and hunching beside me as I lay with Marie between me and the bulkhead to protect her from his restlessness. Then he would crawl out and pace up and down the cabin as I listened for muffled voices.

Somehow the results of every sounding were known instantly throughout the ship. Jehan would climb back into bed with a whispered message for me.

"Sand at twenty fathoms"!

At four bells into the second watch they found bottom at twelve fathoms. This was too close for comfort. There was much shouting and great creaking noises as we took in the topsail and came about, retracing our course. When we had a good seventeen fathoms, the *Rensselaerswyck* headed north, through the night, up the coast of the New World.

Thursday dawned cold and foggy. The latitude was 37 degrees which meant we were passing the Virginias. In vain we craned our necks to see the coast line, only a few miles away. Occasionally a smudge appeared on the horizon but even with a telescope it was impossible to make out any features.

At three o'clock the Skipper identified the first landmark, Smits Island, just east of a place called Cape Charles. We all trooped out eagerly to get our first real look at the New World.

Freezing rain drizzled down my neck and the place looked ominously inhospitable against a gloomy gray background. I went back inside, wrapped myself in my blanket, and sat shivering on the edge of the berth.

"It's an evil place," I whispered.

Jehan heard me. "My dear, it's the weather that's evil, not the island."

I wish he was not always so logical. For no good reason tears ran down my cheeks.

Friday night I was awakened out of a sound sleep by a hand on my shoulder and an almost inaudible whisper.

"Psst, Rachel. It's me, Hendrick." He motioned for me to follow him.

I crept out of bed leaving Marie and her father fast asleep. Quietly I pulled on my shoes and cloak. Hendrick took my hand and we tiptoed through the dark cabin full of snoring passengers.

When we were children, he would lead me by the hand just like this to show me a surprise. Once it was a basketful of newborn kittens. His enthusiasm always made the surprise especially exciting to a little sister. I smiled to myself at the memory.

We stepped out on to the main deck which was lit by a thousand golden stars.

"I just came off watch, Rachel. I couldn't wait to show you something." He guided me over to the rail and pointed in the direction of the shoreline.

At first I could see nothing but blackness. Then a tiny pinpoint of light appeared, then another and another. Soon I was looking at a dozen little bright dots.

"Those are campfires of the Wilden, Rachel. Here, look through this." He handed me a telescope.

With the glass to my eye the pinpoints grew brighter and began to flicker like flames. It was eerie to think there were Indians so close.

"Where are we, Hendrick? Is this still the Virginias?"

"No. This belongs to the Netherlands. We are just coming to the mouth of the South River which the English call the Delaware. Back in '31, my friend, Captain de Vries, put 28 men ashore on this river to start a settlement. I was offered the position of managing it for him, but before I even set sail they were all massacred."

I shuddered. Of course I had heard the story many times. "Thank God you weren't there," I whispered.

"If I had been there, little sister, it wouldn't have happened. There is no more loyal friend than an Indian if you treat him fairly."

I looked through the glass again and tried to believe him.

"If anything should ever happen to me, Rachel, I want you to look for an Indian named Moose Foot. He has been a good friend to me."

"Moose Foot," I murmured. "What an odd name." Of course I had no idea how one goes about locating an Indian.

"How long does it take to get from the South River to Manhattan," I asked.

"Depends on the wind. Could be only two days if we're lucky." He hesitated then cleared his throat. "There's something else I have to ask you, Rachel. Is the Muis going to marry Lanky?"

I laughed. Since we left Ilfracombe, every unmarried man aboard, except maybe Stieffy, has been after the little widow. Lanky was the most persistent, but as far as I knew the Muis was not interested.

"Have you forgotten that you're not a bachelor?" I teased.

"Don't be silly," he said. "It's Stieffy. The poor fellow is really smitten. He told me he's never even been close to a woman before. You know he has the berth right above the Muis. Every night he lies awake trying to think of something to say to her. Finally in desperation he came to me. He's a good man and I promised to help. Do you think it's hopeless?"

I tried to readjust my thinking to the prospect of the inarticulate hog dealer as a suitor.

"It's not hopeless," I said. "After the blacksmith was killed, I remember the Skipper asking the Muis if she would like to change the location of her berth. She said she preferred to stay where she was because she trusted Stieffy."

Hendrick brightened. "That's a beginning. Tomorrow I shall speak to the Muis on Stieffy's behalf."

On Sunday, the first of March, the ship was surrounded by a school of friendly whales, leaping, diving and cavorting playfully as though to entertain us. The children were enchanted and I was astonished by the apparent intelligence of the beasts. A dozen of them escorted the *Rensselaerswyck* for a good two hours.

At sunset we came to anchor behind a sandy hook at the entrance to the great bay which is the mouth of the Hudson. We were now only fifteen miles from the island of Manhattan. In the morning, however, the wind was from the northwest, and the weather so rough we could not make the narrows which guard the entrance to the harbor proper. So we stayed where we were and the ship's boat took a party ashore to shoot geese. They spent the night on the hook. It was bitter cold and I did not envy them.

The next day, to the astonishment of all, my shy little Muis was officially betrothed to the bashful hog dealer. Captain Schellinger broke out some bottles from his private store. Even Lanky swallowed his pride and joined in the general merriment as we drank a hundred toasts to the happy couple. Then we feasted on roast goose and the *Rensselaerswyck* overflowed with joy and goodwill.

I look forward to tomorrow, especially to hearing from you. Has the baby arrived yet? I pray all is well with you both.

Please give my regards to Uncle Gerard and Aunt Hester and of course Gertrude.

Your devoted cousin,

Rachel

Manhattan

Thursday, the 5th of March, 1637,
On the island of Manhattan,
By the Grace of God

Dearest Margariet,

Today I received six wonderful letters from you. You cannot imagine how happy it makes me to hear all your good news. I am glad you have decided to stay with Uncle Gerard and Aunt Hester for a while longer. Leasing a place of your own in Leyden is terribly expensive and buying is all but impossible.

You will be appalled to learn that Hendrick received NO letters from Gertrude! He says that she probably was waiting to hear from him first, but I know he is heartbroken. I have forgiven that sister of yours for not sailing with us. I have forgiven her for not even showing up to see her husband off. But I don't think I can ever forgive her for not writing to him.

Yesterday morning we left Sandy Hook and reached the narrows at noon. There was heavy fog and by four o'clock the main deck was crowded with passengers straining to catch their first glimpse of New Amsterdam. The ship's bell clanged continuously all day. Now another answering bell sounded ahead.

I don't know what I expected. Certainly nothing like Leyden with its beautiful canals and handsome brick houses. With Marie in my arms I stood at the rail beside the Muis who was holding Little Rachel, perhaps for the last time. How I will miss her when she and Stieffy and the others continue up-river to Fort Orange. I must speak to Jehan about a wedding gift.

"There she lies!" someone cried, as the tip of Manhattan slowly emerged from the fog.

My heart sank at the sight. New Amsterdam is nothing but a cluster of wooden huts set haphazardly in the mud around a crumbling fort, its orange, white and blue flag waving pathetically above. One lone windmill faces the sky, bare arms lifeless. How could we have risked our lives a hundred times over, only to reach this God-forsaken place?

Along the shore a score of rowdy settlers stared at us. Some waved and shouted words of welcome. All around me passengers jostled each other as they shouted back.

I began to feel dizzy. Maybe I had been on my feet too long. I must not give up now. A woman is the heart of her family. If she collapses the whole family sinks. I looked down at Jesse clinging to the rail, his dear, pinched, lopsided face creased with worry.

"It'll be all right, Jess." I forced myself to smile. "We will soon be snug in our own little home."

What home? How can I ever make a home in all this mud?

"Wave, Mama, wave!" yelled Jan above me. He had climbed the shrouds and was hanging out half over the water with excitement.

I scanned the rough unfamiliar faces. One woman in a gaudy red skirt had climbed on to the small wooden pier as though it were a stage, and was making peculiar, lewd gestures.

"It's Grietje the whore!" came a shout from the rigging.

"Whore! Whore! Two-pound-butter whore!" chanted another.

At this Grietje turned her back to us, lifted her petticoats up to her waist and bent over. As God is my witness, she did not have a stitch on above the top of her stockings. With one hand she slapped her bare backside and from her upside-down painted grin came a scream, "Bless my sweet ass!" The sailors went wild.

"She'll have her hands full tonight," laughed Stam.

Over the catcalls and whistling, a voice proclaimed that Grietje was the most famous whore this side of the Atlantic. I wonder if she really charges two pounds of butter. What a madhouse! How can I possibly bring up four children in this dreadful place?

Of course both boys were fascinated by the spectacle. Jan is a great imitator. If Grietje had stood on her head, Jan would have stood on his. Fortunately something told him that this performance was not to be copied. He contented himself by whistling shrilly with two fingers in his mouth.

Then an old witch in black hobbled over followed by an ugly three-legged dog. She began to screech and shake her stick at the performance, but she was unable to climb onto the pier and Grietje skipped easily out of reach.

Was everyone here raving mad? I searched in vain for one sympathetic face. The whole town was on hand now, mostly rough-looking men, expressions hidden behind beards that have not known razor in a donkey's age. In the background stood several Indians wearing furs turned inside out. Their faces were hairless as were their scalps, except for a narrow ridge down the middle that stood up like black pig-bristles. They had no expressions at all.

Small boats began to ply back and forth between ship and shore. I watched Hendrick and Stam set out busily. Now the winter afternoon was drawing to a close and long cold shadows crept in to the very marrow of the bone.

Above the commotion, a man's voice echoed across the water. "Have you a Doctor Montagne aboard?"

I heard Jehan answer. Then more shouting. It was my father's friend, Philippe du Trieux.

Jan was almost overboard with excitement. "Mama, they're calling us!"

Somehow they lowered us into a small boat that smelled of dead fish. The dizziness came back and I put my head down on top of Marie. Her bundled warmth felt good against my frozen cheek as I fought to keep the world from spinning.

The next thing I knew we were at the home of Philippe du Trieux and his wife, Susannah. Bone tired, I sat by the roaring fire nursing the baby while Susannah bustled about the hearth where savory odors issued from bubbling pots. A homely redheaded girl gave the children porridge and hot cider and tucked them into trundle-beds in the side chamber. Then Philippe handed me a glass of port. One sip and I was dead to the world.

When I awoke it was pitch-black and at first I did not know where I was. Then I realized that I was in the side chamber with Jehan snoring beside me and the children asleep on trundles. It was Marie's murmuring that roused me. In a few minutes she would start to cry. Oddly enough the loud rumble of Jehan's snoring never disturbs me, but one tiny peep from a babe and I am always wide awake.

I crept out of bed and stole across the icy floor in my stocking feet. In the kitchen the fire was dead, but moonlight filtering through one unshuttered window helped me get my bearings. With a shovel I uncovered red coals banked over with ashes for the night. Logs and kindling were stacked nearby and I soon had a friendly blaze going.

Then I saw my great-grandmother's cradle. I learned later that Jehan had returned to the ship last night for our chest and persuaded Hendrick to search the hold for the cradle, knowing it would give my spirits a lift. Susannah had cleaned it up and lined it with a soft blanket. I fetched Marie, changed her, wrapped us both in a quilt and sat down by the fire to wait for the dawn. It was a long time since I had eaten. Still Marie suckled away contentedly. How wondrous are the laws of nature!

My mother used to say, "When life seems hopeless, Rachel, remember that things are bound to look brighter in the morning."

She was so right. Last night I had been good for nothing, now I was ready to face the world. I gazed with satisfaction at the old oak cradle with its lovingly carved Bible scenes. In a century it had survived the flight from Avesnes to Leyden, and it had survived the worst Atlantic storm in history. Today it would begin a new century with a new infant in a new world.

Suddenly I had the uneasy feeling that I was not alone. Instinctively I glanced at the window and my heart froze. Pressed against the glass was a distorted, savage face. Instantly the face disappeared and there was nothing but night sky with the first pale gray streak of dawn.

Slowly the tug of the child at my breast brought my heart back to normal. By the time Susannah entered a few minutes later I had half persuaded myself that it was a dream.

I liked Susannah immediately. She is only a few years older than I, with a lovely face but a low hoarse voice. I wonder if 13 years in this country could cause one to go hoarse. When I apologized for collapsing last night she gave a husky laugh.

"Poppycock! I've been looking forward to your arrival ever since we got the letter from your Uncle Gerard. You are welcome to stay with us as long as you want. As for collapsing, it was Philippe's fault for giving you that port on an empty stomach. Besides, a good night's sleep is just what you needed. Here, drink this." She fixed me some hot beer. "It's the best thing I know for bringing milk."

I drank gratefully and after a few swallows, felt myself letting down a great surge of milk. Marie opened her eyes wide with astonishment at the sudden windfall. We giggled like schoolgirls at her expression.

"I hear you had a wild reception yesterday," said Susannah preparing breakfast as we talked.

I laughed. It felt so good to find one friendly face in this country that I was prepared to forget yesterday.

"If you had arrived in the morning," she continued, "Director General Wouter van Twiller would have been there to welcome you and Grietje might have behaved better. Unfortunately Wouter is always dead-drunk by four o'clock."

I was appalled. "Jehan has a letter of introduction to the Governor," I stammered. "Is that the same van Twiller?"

She nodded. "The Governor's title is Director General but he's younger than I am and everyone calls him Wouter. He's friendly enough and fat as a pig, but he has no control over what goes on here and doesn't care. He just sits and drinks all day. When God gave out brains he missed Wouter completely."

"How could the Company appoint him?" I asked in dismay. "What happened to Governor Minuit?"

"Peter Minuit was a good man but the Company recalled him for spending too much money. Wouter's not just a fool, he's a thoroughly corrupt fool. He has only one qualification for the position."

"What's that?"

"He's a nephew of van Rensselaer."

At that moment Philippe stomped through on his way out to milk the cows. He is much older than Susannah, with a weatherbeaten face and graying beard. His greeting was gruff but the blue eyes were kind.

Breakfast was a substantial affair and we sat at a long wooden board table down the center of the room. There were four du Trieux children: two-year-old Rebecca, six-year-old Abraham, Sutje, a pretty golden-haired girl of nine, and twelve-year-old Sarah who had wild red hair, long gangly legs and too many teeth. The main dish was an odd-looking yellow porridge which, to my surprise, tasted delicious.

"Mmm, this is good. What is it?"

"Suppawn," said Susannah. "It's ground maize cooked with milk."

I had heard of maize, the Indian corn that grows on long yellow ears, but I had never seen any. Jan managed to gobble down three bowlfuls.

Finally I got up enough courage to mention the face at the window. Jehan looked worried, but Susannah was quick to reassure us.

"The Wilden are like lambs, Rachel. In thirteen years never once has a Christian woman been molested by an Indian."

"Other way round's a different story," muttered Philippe under his breath.

After breakfast we left the redhead in charge and Philippe rowed Jehan, Susannah and me into town. I was a little nervous about leaving a twelve-year-old with seven little ones including an infant.

"Don't worry about Sarah," said Susannah. "She's like a sergeant with a platoon. She'll have them scrub pots, sweep the floor, rock the baby or just march up and down in formation. Her secret is never to do any work herself unless absolutely necessary. She uses all her whirlwind energy in ordering others around. She marks them like a schoolmaster for chores well done, whacks them when they get out of line, and shifts them on to the next task before they get bored."

I thought to myself that Jan would get more than his share of whacks before the day was done.

The du Trieux home is on a hillock overlooking the East River just north of town. Today there were a dozen small boats on the water in addition to the *Rensselaerswyck* and an English vessel. Across the river is a pleasant view of pine forest which looks like mainland but Susannah says is part of a huge island called Long Island.

We beached the rowboat on the Strand and the men set out for the Fort to meet the Governor and to collect our mail. Susannah and I headed for the church to make arrangements to have Marie baptized. Afterwards Susannah would show me the house that Philippe has selected for us to lease until we can build our own.

The weather was mild for March, and New Amsterdam bustled with activity. Many of our fellow-passengers strolled about looking at the sights, and a gang of sailors from the English vessel staggered past, singing at the top of their lungs.

"They're on their way to Boston," laughed Susannah. "It's impossible to get a drop up there, so they drink like fish here."

We saw dozens of strange-looking Indians who stared at us impassively. Some carried beaver skins for trading, others reeled along drunker than the sailors. The colonists themselves couldn't have been more friendly as housewives hurried out to welcome me in accents from all over Europe. Even Grietje, the whore, seemed almost normal this morning with her skirts down and two toddlers in tow. She offered to sell me some peach trees from her husband's orchard.

There are about fifty houses in all, some no more than huts but others wooden homes like that of the du Trieux, with thatched roofs and half garrets. In between are fences but no proper streets, just vast tracts of mud filled with chickens and rooting pigs.

The church is a wooden barn, but the Dominie's cottage next door has neatly-trimmed bushes and a pleasant garden running down to the East River. Dominie Everardus Bogardus is a handsome bachelor in his early thirties. He welcomed us into a surprisingly neat kitchen and insisted that we have a seat and sample his Madeira.

"What a small world this is, Madame Montagne. I was a student at the University of Leyden while Dr. Montagne was on the wild coast of South

America. Now, ten years later and 3000 miles away we shall at last shake hands."

I thought it odd to be sipping Madeira at nine o'clock in the morning, but our host was charming although unlike any man of the cloth I have ever met. When we finally took our leave we ran into Stieffy and the Muis, on their way to ask the Dominie to marry them.

"The river is still frozen over up north so we may be here for weeks," said the Muis after I had introduced Susannah. "Furthermore there is no minister at Fort Orange."

"Harrumph!" boomed Stieffy happily.

I was delighted. "We will hold the wedding-party in our new home," I exclaimed in a burst of optimism.

From the church we turned westward, heading across Manhattan toward the Hudson. On our right were five connected stone buildings belonging to the Company. Susannah pointed to one with goats tied out front.

"That's the Company store. They let you buy on credit," she said, "but watch your account. The bookkeeper has the stickiest fingers in town."

Diagonally across from the store a crowd had gathered around a lopsided wagon loaded with manure. One wheel was stuck fast in a hole the size of a horse-trough. The driver, a tall, angry-looking mulatto, alternated between whipping his beast, tugging it, and shouting profanities. All to no avail.

"That's Grietje's husband," whispered Susannah. "Half Moroccan. We call him the Turk."

Spectators shouted good-natured instructions in half a dozen different languages. This place is more like a modern-day Babel than a Dutch colony. Finally the Turk unyoked his exhausted animal and some bystanders tried to lift the wheel free. Unfortunately there was room for only one man to get a good purchase on the corner of the wagon. Exerting pressure on the flimsy wagon-shafts was useless.

"Unload the stinkin' cow-shit!" cried a voice as the Turk angrily lined the men up for another attempt.

We joined two women who were watching the proceedings at a discreet distance to avoid getting splattered. One was the old witch from yesterday, still accompanied by the three-legged dog which looks more like a dirty, white pig with a black patch over one eye. Susannah introduced her as Madame Vinje-Dam.

The second woman, Madame de Rapelje, had a pleasant face and must have been about Susannah's age. They were both Walloons, and like the du

Trieux, had been here thirteen years. Madame Vinje-Dam proudly informed me that she was the First Lady of New Amsterdam and always sat at the Governor's right hand at official banquets. I nodded politely, but found it difficult to believe that any Governor, however dull-witted, would choose to sit next to such a face. She seemed to have only two teeth, rather like yellow fangs.

"Tchah! Good thing you're French, young woman," she hissed through the fangs. "Dutch girls that come here are all whores."

At that moment two Indians emerged from the store with bolts of red and blue duffel-cloth. The Witch eyed them with disgust and spat pointedly.

"Tell you something else, young woman," she said raising her voice to the screech level. "Never go into the store with Wilden there. Thieving varmints stink worse than bear-dung!"

I wanted to sink into the earth but the Wilden paid no attention and stared without expression at the disabled wagon. Perhaps they do not understand French.

"Tchah! There you are," shrieked Madame Vinje-Dam, hurrying across to the ring of spectators and jabbing a pair of broad shoulders with her stick. After a short argument she limped off, with the dog limping behind and Broad Shoulders in reluctant pursuit.

"Is that her son?" I inquired, glad to be rid of such poisonous company.

"No, it's her husband." The other two burst into laughter at my astonished expression.

"He looks about thirty," I mumbled.

"Poor old Guillaume Vinje died a few years back. That's her new husband, Jan Dam." said Susannah. "She likes to be called Madame Vinje-Dam."

"Women are very scarce, my dear," added Madame de Rapelje with a twinkle. "Widows don't stay single long."

I was still musing on this topsy-turvy society when I received yet another surprise.

"Here comes the Giant," said Susannah.

As we watched, a small, bearded Dutchman approached the accident followed by a tremendous slave, black as coal. He must weigh 300 pounds, all muscle.

"The Company sent a dozen slaves here back in '26," whispered Madame de Rapelje. "The bearded fellow is the overseer."

The Giant looked puzzled at the sight of the lopsided wagon. Susannah said he was slow-witted and could not speak one word of any Christian tongue. When he finally grasped the problem, his face lit up with boyish delight.

At a signal from the overseer the powerful black man lifted the wagon like a toy. Spectators shouted and cheered as others pulled it clear of the hole. Then this marvelous specimen of a man turned toward us and slowly broke into a broad smile of pure joy. Two rows of flashing white teeth extended from ear to ear. We all smiled back happily.

Madame de Rapelje keeps a tavern just opposite the store. With the excitement over she invited us in for a little drop but Susannah refused. We continued westward toward the dilapidated Fort with its four crumbling bastions where pigs dig holes in the ramparts and chickens nest under rusty cannon.

"People steal the posts for firewood," apologized Susannah. "Anyway, there is no ammunition for those guns."

I was appalled. Thank God the Wilden were so friendly. Through a gap in the wall I could see the barracks and a comfortable brick house which was the Governor's mansion.

On the muddy parade ground outside the gate a sergeant was drilling a small company of soldiers. One poor fellow sat to the side on a sort of trestle, holding his sword aloft in one hand and a pitcher in the other. He looked ridiculous.

"He's being punished," explained Susannah. "That's called riding the wooden horse."

Now we turned north up the Heerenstraat. On our left was the broad Hudson which the locals call the North River. A few houses along on our right was the ramshackle ruin that Philippe had selected for us. Susannah had warned me not to expect too much. Still it was a shock. I stared in - dismay.

New Amsterdam has several vacant houses abandoned by disillusioned colonists returning to Europe. None have brick chimneys, only crossed logs coated with clay. Philippe had inspected them all and declared this to be the safest.

"He says it's structurally sound," muttered Susannah. "Let's go round to the back rather than climb up there." She pointed to the front stoop which had caved in, leaving the door a good four feet above ground.

Susannah had obtained the key from the Dominie who was agent for the departed owner, but we didn't need it. The large barn-door in the rear was unlocked. I propped it open and we stepped gingerly into the dark muddy interior. This half of the house was a stable with stalls for livestock.

Near the chimney, up a couple of steps, was a narrow door leading into the front half which had a wooden floor. From the smell you would think the animals lived in both halves.

I quickly opened the shutters but there was not much to see: two rooms, each with a small, high window, but no glass. The larger room had a fireplace and a ladder leading up to a loft. The floors were warped and caked with mud and ancient manure.

"I didn't know it was so dreadful," apologized Susannah.

The du Trieux had been very kind and I hated to appear ungrateful. "It's not that bad," I said. "Let's get a little more light in here." I struggled with the front door. It was a typical Dutch door, the kind where you can open the top half to let in the sunshine but leave the bottom closed to keep the pigs out. Finally the top swung open. I leaned out and took a deep breath.

Across the Heerenstraat is a little cemetery which I had not noticed before and above it is a spectacular view of the most magnificent river I have ever seen.

"People would pay a fortune for a view like this back in Leyden," I said. The sound of my own voice bolstered my courage. "Give me one week, Susannah, and I'll have this place fit for a king."

As we left I took a closer look at the cemetery. Most of the graves were marked only with wooden crosses. I wondered how so many could have died in just thirteen years. At that moment a tall Indian stepped out of the shadows and came directly toward us. Susannah spoke to him in his own tongue but he was looking at me. Then I recognized the face at the window and I froze.

From his belt the Indian took a wooden trinket and handed it to me. It was an infant's toy made of carved animals strung on a bracelet of reeds. Before I could recover my wits he was gone.

"Susannah!" I whispered. "That was the face at the window!"

"Mais chérie," she laughed. "You said it was a horrible face. That was Moose Foot. He has a very kind face."

So this was Hendrick's friend. Susannah was right. He does have a very kind face.

In case your ears have been burning we received a letter from Uncle Gerard who writes: "Margariet is the sweetest daughter-in-law a man could imagine."

Your affectionate cousin,

Rachel

Vredendale

Dearest Margariet,

What wonderful news about the baby! Gerard is a good strong name and I know Uncle must be so pleased. I am sending a gift which is much too large but he will grow into it.

On this side of the Atlantic we are all well and thriving. Jehan is building himself a nice medical practice although his patients never have any coin. They usually pay in wampum, little white shells strung together. Six white shells equal one dutch stuiver. Purple ones are worth twice as much. And a fathom of wampum is equal to four guilders.

You will be glad to hear that Hendrick has finally received a letter from Gertrude. He is very cheerful and has begun work on his tobacco plantation which he calls "Vredendale" or Valley of Peace. It is 200 acres of rich bottom land about eight miles north of town.

Hendrick is only the second colonist to get permission to settle in the north half of Manhattan and the reason for this is peculiar. Remember we all heard about Governor Minuit having purchased the island of Manhattan from the Indians for 60 guilders? Well it turns out that Minuit was duped. He thought that he bought the whole island from the Manhattan tribe, who agreed to move across the East River to Long Island to join their close kin, the Canarsies. What Minuit did not realize was that northern Manhattan was inhabited by Weckquasgeeks who did not sell and had no intention of leaving.

Jehan feels this is a potentially dangerous state of affairs and should be rectified, but Wouter (Minuit's successor), takes no interest. Fortunately Hendrick is safe because he bought his land twice. Back in '32 he bought it from the Weckquasgeek Chief, Rechnewac, who is Moose Foot's brother. Now he has paid Wouter to have it registered properly.

Jehan is worried because Hendrick did not get a ground brief for the land. He says this payment to Wouter is nothing more than a bribe. But the important thing, at least in my opinion, is that the Indians are so friendly. Everyone says they are "like lambs."

In the meantime I have made a tiny but comfortable home out of the house on the Heerenstraat. I got one good day's work from Willem and Tobias who were able to rebuild the front stoop before Hendrick whisked them off to Vredendale. Then the Company store had just enough tiny panes of leaded glass for our two windows. Isaack installed them for me and he also made a new frame for Rembrandt's sketch of Papa.

With the Muis to help me, the house was scraped, scrubbed and scoured from top to bottom before our belongings were delivered from the *Rensselaerswyck*. Now sunshine streams through my glistening window-panes onto a floor of fresh white sand, and from the newly whitewashed wall, Papa smiles triumphantly down upon his children and grandchildren.

On Sunday, March 22, the Muis and Stieffy were married here and the little house overflowed with merriment.

Three days later the *Rensselaerswyck* set sail for Fort Orange. From the stoop I watched her slowly tack back and forth on her way up-river. For weeks I had been dreading this farewell. But standing there, watching the sun set over the mighty Hudson, it was impossible to be miserable.

Fortunately Hendrick was not needed for the journey to Fort Orange. He and Isaack work all day with Tobias and Willem at Vredendale. At night they sleep under the stars. (Wouter has promised to lend Hendrick some of the Company slaves when they are not needed in town.)

Even Jehan has fallen under the spell of Vredendale. When he has no patients he spends the morning up there overseeing construction. Some-times he sends Isaack down to help me. People say it is a shame that Isaack is not a born leader like Hendrick, but for me it is a blessing. Around the house a willing worker with a strong arm beats a born leader any day.

Did I tell you that Hendrick has bought a somewhat battered yawl called the *Yellow Swan*? After church Sunday he took Jan and me for an outing and I got my first look at Vredendale. He let Jan hold the tiller as we sailed up the East River but took it back when we reached the wide place called Hell Gate Bay.

"There's the famous Hell Gate." Hendrick pointed to our right at the narrow passage leading out to Long Island Sound.

"It doesn't look a bit dangerous," I said with surprise, having heard so many tales about the perils of Hell Gate.

"That's because it's slack water. Right now we could sail through easily, but we'd never get back. In twenty minutes the tide will rush out through that passage with a roar like the highest waterfall. Below the surface are a hundred treacherous rocks and anything caught in the maelstrom would be battered to pieces in the wink of an eye."

Jan whistled with two fingers in his mouth but I shuddered. Hendrick assured me that there was no danger if we kept to the Manhattan shoreline. Later, on our way home, the roar was astonishing. A column of spray rose high in the air to hide the whirlpool that was Hell Gate. It was hard to believe it was the same place.

Opposite Hell Gate a broad creek leads inland to the center of Manhattan. Hendrick said that the point of land North of the creek has just been granted to Jacob van Curler, a cousin of the Governor.

"Our first neighbor, Rachel! He is going to call his bowery Otterspoor. Now look to your left. You can't see it but there is a Weckquasgeek village through those trees. Chief Rechnewac lives there. So does Moose Foot."

When the creek narrowed we beached the yawl and Hendrick led us up onto a bluff where we had a magnificent view of the countryside. There is a mountain about a mile to the north of us.

"That's Slangberg, Sis, the highest mountain on Manhattan. I own all the way from here to the foot of Slangberg."

To our right lie the woods of Otterspoor. Beyond is the Great Kill, the meandering stream that runs from Hell Gate Bay around the north end of Manhattan to join the Hudson. To our left is a chain of high cliffs broken by a ravine through which we could just catch a glimpse of the silver waters of the Hudson itself. And beneath us, on a tapestry of velvet green, lies the rich bottom land which is Vredendale.

Hendrick pointed with pride to the partially-constructed stockade and the large pile of bricks for the center wall and chimney. Today being Sunday there were no workmen about and deer grazed beside the stacked timber. At the sight of the animals Jan shot off down the slope before I could stop him.

"Let the lad go, Sis. There's nothing to harm him. Besides, I have this just in case." He patted his gun.

The deer bolted gracefully into the woods long before Jan reached them. Undaunted, he scrambled up the side of the stockade like a young animal.

"Do you see that well-worn path running along the edge of my land, Rachel? That's the Weckquasgeek Trail. It leads all the way from New Amsterdam up to the Wading-Place at the north end of Manhattan. There, at low tide, you can cross over to the mainland where the trail continues north 150 miles to Fort Orange and beyond. Mark my words. One day that trail will be a wagon road and people will drive all the way from New Amsterdam to Fort Orange."

"Don't you need a watchman here on Sundays?" I asked. "Madame Vinje-Dam says the Wilden are all thieves."

"Blikskaters! I'd a lot sooner have Wilden for neighbors than that poisonous Witch. Besides, I don't need a watchman. Moose Foot keeps an eye on things for me. Look at that lovely waterfall down there. I shall call it De Forest's Fountain." Then he hesitated. "Do you think Gertrude will like it here, Sis?"

I looked up at the cry of an eagle soaring above us in the sunshine. Gertrude is so beautiful and so sophisticated that it is difficult for me to picture her living in this rough country.

"Hendrick," I said, "there isn't a woman in the world who wouldn't give her eye teeth to live in this paradise."

At that moment a flock of blackbirds rose into the air with a cry of warning. Then I saw the mountain lion streaking through the tall grass toward the stockade.

"Jan! Jan!" I screamed, and plunged down the slope.

There was a loud click behind me as Hendrick's gun misfired.

"Sang de Dieu!" he swore loudly.

The huge cat leapt up on to the palisade fence only yards from the boy. I was flying down hill, miraculously still on my feet, but Hendrick was faster. Now he passed me, yelling at the top of his lungs and waving the gun as he ran. Distracted, the creature turned its head in our direction. Unfortunately Jan chose that moment to jump. Instantly the animal crouched, ready to spring. Hendrick was only a hundred yards away now. He roared as the cat sprang.

In mid-air, the animal's body, fully extended, suddenly buckled, spun around and dropped to the ground with an arrow through its neck. Moose Foot emerged from the woods just before I tumbled head over heels into a bramble patch.

By the time I had picked myself up, the Indian had retrieved his arrow and slung the dead cat over one shoulder. Then he and Jan walked toward us side by side.

Please give little Gerard a big hug for me.

Affectionately,

Rachel

Malaria

Dearest Margariet,

My news is so sad that I scarcely know how to begin. Hendrick is dead. My strong, handsome brother died of swamp fever. I will try to recount the sequence of events as best I can.

In June the *Rensselaerswyck* returned from Fort Orange and headed down the coast to the Virginias for one last trading expedition. This time Hendrick was needed and he left Vredendale in charge of Jehan.

So it came to pass that I was alone with the children when the *Rensselaerswyck* returned from Virginia. It must have been midnight when I was awakened by a loud knocking. I pulled something around me and cautiously opened the top half of the door.

It was Potty, a seaman from the *Rensselaerswyck.*

"Skipper sent me to fetch the Doctor, Ma'am. Ship's mate is took real bad with swamp fever."

It was swamp fever that killed my father in South America. I forced myself to speak calmly. "Dr. Montagne is up north, Potty."

"Skipper says if I don' find the Doctor I has to fetch the chirurgeon. Mate needs bleedin' straight away."

"Oh, no!" I cried in a panic. "The chirurgeon is useless. He can't even give a decent shave. I'll get the Doctor, Potty, but it will take a while." I gave him Jehan's medicine chest. "Take this with you. The Doctor will need it. In the meantime tell them to put wet compresses on Hendrick's head and neck. But don't let them bleed him."

He nodded, hoisted the chest onto his shoulder and disappeared into the night.

As I pulled on my clothes and heavy shoes I realized that I had been foolish to let Potty go. Of course I could not have sent him after Jehan. He would never be able to find Vredendale in the dark. But he could have accompanied me to the du Trieux home where I was sure Philippe would be willing to row up-river. Well, I would just have to find the du Trieux home by myself. After all, I'd done it a dozen times in daylight.

When I reached the front gate I stopped to listen and peer cautiously in both directions. Not a light showed anywhere except for my own lantern. Wind rustled through the branches and the moon cast ghostly shadows in the cemetery. I decided to save time by going up the Heerenstraat and cutting through the sheep meadow.

The sky was bright with stars as I hurried along trying not to trip over roots and holes in the road. An animal scurried across in front of me. Then I heard a voice to my left. I froze but it was only the hoot of an owl. My heart was hammering and I could feel eyes watching me from the shadows. The owl hooted again. This time there was an answering hoot from the right.

A hundred yards north of us is the Black Lion Tavern. According to Susannah, there are all kinds of illegal goings-on inside. Marie, the buxom serving wench, is the daughter of Philippe du Trieux by his first wife and he and Susannah are estranged from the girl. The du Trieux have been so good to us that I have purposely avoided the Black Lion.

Now I could see a faint light through the half-closed shutter. This was no time to stand on ceremony. I knocked.

Marie answered the door in her nightdress and pulled me inside where the remains of a fire still glowed. An Indian slept by the hearth and another sat, dead drunk, at the table. When I explained why I was there she quickly shook the Indian by the shoulder addressing him in his own tongue. I caught the word "Muscoota" which is the native name for Vredendale.

The Indian, whose name was Kumtassa, was alert and on his feet immediately. After a few words with Marie he turned to me and announced solemnly in good Dutch, "Kumtassa run like wind." Then he was gone.

"We used to play together as children," said Marie. "Now he's the best runner the Weckquasgeeks have. He'll do the eight miles to Vredendale in half the time it takes a man to row."

My hands were still shaking and she insisted that I have a glass of port before being escorted home by the quiet, gray-haired tavern keeper.

Safely back in my own kitchen I found I could not sleep, so I made up the fire and sat with my knitting to wait for the dawn.

Would Kumtassa be able to find Jehan? Would Jehan agree to go off in the middle of the night with a strange Indian? Would he think it was a trap?

I should have given the Indian a note to carry. How long would it take them to reach the harbor?

I thanked God for the Jesuits' bark in the medicine chest. If Jehan had had this new drug years ago in Guiana, my father would be alive today. The Jesuits in Peru learned about the bark from Indians and it was barely two years ago that the first samples reached Europe. Today the only Jesuits' bark in New Amsterdam is in Jehan's medicine chest.

It was still dark when Marie tapped at the door. She had seen my light and wanted me to know that Kumtassa was back. He had had no trouble finding Jehan and they came down together in the *Yellow Swan*. Jehan was this very minute on board the *Rensselaerswyck* with Hendrick.

After she left I fell asleep in the chair, thoroughly convinced that, in spite of her reputation, Marie was one of the truly kind people in this world.

The children were still asleep when Jehan staggered through the front door at dawn.

"It's malaria, Rachel." His voice cracked with weariness as he leaned against the table for a minute. Then he shook himself and sat down.

"I need a drink," he said.

"Will he be all right, mon vieux?"

"Yes." He looked me directly in the eye. "Thanks to the Jesuits' bark, Hendrick will recover. Now may I have that drink?"

"You need food and sleep," I said. "Why don't you bring him here so I can take care of him?"

"He is violent, my dear. It took two men to hold him while I forced the medicine down his throat. When the fever breaks he'll come here."

I brought ale and a bowl of cold suppawn. "How in the world did Hendrick catch malaria?" I asked. "I thought it came from tropical swamps like Guiana."

"Virginia is full of swamps. Stam says there was a dreadful swamp on Smits Island near where Hendrick went ashore."

Smits Island! I remembered my terrible premonition of disaster the day we saw Smits Island from the *Rensselaerswyck*. But this was no time to speak of premonitions.

Jehan refused to rest. When he had eaten he went straight back to the *Rensselaerswyck*.

"I must be there when he wakes up, Rachel."

After the children had their breakfast, I went out to the yard, caught one of our newly-acquired chickens and wrung its neck. The miracles of modern medicine are one thing but a good chicken broth still cures more ailments than meet the eye. Two hours later I left Jesse in charge and carried a pot of fresh broth to the Strand, where I found a boatman willing to row me out to the ship for a stuiver.

Hendrick did not recognize me. He was wrapped in blankets from head to toe, shivering with cold in the middle of July. Stam sat with him while Jehan slept on the next bunk.

"One minute he's freezing," said Stam, "The next he's burning up. I don't hold with this newfangled Jesuits' bark. If you ask me, the Doctor should give him a good bleeding."

At the sound of voices Jehan got stiffly to his feet. "Rachel thinks chicken broth cures everything," he said gently. "You spoon, my dear. Stam and I will hold him."

Hendrick did not fight us, but his whole body shook so badly that half the broth spilled over the bed. In no time we were all exhausted and very little broth was inside the patient.

Four times a day Hendrick was given a mixture of Jesuits' bark, saffron and snake-root in red wine. The medicine was slow taking hold, however, and Jehan decided to sleep on board himself until it began to work.

Every morning I brought fresh broth and apple juice, but Hendrick got worse, not better. A severe bowel flux developed and he vomited constantly. Apparently it was a particularly stubborn form of malaria. Then on the third day his urine turned black.

"The Jesuits' bark is bound to cure him," Jehan said calmly, but the pulse in his throat was pounding and he did not look me in the eye.

Sometimes Hendrick recognized me, sometimes not. One day he suddenly sat up and began to speak quite coherently.

"Rachel, do you know what's wrong with me? I've been poisoned by bastard mosquitoes!" He put his head down, smiled and fell asleep.

Later Stam confirmed that Hendrick had red mosquito welts on his neck which had since disappeared.

"Jehan!" I exclaimed. "Didn't you tell me that Father had mosquito bites on him when he came down with the fever on the Oyapok? Maybe Hendrick's right. It's mosquitoes that cause malaria, not the poisonous air!"

"My dear," said Jehan patiently, "Doctors of medicine at all the best universities have been studying the cause of malaria for years. Are you suggesting that Hendrick, who never got through the first year of Latin school, has solved something that has escaped the finest minds of Europe?"

Put like that the idea was ridiculous and I never mentioned it again.

Jehan did bleed Hendrick but only in moderation. He said it was more important to keep the hard-earned liquids in his body. Stam never agreed with this policy. One day when Jehan was absent Stam persuaded the Skipper to send for the chirurgeon who took a large quantity of blood from the jugular vein in the neck. When I arrived a few minutes later, Hendrick was more lucid than I had seen him in days. He recognized me and smiled, but seemed to think we were children again back in Leyden waiting for Father to return from the Oyapok.

"Don't worry, little sister." He squeezed my hand. "I'll take care of you till Papa gets back."

I was able to get him to drink something before he fell back into his tortured sleep. Early the next morning God took my brother out of his misery forever.

Jehan still cannot speak about Hendrick's death. For him it is like Papa's death all over again. It would be better if he could break down and cry instead of keeping it all pent-up inside himself. It is easier for me. God gives women so many tasks in this world that they are forced to pull themselves together and go on living.

Susannah helped me prepare the body. She also helped bake the sweet dood-cakes for the funeral. Isaack spent hours at the Black Lion. Marie told me later that he drank too much and cried like a baby.

Funerals are very important occasions here because there are so few social events. Jehan was determined to give Hendrick the best. He laid in beer, ale, brandy, tobacco and a supply of clay pipes for the men, as well as Madeira for the women. He even arranged for silver spoons to be given as memorials to the pallbearers.

Dominie Bogardus stayed the night with us and took turns watching the body throughout the long hours. No prince of Europe could have a finer eulogy than he gave Hendrick the next day.

In New Amsterdam, women do not accompany the body to the grave. From the stoop I watched as they carried the coffin to the little cemetery across the road where Moose Foot stood unnoticed in the shadows. There the men gathered with bared heads while the Dominie said a final prayer and they laid Hendrick to rest for all time.

I have written to Gertrude and I have sent her Hendrick's gold ring. I feel so sorry for her now and I am thoroughly ashamed of all the mean things I ever said in the past.

Jehan is writing to Uncle Gerard.

Very much love,

Rachel

Tiger

This 24th day of October
In the Year of Our Lord 1637
On the island of Manhattan

Dearest Margariet,

Thank you for your beautiful letter about Hendrick. You are right. He was a wonderful person. And he lived a great life, an exciting life, the kind of life he always wanted to lead.

You ask what has been done about Vredendale. For the first few weeks none of us could even think about Vredendale. Willem and Tobias were up there supposedly working, but you know how little gets done without an overseer. Of course the property now belongs to Gertrude and she has not yet answered Jehan's inquiries as to her wishes.

Jehan wants Isaack to buy Vredendale from Gertrude and run it himself, but Isaack is so lost without Hendrick that he has no will power for anything else. I am the only family he has left now, and he can hardly bear to let me out of his sight. This is in spite of the fact that I give him all the worst chores around here. I even made him dig a new privy, and plant flowers where the old one used to be. If Governor van Twiller had any brains he would make it illegal to build outhouses by the road. They leak and stink and it is disgusting to see the pigs rooting about in the muck.

What I wanted was for Jehan to buy Vredendale from Gertrude, but I was sure it was impossible. His medical practice would be ruined if he lived so far out of town. Still, it would be wonderful to bring up our children in a paradise like Vredendale. Of course I said nothing. The surest way to set a husband against a plan of action is to suggest he adopt it.

Then one hot Sunday in August, Dominie Bogardus joined us as usual for a cold supper and afterwards we sat out on the stoop to catch the river breeze. Jehan and Isaack smoked their pipes while the Dominie sipped his Madeira.

"Perhaps you went a little too far with your sermon this morning," said Jehan, very tactfully, considering that the Dominie had called Governor van Twiller a scoundrel and a half-wit from the pulpit. "I know the Governor never attends services but he is bound to hear about it."

"The man *is* a scoundrel and he *is* a half-wit," insisted the Dominie, holding out his empty glass to be refilled. "Oh yes. I'll be dismissed soon for insubordination, my friends. But when I go I'll drag that oaf down with me. Now tell me what has been done about Vredendale? I hope you have not been neglecting your duties as overseer, Jehan."

"Vredendale belongs to Gertrude, Hendrick's widow, back in the Fatherland," explained Jehan.

"Poppycock! What use is it to the pretty widow? Isaack must buy the place from his sister-in-law and run it himself."

We all turned to Isaack who was shaking his head miserably.

"Andries Hudde told me that he was interested in buying the property," offered Jehan. (Hudde is van Twiller's chief Councillor.)

"God's wounds! The man is a speculator, Montagne, and too cocky for his own good. He already owns 1000 acres on Long Island. Vredendale is the choicest piece of land in the Colony. One day it will be worth a fortune. Do you think it would please Hendrick to see that fortune in Hudde's pocket?" Regardless of how much he drinks, the Dominie is an eloquent speaker.

"Suppose I buy the bowery myself," suggested Jehan out of the blue. "Would you be willing to live eight miles from town, Rachel?"

I could hardly believe my ears. "What about your practice, mon vieux?"

"Eight miles is not the end of the world. Besides, I will be a tobacco planter, not a doctor. What do you say, Isaack?"

So everything fell into place. Jehan wrote Gertrude another letter with an offer to buy Vredendale for himself and we threw ourselves into finishing the living quarters. When we were short-handed I left the children with the bossy redhead and spent the day up there working alongside the men. It is as though we were doing it for Hendrick. The harder we worked, the more enthusiastic we became.

Except for Susannah there is only one friend I will miss in New Amsterdam, a lively Scandinavian girl named Anneke Jans. Anneke's husband, Roeloff, died earlier this year from a stone in the gut, leaving her with five little children and 62 acres. Still she managed to find the time to cheer me up when Hendrick died.

"Tchah! You're a fool to even speak to that whore," hissed Madame Vinje-Dam, who makes a daily habit of stopping in for a wee drop and a pipeful. "Why do you think Wouter granted that land to her husband when the rest of us were forced to lease from the Company? Horse piss! Roeloff couldn't even read or write. He had nothing to offer but that trollop and her petticoats!"

I wish I had the nerve to shut the door in Madame Vinje-Dam's face, but I never did. Neither, apparently, did any of the other housewives on her rounds. Up and down the street she hobbles, dressed in black, with that ugly three-legged animal hobbling behind. While she is indoors, he stands guard on the stoop so you can always tell where she is. Once I asked Susannah how she put up with the dreadful woman.

"After 13 years one learns to accept most anything, Rachel. And she does bring the latest news."

I still have not learned to accept Madame Vinje-Dam. As for Anneke, she is not only beautiful, she is intelligent, capable, and full of fun. I like her and I do not care a whit how Roeloff came by his 62 acres.

One glorious Sunday morning Anneke and I and the children went oystering after church. We left the two infants with her mother, Tryntje Jonas, who has her own pocket-sized house and garden up against the Fort wall. Tryntje is the town midwife, a trim energetic little woman in her fifties.

"Jehan thinks very highly of your mother," I remarked, as we waded along behind the younger children. We were in a cove of the Hudson, not far from Anneke's farm, just north of town. "He says her percentage of live births is way above average and her record on childbed fever is astonishingly good."

"Ma has a secret weapon," chuckled Anneke. "Years ago she visited a lying-in hospital in the Fatherland where she watched medical students dissect corpses one minute, and deliver babies the next. She thought the smell of death on their filthy smocks scared the newborns, who died like flies. When she spoke to the doctor in charge, he said that infants had no sense of smell and she was a superstitious busybody. Ever since, she's worn a clean, sweet-smelling apron to welcome each new babe into this world. It seems to work." We laughed at the picture of the perky little midwife defying the great university scholars with her secret weapon.

Oystering is fun. Warm sunshine on head and shoulders counteracts the cold salt water lapping at the ankles. The younger children splashed and giggled, bare toes squishing happily in the mud. Even Jesse easily detached good-sized oysters from the thousands exposed by the tide.

Sarie and Tryn, Anneke's two oldest, together with Jan, soon filled their buckets and raced along the beach far ahead of us. Now they were climbing out on a rocky promontory toward what looked like the burned-out hull of a ship.

"That was Captain Block's ship, the *Tiger*," explained Anneke.

I was fascinated. Of course I had heard about Captain Block who explored the river just a few years after Hudson. The *Tiger* had been destroyed by fire, and the men stranded on Manhattan for the winter.

"It burned right to the waterline," said Anneke. "At high tide you can barely see the wreck. Over there is where the men dug shelters. They'd never have survived if the Wilden hadn't supplied them with food. In the spring they built a new ship called the *Restless*."

"Jehan says the *Restless* was the first ocean-going vessel built in the New World."

Anneke nodded. "Did you know that one of the sailors on the *Tiger* had smuggled a woman on board and the poor thing gave birth in that shelter without a single female to help. That baby was the first Christian born in the Colony."

"I thought Madame Vinje-Dam's son was the first."

"He was!" laughed Anneke. "The sailor's name was Guillaume Vinje and the stowaway was Madame Vinje, only of course they weren't married then. Hard to believe, isn't it?"

I struggled to reconcile the picture of that pathetic stowaway and today's bitter old Witch. Thank God I never did shut the door in her face.

At that moment a commotion broke out ahead. Tryn began screaming hysterically and Sarie was shouting, "No! No!" as she stood with one foot on the rocky promontory, the other balanced precariously on the hull of the *Tiger*. Jan had disappeared inside.

"There is no inside to that wreck, you know," said Anneke.

I ran. Dear God, my feet kept sinking in the sand. It was like a bad dream where I was racing as fast as I could and getting nowhere. They say if you drop a cat in the water it swims by instinct. Blessed Jesus, don't let him drown.

Jan was not in trouble. By the time I reached the rocks he had crawled out, soaking wet, with the body of a small animal in his arms.

"It's dead!" shouted Sarie. "Throw it back!"

Her sister was still screaming and prancing about like a spooked colt.

"Houd op, Tryn!" yelled Anneke.

"Potverdikki! It's a puppy and I saved him!" announced Jan, proudly carrying the lifeless body toward us.

"That's not a dog, Jan," I gasped, catching my breath. "It looks more like a drowned rat."

"He's alive, Mama. He was swimming."

"If it's alive it'll bite you," I snapped. "Drop it this minute, Jan! People die from rat bite."

He shook his head stubbornly. Then he gently placed the drenched, moth-eaten package on the ground. It was alive, but barely so.

"Good heavens!" exclaimed Anneke. "The boy's right. It *is* a dog. Look at the tail!"

The poor thing tried gamely to stand but wobbly legs buckled and sent him sprawling. One shoulder was ripped, probably from a fight with some animal. The head was grotesque and ludicrously large for the scrawny body. Only the eyes and an occasional feeble wag of the tail betrayed the fact that this miserable creature was indeed some form of dog.

"The head looks a little like a bull mastiff pup," said Anneke. "But he's not long for this world. The kindest thing would be to put him out of his misery."

Jan promptly picked up the dog and turned to face us, legs planted stiffly apart. He had the same steady blue eyes as Hendrick and the same obstinate set to his chin.

"My papa'll sew him up," he said, firmly. "I'm gonna call him Tiger."

I looked again at the mangy creature. Flies were beginning to cluster around festering sores on the shoulder but the eyes were not those of a wild animal. They were eyes that had trusted mankind for centuries.

"Well, bring him along then," I said. "The poor thing probably hasn't eaten in a month of Sundays."

No one but Jan ever expected Tiger to survive, but survive he did. In two weeks his wounds had healed and there was enough flesh on his ribs to make it clear that he was a dog, if an ugly one. He and Jan were inseparable.

"That mongrel is one half bull mastiff," declared the Dominie, "and one half debatable. A full grown bull mastiff is a match for anything, Rachel."

He thought Tiger's mother could be one of the Indian mekane; mean, vicious beasts that slit the throats of livestock and are more akin to wolves than domestic animals.

"Watch that pup, Rachel. If he takes after his dam, he will have to be destroyed."

Tiger showed no sign of either heritage. The only livestock we had was a brown and white cow with the colorful name of Rainbow, and a dozen chickens. He made several efforts to frolic with Rainbow before resigning himself to the fact that she had no intention of ever frolicking with anyone. The chickens he ignored. Many's the time I saw him lying in the yard gnawing at a bone, with poultry pecking the ground a few inches from his busy jaws.

There was one bossy red hen that finally tried his patience. Maybe she pecked at one of his old wounds. I ran out at the sound of barking and hysterical squawking to find Tiger covered with feathers. I expected the hen to be good for nothing but the stew-pot, but I was wrong. She was furious but unharmed. Tiger had only snapped noisily. Some instinct had kept him from actually closing his jaws on the bird.

One Saturday, a few weeks after the oystering expedition, Anneke arrived loaded down with pheasant.

"I can't believe it's the same animal," she declared, as Tiger escorted her cheerfully from gate to door. "He won't make much of a watch dog if he's this friendly to everyone. How would you like pheasant for Sunday, Rachel? Andries Hudde brought these today. It's the third lot I've received this week."

Of course I was delighted. "I didn't know you and Andries were so friendly," I said.

"We're not. He wants to marry me, that's all. Shall I help you pluck?"

"Are you going to?"

"Going to what?"

"Marry Hudde."

"Of course not. As a matter of fact, I think he's more interested in my 62 acres than he is in me."

Since the day they put her husband safely underground, every bachelor in New Amsterdam has bent over backwards to win Anneke's favors.

"So far I haven't let one of them past the door," she laughed. "But I'll have to choose soon."

"Madame Vinje-Dam says Andries Hudde is the best catch in town," I contributed, moving the kettle to the center of the hearth.

"Yes. Andries says so too. Know what he told me? He said it was highly unusual for a gentleman like himself to marry a woman who can't read or write, but because of my other 'fine qualities' he's happy to overlook this."

We burst into laughter at the picture of the cocky suitor and his tactless wooing. In the Fatherland such a marriage might be unheard of, but in this country Hudde would be getting much the better of the bargain.

"There's one bachelor here who doesn't even know I exist, Rachel."

"Impossible," I said. "Who?"

"Dominie Everardus Bogardus. He's the one I'm going to marry."

"Anneke, the mice have got at your brains! The Dominie drinks like a fish."

"All men in this country drink too much. I'm used to it. You don't think Roeloff sipped goat's milk, do you? Besides there's nothing else for a bachelor to do here. I'll provide other diversions."

I chuckled. "Do you realize that the Dominie is in danger of being recalled because of the dreadful things he says from the pulpit about the Governor?"

"Of course I do and I admire him for it. He's the only one with the guts to stand up publicly and tell the world what a fool Wouter is. But it doesn't matter. If Everardus is dismissed we still have my 62 acres. And if he's not dismissed we'll lease the land and I'll help him charm parishioners."

In my opinion Anneke would make the ideal wife for anyone. She has the sort of extraordinary beauty that transcends all social barriers. But the town gossips would be horrified.

I thought about tomorrow. It is the custom on Sunday to draw the ruffled curtain across the fireplace so the hearth too can have its day of rest. However, the fact that I serve only cold food never stops the Dominie from joining us for Sunday supper.

"I'm going to roast the pheasant now and serve them cold tomorrow," I said. "Everardus will be here, Anneke. Why don't you join us?"

She dunked a bird in the boiling water and began to pluck. "I thought you'd never ask," she laughed.

Margariet, if you are in contact with Gertrude, please encourage her to answer Jehan's letter with regard to our purchasing Vredendale. He is becoming exceedingly anxious over the matter.

Your affectionate cousin,

Rachel

By the Waterfall

April 15, 1638
Vredendale
The island of Manhattan

Dearest Margariet,

By mid-winter Vredendale was halfway habitable and we moved up the East River, lock, stock and barrel. So began the busiest days of my life and, surprisingly, some of the happiest. People think happiness can be measured by material possessions or prestige but they are so wrong. Happiness comes from knowing exactly what you want in this world and working as hard as you can to get it.

My father gave his life to founding a colony in the New World. Hendrick gave his to carving a bowery from the wilderness in the very heart of that colony. He is here beside me every day.

Now it is my task to turn the bare boards of Vredendale into a comfortable home. My day begins before dawn and by sunset I ache in every bone. When the supper is cleared away and the girls are asleep, I rest by the hearth with my knitting.

In winter the snow outside can be two feet deep and we hear wolves howling from the rocky heights to the west. Then Isaack throws huge hickory logs on the fire until it blazes halfway up the great brick chimney. Candles burn in brass holders on the long table where Jehan helps the boys with their Latin. On the high-backed cupboard my blue and white dishes gleam in the flickering light, and from the wall the sketch of Papa smiles down upon us all. I am exhausted but I am at peace with the world.

Our only neighbor is Jacob van Curler of Otterspoor, a good-looking bachelor who frequently joins us for meals. Although a distant cousin of the Governor, he is not at all like the sodden, dim-witted Wouter. Jacob reminds me of Hendrick: energetic, manly, always joking and full of fun. Jehan and Isaack both like him but there is something about the man that bothers me. If anything he is too masculine.

One Sunday as we were leaving for church, Jacob helped me into the *Yellow Swan*. His arm beneath mine was like a rail of iron. Of course any man who has been in this country for years, swinging an axe among other things, is bound to have an arm of iron. Nevertheless it set me to musing about the astonishing differences God has created between men and women. I was irritated with myself and made a point of not allowing him to touch me again.

Naturally I have not said anything about this. It is too ridiculous. I continue to invite him to meals, accept his help around Vredendale and parry his teasing banter just as though he were Hendrick. For some reason I am reminded of the long-forgotten words of an elderly busybody in Leyden.

"Marry an older man, my child, and you will repent when you reach your prime."

Well, she was wrong. I am 29 and I still love Jehan as much as I did at 16. He is the only man I have ever known. It is true that I sometimes wish he were less logical and more exciting. Maybe it is hard for a man to be exciting at 45. Anyhow Jacob is only 27 and means nothing to me. Still I am glad that Jehan is always on hand so I never have to spend any time alone with our new neighbor.

Ever since Hendrick's death Moose Foot has brought us his beavers. The Company store pays Christians substantially more per skin than it pays Indians, so only Wilden from a great distance deal directly with the store. Most colonists have their own group of longstanding Weckquasgeek or Canarsie friends. We have two, Moose Foot and Kumtassa, the runner. Every Friday Isaack takes the furs into town and returns with supplies and news.

"Your friend, Anneke, is finally betrothed to the Dominie!" he announced at dinner one Friday.

"That *is* good news," I said. "Who told you?"

"Everyone. Half the town's against the marriage and half for it," he paused to sneeze and blow his nose. "Madame Vinje-Dam says it's a disgrace for a representative of God to marry an illiterate whore."

"That Witch should be gagged," I snapped. "And please don't sneeze into the fish."

"My dear," interrupted Jehan, "Isaack brought me a note from Everardus. It seems that Wouter has forbidden the banns. What kind of fish is this anyway?"

"Bullheads and perch. Jan caught them this morning."

"The ones with the whiskers are bullheads, " explained Jan proudly.

"Very sweet taste, Son."

"Mite bony, these perch," muttered Isaack under his breath but Jan ignored him.

I coulda catched a hundred!" he boasted.

"Caught," corrected his father. "You could have caught a hundred."

"Maybe two hundred!" said the boy.

"About Wouter," I continued, "he's just jealous. Can't you speak to him, mon vieux?"

Jehan promised to stop by the Fort after Sunday service. But by Sunday there was no need to persuade Wouter of anything. As we sailed down the East River on our way to church, the *Soutberg*, out of Amsterdam, was about to drop anchor and the exciting news was already hopping from one small boat to another.

After five years, Governor Wouter van Twiller has been sacked! I think it is the first sensible move the Company has made. That very morning Dominie Bogardus published the banns from the pulpit while a radiant Anneke, head held high, sat in the front pew with her five children beside her.

Wouter himself does not seem overly affected by his changed status and if anything he is more popular than ever with the colonists. He has arranged to lease the Company bowery, just north of town, so he can spend his days drinking himself under the table up there instead of at the Fort.

The new Governor, Willem Kieft, is due here shortly. I pay little attention to the ugly rumors about him. He has to be better than fat, stupid Wouter, but Jehan is worried sick.

"The problem, my dear, is that we have no ground brief for Vredendale. Who knows how this new man will view the commitments of his predecessor? Another thing. Why haven't I heard from Gertrude about my offer to buy the bowery?"

We received a long sympathetic letter from Uncle Gerard who mourns Hendrick as though he were his own son. He has been to Amsterdam and seen Gertrude. He says she has recovered quickly from the shock of widowhood and is once again the belle of the city.

"Give me one good reason why Gertrude hasn't answered my letters," repeated Jehan. "And don't tell me that she is distraught by her bereavement."

"Maybe she's too busy, mon vieux."

"Poppycock!" he said.

When the Honorable Director General Willem Kieft arrived, van Twiller gave a welcoming banquet and everybody who was anybody was invited. The dinner was magnificent. Wine flowed like water, and silver gleamed in the light of a hundred candles. The Company slaves, dressed in elaborate livery, served venison, turkey, bear steak and lobsters three feet long. The pièce de résistance was a roast haunch of buffalo carried in on a six-foot trencher by the marvelous smiling Giant.

Governor Kieft is a small fussy man who is given to massaging his elbow. When we were introduced he did not look me in the eye. In fact he ignored me entirely and concentrated on Jehan who was as usual the most distinguished-looking gentleman in the room. I suspect that our new Governor has no use for women.

At dinner I was seated next to the smooth-talking bookkeeper, Cornelis van Tienhoven. He is a large man with cold eyes and an excellent set of teeth which he likes to show off with a forced smile. During dinner he put his hand on my knee under the tablecloth. Furious, I dislodged his fingers only to have him replace them higher up. Desperate not to cause a scene I slipped a carving knife into my lap and he put his hands hurriedly onto the table, all the while smiling like a great shark. From the Governor's position at the far end of the table he must have appeared the soul of congeniality.

On my other side was the cocky Andries Hudde.

"Madame Montagne," he said cheerfully, "I have just received a letter from your charming sister-in-law."

This was certainly a surprise as we have yet to hear from her ourselves.

"I didn't realize that you knew Gertrude, Monsieur."

"Our grandmothers came from the same village," he said. "The last time I saw Gertrude she was a chubby little girl of ten. When Hendrick died I naturally wrote to offer my condolences."

There was something very suspicious about this but I was too busy fending off Sharkface to pay much attention to Hudde.

Anneke and the Dominie sat across from me. She was the most beautiful woman there, and he looked happier than I had ever seen him. Even Madame Vinje-Dam was on her best behavior, cackling and hissing quietly from her seat at Wouter's right. One way or another we were all trying to impress the new Governor who spent the evening stroking his elbow and sniffing delicately as though there were a bad smell in the room.

The next morning two soldiers arrived at Vredendale to summon Jehan to the Fort. It seems that Governor Kieft wants my husband to be his sole

Councillor. Where van Twiller had a Council of four to advise him, Kieft prefers only one. The pay is to be 35 guilders per month and Jehan has one week to make up his mind.

"I don't like the man, Rachel. As for a Council, do you know what he told me? When there is a decision to make he will have two votes and I will have one. Per Deus immortales! What kind of a Council is that?"

"Would it mean living in town?" I asked.

"No. When I told him that I had no intention of leaving Vredendale, he said the position required only one or two days a week for which I will have a private room at the Governor's mansion. The rest of the time I will be free to attend to my own affairs. I stopped in at the parsonage afterwards. Everardus thinks I should accept."

"Of course you must accept," I said firmly. "If you are the Governor's Councillor, our rights to Vredendale will be safe. If you turn him down, anything can happen. Besides, he knows nothing about this country and needs advice badly."

And so it came about that my husband is now the number two man in the Colony, second only to the Governor himself! The first council meeting was Thursday morning, April 8th, and Jehan left for town Wednesday afternoon. I would give anything to be able to erase the next few hours from my life.

The *Yellow Swan* glided smoothly down the creek as I waved goodbye from our newly painted dock. On every side the sturdy forest was sprinkled with the young green magic of sweet-smelling springtime. A bright colored kingfisher dove from on high into the placid water at my feet, and the music of a hundred song-birds rose above the distant roar of Hell Gate. It was just such a day one year ago that Hendrick had first brought me to Vredendale. On an impulse I decided to look for the little waterfall he had pointed out from the bluff.

I soon found the stony brook which runs somewhat south of our creek, eventually joining it near Otterspoor. Like a young girl I sprang from one rock to the next, gradually working my way down stream. I was a fearless explorer braving the North American wilderness.

The waterfall, when I reached it, was enchanting. I stood on a rock below the cascading water, droplets of spray on my cheek. I was as free as the eagle that soars the heavens. The whole world was my garden.

I do not know how long I stood there or when Jacob van Curler arrived. Perhaps he spoke and I did not hear over the noise of the water. Suddenly there was a hand on my shoulder. Startled, I lost my balance and would have had a dunking if he had not caught me. He picked me up with those arms of iron and carried me across to the mossy bank.

It is difficult for me to explain what happened next. In some twisted way it was as though weeks of jesting banter with Jacob had become weeks of unconsummated lovemaking. His fierce urgency swept away my wits. Sweet Jesus, how could I have been so insane!

When it was over and I had recovered my breath, I was furious with Jacob and furious with myself. What a fool I was! I stood up and pulled my clothes together. Jacob rolled over onto his back, handsome blue eyes mocking. I never really liked this man, now I hated him.

"Don't ever set foot on Vredendale again, Jacob van Curler!"

He sprang to his feet, awkwardly buttoning himself, and began to apologize. I stopped him, more civilly this time.

"It was as much my fault as yours, Jacob, but it must never happen again. Jehan is a good man and a good husband. How could I have done this to him?"

Jacob swore that it would never happen again but I was adamant that he stay away from Vredendale. Reluctantly he agreed.

On the way home my mind raced in circles. I owe it to Jehan to see that no one ever suspects. Suppose . . . ? No! That does not even bear thinking. It would be two weeks before I could be sure. Please, Sweet Jesus, spare me that.

Then, to my horror, I noticed an Indian standing above the falls. At first I thought he was speaking to me, then I realized that he was talking to himself or perhaps to some imaginary spirit in the treetops. How long had he been there? What had he seen? I looked back but Jacob had disappeared.

The waterfall must be very close to the little cluster of wigwams just across the creek from Otterspoor. Thank heavens I did not recognize the Indian and thank heavens he did not appear to notice me. Perhaps he really was deranged. People would never believe the gossip of a deranged Indian.

To my surprise, no one at Vredendale was even aware that I had been missing. We have a maid now, Ariaen, a lazy overweight girl who will not scrub a pot unless I have my eye on her. Her only redeeming feature is that she is good with the children. Women are much more suspicious than men. When Ariaen is missing I always imagine her out in the barracks with Tobias. But even she did not seem to notice anything out of the ordinary today.

Jehan returned the next evening. When we were finally alone he lit his pipe and told me the story of his humiliating defeat at the first council meeting. It seems that the new Governor has decided to promote Sharkface, the lecherous bookkeeper, to the all-important position of Secretary. I never told Jehan about the fingers under the tablecloth and this was certainly not the time.

"It's the worst move Kieft could make, Rachel. People here despise van Tienhoven."

"The Governor can't possibly know the man, Jehan." I attached new yarn to my knitting. "Susannah says he's been cheating on the books for years."

"There is no proof of that, my dear."

"Of course there is no proof because Wouter was always too stupid, too drunk and too dishonest to care. Did you tell Kieft how he molested the twelve-year-old de Rapelje girl?"

"The Governor is not interested in that side of the man. Van Tienhoven is clever, very clever. I suspect he has a contact in the Netherlands who recommended him. He has spent the last two weeks showering the Governor with flattery.

"I tried every argument I could think of, my dear, but it was like hitting my head against a main dike. When I proposed Andries Hudde for the position, Kieft just laughed. What's more he positively relished seeing me upset. He has promised van Tienhoven 36 guilders a month as a deliberate slap in the face at me. I am sorely tempted to resign, Rachel."

Jehan was promised 35 a month. Clearly this new Governor has a cruel sense of humor. Still it cannot be right to resign after one week. I tried to take his mind off his humiliating defeat.

"What else went on at the meeting, mon vieux?"

The selection of lesser officials had apparently gone about as expected. Philippe du Trieux was appointed "Court Messenger," an elaborate title for the relatively minor position of serving summonses and delivering official communications.

"I don't like Kieft, Rachel, but he's an improvement over Wouter. He does not drink and he is not lazy. He is planning a whirlwind of reforms around here, most of which are good, but they are not going to sit well with colonists who are used to doing as they please."

Kieft intends to put a tax on tobacco, which I think is unfair. However Jehan says it is a sensible idea and I must not be prejudiced by the fact that tobacco will be the principal crop of Vredendale.

The funniest regulation is one forbidding intercourse with the Wilden. With so few European women, this is going to be impossible to enforce. In fact many of the early colonists have settled down happily with Indian common-law wives. Rape of Indian squaws is a frequent problem and, according to Philippe, the worst offender is the slippery Sharkface. He is said to dress up like an Indian, with nothing but a small patch over his loins, and gallop through the fields lusting after Indian maids. Philippe says there has never once been a case of a Christian woman being raped by an Indian. It makes you wonder who is the more civilized.

Where Wouter has been content to live and let live, Kieft intends to supervise everyone and everything. The town bell used to ring once a week for Sunday service. Now it rings constantly, to call the men to and from the fields, to summon the accused to court, and at nine o'clock to announce bedtime. Kieft even plans to require permits to leave the island of Manhattan. And of course he is determined to stop the sale of liquor and guns to the Wilden.

"Don't worry, my dear. I will not resign without giving the position a fair trial. I shall ignore this morning's unpleasantness and do my best to work with van Tienhoven for the good of the Colony. Now tell me what has been going on here while I was away."

I gave him a few details of my efforts to start a kitchen garden when he interrupted. "By the way, Rachel, I ran into Jacob van Curler in town this morning."

I dropped a stitch. Carefully I forced myself to go back and pick it up.

"What did Jacob have to say, mon vieux?"

"He was with Claes, the wheelwright. He has just agreed to lease Otterspoor to Claes and move back to town. He says it's too lonely way out here for a bachelor. Jacob was a good neighbor, Rachel. We are going to miss him."

I did not answer.

Two weeks later my monthly courses returned. God had forgiven me! I was so elated that I decided to pay a welcome call on our new neighbor, the wheelwright's vrouw. With a basketful of freshly baked cookies over my arm I set out for Otterspoor, a pleasant half mile walk along the creek. The prospect of a woman to visit was appealing. Rumor had it that she was old and bad-tempered. Still she couldn't be as dreadful as Madame Vinje-Dam.

Alas, in comparison with Claes's vrouw, Madame Vinje-Dam was a model of charm itself. My new neighbor was not only unfriendly, stupid and vicious of tongue, she was unspeakably vulgar. I departed after ten minutes feeling quite unwelcome and determined never to return.

As I left, an Indian came through the gate, leading two horses and muttering to himself. My heart sank as I recognized the witness from the waterfall. It is against the law to allow an Indian to ride or even to handle a horse, so I pretended not to notice him as my new neighbor spat and slammed the gate behind me.

Indians do not make good servants because they insist on feeling superior and refuse to take orders. Perhaps a deranged Indian was different.

By the creek I ran into Claes. He was in his sixties, but spry enough and quite shrewd. He told me that the Indian lived in the area and came in occasionally to do odd jobs. They call him the Crazy One. It seems that years ago, when he was a young boy, the Crazy One accompanied his uncle to the Fort with some beaver skins. On the way they were set upon by three of Governor Minuit's men who killed the uncle and stole the furs. The boy escaped but ever since he has carried on a one-sided conversation with the murdered uncle. I plan to worry no more about the witness by the waterfall!

Margariet, I have just reread this letter and cannot believe I wrote what I did. If you were here I could never have told you all this.

Your affectionate cousin,

Rachel

P.S. For God's sake please destroy this letter.

Evicted

The 15th day of May
In the Year of Our Lord 1638
At Vredendale
On the island of Manhattan

Dearest Margariet

You have probably already heard the bad tidings. Andries Hudde is about to sail for Europe to marry Gertrude. They plan to live here at Vredendale!

"There must be some mistake," I said when Jehan brought home the news. "Andries has been in this country for nine years. He told me himself that he has not seen Gertrude since she was a child."

"My dear, he has managed to woo her with his pen. The man is strutting about town like the only cock in the barnyard, waving her latest letter under everyone's nose."

I still would not have believed it if there had not been a short note to us from Gertrude in the same post. It was a single page thanking us for the temporary care of her bowery and requesting that we vacate the premises as soon as possible because she and her new husband intend to live here.

Margariet, that girl must be demented! She refused to come to this country with Hendrick until he had built her a home. She practically never wrote him. She never answered our letters and now she cannot even wait until her year of mourning is up before announcing her betrothal to a man she has not seen since she was a child.

As for that schemer, Hudde, he's worse than she is! He's only marrying Gertrude to get his hands on Vredendale which is the finest piece of property on Manhattan. In fact it is the only rich bottom land on the whole island. The rest is nothing but rock. Furthermore, I'm not leaving Vredendale! Every stuiver we own is tied up in this bowery.

"You have influence with Kieft," I stormed at Jehan. "Well, it is time to use it. What is the good of being the Governor's Councillor if you let your family be thrown out of their home?"

"My dear, this is not our home," Jehan stated patiently. "Vredendale belongs to Gertrude. I told Hudde this morning that we were more than willing to buy it from him."

"What did he say?"

"He said he wouldn't sell for 3000 guilders."

"Three thousand guilders!" I echoed in astonishment.

"It's worth less than half that. But remember that Hudde is angry. If it had not been for me he would probably be Kieft's Councillor today. He also thinks that I am responsible for his not getting the position of secretary, which is not true. The man hates me, Rachel, and he is never going to sell us this place."

I am in favor of digging in our heels and trusting that no one will forcibly evict us. Jehan says that I know nothing about the law and whatever we do has to be done legally. In the meantime, Hudde has hired his own overseer and is anxious to see him installed before he sets sail.

Governor Kieft sympathizes with us but refuses to interfere. "You see how right I was, Montagne, not to appoint Hudde secretary. However he is certainly knowledgeable about land. On his return from Europe I will make him my chief surveyor."

When Dominie Bogardus heard about our troubles he promptly rowed eight miles up the East River to offer his support. Unaccustomed to such exercise he had to refresh himself with Jehan's Madeira before exhorting us to stand firm.

"In the eyes of the Lord, Vredendale belongs to you, not to that interloper, Hudde, or that gad-about, Gertrude. Stand firm, my children, and the will of God shall prevail!"

Jehan was not impressed by this logic. He thinks we should buy land on Long Island and start all over again. Isaack is in a state of shock. It is hard to say what he thinks.

I love Vredendale, Margariet. I love her tall brick chimney and her beautifully thatched roof. I love the dogwood trees in the yard and the honeysuckle that is just beginning to climb the stockade walls and the miraculous tulips beside the front stoop. I keep thinking about Hendrick and my father and all the hard work that Jehan and Isaack and I have put in over the past year. Even the roar of Hell Gate in the distance has become a familiar friend.

My mother used to say that all life is a race. Just to stay even you have to work as fast as you can. Pause, and you sink.

I have not given up, but I am sick at heart. I cannot bear for this all to be taken away from us.

Affectionately,

Rachel

Auction

This 14th day of October
In the Year of Our Lord 1638
At Vredendale
By the Grace of God

Dearest Margariet,

I have waited to write until things have been settled which, thank God, they now are.

It was after a long discussion with Sharkface that Jehan came home with a plan for acquiring the bowery legally. It involved borrowing a vast sum of money and it meant returning, temporarily, to the little house on the Heerenstraat. I confess I did not have much faith in the plan. Isaack and I agreed only because we could think of no alternative.

Jehan used the money to settle all outstanding debts on Vredendale, including 110 guilders each to Willem and Tobias for their wages to date. I thought we should leave the debts for Hudde to inherit but it was part of Jehan's plan that the estate should owe us as much as possible. Then with a heavy heart we moved all our belongings into town on barges.

The law here is like the Netherlands in that a betrothal is just about as binding as a marriage. On July 20, Governor Kieft signed a ground brief giving Andries Hudde the 200 acres formerly belonging to Hendrick de Forest. This is the first recorded transfer of property on the island of Manhattan.

Jehan has kept a careful record of all our expenses in the construction and maintenance of Vredendale. From these he subtracted the income due Hendrick from our first tobacco crop, also the amount raised from the sale of Hendrick's clothes. He now presented Hudde with a bill for the difference which came to 680 guilders.

"Ga de pot op!" muttered Hudde under his breath, and he sailed for Europe without paying a stuiver.

We waited until September. Then Jehan started proceedings against Dominie Bogardus who was appointed Gertrude's agent in this country.

The court ruled that Vredendale be sold at auction to the highest bidder. Out of the proceeds, 680 guilders would go to Jehan, the remainder into Gertrude's estate.

The auction was held October 7th, on the parade ground. This was the opportunity we had been waiting for and we discussed at length how much Jehan should bid. There was some chance that no one would bid against us if we offered a fair price, but every potential buyer in New Amsterdam was on hand ready to grab at a bargain. In fact it looked as though every man, woman and child was there just to watch the spectacle.

Sharkface handled the proceedings. First he read a description of the property, buildings and livestock, including three cows, a year-old bull, two goats, six hens, two cocks and about 20 chickens. Also included was a quarter share in 600 tobacco plants for this year. It was stipulated that the purchaser pay one third down immediately, the second third in six months and the final third at the end of one year.

At this point the secretary declared the auction open with a minimum bid of 800 guilders. The bidding was brisk at first as people with no intention of buying could not resist such a bargain.

At 1200 there were only two bidders left, Jehan and an unattractive fellow who was probably an agent, but for whom?

Jehan had decided ahead of time that he would bid no more than 1500. Surely this agent would not go so high. But when my husband eventually bid 1500 the agent promptly said 1550. There followed a long silence.

"1550, going once!" announced Sharkface.

I had to bite my lips to keep from calling out.

"1550 going twice!"

More silence.

"1600," cried Jehan. Bless his heart.

It was now a cat-and-mouse game with the price rising fast. When Jehan bid 1800 I knew from his face that this was his last bid. He was finished and the agent would take Vrendale for 1850.

But the agent did not bid again. He hurried away, and the next thing I heard was "Sold to Doctor Montagne for 1800 guilders!"

Tears of joy ran down my face as I hugged Susannah and Anneke. The Dominie had his arm around Jehan's shoulder. Now, instead of Hudde owing us 680 guilders, we owe him 1120. But we have six months before any money is due. Vredendale is ours, and what's more, we have a ground brief to prove it.

A week later the forests on either side were a glorious mass of red and gold as we sailed up the East River once more. We waved as a Weckquasgeek dugout sped past, laden with beaver skins. Hell Gate roared its welcome and a shimmering rainbow danced in the spray from the whirlpool. God smiled down upon Vredendale on the island of Manhattan.

Affectionately yours,

Rachel

P.S. I do not know what is going to happen when Hudde and Gertrude return, but I do not feel a bit sorry for either of them. Hudde has a thousand acres on Long Island, much closer to town than Vredendale. Let him build there!

Scandal

The 23rd day of October
In the Year of Our Lord 1638
At Vredendale

Dearest Margariet,

I've just received your letter with advice about dealing with Gertrude and her new husband. Do not worry. I shall be very civil to them both as long as they do not try to take Vredendale away from us again.

On that other matter, concerning our handsome ex-neighbor, there has been a complication. For God's sake, Margariet, make certain that you destroyed that letter.

In case I have not mentioned it, court is held here every Thursday. Disgruntled colonists air their grievances and a black-robed Kieft metes out rough justice. Slander cases are the most common and the taverns of Manhattan soon buzz with every embarrassing detail. I used to thank heaven that we lived so far from town. With Jehan being Governor's Councillor, I was confident that we could keep the family name out of the mud, but I was wrong.

One morning I was on my way to the barn to see why the milk was so late, when I heard Tobias's voice.

"My money's on that good-looker, Jacob van Curler," he said as my heart skipped a beat.

Then came Ariaen's high-pitched giggle. At the sight of me they both looked embarrassed. The woman went back to her milking with a guilty smirk and Tobias's birthmark glowed purple as he busied himself with the horses. I pretended not to notice.

"There's no milk for the suppawn, Ariaen," I said mildly, helping myself to a full pail.

Why was I always the last to hear anything around here? Now that I thought about it, Jehan had been looking grim all week. I meant to ask him what was wrong but we were both so busy. He left for town last night saying he needed a full day to prepare for tomorrow.

After breakfast I cornered Isaack. He may be twice my size but he's still my little brother and in no time I had the truth out of him. It seems that Jehan, my calm, dignified Jehan, had been accused of striking an old woman. Furthermore he as good as admitted it. I was dumbstruck!

What happened was this. During court last Thursday, our new neighbor, Claes, the wheelwright, announced that he was bringing charges against Councillor Montagne for striking his vrouw. Whereupon Jehan, instead of denying it, said he was filing a countercharge of slander against Claes for remarks uttered by said vrouw. At this point the Governor stepped in and ordered both cases postponed one week.

Sweet Jesus! That crazy Indian had been a witness after all!

"What did Claes's wife say, Isaack?"

"What difference does it make? Claes should have walloped that dreadful woman black and blue long ago." He pulled out his handkerchief and honked into it.

"What did she say?" I repeated.

"No one knows for sure yet, but she must have referred to you. Every time someone gets angry around here he calls the other fellow's wife a whore. Don't worry. No one's ever going to believe anything like that about you."

Dear, sweet Isaack. Do men always have such faith in their sisters?

"Jehan would never strike a woman," I said aloud, "regardless of what outrageous lies she might tell."

But suppose, I asked myself, suppose the woman were speaking the truth, and Jehan realized that she was speaking the truth?

Isaack did not have to tell me that the case was the talk of New Amsterdam. There must be a hundred different versions by now of that dreadful woman's story. But Claes is not a talker and his vrouw rarely leaves Otterspoor. No one could be sure which tale was correct until the next day when Jehan sued for slander. At all costs he must be prevented from bringing charges. Isaack would have to help me.

An hour later my brother left for town with a list of arguments for Jehan. Then he spent the night at the du Trieux home, attended the court proceedings in the morning and hurried home here with the news.

Jehan did plead guilty to the charge of striking an old woman, but the counter charge of slander was dropped. He was sentenced to pay six guilders to the poor, and the case was closed if not forgotten. Except for

Isaack, no one suspects that I even know about the charges. Ironically, Isaack is probably the only person who is completely sure that I am innocent.

I made a bad mistake and I am paying for it. But confessing the truth would only make things infinitely worse. I vowed to be a loving wife to Jehan and charitable to all who fall from the straight and narrow. For the rest I will hold my head high and say nothing. In the course of time the gossip will die for lack of fuel.

A few days later, Claes's vrouw was found dead with a bottle of Dutch gin in her hand and a thousand cockroaches in her pantry. None who knew her shed a tear. But Jehan's treatment of this old woman is being held against him. God forgive me for letting him take the blame alone.

Gossip about the indiscretions of the Montagne family was soon overshadowed by the double slander case of Dominie Bogardus and his wife, Anneke. Marriages to men of God are not always made in Heaven as Anneke soon discovered. She was able to transform the bare parsonage into a warm and hospitable home. She managed children, housework and garden, apparently without effort, and served sumptuous repasts to a parade of parishioners, herself always as fresh as a wild rose in the cabbage bed of Manhattan society.

The Dominie, however, she could not transform. His temper was as fiery as ever. Although devoted to his petite bride, he remains equally devoted to his brandy and Madeira.

As predicted, Anneke's sudden rise to the top of New Amsterdam's social ladder set tongues wagging furiously. Once more the old questions surfaced. How had her late husband come by those 62 acres? What was the relationship between Anneke and ex-Governor van Twiller? And why was she on such good terms with Grietje, the whore?

Through it all, Anneke marched the streets of New Amsterdam with head held high. Marched is the wrong word. Anneke does not march earnestly through this world like your typical minister's helpmate. Rather she trips lightly round the potholes of Manhattan, rainbow-colored petticoats swirling gracefully above dainty ankles, a pleasant sight for sore eyes and more grist for the gossip mill.

All would have faded with time if Bogardus had not been provoked into suing for slander on two counts. The court proceedings dragged on for weeks, putting the sordid details, not only on the tip of every tongue, but indelibly into the records.

It all started with Grietje, the whore, and her unsavory husband, the Turk. Apparently Giretje sometimes does business on credit. Any customer that fails to pay up can look forward to a very unpleasant visit from the pistol-waving Turk.

Before leaving for the Fatherland, Andries Hudde mortgaged his Long Island property to raise money for his upcoming marriage. That very same day Grietje presented Andries with a large bill for back favors. He claimed it was much more than he owed but he paid up to avoid trouble.

When she tried the same trick on Bogardus at the time of his wedding, the Dominie said he did not owe her a stuiver and he did not intend to be blackmailed. It was not much money and Anneke begged him to pay up to keep Grietje quiet. The Dominie said it was the principle, not the amount. He refused.

When she failed to collect, Grietje took her revenge by circulating the rumor that the Dominie owed her money. He naturally sued for slander and Anneke vowed she would never speak to Grietje again. The gossips speculated happily about Bogardus's bachelor exploits, but the Dominie was a popular figure and his reputation suffered little. New Amsterdam is a far cry from Puritan New England.

It was not long before the attack shifted from the Dominie to his wife, whose reputation was more vulnerable. One day in the Strand, the Turk proclaimed loudly that Anneke was not only a whore, but an ungrateful whore. He said Grietje had befriended Anneke when she first came to Manhattan from Fort Orange. Now that she was married to the Dominie, Anneke was too uppity to speak to her former benefactor. Dominie Bogardus sued again, this time on behalf of his wife.

Both Jehan and I tried to persuade him to drop the charges. Anneke also pleaded, but the Dominie is a stubborn man. He said Grietje and the Turk had plagued Manhattan society long enough under Wouter's protection. With Wouter gone it was high time to get rid of these two, and he refused to withdraw his suit. The Turk was asked to present proof of his accusation, witnesses were called on both sides and the whole Colony as far away as Fort Orange gnawed with relish on every spicy detail.

The case revolved about an incident that occurred in front of the blacksmith's shop, normally the loitering place for the rowdy. Here, according to Grietje, Anneke had been seen lifting her petticoats, the time-honored invitation of the whore. And the object of her solicitation was none other than our ex-neighbor from Otterspoor, the good-looking Jacob van Curler.

Official sympathy was, of course, all with Anneke. The Dominie was allowed to bring witnesses to testify as to the unsavory character of Grietje as well as those to testify to the innocence of his own wife.

In the meantime it was very hard on Anneke. I visited her as often as possible with as much support as I could muster. "There," I thought, "but for the grace of God, go I."

Lawyers are not allowed to practice in court so everyone pleads his own case. Grietje and the Turk were no match for the Dominie, whose star witness was Jacob van Curler, himself. According to Jacob, Anneke had come to his home on the day in question, only to depart in a great hurry upon discovering Grietje within. The purpose of Anneke's visit, or for that matter the reason for Grietje's presence, was never mentioned. Jacob claimed that he ran after Anneke in order to ask her "to dine with him that noon." He caught up with her in front of the blacksmith's just as she was lifting her skirt to avoid an "uneven place in the road."

At this the packed courtroom roared with laughter because the streets of Manhattan are nothing but mud and potholes.

Next Hendrick Jansen, locksmith, testified that he happened to look out the window of his shop just as the Dominie's wife passed the blacksmith's. He also saw her discreetly lifting her skirts to avoid being splattered.

If future generations ever read the minutes of these sessions they will wonder why everyone was so concerned about Anneke Jans's petticoats as witness after witness testified to her refined mannerisms at that "uneven place in the road."

Interspersed with these chaste accounts of Anneke's petticoats, were sensational details of life chez Grietje and the Turk. Hendrick van Borsum, Master Carpenter, testified that he had been working at the Fort one day when Grietje arrived with her two infants, screaming that the children were bastards and she was going to "dash their brains out against the Fort wall." Restrained from carrying out this threat she then shouted that she had been "the whore of the nobility for long enough." From now on she was going to be "the whore of the rabble."

Lysbet Dirks testified that she had acted as midwife at Grietje's last confinement. (Anneke's mother, the official town midwife, refused to attend Grietje.) When the baby was born Grietje asked Lysbet whether the child looked like the Turk or like Andries Hudde.

"If you don't know who the father is, how should I?" was the indignant reply. "But his skin is kinda brown."

Fortunately for Andries, he and Gertrude are still in Europe.

Perhaps the most intriguing tidbit was the account of how Grietje measured the male organs of certain well-endowed patrons by making notches on her broomstick. Rumor has it that the Turk holds the record.

After all the witnesses had been heard and the evidence thoroughly sifted, Grietje was ordered to make a public acknowledgement at the toll of the bell that she had lied falsely, and that the minister was an honorable man. Antony Jansen, the Turk, as husband and guardian of Grietje, was required to appear in court and acknowledge that he knew the minister's wife to be a virtuous and honorable woman.

This is by no means the first time that Grietje and her husband have been in court. Hardly a week goes by without one or both of them being called on some violation or slander charge. Drunken brawls are the most frequent. The Turk also has an unfortunate habit of pointing a loaded pistol at his neighbors when he loses his temper.

New Amsterdam colonists are by and large a rowdy lot, but this pair is too rough even for New Amsterdam. The court has ordered them banished from Manhattan. Grudgingly, they have agreed to buy land on Long Island.

Thank God it is all over.

> Your affectionate cousin,
>
> Rachel

Little Deer

This 1st day of November
In the Year of Our Lord 1638
At Vredendale

Dearest Margariet,

Jan has a new friend, a young Weckquasgeek named Little Deer. He first appeared on a Sunday afternoon when the boys were fishing from the dock. I noticed the Indian standing motionless by the water's edge, almost invisible in the dappled shade from the birches. He looked harmless enough, maybe a year or two older than Jan who is now eight, but I left the gate open to keep an eye on the situation.

As I watched, Jesse landed a fish and struggled for some time to remove the hook.

"It's stuck in his gut," he cried finally, panic creeping into his voice. Jesse is much too tender-hearted for a boy.

"Pull harder, domkop!" shouted Jan. "Here, gimme that!" He slammed the fish's head against the dock, yanked the hook free, removing half the jaw in the process, and nonchalantly tossed the bloody remains into the basket.

Jesse gagged, grabbed his crutch and set off for the house at a rapid hobble. When I looked back, the Indian had taken over the discarded pole, handling it as naturally as if he had been born fishing with hook and line instead of Weckquasgeek spear and net. Side by side, he and Jan pulled in perch and bullheads without ever exchanging a word.

It was a few days later that Jan came home with the knife wound. He had been scaling the stony face of Slangberg when he noticed his Weckquasgeek friend above him. With one eye on the Indian he never saw the snake sunning itself on a rock. It struck him on the shoulder.

In an instant Little Deer was on the spot. Without so much as a by-your-leave, he grabbed Jan's arm, cut an incision in the wound with a wicked-looking knife and sucked out the poison, which he then spat noisily in the direction of the vanished snake.

Willem was the first to greet Jan when he returned. He says he saw no proof of snake bite.

"Them savages just enjoy slashing Europeans to find out what color the blood is!"

Neither Willem nor Tobias has ever gotten over their loathing of Wilden. As for Jan, he maintains that Little Deer saved his life. It is difficult to know where the truth lies.

Every Indian youth has an uncle who is responsible for his education. It turns out that Little Deer's uncle is Moose Foot. After the snake-bite incident Little Deer decided to take Jan under his wing and pass on what he learns to this promising Swannekin, which is Algonkian for European, meaning person from the salt water.

At first it was mainly running. Sometimes I watch them from the loft window, Little Deer always a few paces in the lead. The idea is not to go as fast as possible but to maintain a steady speed over the long haul. In hot weather they swim naked in the creek. Jan has mastered the overhand crawl of the Wilden, which is much faster than the sedate European breast stroke.

Inside the stockade Little Deer rarely says a word although he seems to understand Dutch. Outside he is a patient but strict taskmaster. If his pupil so much as snaps a dead twig he is made to retrace his steps. Jan says that the Weckquasgeek can approach a deer from down wind, so close as to be able to slap the animal on the rump before it bolts. The nearest he himself can get is twenty paces.

It is an odd relationship, but Jehan says there is no harm in it providing Jan keeps up with his Latin and does his chores.

It was not long after Little Deer began coming to the house that the *Yellow Swan* disappeared. There was a severe windstorm during the night and Jehan suspected Willem of not mooring her properly. Willem, of course, was certain she had been stolen by Weckquasgeeks if not by Little Deer himself.

The men spent the day searching the creek and nearby coves with no success. Jehan even swallowed his pride and borrowed a rowboat from Otterspoor. He and Jan circled the islands in Hell Gate Bay and the East River, then rowed into town where no one had seen strake nor wake of the missing yawl. It seemed likely that she had been dashed to pieces in Hell Gate and the remains washed out into Long Island Sound.

"Devil's Frying Pan got her," muttered Philippe, when he heard the story. All the large rocks in Hell Gate have their own weird names. "Lucky no one was hurt," said Susannah. "Last year two boys fishing from a row-boat disappeared. All they ever found was an oar."

Not wanting to leave any stone unturned, Jehan tacked a notice to the Fort gate offering a reward of ten guilders for the return of the *Yellow Swan*. He did not have much hope.

In the meantime, with the men off searching for the yawl, and Jesse and the girls napping, I decided to tackle the clutter in the loft. Ariaen slept up here until last week when she left to be married. I was glad to be rid of her even though it meant more work for me.

We do not have a separate cookhouse yet, so the garret is used to store everything from powder and shot to sacks of corn and rye flour. In winter the place is draped with drying clothes and the chimney serves as smoke-house to hang sausages and strips of dried beef.

I was moving a barrel of salted eels when Tiger began to bark. We never have any trouble with Weckquasgeeks but Indian dogs are another matter. From the loft window I saw six of the vicious beasts slinking through the cornfield toward the meadow where the cattle graze. This meadow is bound on one side by the creek, on one side by the stockade itself, and on the other two sides by a none-too-firm rail fence. Tied to a stake in the center was Tiger, barking fiercely.

At first warning the men usually come running with clubs and guns. One shot over their heads would send the savage creatures scurrying back into the forest. Jehan is determined to maintain good relations with the Weckquasgeeks and has given strict orders not to harm their dogs. When Willem accidentally killed one, Jehan compensated Chief Rechnewac and deducted half the amount from Willem's wages.

Now the bloodthirsty creatures were growing bolder. I shouted and shook my broom out the window. For a moment they hesitated, then some instinct told them that the angry men with clubs were not coming today. If I did not do something quickly, I would soon have three dead cows and one dead bull mastiff on my hands. I began to load the long gun.

Tiger seemed to understand that it was all on his shoulders today. Head low, ears back, he told the enemy just what he would do to the first one that came any closer. Full grown now, he was bigger and stronger than any of his individual attackers. But one dog tied to a stake is no match for a pack of six.

Carefully I aimed the gun, not over their heads but directly at the animals. It would only fire once so I would not get another chance. No one could dock my wages.

I never pulled that trigger. Suddenly, with one powerful lunge, Tiger wrenched the stake from the ground and flew at the enemy, rope and stake whipping after him like the tail of some monstrous serpent. The topmost rail crashed to the ground as he cleared the fence, still flying with murderous fury. For one moment the brutes stared in horror at this fiendish apparition. Then they turned tail and fled like the cowards they are, into the wilderness. Tiger chased them to the edge of the clearing. Satisfied, he blatantly cocked a leg at every tree-trunk along the border before trotting briskly back to his charges.

In his absence Rainbow had stepped over the fallen rail and was grazing contentedly outside the enclosure. Tiger signaled her curtly to get inside. She craned her neck to give him a look of patient incomprehension and returned to her munching. Having vanquished the enemy horde, he was in no mood to be defied by a foolish cow. A few sharp snaps at her hindquarters quickly persuaded Rainbow to get back where she belonged.

I brought the hero a generous soup-bone and was just struggling with the fence rail when Jehan and Jan returned from town with a report on the missing yawl.

"If she doesn't show up by tomorrow, my dear, we shall have to buy a new one. Nothing so grand as the *Yellow Swan*. A good sturdy rowboat with two sets of oarlocks should be adequate until our finances improve."

The next day there was still no sign of the yawl and Jehan prepared to walk down the Weckquasgeek trail to call on the shipbuilder.

"I can't stomach borrowing Claes's rowboat two days running, my dear, and it's worth one's neck to ride a horse on that trail."

"Why not send Isaack?"

"He wouldn't get as good a price."

At that moment Jan came dashing though the cornfield, shouting with excitement. With him was Little Deer, quiet and self-contained as always. It seems that the Indian had offered to speak to his grandmother, Old Nehooma, who was so wise that she would be bound to know exactly what had happened to the *Yellow Swan*.

In the last few weeks we have learned something about Little Deer's family, who live in the Weckquasgeek village of Shorakapkok at the north end of Manhattan. His father was killed fighting Mohawks and his mother is overseer of the village field hands, all of whom are female. Indian braves do the hunting and fighting. Raising crops they leave to the squaws.

Jan has seen Old Nehooma and insists that she has yellow eyes. He thinks she is blind but is not sure. She has her own hearth in the long house at Shorakapkok where even Chief Rechnewac will occasionally seek her advice.

Of course it would be absurd to ask this old woman, she is probably Little Deer's great-grandmother, to locate our yawl. However, one thing one must never do is ridicule an Indian. Jehan thanked Little Deer politely and said that he would be most grateful to have Nehooma's opinion. So the boys ran off eagerly toward Shorakapkok and as soon as they were out of sight Jehan set out for town to order a new boat.

The boys returned first with a peculiar tale. They had found Old Nehooma squatting by the fire, smoking her copper pipe. Little Deer explained about our yawl disappearing from Muscoota the night of the windstorm. He said that Old Nehooma's wisdom was so well-known that the famous Swannekin, Doctor Montagne, was hoping she could help him locate this valuable boat.

Jan watched the flames reflected in her yellow eyes as she stirred the fire. The lines on her face were not the soft wrinkles of a European grandmother. He said they looked like cracks in the bottom of a dried-up creek bed.

The old woman remained silent for a long time and when she finally did speak Jan could not understand a word. Then she turned and motioned for him to approach. He was surprised because he didn't think she knew he was there. When he squatted down beside her, she put her hand on his head and muttered something in a sad, far-away voice. Then both boys thanked her and took their leave.

Once outside, Little Deer explained that Grandmother had seen the *Yellow Swan* in the fire. She said the storm blew the yawl down the creek into Hell Gate Bay. When it reached the whirlpool it was damaged by rocks but not destroyed. It did not go through Hell Gate but was driven aground in a swampy cove on the far side of Tenkenas Island. The sad message at the end was one of her favorite complaints. She said that when Jan was a grown man there would be no more Weckquasgeeks on Manhattan.

The boys then hurried up to Paparinemin, the Wading Place, where Moose Foot was launching his dugout. He volunteered to investigate Tenkenas Island and said he would meet them back at Muscoota. Little Deer stood quietly as Jan related the story with his usual enthusiasm. Then the two went down to the dock to wait for Moose Foot and the yawl.

I did not have the heart to tell them that Old Nehooma was simply imagining things. They would be disappointed soon enough. Jan should have had the wit to tell Moose Foot that he and his father had already rowed around the far side of Tenkenas.

Jesse soon limped down to join the others who were skipping stones into the water. It is strange that you never see a lame Weckquasgeek. In fact Wilden never have club feet or cross eyes or hunchbacks or cleft palates or any other afflictions so common to Europeans. The only ailments that seem to affect them are connected with cleanliness, or lack of it, namely foot infections and head lice.

I needed a suitable gift for Old Nehooma. With the idea of sending her some of my crab-apple preserve, I climbed the ladder to the loft. At that moment I heard shouting and ran to the window. Jan was jumping up and down on the dock yelling at the top of his lungs.

"Mama! Come look!"

There, paddling slowly up the creek, was Moose Foot towing the *Yellow Swan*.

That night in bed Jehan and I reviewed the whole sequence of events. Moose Foot had found the yawl, mast broken, lying bottom side up exactly where Grandmother had predicted. I insisted that we send her ten guilders worth of wampum in addition to my jars of crab-apple preserve.

"Of course we will send her the reward money, my dear." His chest rested against my back with his hand on my shoulder. "But I do not believe for one moment that the old woman saw the *Yellow Swan* in her fire. Nehooma has lived her entire life on Manhattan." His hand moved slowly down my arm. "She knows this island inside out, Rachel. Well, boats have gone adrift before."

My arms were folded tightly across my breast. Should I stop him? Jehan never forces me.

"Suppose," he continued, "suppose that fifty years ago a dugout, beached in our creek, washed away in a windstorm like we had the other night. The combination of wind and current might drive it ashore in that particular cove."

How can men carry on intelligent conversation at such moments?

"I think Old Nehooma did see the yawl in the fire," I whispered.

"No, my dear. She was only remembering an event from her past," he said, kissing the back of my neck. He always smells of good leather and tobacco.

"When we get another windstorm, my dear, I shall do an experiment to prove it."

I wriggled my stern backwards and he stopped talking.

The next day Jehan and Isaack took the damaged yawl to the ship-builder who agreed to make her as good as new for 18 guilders. While they were gone Jan and I walked up to the top of the bluff where Hendrick had first shown us Vredendale. If Nehooma was right about the *Yellow Swan* there might well be some truth in her other remarks. I made him repeat carefully the old woman's every word.

"Maybe it's true that the Wilden will eventually leave Manhattan," I said.

"I hope not, Mama. I like Weckquasgeeks much better than Christians."

"This whole valley will one day belong to you, Jan."

He nodded and we stood gazing quietly at the peaceful bowery spread out beneath us in the sunshine. In the distance three miniature cows stood motionless as though painted on a landscape of rolling green. Only a thin curl of white smoke from the toy chimney moved against a cloudless sky.

Neither of us mentioned Jesse. It was tacitly understood that he would never be strong enough to run a tobacco plantation. Please God, let him live to grow up.

"Don't forget that we have a ground brief for Vredendale now, Jan. As soon as the mortgage is paid off it will be ours forever. When your father and I are gone there may come a time when you need money. You must never sell one acre. Your grandfather and your uncle gave their lives for this land. Some day you will pass it on to your son and he to his son and so on forever."

A week later we had a similar windstorm and Jehan had an empty herring barrel ready with the initials J.M. painted all over in bright colors. In the evening he released the barrel from our dock and in the morning he hurried to the swampy cove on the far side of Tenkenas. It was not there. In fact not one stave of that barrel was ever found anywhere.

Your affectionate cousin,

Rachel

Fire

The 12th day of November
In the Year of Our Lord 1638
At Vredendale

Dearest Margariet,

We had a scare last week. Philippe du Trieux rowed up here on Wednesday with pumpkins for sale. He brought eight-year-old Abram and ten-year-old Sutje.

I bought a dozen pumpkins and produced cider and olykoeks for the youngsters while the men lit up their pipes and sat on the stoop to discuss politics. Philippe is disgusted with the new Governor.

"Man's an ass!" he growled.

"No public official is perfect," said Jehan. "Surely Governor Kieft is a vast improvement over Wouter van Twiller."

Philippe said that the Wilden loved Wouter.

"Of course they loved him," countered Jehan. "Every Indian Chief within fifty miles of here drank himself silly under Wouter's table."

"Kieft treats 'em like dung, Montagne. They're gittin' surly."

"The Governor is merely trying to enforce the law, my friend. You know as well as I that it is illegal to sell a gun to an Indian."

"Hah! He still gets his gun, only now he pays twice over and winds up angry as a she-bear with cubs. Wilden make bad enemies, Montagne."

"The Weckquasgeeks up here are very friendly," I ventured. "Chief Rechnewac, himself, brought me two fat turkeys only this morning."

Jehan smiled. "We have our mid-day meal in the fields with the men. Rachel cooks enough for an army and it is a rare day when one or two Indians do not sit down to share with us."

"Better outdoors than in!" Philippe muttered with a grimace.

The Wilden do have a powerful odor, a combination of sweat and rancid bear-grease. I never turn anyone away, but I am always thankful when they join us in the open air.

"Philippe is right, my dear. Van Twiller, inept though he was, did maintain excellent relations with the Wilden. Kieft, in his effort to bring order out of chaos, has been treading on their toes." He turned to Philippe.

"I am going to the Fort this evening, my friend. I should like you to accompany me to discuss this with the Governor."

"I'm no good with fancy words, Montagne."

"That is not important. What matters is that you have been here since the beginning and can vouch for the relations between the races."

"That I can. Fourteen years Weckquasgeeks and Canarsies lived among us like lambs. Many's the family would have starved without their help."

The conversation shifted to the new settlement on the Delaware. Our first Governor, Peter Minuit, is now in the employ of Queen Christina of Sweden. Accompanied by 50 Swedish colonists he recently landed on the South River and proclaimed the place "New Sweden."

"Leave 'em alone," was Philippe's opinion.

"Impossible," said Jehan. "The South River belongs to the Netherlands, and the Swedes must either swear allegiance or be evicted."

"What about the English trespassers on the Connecticut?" I countered.

"The problem, my dear, is that we do not have enough colonists here for one river, let alone three. New England, with her miserable winters, already has a population of ten thousand. It is not surprising that a few have strayed down onto the Connecticut and built themselves a village called Hartford. But they must be made to swear allegiance to the Netherlands."

While the men debated the best method for dealing with Swedish and English trespassers, I watched the youngsters romp in a pile of autumn leaves. Little Sutje du Trieux has the most fascinating golden ringlets. Head first, petticoats flying, she somersaulted into the crackling heap. Then she gave herself a good shake, like a wet dog shedding a spray of leaves and twigs. Lo and behold each shiny curl sprang back instantly into its perfect position.

Jesse awkwardly raked more leaves onto the ever-growing pile as Little Rachel and Marie, heads down, rumps in the air, struggled comically to imitate the somersault. Then Sutje pulled the little ones away while Abram du Trieux and Jan took turns leaping into the leaves from the big elm. Jan naturally embroidered his act with a few acrobatic swings for Sutje's benefit, and she showed her appreciation with squeals of girlish glee. Those curls will break their share of hearts in a few years.

Thursday morning when Tobias unlocked the gate he noticed a faint red glow in the northern sky.

"Looks like them savages is havin' a fire, Ma'am."

My first thought was to dispatch Willem and Tobias to help, more as a gesture of good will than anything else. There were hundreds of Wilden in the area, much more capable than they of dealing with a run-away blaze.

"Can't do that Ma'am. Can't leave you alone with all them youngens."

Philippe and Isaack had both accompanied Jehan to the Fort the night before, leaving Abram and Sutje here. This left me with six children in all. I enjoyed having them although Sutje was more decorative than helpful.

"I hope the flames are not near Shorakapkok," I said. "Those bark wigwams will go up in a flash."

Tobias suggested that Willem climb Slangberg to have a look. "He can see what's what easy from there, Ma'am. I'd go myself but his legs is younger."

With difficulty I restrained Jan and Abram from dashing after Willem who strode off in high boots to protect against snake bite.

"We need you boys to fill the water barrel in case the fire heads this way," I said handing them each a leather bucket. Of course it did not occur to me at this point that Vredendale was in any danger, but the water barrel did need filling anyway and this made it sound more important.

The men had planned to cut wood today. Logs for the fireplace were neatly stacked in cords in the woodshed, but the actual cutting was done just outside the north gate. When I looked out a few minutes later, the sky was still pink but not threatening. The fire was obviously miles away. Nevertheless Tobias had abandoned his axe and was dragging every tub and hogshead out of the barn.

"Just a precaution, Ma'am. Savages is kind'a slow curbin' them flames."

Soon we were all busy with pots, pails and kettles, shuttling back and forth from the creek. Then Willem reappeared, running and flailing his arms like a madman.

"Savages is burning us out," he gasped, still waving his hands. The missing fingers added emphasis to the horror in his face.

When he got his breath back he told us that the Wilden were fanning the fire instead of trying to control it. Dear God, I wish Jehan were here. Willem must be demented. He has far too much imagination for eighteen.

"I'm sure there is a logical explanation," I stated as firmly as possible. "Tobias will go up to Shorakapkok to speak to the Wilden and Jan will go along to translate."

"Can't get through!" cried Willem, rolling his eyes. "Flames is right across the island. Them savages is lined up along the far side wavin' blankets to make it burn."

I must remain calm. Philippe said the Wilden were angry with Kieft's new regulations. Could their anger be so great that they were willing to burn the whole island of Manhattan? Impossible. Moose Foot would never let anything happen to Vredendale.

"Chief Rechnewac brought me two fat turkeys just yesterday," I said feebly.

Willem pounced on this. "That's how savages puts you off guard. They acts friendly like. Then the next minute they stabs you in the back." His face was covered with sweat.

Tobias pointed to a cloud of dark smoke beginning to rise above the treetops. "Wind's from the north, Ma'am," he said. "With dead leaves everywhere, them woods is one big tinderbox. We best get the animals and youngens out of here. Me and Willem'll stay as long as we can."

He suggested that the children and I row out to Tenkenas Island in Hell Gate Bay, but I had no intention of leaving Vredendale in charge of indentured servants. In the first place, if the fire did reach us we would need every possible pair of hands. And in the second place, I knew perfectly well that if I left, the two of them would not be far behind.

I wish Moose Foot would appear. Suppose he was off hunting up in the Land of the Tall Birch. Wait a minute! Willem said the fire was started along a line this side of Shorakapkok. But Moose Foot and Rechnewac live in a tiny village called Konaada Kongh between here and Hell Gate.

"You must be mistaken, Willem," I said. "Weckquasgeeks would never jeopardize Konaada Kongh."

"Hah! That village ain't but a dozen wigwams. Savages'd sacrifice 'em easy enough to wipe us Christians off Manhattan."

I told myself not to panic. There were acres of cleared land between us and the forest. We had unlimited water from the creek and seven pair of hands counting the four older children.

The fields were covered with dried cornstalks and stubble. Between stockade and farmland was a strip of ground 20 feet wide and strewn with half split logs, chips and sawdust.

"Flames'll race straight across them fields, Ma'am." Tobias shook his head gloomily. "What we need is a good 40 feet of bare earth round the whole stockade."

"Twenty feet is better than nothing," I shouted, grabbing a large branch and dragging it away. Soon everyone was frantically dragging, lifting, pulling. Tobias tried to harness Mitternacht for the heavy timber but the horses smelled the fire and were so terrified as to be useless.

It took both men to lift the bigger logs. I got a rake and broom and made a pile of sawdust and leaves to be burned. What I pictured was a strip of mud around Vredendale. Surely a fire could not cross 20 feet of mud. How many buckets of water will turn dry ground into mud?

"Lieve God in Hemel!" Willem pointed as a huge tongue of flame shot high above the horizon before being sucked back into the cloud of smoke.

We stared in horror then redoubled our efforts. Surely they must see the smoke from the Fort by now. But any troops would arrive too late to save Vredendale. Sweet Jesus, help us.

Tobias set a ladder against the house. "One spark on that there thatch and we're all goners," he growled, handing Jan a bucket. "Here, you monkey, give them reeds a good wet-down."

Jan scurried nimbly over the roof as Abram raced up and down the ladder exchanging full bucket for empty. I wondered what was happening at Otterspoor. Thank God Claes had two grown sons to help him.

Then the deer came. Just a handful at first, soon a steady stream racing diagonally across the fields. Now there were thousands stampeding directly toward us, only veering into two groups at the last minute to avoid the stockade. It was an astonishing sight. I never imagined that there could be so many deer on Manhattan.

Little Rachel and Marie began to cry. They were in the child's pen by the front stoop, with Tiger tied to the post. It was already too late to get the animals to Tenkenas. Soon it would be too late for all of us.

Creating a strip of mud was slow work. Where there was too much grass, Willem swung away with a pickaxe, then turned the earth under. Tobias cut down some of the closer cornstalks and threw them on to my bonfire. Sweat made his birthmark shine bright purple.

"Why not burn off th' whole field, Ma'am," he said, "before the flames gits here."

Of course! Why didn't I think of it before? Fight fire with fire! Thank God for Tobias.

However, it was not as easy as it sounds to burn against the wind. The men put torches to the first two rows and the rest of us fanned with blankets until our arms ached. All we got was smoke in the face. The flames would not go in the right direction and I began to fear that Vredendale would be destroyed by sparks from our own efforts.

My eyes stung from the smoke. At one point my skirt caught fire. Then Tiger began to bark as though we were being attacked by a hundred savage dogs. Over the sound of barking and wailing infants there was a growing roar in the distance like a cyclone approaching. Was it the fire or only the roar of Hell Gate?

Suddenly, without warning, we were surrounded by Indians carrying burning brands. For one horrible moment I thought they were putting the torch to Vredendale. Then I realized that they were burning back toward the forest fire. In no time they had the cornfield ablaze, all the while running up and down this end to stamp out sparks.

Tobias and Willem helped fan the flames but I went and sat on the stoop with Marie and Little Rachel in my arms. Now that the danger was over I felt dizzy and put my head down on top of the children. Tiger stopped barking and licked my ear.

"Doucement, Tiger, doucement," I whispered.

By the time Jehan and Isaack returned from town it was all over. The forest still burned in patches, but the advancing flames were checked where they met the brush fire from our fields, now black and smoking.

Moose Foot told me later that before the Swannekins came, the Wilden used to burn off the whole island of Manhattan every few years. Now they only burn the north end. The fire cleans off the floor of the forest and makes it easier to hunt. They always burn after harvest by which time the young animals are old enough to flee the flames.

He explained that a fast fire like this does not harm the big, healthy trees. In fact they are all the better for having the underbrush removed. The greatest danger to a beautiful forest comes when it has not been burned for a long time. Then if lightning strikes there is so much dead wood and debris piled up from years of neglect that everything is destroyed, even the greatest oak.

We brought out a keg of beer for the fire-fighters and the youngsters proudly drank their share alongside the Wilden. Jan and Abram were so dirty it was hard to tell them apart. Sutje was cleaner but one side of her beautiful hair was black.

"Potverdikki! She burnt her curls," announced Jan.

Sutje giggled and dunked her face in a hogshead of water. Then a quick scrub with her apron and a shake. Even the Wilden smiled with childish pleasure as the soot disappeared and each golden ringlet sprang like magic to its appointed place.

Affectionately,

Rachel

Newcomers

This 19th day of September
In the Year of Our Lord 1639
At Vredendale

Dearest Margariet,

I am so happy that you are expecting again. May God grant you an easy delivery and a big, healthy child.

Gertrude and Andries Hudde have arrived and so far there has been no trouble over Vredendale. When I learned they were due I had the little house in the Heerenstraat put into shape. Then, the first Sunday, I went to call. Andries had gone to inspect his Long Island property, leaving Gertrude alone and pathetically glad to see me. She is still a great beauty but full of complaints.

"Manhattan sounded so grand when Andries described it, Rachel. How could I have left Amsterdam for this Godforsaken mud-hole?" We sat on the stoop sipping the apple juice I had brought.

"You'll get used to it," I said. "Look at that magnificent river, Gertrude. This is the best view in town."

She was not interested in views. "And I don't want to live on Long Island, Rachel. If I have to stay in this dreadful place I want to be within shouting distance of the Fort."

Hudde's Long Island property is less than two miles from town. If Gertrude is afraid to live there she certainly is never going to covet Vredendale. To hide my relief I glanced across the road at the little cemetery. She followed my eyes.

"I thought it would bother me to be so close to Hendrick's grave, but it doesn't." She patted her flat little stomach. "If it's a boy, we've agreed to name him Hendrick."

Of course it is only right that they call their first born after Hendrick, nevertheless I was pleased. Jehan may still be at loggerheads with Andries, but Gertrude and I have made our peace.

It was the next Thursday that Jehan brought home word of the Governor's fateful decision to tax the Wilden.

"My God, Rachel, Kieft will plunge the whole country into war if he goes on like this!" Jehan sucked on his pipe then tapped it impatiently against the chimney. When he is upset the only thing that gives him any peace is that pipe.

New Amsterdam badly needs money to repair the Fort among other things. At least there is no dike tax here like there is in the Fatherland, but to tax the Wilden is outrageous.

"How can anyone possibly justify taxing Indians?" I asked.

"Kieft says the Fort is here to protect the Wilden as well as Christians. Come harvest time he will send the Company yacht round to collect corn from every tribe in the neighborhood. My God, this is going to cause trouble!" Jehan tapped the chimney again. This time the clay pipe smashed into a hundred pieces.

The next morning Moose Foot arrived with a pile of beavers slung over his shoulder. He already knew about the tax.

"Kieft want corn, him pay," he said in his deep, deliberate voice. "No wampum, no corn."

I brought refreshments and we sat down to the serious business of bargaining.

"Doctor Montagne will surely persuade the Governor to change his mind," I lied hopefully. "This beaver has an arrow hole in it, Moose Foot." I opened my wampum box and offered him a half length.

He shook his head. "Wampum no good," he said pointing to some broken shells.

That is the trouble with wampum. A guilder is a guilder forever, but wampum tends to lose its value. I ended up exchanging a full length of defective wampum for the beaver with the hole in it.

When we had exhausted the furs and incidentally all the wampum, Moose Foot returned to the subject of politics.

"Wise Sachem like great tree," he said. "Whole tribe rest in shade of great tree. Under blue sky, under black cloud, wise Sachem keep peace."

He cannot understand why the Company does not exchange Kieft for a wiser Sachem. Matter of fact, neither can I.

The thought of the impending tax threatens our world like a fault in a great dike. Many already are pulling up stakes and preparing to return to the Fatherland leaving more vacant houses to add to the general gloom.

A week later there was much excitement with the arrival of the *Fire of Troy*, carrying two wealthy Danish families with livestock and farm-hands. Eager to encourage settlers of this caliber, the Company has relaxed its restrictions, permitting the newcomers to buy land, even on Manhattan. Kieft has been instructed to give them every assistance and has put them up temporarily in the Governor's mansion. Jehan brought home glowing reports.

"A few more colonists like these two, my dear, and New Amsterdam could land on its feet after all." It is the first time he has been enthusiastic about anything since the proposed tax on the Wilden.

I did not see the Danes until Sunday service. Jochem Pieterse Kuyter is tall and thin with a spine like a ramrod. They say he served in the East Indies with a commission from King Christian of Denmark. The more scholarly Jonas Bronck is on the portly side, with gold-rimmed spectacles and a gold tooth that gleams when he sings the hymns. Both men are in their forties.

The two wives are much younger. Dressed in the latest European fashion, they sat in the front pew of the women's section, next to Gertrude, who appears to have met them in Amsterdam. All three rigidly ignored the whispers and stares of the dowdy congregation behind. Thank heavens the Dominie was halfway sober for once.

Afterwards, in the churchyard, I went up to welcome the newcomers. Vrouw Kuyter speaks little Dutch but Bronck's wife, the former Antonia Slagboom of Amsterdam, had plenty to say and said it.

"This church is a disgrace to the Fatherland, Madame Montagne," she sniffed, as though it were my fault. "And as for this mud," all three clutched their elegant skirts with expressions of horror, "I am appalled that in 14 years not one single street has been paved!"

Those stylish hemlines will be well up by next Sunday.

"She's a member of the wealthy Slagboom family of Amsterdam," confided Susannah later, "They say she brought every conceivable luxury with her, even a set of alabaster wineglasses!"

We were dining with the du Trieux as usual on Sunday. Today the household was especially chaotic because the efficient redhead with too many teeth was missing.

"Gotchoo!" sneezed Isaack as he rescued his beer from a goat that had strayed through the open door. "Where's Sarah?"

"At the Governor's mansion minding snively Danish brats." Susannah gave me a meaningful glance as she swept goat, hens, puppies and children into the yard. She has her heart set on marrying Sarah off to "a nice French boy like Isaack." As far as I know, my brother, at 23, has never even looked at a girl, much less a flat-chested, bossy fourteen-year-old with buck teeth. In this country Sarah will be grabbed up soon enough, but not by Isaack.

"Did you know that Bronck brought a hundred books with him," Susannah chattered on as we laid the table.

"If true he will have the largest library in the Colony," contributed Jehan from behind a cloud of pipe smoke.

"Gertrude says they were quite friendly with the Broncks in Amsterdam, mon vieux," I said.

"A slight exaggeration, my dear. Hudde managed to borrow 200 guilders from Bronck before they embarked, repayable in Manhattan. Now Bronck wants it back."

"Where's Hudde going to get 200 guilders?" laughed Susannah. "His land is already mortgaged to the hilt."

"Hudde spoke to me after church," continued Jehan. "He asked me to advance him the 200 so he can repay Bronck. I agreed."

For once I was speechless but not Susannah.

"That slampamper only married Gertrude to get Vredendale," she cried. "He's going round town now, saying that you stole it from him, Jehan. I wouldn't lend Andries Hudde so much as a stuiver if my life depended on it!"

"Hudde and I have had our differences, Susannah," Jehan always spoke calmly, "but he's a good colonist and God knows we need them here. Furthermore, I am not lending him the money. I am merely advancing him 200 guilders against the final payment on Vredendale which is due in October. In exchange, Hudde will sign a statement proving beyond a shadow of doubt that the land is ours."

"Hah!" said Philippe scratching his beard. It was a "hah" tinged with respect.

"That is very generous and clever, mon vieux," I said trying to look equally impressed. "But we don't have 200 guilders."

"My dear, I can easily raise 200 guilders."

That is true enough. He has several times borrowed money, always with Vredendale as collateral. Jehan loves legal niceties but we rarely see eye to eye in this matter of increasing the mortgage.

"Unfortunately, my dear, you do not have the legal background to appreciate the situation." Jehan spoke gently but I knew the discussion was closed.

"Do you think the newcomers will build on Long Island?" asked Susannah, tactfully changing the subject.

"Only a fool'd build anywhere today," muttered Philippe. He is convinced that the whole Colony will go up in flames the minute Kieft tries to tax the first Indian.

"I'm taking the Danes to look at Shorakin, tomorrow," announced Jehan. This was a pleasant surprise. Shorakin is the large tract of land north of Slangberg.

"Mangeons!" called Susannah throwing open the big front door. A rush of youngsters to the dinner table put an end to all serious conversation.

And so we have acquired two new neighbors. Kuyter was granted 400 acres about a mile northeast of us, and Bronck decided to settle directly across the Great Kill from his friend. He has purchased 500 acres from the Wilden and is the first European to build on the mainland. Both have bulging pockets, and easily persuaded Kieft not to enforce the Indian tax until their stockades are completed.

Kuyter has twenty men working for him. Jehan says a well-constructed stockade manned by twenty men is safer than Fort Amsterdam. Bronck's stockade is even larger. Inside he is building a great stone house with a red tile roof for the elegant Antonia and her alabaster wineglasses.

Both Danes are devout Lutherans. Fortunately their religious scruples include a firm determination to treat the Wilden fairly. There are reports from town of growing discord between the races but life here in the north remains peaceful.

Kuyter calls his bowery Zegendale. He commissioned Jehan to construct a map of Manhattan and insisted on marking in his property in large letters as though it were 400 square miles instead of acres. Jehan says the man has delusions of grandeur.

We continue to see a great deal of Little Deer. Sometimes he joins us for a meal and sometimes Jan eats at Shorakapkok. Indians eat the entrails along with the meat, and they consider dog flesh a delicacy. Just the thought turns my stomach though it never seems to bother Jan.

The tax on Indian corn will be enforced next month. I dread the outcome.

Your affectionate cousin,

Rachel

Raritans

This 14th day of July
In the Year of Our Lord 1640
At Vredendale

Dearest Margariet,

The Indian tax has now been enforced and so far there has been only one incident. Raritans attacked the Company yacht, *Vrede*, as she was on her rounds collecting taxes and furs. No one was seriously hurt but a few soldiers got a proper dunking. We were lucky this time. The Wilden, at least, looked on the whole episode as a lark. When an emissary was sent to the Raritans demanding satisfaction, they just laughed. Unfortunately Governor Kieft did not forget or forgive.

Last night Jehan bought home a dinner guest, Captain David de Vries. I had never met him although I had heard a great deal about him from Jehan. When we arrived in this country the Captain was on his way to the Fatherland to offer his services to the Company as Governor in place of the besotted van Twiller. Since his return he has been occupied establishing a bowery on Staten Island. Jehan says he is the best colonist we have and if the Company Directors had any sense, de Vries would be Governor today instead of Kieft.

I usually serve a roast for company but it was too late and I had to stay with the samp hutspot which had been cooking all day. Together with fresh pumpkin bread and our best wine it made a delicious meal if not an elegant one.

In his forties, with angular but handsome features, the Captain exuded strength, physical strength as well as strength of character. At the same time he had the magnetic charm and courtly manners that had made him the welcome guest of princes.

"Madame Montagne, I was told that you were the most beautiful woman in the Colony. My sources do not exaggerate."

"Captain de Vries, I was told that you were the man most capable of governing the Colony. I only regret that the Company Directors have been so lacking in vision."

It was a magic evening. Perhaps I drank too much wine because life never seemed rosier. How could we be in any danger with a man like this on our side?

What really won my heart was the Captain's obvious interest in the boys. Of course Jehan insisted that they recite some Latin. Jesse was impressive but Jan stumbled and was vexed with himself.

"Never mind, lad," consoled the Captain. "My Latin is so rusty, I can hardly tell an ablative absolute from an Indian war whoop." Then he asked the boys a question in Weckquasgeek. Jan brightened and answered with surprising fluency.

De Vries was pleased. "God willing, it is boys like you who will be running this country one day, Son."

Samp hutspot usually tastes better than it looks. Today, it slid effortlessly from the pot, golden crust miraculously intact, amid the "oohs" and "ahs" of the hungry. I swept the platter nonchalantly to the table as though such perfections sprang daily from my oven.

"I would have served venison, Captain, if I had known you were dining with us."

"Then I am thankful that you did not, Madame. My men prepare only game." Hot savory gravy bubbled from the hutspot as he pierced it with his knife. "You don't know how fortunate you are, Montagne. I have tapestries for my walls and Turkish carpets for my tables. Yet without a woman my home lacks a soul. This is positively delicious, Madame." We set to with a will.

After a lengthy silence broken only by an occasional "pass the bread," Jan asked the Captain if the Indians all spoke the same language.

"All the tribes near Manhattan are closely related, young man. Weckquasgeek, Canarsie, Siwanoy, Raritan, Hackensack, Tappan, they all speak almost the same tongue and are part of a large nation called Algonkian that settled along the Atlantic seaboard hundreds of years ago. Their dreaded enemies are the bloodthirsty Mohawks, newcomers from the West, who took over a valley near Fort Orange. They are part of a completely unrelated nation called Iroquois and their tongue is as foreign as Greek is to Dutch. Take the word for woman, which in Algonkian is "squaw." The Mohawk word is "ye-oh.""

"Generations of soft living in this land of plenty, left our local tribes no match for the ferocious newcomers," continued the Captain. "Bloody battles followed and the Algonkians eventually fell under the domination of the Mohawks shortly before we Europeans arrived. Today, the very glimpse of a Mohawk war canoe causes even Weckquasgeeks to abandon their villages and flee into hiding. Once a year Mohawk emissaries come down the Hudson to collect tribute from the local tribes, who pay rather than subject themselves to the murder and destruction that would follow if they refused."

I had not realized that our Wilden were accustomed to paying an annual tax to the warlike Mohawks. "That must be why there has been so little resistance to the Governor's tax," I said aloud.

De Vries nodded. "The Wilden are angry about Kieft's tax, Madame, but they are even angrier over the gun law. The Mohawks get all the guns they need from the Dutch at Fort Orange which is too far away for Kieft to have much control. Thus our local tribes are desperate for guns to keep the balance of power from tipping even further against them."

"Surely the answer lies in better control at Fort Orange," suggested Jehan sensibly, as he refilled the Captain's wineglass.

"No good, my friend. The Mohawks can always obtain arms through their contacts with New England or even New France."

"After the way the English massacred all their Indians it's a wonder they have any contacts there," said Isaack.

"The English massacred Pequots, my friend, and Pequots are Algonkians. The more Algonkians that are murdered the better, from the Mohawk point of view," said de Vries. "Furthermore, it is almost impossible to enforce the gun law here on Manhattan, let alone at Fort Orange. This morning a Raritan offered me 20 beavers for a gun worth three. I refused, but I'll wager all the tobacco on Manhattan that he finds a seller before nightfall."

"Then where does the answer lie?" asked Jehan, thoughtfully stroking his chin.

"The answer, my friend, is to treat the Wilden fairly, something our friend, Kieft, has no intention of doing. Did you hear about my pigs, Montagne?"

"The Governor told me this morning that Raritans had stolen some pigs from Staten Island."

"Raritans, my foot! It was sailors from the *Vrede*. One of my men saw the whole thing from a distance. Yesterday I reported the matter to Kieft who promptly blamed Raritans. In fact it was only by withdrawing my complaint that I dissuaded him from sending an armed expedition to punish the whole tribe. The man is sick, Montagne. That lecherous Secretary was there too and he's worse. Why should van Tienhoven be so anxious to spill Raritan blood?"

After supper the men lit up their pipes and the Captain related some of his adventures at sea for the children, who were enthralled. When the girls had gone to bed, the boys persuaded him to tell the story of his ill-fated plantation on the Delaware back in '31.

"Swannendale, we called it, lads, as sweet a piece of land as you'll find anywhere. We built a house and stockade, and had already put the first seeds in the ground when I returned to Europe for supplies, leaving 34 men behind. Your Uncle Hendrick was to manage the plantation for me. Until he should arrive I left Gilles Hoosett in charge, a good man but not a wise one as you shall see.

"Tacked to a post," he continued, "was a tin emblem of the Netherlands. One day an Indian Chief helped himself to the emblem in order to make a pipe. Gilles viewed this as a national insult which was foolish, and publicly rebuked the Chief which was even more foolish. Members of another tribe tried to compensate for the insult by murdering the Chief and presenting the Dutch with his bloody corpse. Too late, Gilles realized his error."

"A few days later all but two of the men were in the fields. Gilles and one other who was ill were indoors. Three Indians approached the house with furs for trading and persuaded Gilles to chain the dog. Once inside they had no trouble killing the two Dutchmen but there were 25 arrows through that bull mastiff's body before he finally succumbed. In the meantime other Indians went into the fields pretending to be friendly until they were close enough to murder every last man."

Oddly enough I felt little emotion over Gilles Hoosett and the slain men, having heard the story so often from Hendrick. I was more shocked by the picture of a bull mastiff like Tiger, fighting fiercely at the end of a chain, with 25 arrows through his body.

"When I returned," continued the Captain, "I found Swannendale in ruins, the fields strewn with limbs and torsos."

"But how did you know?" interrupted Jan. "If everyone was dead how did you know what happened?"

"Good question, young man. Now picture the position. There we were with the ship's cannon and plenty of guns. No Wilden to be seen but they couldn't be far off. What should we do?" He looked at the boys expectantly.

"I'd march into the woods and shoot 'em all dead," said Jan stoutly.

"Not me," said Jesse sensibly. "I'd weigh anchor and get out of there fast."

"No good, boys," said the Captain. "You would leave nothing but bitterness behind. What I did is this. I located two braves and persuaded them to come aboard and tell me the story. Using them as intermediaries I was able to arrange a peace treaty which we sealed with gifts on both sides. When we finally departed three days later, we left in friendship."

How could the Company have been so short-sighted as to turn down this man for Governor?

Continued one week later

There was another incident the next day and this one was worse. During breakfast Kumtassa arrived with a message from the Governor. The Dutch ship, *Neptune,* was in harbor and Dr. Montagne's presence at the Fort was required immediately. Mystified, Jehan swallowed down the remains of his suppawn and set off in the *Yellow Swan* with Isaack and Kumtassa.

Willem and Tobias have left us now to strike out on their own, having finished their three years. The temporary replacements require constant supervision and by late afternoon I was exhausted. Why was Jehan so long getting home? Why did the Governor required Jehan's immediate presence at the Fort and what did the *Neptune* have to do with it? I was beginning to suspect Kieft's every move. How could the Company have preferred him to a man like Captain de Vries? Jehan said it was because Kieft's grandfather had been an Amsterdam patrician. How foolish men are.

Why was Kieft so anxious to blame Raritans for de Vries's missing pigs? His idea of sending an armed expedition to punish the tribe was unthinkable. If a Weckquasgeek stole our pigs Jehan would report it to Chief Rechnewac, who would punish the offender, and either return the pigs or give us proper compensation, ending the matter.

The Raritans live across the harbor, west of Staten Island. There is no way to get there by land and the *Vrede* is too small to carry an expedition. It would require a full size ship like the *Neptune* to send . . . No! It can't be. I am imagining things. Besides, it was not Raritans who stole the pigs. It was Kieft's own men.

"Mama, Uncle Isaack and Papa are home." Little Rachel put her head in the door. She and Marie were watering my vegetable garden.

She was wrong. Isaack stumbled in alone.

"Jehan is spending the night at the Fort," he said. "My feet are killing me, Sis." He threw himself into a chair and mopped his head with his handkerchief. "Eight miles is a long walk."

"You're getting old," I snapped. "Jan and Little Deer go that distance on the run." I poured him a beer.

"Not with a gun and heavy boots, they don't." He drained the wooden can and I refilled it. "It's hot as Hades out there today."

I dried my hands and pulled up a chair. "Tell me what happened," I said.

"Kieft sent an expedition to teach the Raritans a lesson."

"Sweet Jesus! In the *Neptune?*"

He nodded. "They had a meeting. Kieft, Jehan and that sharkfaced Secretary, van Tienhoven. Jehan says the other two had already made up their minds and wouldn't listen to him. The ship had been conscripted before we arrived."

"What about Captain de Vries? Couldn't he stop them?"

"De Vries left for Fort Orange this morning and doesn't know anything about it." Isaack pulled off his boots and massaged his stockinged feet.

"How big an expedition?" I asked.

"Fifty. A few bad actors out for a lark and the rest soldiers. The whole town watched as they marched from the Fort across to the Strand. Sharkface led them himself with the Witch egging the men on and behaving even worse than usual."

The Secretary had recently married one of the three ugly Vinje girls, which meant the Witch was now his mother-in-law. They deserve each other in my opinion.

"What did Madame Vinje-Dam do?" I asked.

"She screamed at the men to bring her back a pair of Raritan testicles. Sharkface pretended not to hear but the others guffawed, and a lout named Loockermans promised to deliver the balls."

I had my mouth open to ask more but shut it in dismay.

"After they set sail," continued Isaack, "a group of us watched for a while from Weepers' Point. It's two hours to the Narrows and as long again to the Raritan so the *Neptune* won't be back till after dark. Jehan sent me home to let you know what's going on. He has to be on hand when the men return."

"What's the expedition supposed to do?" I asked.

"The *Neptune* will put the men ashore at the mouth of the Raritan. There they march inland to tribal headquarters where Sharkface demands satisfaction for the attack on the *Vrede* and the stolen pigs."

"But they didn't steal the pigs!"

He shrugged. "Maybe. Maybe not."

"Suppose the Wilden refuse to pay? What then?" I persisted.

"Kieft's orders are to cut down their corn, and take prisoners, but no bloodshed."

"How can they take prisoners without bloodshed?"

There was no possible answer to this.

That night I could not sleep with this foolish expedition racing around in my head. Furthermore it was unbearably hot. After tossing and turning for what seemed like hours I finally decided to sit out on the stoop and watch the stars. Tiger joined me. Together we listened to the shrill music of the cricket and the throaty "nee deep, nee deep" of the bull frog.

A small animal scurried through the bushes and Tiger lunged furiously in pursuit. Then he located something under the barracks. I wondered if he carried on all night like this or if he was just trying to impress me with his alertness. I whistled and he returned obediently.

"Doucement, Tiger." I scratched his head absentmindedly.

The Wilden would surely retaliate. From the mouth of the Raritan it is only a few strokes of the paddle to Staten Island and de Vries's plantation. The Captain had gone up-river. Suppose he were to return and find everything in ruins just as he did at Swannendale? Sweet Jesus! That could not happen twice to any man.

A whippoorwill began to call. The dog ignored it just as he did the crickets and the frogs. When the cat materialized like a black spook out of the darkness, he ignored her too. She rubbed herself against my ankle and Tiger's huge paw before wandering off into the night.

Above the big elm hung Orion's belt with its three bright jewels of gold. For how many thousands of years have men gazed at the stars and dreamed of a new world? Have we found that new world, only to destroy it?

Suddenly Tiger tensed, head cocked in the direction of the Creek. Then a low growl and silence. I strained my ears for any sound. Nothing but crickets and rhythmic snores from the barracks. Could it be a wild animal come to drink by the dock?

Tiger gave a short warning bark. I followed him to the gate and peered through the porthole. In the moonlight, clear fields stretched all the way to the creek except for the one stand of seven birches which I had begged Jehan not to destroy. About thirty paces from the stockade, they look in daylight like seven graceful sisters springing from a single root. By night they cast an ominous patch of black. Could some invisible enemy lie hidden there? The moon passed from behind a cloud revealing seven separate tree trunks with nothing between.

Then I heard the squeak of a rusty oarlock and the dog began to bark in earnest. The men would be out here in a minute, guns loaded. I grabbed his collar.

"Doucement, Tiger."

Slowly a boat emerged from the shadow into a stretch of silver water. It was the *Yellow Swan* with her sails furled and Jehan at the oars. I waited for the yawl to be tied before opening the gate. Then I raced after the bounding Tiger.

"Why are you not in bed, ma petite." Jehan had his arm about me as we walked up the path, Tiger in the lead.

"I couldn't sleep. Isaack said you were stopping at the Fort."

"After what Kieft has brought about this day, Rachel, I prefer never to spend another hour in his company."

We sat together on the stoop, beneath the stars, and he told me the whole story. The ship had put 70 men ashore on the Raritan, fifty soldiers plus twenty volunteers from the *Neptune*. Sharkface led them to Raritan headquarters where he demanded compensation for the attack on the *Vrede* and the stolen pigs. The Wilden denied all responsibility for the pigs. As for the attack on the *Vrede* they just laughed.

"Our men were spoiling for action, Rachel. Van Tienhoven could have controlled them but he deliberately turned his back, leaving them to cut down Raritan corn. He was barely out of earshot when the troops fell on the Raritans. Three Raritans were killed and one Dutchman, the supercargo of the *Neptune*. Loockermans managed to capture the Chief's brother. Once aboard the *Neptune* he amused himself by torturing the prisoner in the genitals with a split stick."

"Sweet Jesus!" I winced. "The man is an animal."

"Every right-thinking man in the Colony agrees with you. Kieft has overstepped himself this time and he knows it. If the Wilden do not retaliate there will be no more foolish expeditions."

And so an uneasy peace has descended upon our world. I pray there will be no more incidents.

Yours affectionately,

Rachel

The Wind Will Blow

The 15th day of October
In the Year of Our Lord 1640
At Vredendale

Dearest Margariet,

I am so happy to hear of the safe arrival of little Agnes. Under separate cover I am sending a blanket. Of course Crispin was hoping for another boy to take the place of poor Gerard. Men always hope for a boy.

There have been no more incidents since my last letter and I pray that the trouble between the races is over.

Last Monday evening Little Deer brought a mysterious message from Old Nehooma.

"The wind will blow and the leaves will get wet."

Jehan was reading *Horace* with the boys. I am always amazed that he can make Latin even halfway palatable to youngsters.

"This next paragraph, boys, is not suitable for a lady's delicate ears. We will have to do a written translation."

This was certainly my cue. "Mon vieux," I protested over the whir of the spinning wheel. "Do you really think children should read such things?"

The boys peered suspiciously at my "delicate ears," and Isaack blew his nose in an effort not to laugh.

"It's quite all right for men, my dear," answered Jehan and even Jesse seemed to throw his shoulders back.

At that moment there was a pounding at the north gate. We never have visitors after dark so Jehan took down the long gun, but it was only Little Deer delivering the brief message from his grandmother.

"The wind will blow and the leaves will get wet," repeated Isaack, after the Indian had gone. "What kind of nonsense is that?"

"It must be important," said Jan. "Everything Old Nehooma says is important."

"What does it mean?" I asked.

"My dear," said Jehan, "it means that the old woman is growing senile. Maybe there will be another windstorm tonight and she is hoping for another reward. In any case, if every leaf in the forest gets soaked we can do nothing about it. Now let us finish this paragraph, lads, and then to bed."

The boys returned to their *Horace* but my mind stayed with the cryptic message. I did not believe Old Nehooma was senile. Had the meaning been twisted in translation? Wilden never use two words where one will do. The original must have been something like "Wind blow, leaves wet." Where did that get me?

I pretended not to hear the muffled giggles coming from the Latin table. Those Roman poets can be quite outrageous. What earthly good is *Horace* to boys growing up in this New World?

It is six miles from here to Shorakapkok. Why had Little Deer done the round trip in the dark, instead of waiting until morning? Perhaps tomorrow would be too late.

Isaack went out to stoke the fire in the tobacco house and I followed him as far as the stoop. I never go into the tobacco house if I can help it because it has no windows. The very possibility of being shut up in a place without windows still frightens me.

Warm raindrops began to fall with a gentle whisper on every leaf and blade of grass. The night air smelled sweetly peaceful. I pictured Old Nehooma, far away in her wigwam, squatting by her hearth, staring into the flames with those yellow eyes. What was she trying to tell us?

It was three years since Little Deer's grandmother had located our missing yawl and I still had never set eyes on the old woman, although I continued to hear about her from Jan and Moose Foot. Jehan thought she was a shaman or witch-doctor. Once when he had a toothache, she sent a paste of herbs that cured the pain.

In Weckquasgeek society the older matrons are much respected and play an important role in politics, being the ones to choose the Sachem. According to Moose Foot, Nehooma was largely responsible for appointing Rechnewac. But that could have been years ago. Was she still so influential?

Grandmother was already an old woman when Hendrick Hudson explored this river the year I was born. Moose Foot said she often told the tale of her two nephews who were taken hostage aboard the *Half Moon* and given gifts of red coats. When the ship reached the highlands the braves escaped through a porthole, shouting taunts at their captors as they swam for shore, still wearing the red coats.

"The wind will blow and the leaves will get wet." In the far corner of my mind something clicked, and for a fraction of a second the solution flitted to the surface then disappeared again. It was as though I were trying to recall someone's name and all I could remember was one letter. Maybe if I stopped concentrating and tried to make my mind a blank it would return. Nothing came except the certainty that I knew the answer and it was in some way connected with Isaack. Later in bed I continued to wrestle with the problem but fell asleep no wiser than before.

In the middle of the night I was awakened by the sound of wind howling through the stockade. I had forgotten all about Old Nehooma, but one side of me was too warm where it pressed against Jehan. Our mattress sags badly and no matter where we start the night, we both end up together in the middle. Rain beat noisily upon the windowpanes as I inched my way up the slope to a cooler spot. I took a deep breath of night air and was just about to pull the covers over my head again, when it all came back in a rush.

"The wind will blow and the leaves will get wet."

Wide awake now, I pushed the blanket away and strained my ears but I could hear nothing over the roar of the storm. Jehan was snoring unconsciously beside me as I tried to think. Whatever the danger, the time was now. Isaack was the key. In my mind's eye I followed my brother out into the windowless tobacco house where the odor was stifling and hickory smoke always made my eyes run. Hanging from every rafter were rows and rows of tobacco leaves in various shades of brown and gold.

Tobacco leaves! That was the answer! Suppose the wind blew the roof off the tobacco house. Rain would ruin our whole crop. But that was impossible. Jehan just had a brand new tobacco house specially built by a fat English carpenter named Morris.

"No one understands tobacco better than the English, my dear."

Still it would do no harm to check. Carefully I crawled out of bed and pulled on my shoes in the dark. Then I heard it! A muffled crash from the direction of the barracks.

"Jehan, wake up!" I shouted, pulling off the blanket. "Hurry! There's been an accident!" I threw a cloak over my shoulders and ran out into the rain.

The tobacco house stands next to the barracks. At least it used to stand next to the barracks. Now it lay on its side, posts every which way, while a driving rain pounded the jumble that was once neatly strung tobacco.

I was banging on the barracks door when Jehan arrived with a lantern, fuming that he was going to sue that fat English carpenter for every pound in his fat English pocket.

Someone produced knives and the men cut strings of tobacco from the tangled hodge-podge and carried them into the cook-house. A few entire poles were rescued and balanced on the kitchen rafters with their leaves hanging intact, but most of the tobacco had to be separated and restrung which was my job. Each load to arrive was progressively muddier.

"It's no use, my dear. Come to bed," said Jehan, dropping the last soggy clump onto the table. "The whole crop is worthless."

I would not give up. We had hoped to get 500 guilders for this tobacco. Long after the men finished, I remained in that cook house tending the fire, separating leaves, cleaning, restringing and brooding.

Mold was the enemy. If the leaves did not dry properly, mold would be fatal. Jehan had already borrowed 200 guilders against this crop from the wealthy English merchant, Isaac Allerton, the same man who had lent us money before, always with Vredendale as collateral. Somehow we were never able to reduce the mortgage. Instead it kept growing.

Why is it that New Amsterdam tobacco never fetches the high prices of Virginia tobacco? Jehan says the flavor will improve as the soil gets used to the crop. Maybe he is wrong. People assume that we are wealthy because Jehan is the Governor's right-hand man, but 35 guilders a month does not go far. True, there are occasional gifts which Jehan is always reluctant to accept.

"Government officials should not be allowed to accept gifts, my dear."

"Nonsense, mon vieux. Politicians have always accepted gifts. How can anyone expect to live on a Councillor's salary. Besides, you never let the gifts sway your judgment."

We are also in debt as a result of buying on credit from the Company store, but at least the Company is not going to foreclose on our land. Dear God, it would be a sin to lose this beautiful bowery, but if Allerton chose he could take it away from us tomorrow. My eyes began to weep from the smoke. They say tobacco cannot be wet washed but I must get the mud off. Suppose we only get 10 percent of the crop's value. Ten percent is better than nothing.

I was still there when Isaack came out to milk the cows. He wanted to repair the tobacco house but Jehan refused.

"The wreckage must not be touched until it has been inspected by an independent authority."

It was weeks before that independent authority arrived, but Mister Allerton appeared bright and early Thursday morning to view the damaged tobacco.

Allerton was one of the English Puritans who lived in Leyden before coming to this country. For a while he was Assistant Governor of the Plymouth Colony under Bradford. Then he had a falling out with the New England authorities and became the first Mayflower passenger to settle on Manhattan. He had a son, Sacky, who was the same age as Jan.

Jehan was not here when Allerton arrived so it was I who took him out to view the tobacco. He shook his head sadly at the sight.

"You will be lucky to get 30 guilders for this, Madame Montagne." His teeth clicked when he talked.

"I expect 100 at least, Mister Allerton," I lied graciously. "But please do not worry about your investment. Dr. Montagne will return the advance next week together with the interest on the mortgage."

"I am glad to hear that, Madame," click, click, "because my partner, Govert Loockermans, is anxious to foreclose."

My heart sank at the mention of that brute Loockermans who used a split stick to torture the Raritan in the genitals. How could a gentleman like Allerton be in partnership with such a fiend?

"Govert has a good head for money," he answered my unspoken question.

I was determined to be pleasant. After the inspection we returned to the house where I served him peach cobbler and some of Jehan's best Madeira. We talked about Leyden.

"It was our home for nine years, Madame, and the Dutch were exceedingly hospitable. Did you know that on the very day we departed your father saved my little girl from drowning?"

"Good gracious!" I exclaimed. "Was your daughter named Remember?"

When he answered in the affirmative I fetched Rembrandt's sketch from the attic where it was rolled up waiting for the frame to be mended. Allerton stared in silence at this scene from half a life-time ago. Sunshine seemed to dance on the Rapenburg as my father held aloft the dripping child. I wondered if . . .

He read my mind. "She was one of the fortunate ones, Madame. Remember is a grown woman today with a family of her own." He told me of the first terrible winter in New England when so many of the Mayflower passengers died, including Remember's mother.

"Then I married Fear Brewster, the mother of my son, Sacky. He was barely weaned when she too died."

Fear and Remember! What tragic, poetic names these Puritans give their children.

"My husband studied English in Leyden under a William Brewster," I said.

Allerton nodded. "My late wife's father," click, "now Governor Bradford's right-hand man," click, click. He turned back to the picture. "Tell me, Madame, who made this excellent likeness of the great Jesse de Forest?"

I told him about Rembrandt, the miller's son, who was at the University with Jehan.

"Now I know why your good husband never mentioned this sketch. He was afraid I would try to buy it. Rembrandt is a famous artist today, Madame. This would fetch a good price in Europe."

"We would never part with a picture of my father, Mister Allerton."

"Not even for 50 guilders, Madame?"

Fifty guilders! This was astonishing. I had no idea that a sketch could be worth so much. But I did know that when a man like Allerton offered 50 guilders, he was willing to pay more.

"If we were interested in disposing of the picture, Mister Allerton, we would send it to my uncle in Leyden to sell."

"Well put, Madame," click. "But for me there is a sentimental value here as well. I will give you 75 guilders for the sketch."

His protestations of sentiment did not impress me but 75 guilders did. How much was it really worth? From long experience I knew the best way to deal with any man was to let him think he was vastly more intelligent than a mere woman.

"My husband cares nothing for money, Mister Allerton." This was true enough. In fact it was why we were in danger of losing Vredendale in the first place. Give Jehan his philosophy, medicine, science, and he was content. To me the land was what counted. I would sell a thousand pictures to save Vredendale, but I must not let my face show it.

"Dr. Montagne is an outstanding Councillor, Madame," click, click. "But in matters of business I prefer to deal with someone who understands the value of money."

And so we fenced back and forth, I pretending lack of interest, he gradually raising the bait. I was treading a delicate path but I knew what I wanted.

Finally, praise be to God, I sold the sketch, together with the damaged tobacco in exchange for the 200 guilder advance and, more important, the word of a gentleman that neither Allerton nor his partner would ever foreclose on Vredendale!

Jehan would be upset, but if I said nothing it could be months before he noticed the picture was missing. Six weeks had already passed since I asked him to mend the frame.

I was sure my father would approve. As I handed over the sketch I took one last look at the expression of triumph on his face. It was as though the great Jesse de Forest knew that he had single-handedly saved Vredendale for his children and their descendants forever.

Give little Agnes a big hug from me.

Yours affectionately,

Rachel

PART TWO

—

Jan's Story

Introduction

To my children and grandchildren:

In 1654 I visited Leyden where I stayed with my mother's cousin, Crispin de Forest, and his wife Margariet, who was Mother's best friend. Margariet told me that she had saved all Mother's letters and promised to have them sent to me before she died. It was many years before I received the letters. Every time I read them I have the feeling that they contain the unfinished story of the courageous woman who was the heart of our family. Now in my 35th year, I shall attempt to finish the story.

Cousin Margariet told me that there were actually three additional letters that were lost. She remembered that one of them dealt with the hanging of the Giant. Mother was very fond of the huge black slave so I will start my story with this.

The Day They
Hanged the Giant

When I was little I used to think the Giant was the biggest man in the world, with skin as black and shiny as fresh tar. Simon Congo, Jan Premero, Jan t'Fort Orange, Big Manuel and the Giant were the slaves who helped build Vredendale back in '37. Tobias used to say, "them slaves is stupid as sheep and lazy as bears in winter," but Vredendale never would have been built without them.

Most of the slaves spoke a little Dutch. Not the Giant. However he was stronger than the other four put together.

I remember asking Tobias, "If you can't understand their language, how do you know that they are so stupid?"

"Boy," he said. "Them slaves don't have no language. Just heathen gibberish."

Tobias claimed that the Giant had nothing upstairs. Mama said he was simple. Jesse and I thought he was wonderful.

Every noon, when the long trestle table was being set up for the midday meal, the Giant would lift me and Jesse each up on to a broad black shoulder. "Giddap! Giddap!" we yelled and away he galloped, round and round the stockade, us shrieking with terror and delight.

Finally he would plunk us down near the food and make himself comfortable under the great elm with a mountain of bread, meat and cheese and a big wooden can of beer. Jesse and I squatted beside him, too fascinated to eat.

It always happened the same way. First he would throw his head back and drain the can, which I quickly refilled as the vittles vanished down the mighty gullet. After the second beer came the moment we were waiting for. A puzzled look would cross his brow. Then his insides apparently assured him that all was well and he started to smile. When the Giant smiled it was like the sun bursting out from behind a cloud. He had about a hundred big white teeth, stretching from one ear to the other. It made me feel so good just to watch. Jesse and I smiled back at him as hard as we could until our jaws ached. I thought the whole world must love the Giant.

I remember the first time Little Deer saw the big slave. We had been running and the Indian reached the stockade before me, just as the Giant came out carrying a huge portion of damaged roof on his head. Little Deer had never even seen a black man before and the sight of this 300-pound Goliath with what looked like a whole house on his head, must have been a shock. When I arrived they were both standing stock-still staring at each other. Then the Giant saw me and began to smile.

Wilden rarely show any emotion. It is as though they are continually on guard not to change expression for fear of ridicule. The Giant's magnificent smile broke through that guard. For one moment in time, the three of us, from three different worlds, beamed at each other with the pure joy of being alive.

When I was eleven the slave, Jan Premero, was killed in a brawl. Nine of the Company slaves were involved, including the Giant, but nobody would admit to wielding the knife stuck through the dead man's ribs. Of course Governor Kieft had no intention of executing nine valuable slaves. After weeks of wrangling, the court still could not identify the culprit, so it was ruled that the prisoners draw lots and allow divine providence to determine who should hang. The Giant got the short straw.

At Vredendale we were all furious. The Giant was the gentlest of men and never even looked angry. Mother said he was an innocent child of God and Kieft was a miserable tyrant who just wanted to display his authority with a public hanging. Papa said she had better watch her tongue but he did his best to persuade the Governor to modify the sentence.

After church Sunday, Abram du Trieux and I sneaked off to visit the prisoner. It was easy enough to get into the Fort but the guard would not let us in the jail. So we went round back and peeked through the iron bars on the window.

There on the stone floor sat the magnificent Giant, head slumped against his chest. It was January but he wore only rags of duffel and his feet were bare. By the door was a bowl of water and a stinking bucket of urine.

"Psst! Mijnheer Giant, it's me, Jan Montagne," I whispered.

He looked up. I never noticed before how big the whites of his eyes were. Now there were pink rims around the white and his beautiful, black, shiny skin was all dusty. He got to his feet stiffly and hobbled to the window. We had brought four olykoeks which he swallowed whole without a word. I hoped he would smile but he only stared at us with the whites of his eyes.

"Hey! You young'uns! Get away from that window," shouted the guard. We ran.

Back at the du Trieux house, Sarah, Abram's redheaded sister, scoffed at our efforts. "When did sugar ever fill a man's stomach?" She sliced bread and meat and wrapped it in a napkin. "Here, give him this."

"Can't," said Abram. "Guard'll skin us alive."

"Scaredy-cat!" she shouted. Then with the napkin and a blanket under her apron she marched into the Fort right past the guard who kept his eye on us and ignored her.

"If you ask me Jan t'Fort Orange did it," she told me on the way home.

"Did what?" I said.

"Murdered Premero."

"How do you know?"

"Because."

"Because what?"

"Just because."

Sarah could be stubborn as fresh milk in a new churn, but she was no fool. That night I discussed it with Papa.

"It doesn't matter any more who committed the murder, Son. All nine suspects signed a confession and agreed to abide by the luck of the draw. The only thing that can save the Giant now is a pardon from the Governor."

But the pardon never came. The night before the hanging, Papa took the yawl into town. He told us that, as Councillor, he was required to be there, but that under no circumstance were any other members of his family to be present.

"And that means you, young man," he said, pointing at me. Then he turned to Mother. "Don't worry, my dear. The Governor is bound to issue a last minute reprieve."

The next morning Jesse pulled my blanket off as usual at dawn. He was always a poor sleeper, coughing and fretting all night long. I was just the opposite and never even heard the cock crow unless someone woke me. I got furious with Jesse sometimes, but it never did any good. By the time I had thrown my boots at him and recovered my blanket I was up anyway.

Since the day Willem and Tobias left us, one of my chores was the milking. "They're gonna hang the Giant today," I told Rainbow, leaning a sleepy forehead against her broad flank. The stupid cow was not interested, but Tiger thumped his tail sympathetically. "They should hang Kieft instead," I muttered. The dog agreed and rested one huge paw on my knee.

Then Little Deer arrived. He was my best friend. Nothing was said but I knew he was on his way to the Fort to watch the hanging. And I knew I was going with him.

We took the milk inside and Mother insisted that Little Deer join us for breakfast. She always said he had better manners than most Christians.

My sisters were delighted and chattered to the Indian merrily, not at all perturbed by the fact that he never uttered a word in response. Little Rachel kept refilling his bowl of suppawn until he put his hand firmly over the top.

After breakfast Uncle Isaack lit up his pipe and Little Deer and I set off. I had already whispered the plan to Jesse who promised to keep my absence from being noticed for as long as possible. First I tied up Tiger. When he was a pup, he had an argument with a big red hen and he never forgot it. He was used to our chickens by now, but he still quarreled occasionally with the two big reds. I could not possibly trust him to behave on the Heerenstraat with all the poultry in town running loose.

It is eight miles along the Weckquasgeek trail from Vredendale to New Amsterdam. With no wind we ran easily, Little Deer a few paces in the lead. We had barely done a mile when Tiger bounded past, a length of frayed rope dangling from his collar. Eagerly he took his place ahead of Little Deer. I was annoyed but we ran on in formation as if nothing had happened.

The halfway point is Turtle Bay on the East River, where Claes the wheelwright had a cabin. He used to live at Otterspoor, on the creek near us, but after his wife died he built this cabin and left his two grown sons to manage Otterspoor. I asked the old man if he would keep Tiger for a few hours. He agreed but warned us that we were foolish to watch the hanging. He had seen one when he was a boy in Switzerland.

"If I never see another it'll be too soon," he said gruffly.

So we left Tiger locked in the wheelwright's cabin and set off again. Another few miles and the forest thins out and becomes farmland. At the cattle barrier we slowed to a walk. This was long before the Wall was built. It was not even a barrier at all in those days, just a row of branches to keep animals from straying. I prayed that Papa would not see us.

Opposite Marie's Tavern Little Deer pointed back toward the cattle barrier. I turned just in time to see Tiger leaping over the branches. Furious, I grabbed his rope. There was no way to get rid of him now. As inconspicuously as possible the three of us proceeded down the Heerenstraat toward the crowd at the Fort.

I have to admit that Tiger was on his best behavior. Almost immediately a large, snow-white goose crossed our path, herding a flock of goslings. She hissed and scolded the dog. He pretended not to hear and stood patiently on three legs while the plucky brood marched beneath raised forepaw. With her family safely past, the goose spat out one last parting insult. Then we hurried on through mud and potholes, pigs and poultry, until we merged with the crowd.

The area around the Fort was roped off to keep spectators back. This was the first hanging ever held in New Netherland, and every man, woman and child was there to see it. We worked our way almost to the Fort wall where we climbed onto the roof of a shed, hauling Tiger up with us. By lying flat on our stomachs, and sticking our noses over the edge, we had the best view of all.

Directly ahead was a tall crane. A ladder leaned against the wall with a soldier on either side, and about forty paces to the left stood a raised platform with chairs for officials. Extending in a large semicircle from the corner of the Fort around behind the platform, all the way to our shed, was a colorful, noisy wall of friendly burghers and curious Indians. And just six feet below our noses was a huge coil of rope guarded by two soldiers.

When Little Deer realized what the rope was for, he wanted to slip down and slash it with his knife. "Weckquasgeek move like shadow," he insisted, which was almost true. He might even get away with it, in spite of the spectators, if it were not for those two soldiers. As it was, he would be thrown in jail and the Giant would still be hanged by the neck until dead.

I wished I could think of some way to save the huge friendly slave. Famous generals do not give up just because they are outnumbered. That is when they fight their greatest battles. The enemy today had fifty soldiers with guns. What did I have? One large bull mastiff and one young Weckquasgeek with knife.

At that moment came a roll of drums and a sudden hush as the gate opened and out marched a parade of black-coated officials. The Governor was in the lead with Papa just behind. I shrank down but they were not even facing this direction. Then came Sharkface and the Dominie and a few others that I did not recognize. With great dignity they took their places on the platform and I went back to my problem.

Once I asked Papa what we could possibly learn by studying so many famous generals, all dead.

"Strategy, my boy. Strategy!" he exclaimed.

Well, now was the time to profit from all that strategy. When famous generals were outnumbered they always had a secret weapon up their sleeve. Odysseus had his wooden horse and Hannibal his elephants. Drake used ships of fire, and the Prince of Orange unleashed the whole North Sea. What could I do with a dog, an Indian and a sharp knife?

Then it came to me. If I succeeded, Papa would whale the tar out of me. And if I failed I could spend the rest of my life in jail, but I had to try.

One glance at Little Deer was enough as I handed him Tiger's rope. Sometimes he seems to read my mind. He knew I was going to give him his chance to "move like a shadow." First I crawled backwards down the roof and dropped to the ground. Once in the road I grabbed the biggest, fiercest, red hen I could find, and stuffed her head under my arm. Climbing onto a shed with a struggling hen is no easy task and Little Deer had to practically choke Tiger to keep him quiet. He twisted the collar while I jabbed the dog in the muzzle with the furious hen. Then I flung the bird as far as I could toward the platform of dignitaries. At the same time Little Deer released Tiger who flew through the air after the bird like an animal demented. And I leapt after them both, shouting at the top of my lungs and grabbing for the rope.

The commotion was unbelievable. Every eye in New Amsterdam was upon us. At first there was sort of a general gasp of astonishment, then people began to laugh. It must have been some sight. The bird was flapping and squawking with rage, Tiger was yelping insanely and I was apparently trying to separate the two, all the while yelling like a madman.

I normally speak to Tiger in French. Today I shouted in Dutch so more people could understand. "Let go, you miserable mongrel, you stom, hard-nekkig beest!"

I did not dare look behind me at the pile of rope but I did glance ahead at the officials. The only person not amused was Papa. He was angry, so angry that he stumbled off the step. In high good humor Kieft leaned down to help him up.

"Behave yourself, domkop," I yelled at the dog, dragging him away as the hen made a frantic escape under the platform. Tiger had chicken feathers all over his muzzle and looked as guilty as I looked ridiculous. Soldiers and citizens alike were doubled up with laughter at the sight. Even the Indians smiled.

With the rope now firmly in hand, I escaped into the crowd, avoiding familiar faces, and soon doubled back to the shed.

"Doucement, Tiger!" I whispered in his ear. "You did a good piece of work just now. Doucement, boy."

We scrambled up to find Little Deer gone. I crept forward and peered over the edge. Everything looked exactly the same. The pile of rope was the same. The two soldiers were the same. Now the laughter was dying down as the audience waited for the real show to begin.

Then Little Deer crawled up beside me and I could read success in his eyes. During the confusion he had slipped down from the roof and glided like a shadow behind the two soldiers who naturally moved a step forward in the direction of the commotion. Three times he plunged his knife into that coil of rope. He said the guards were so close he could have reached out and touched them, yet they noticed nothing. Neither did the audience.

Instead of returning immediately, Little Deer circled around the edge of the crowd ready to make good his escape, but nobody was suspicious. A dog had chased a chicken. That was all.

Would three slashes have any effect on the rope? I was not sure. But I was elated with the knowledge that we had put on a good performance even though it would get me a sound whipping tonight.

Another roll of the drums brought a hush as the gate opened and a dozen soldiers led out the prisoner. He towered above them. Next came Fort Orange, the appointed hangman. It was just like Kieft to get a slave to do his dirty work. I glanced at Papa who was pleading with the Governor. Kieft shook his head. There would be no last minute reprieve. Then Dominie Bogardus rose to say a prayer.

"Almighty God, guide us thy servants in this world of trials and sorrow . . ." His voice droned on but everyone was watching the Giant. Hands tied behind, he raised his face to Heaven and began to sway back and forth, chanting in a sing-song tongue. Did Africans pray to African Gods? Women began to sob. I felt tears in my eyes.

The official prayer ended and the Dominie took his seat. At a signal, soldiers brought the coil which proved to be two separate ropes. Had Little Deer slashed both or only one? The prisoner was fitted with two halters, each attached by its own rope to the crane. Then he was blindfolded and forced to climb to the top of the ladder.

The hangman began to operate the crane, slowly taking up the slack in the rope. The crowd held its breath as that colossus of a man strained to keep his balance against the pull on his neck. With hands tied he had no chance. Women screamed and men groaned as the Giant plunged into space.

For a minute the body swung violently in mid-air. Then both ropes broke and it plummeted to the ground. There in the mud it twisted and twitched. Nobody breathed. God in Heaven! Now the Giant was struggling to his knees. Slowly he began to crawl away from his tormentors.

In a flash Kieft sprang to his feet and ordered new ropes prepared so justice could be done. But the crowd had had enough. Men and women cried out for mercy. The roar grew louder and more menacing. I know I stood up on the roof with tears streaming down my face, shouting that God would punish Kieft with the fires of eternal hell. Little Deer pulled me down but it did not matter. Nobody could hear with everyone yelling at once.

Then Papa stood up and raised his hands for silence. When the noise subsided he announced that the Honorable Director General Willem Kieft, in his wisdom and mercy, had decided to pardon the prisoner.

Pandemonium broke loose. People began stomping and clapping and shouting and hugging each other. The officials, in their sober black, quickly disappeared into the Fort before the crowd rushed on to the field.

We jumped down into the mass of well-wishers around the crane, as Fort Orange helped the dazed Giant to his feet and led him away. Everyone was talking at once. I heard someone say it had to be a miracle because the ropes were tested only yesterday to lift a seven-hundred-pound cow. All agreed that it was a great show, well worth standing around all morning to wait for. There was humor, drama, suspense and, best of all, a happy ending.

Now it was time to celebrate, and every tavern in town was soon overflowing. Little Deer and I had no money so we started back up the Heerenstraat, Tiger tugging us along happily. We had barely reached the cemetery, when a soldier hailed us to say we were wanted at the Strand. He escorted us to the East River where Papa sat in the *Yellow Swan,* grimly waiting to cast off. Without a word he indicated that we were to come aboard.

We sailed in complete silence, Papa at the tiller, Tiger standing in the prow, nose high in the wind like a ship's figurehead. I knew I was in for trouble, first for disobedience, then for disgracing the family in public. Should I tell the whole truth? I looked at Little Deer, who sat calmly with arms folded as though invisible rope-slashing were all part of his daily routine.

When we were well out of earshot Papa seemed to relax. "Why did you shout at Tiger in Dutch, Son?"

"Because more people . . ." I stopped. Papa must have seen everything. The officials had been directly facing that coil of rope. Did the others see? Had Papa stumbled and pretended to be angry to distract their attention?

He smiled. "When you shouted in Dutch I knew something was wrong," he said. "I looked past you and there was Little Deer by those ropes. The least I could do was divert the Governor, which was not difficult. When he saw that I was angry because it was my son out there, he was delighted. A man who has no son of his own pretends to admire your son's virtues, but is really happiest to witness his misbehavior."

All my life Papa had represented authority. He was my teacher, the one who corrected me, the one who meted out the punishment. Today he was my partner. I was on top of the world.

"That red hen was my secret weapon, Papa," I said.

Happy Squirrel

People used to say that my father was not decisive enough. The trouble was he could always see both sides of a question and spent hours weighing the pros and cons. Jesse was the same. Not me. I jumped right in without waiting to analyze, which is why I was so poor at chess and Papa and Jesse were so good. But real life is not like chess. The world cannot always wait for all that analysis and most of my fast decisions turned out well in the end. Only a few were terrible. The worst was where I did nothing but gawk until it was too late.

It was the spring of '41, the day of the du Trieux party announcing Sarah's betrothal to Uncle Isaack. I never could understand what he saw in that bossy redhead. She was only fifteen, smart enough, but homely as a stack of toadstools. Not a bit like her little sister, Sutje, with the golden curls.

Madame du Trieux borrowed all sorts of things for the party and Mother sent me into town with a bagful of silver spoons. I had only gone a few miles, spoons jangling from my belt, when I heard a cry.

Stopped dead in my tracks, I wondered what kind of animal could make such a human sound. Due west of me there was a clearing and I decided to investigate. After stuffing the spoons into a hollow tree, I left the trail and made my way cautiously through the undergrowth. Far ahead something was moving noisily. When I reached the edge of the clearing I peered out at an amazing sight.

There was Sharkface van Tienhoven, the Company Secretary, prancing through the wild flowers, naked as a jaybird except for his belt and clootsap. As I watched he pulled that off and his pik stood up straight like a bull after a cow.

Then I saw the Indian girl, half-hidden in the long grass. I did not know she was tied. She was not screaming. I thought she was just lying there while he hopped around doing his crazy dance. He jumped on top of her like an animal, grunting and groaning, white buttocks pumping up and down above the daisies.

What did I do? Nothing. I just stood there staring in guilty fascination. Finally the man rolled over, stretched and got to his feet. He replaced the cloot-sap and headed in my direction with a wide shark-like smile of satisfaction on his face.

I stood stock-still without breathing, eyes half-closed so as not to catch the light. There was nothing but leaves between us. He was so close I could almost see his tonsils. Then he apparently had a change of heart and returned to pull up one of the four stakes to which the girl was tied. Instantly she slashed out at him with the stake in her one free hand.

"Bloody she-wolf!" he yelled.

For a moment I thought he was going to kill her. I shouted and ran toward them. Without turning around Sharkface dashed into the forest.

Not until then did I recognize Wehtah, Little Deer's sister. There were red welts on her face and arms. How did he ever catch her in the first place? My God! Why didn't I shout sooner? How could I have just stood there, pop-eyed like a bullfrog?

With my knife I cut the ropes around her wrists and ankles. Any Dutch girl would be screaming her head off. It was not fear in Wehtah's eyes, but fury. She said she was going to kill the Swannekin pig. All she wanted from me was his name.

I lied and said I had not seen his face. How could I admit that I had watched the whole thing? Besides, Wehtah had recently married a young Weckquasgeek brave. Taking revenge on van Tienhoven could only lead to tragedy.

There was a little brook flowing through the clearing and Wehtah knelt down to slap cold water on herself. I took off my shirt and offered it to her but she refused and ran off toward Shorakapkok. I retrieved the spoons and headed for town.

I never told a soul what I had seen that day. Little Deer came by later to thank me for helping his sister. He was my best friend but I could not tell him the truth either.

For a while I brooded, angry and ashamed of myself. But such is the nature of youth that my guilt was soon washed away by the excitement of day-to-day living. When Wehtah's son, Happy Squirrel, was born that autumn, there was no connection in my mind with previous events. As a matter of fact I was there at the Weckquasgeek planting-ground the day Happy Squirrel came into this world.

Mid-morning the field workers always stopped for refreshments and a gnarled old warrior told stories and jokes while they rested. Little Deer and I naturally timed our visits to coincide with the food. I never could understand the jokes but I disposed of large quantities of hickory drink and apple yockey.

This particular day we arrived early. Rows of girls were picking the last of the summer corn, singing as they broke the stalks to the beat of the song. Tattita, Little Deer's mother, was the overseer. I used to think it was because she had the loudest voice.

At one point Wehtah left her place in the far row and squatted down behind a bush. No one paid any attention. Then she was back in line, working and singing with the others, only now there was a tiny papoose fastened to a board on her back. No fuss and no help from anyone. When refreshments arrived the girls crowded around the new baby but I was more interested in the yockey. It was another month before I had a good look at Happy Squirrel.

I never have understood why Christians cannot have babies like Wilden. Even in winter the squaw just wipes the new papoose off with snow, wraps it on a board and that's that. Christians always have help and still they suffer and die like flies. When we lived on the Heerenstraat there was a woman who screamed for two days trying to give birth. She had four people with ropes helping to pull. They buried her in the cemetery right across from us. You can always tell when someone dies in childbirth because they wrap the body in a white shroud instead of black.

In April, when my little brother, Will, was born, Tryntje, the midwife, arrived wearing a purple apron and carrying her black bag full of torture instruments. She was supposed to be the best midwife this side of the Atlantic, but it was still scary. Mother did not scream much, but when she did, the noise raced up and down your spine like the zing of a broken sawblade whipping back at naked fingers.

Jesse got the shakes. He sat at the table with the leather volume of *Horace*, only he was not reading. He was clutching the book to his chest. I would have been outdoors but it was pouring rain so I spent the time cleaning my gun. Sarah was there minding the girls, who were both in tears. She insisted that Little Rachel knit.

"Three more inches on that blanket and fifteen more screams and the baby will be here," she lied. "Keep winding that wool, Marie. Do you want a baby sister or a baby brother?"

Another piercing scream from the bedroom. *Horace* fell to the floor. So did one knitting-needle and the ball of wool.

"Only fourteen to go," shouted Sarah. "But drop any more needles and it goes back up to twenty!"

"Poppycock!" I said, picking up *Horace.*

"YOU are a troublemaker, young man," she yelled. "Go chop some wood!"

Of course I was the only one not making any trouble. "I can't," I said sensibly. "It's pouring."

"Out!" she yelled. "Out this minute!" She picked up the poker and started toward me.

I looked at Papa who was pacing up and down, face twisted as though he were the one in pain. I went out and slammed the door behind me, but I was not going to chop any wood. I went over to the barracks and watched the men play cards. When I came back an hour later, everyone was smiling and I had a new baby brother.

"A great strong knaap he is, too," announced Tryntje, pointing to a tiny bundle in the oak cradle. "Eight pound if he's an ounce!"

He looked kind of puny to me but I knew better than to say so.

Anyhow, in the autumn, after Wehtah's papoose was born, I got to puzzling over the differences in birthing between Swannekins and Wilden. Then I happened to meet Tryntje trotting along the Heerenstraat and I figured if anyone knew the answer it must be the Company midwife.

"What a half-wit!" she snorted. "It says right in the Bible. That was Eve's punishment for tasting the apple. Indian squaws don't suffer because they ain't descended from Adam and Eve."

"I thought everyone was descended from Adam and Eve."

"Hah! A lot you know, boy. Just look at the snake if you want more proof."

"What snake?"

"The snake that tempted Eve, of course. Every Christian woman's born hating snakes. Same as we're all born with original sin. Well, Indian squaws ain't afraid of snakes. So they ain't descended from Adam and Eve."

It was hard to argue with Tryntje, particularly now that Dominie Bogardus was her son-in-law. That night I discussed it with Papa who was not so positive.

"Most people here believe as Tryntje does, Son. They say it is the only explanation for the difference in birthing."

"What do you think, Papa? I mean about Adam and Eve?"

"I am not sure, Son. Sometimes I wonder if the chair can be the culprit. The Wilden have always squatted comfortably on the ground, while for hundreds of years we have been sitting on chairs. Maybe this has caused a change in our pelvic muscles. Today most adult Europeans can't squat for long without discomfort and most European women can't give birth without misery."

Mother did not hold with the chair theory. "Stop filling the boy's head with that nonsense, mon vieux!"

Matter of fact, I didn't think too much of the chair theory either.

Then came the day I got my first good look at Happy Squirrel. I had gone up to Shorakapkok to watch Moose Foot work on his new dugout. He had selected a tree the week before. Yesterday it came down, not with an axe either. Oh, Moose Foot had an axe, but he wanted Little Deer to learn the same way he himself had been taught. He felled the tree by gradually burning a wedge deeper and deeper into the trunk.

Today he started to hollow out the insides with hot coals. For a while we helped scrape away charred bits but mostly it was a matter of waiting patiently while the coals did the work.

Moose Foot never took his eye off the embers, but Little Deer and I wandered around the village. First we watched Wehtah's husband build a new wigwam. Strange that it takes a week to build a dugout and only hours to build a house. You put up two rows of saplings and tie the tops together. Then you cover the whole thing with bark leaving a hole for the smoke and you're done.

Most Christians never go inside a wigwam because they can't stand the stink. I hardly notice it myself. Little Deer's wigwam was a hundred feet long with a door at either end and lots of hearths, one for each family. Mostly it was empty except in bad weather when you have to be careful not to step between anyone and his fire, which is considered rude.

Next to the new wigwam was a pen with a bear-cub to be fatted. The wolf-like dogs jumped around us yapping and growling as we fed scraps to the cub.

Shorakapkok is built in the shelter of a steep cliff where Little Deer and I often explored for caves. Tattita, Little Deer's mother, was squatting in the sunshine at the foot of the cliff, pounding corn. For a pestle she used a heavy block of wood tied to a live sapling to produce the spring power. In her hands it flew up and down as fast as Mother's spinning-wheel.

Leaning against the rock-face were three papooses strapped to their boards. Weckquasgeek children spend almost their entire infancy on these boards. Some say that's why their backs are so straight. There are no napkins to change and the poop just slides right out the bottom. Mother used to say it was disgusting, but it seemed sensible to me and the babies never cried.

As we approached, I noticed that the tiniest of the three was light-skinned and I wondered why a Christian child should be fastened to a board. Then Wehtah and two other girls ran over to shoulder the infants, and the truth struck me. Happy Squirrel was Sharkface's bastard!

My mind flew back to that dreadful day at the clearing. What a domkop I was. Again the feeling of guilt rushed over me, and time stood still. Dried ears of corn, strung like ropes between wigwams, swayed in the breeze. Brown-skinned children ran naked, back and forth through the mud. And Tattita's pestle flew up and down, up and down, as I tried desperately to pull my wits together.

Then Wehtah deliberately danced around so that Happy Squirrel was facing us. Little Deer tried to make him smile but I just stared. Happy Squirrel stared back with wide solemn eyes.

That night I decided that God knew what he was doing when he gave Happy Squirrel to Wehtah. Indians love children. They never beat or even spank a child. The only punishment is mild ridicule. Maybe that is why they grow up with no fear of physical pain. Weckquasgeeks have a wonderful childhood. Better to run wild and free at Shorakapkok than to be brought up a van Tienhoven.

The Crazy One

In the matter of education I had the best of two worlds, Christian and Weckquasgeek. The former came mostly from Papa but the really important things in life, like how to survive in this world, came from Moose Foot. His lessons were more adventures than work and they usually dealt with hunting. Good hunting is every Weckquasgeek's goal in life. Where a Christian will say "Good day" an Indian will say "Good hunting." Even Heaven is known as the "Happy Hunting Ground."

One day in particular stands out after all these years. Little Deer and I were learning how to trim arrows with hawk feathers.

"Wouldn't turkey feathers be easier to come by?" I asked, naively.

"Mattaka!" scoffed Moose Foot. "Turkey kill only worm under foot. Hawk fly swift, strike hard."

He said that eagle feathers were even better. An eagle's eyesight is so keen and his wings so powerful that he can dive from the blue sky in seconds to snatch his prey. The whole northern half of Manhattan is ruled by Old White Face, who lives with his mate high on the rocky cliffs west of Vredendale. Moose Foot challenged us to bring him two tail feathers from Old White Face without harming the bird.

I would have been at a loss, but Little Deer as usual knew exactly how to proceed. First we had to "borrow" one of Mother's chickens. This was back in the days when Willem and Tobias still worked at Vredendale.

"Blikskaters! What you after, boy?" Tobias emerged from the barn just as I prepared to nap the bird. Sweat made the birthmark on his face shine bright purple.

"We're off to catch an eagle, Tobias," I said, helping myself to two empty corn sacks. I knew better than to put a finger on the chicken while he was watching.

Fooling Tobias was the best part of any adventure. We filled the sacks with leaves and ran through the stockade shouting the war cry, "Kowamo! kowamo!" He never took his eye off Little Deer, who made a decoy circle of the barracks while I easily bagged the chicken.

"Stop that childish racket!" Mother appeared on the stoop as we ran through the gate, increasing the volume of "Kowamos" to drown out the furious squawks from my sack.

The next step was to select an open expanse of beach near the mouth of the creek. Here we buried Little Deer in the sand, except for his face and hands which were protected by a mask and gloves of deer hide. We worked quickly, all the while scanning the sky to be sure that Old White Face did not see what we were up to.

I tied the chicken to two stakes so that it hopped around like a wounded bird on top of Little Deer's buried stomach. Then I hid in the bushes with blanket and knife. Patience is not my strong point. After an hour of sun in the eyes and nettles under the collar, the only thing that kept me from giving up was the thought of the sand flies crawling over Little Deer's face.

We expected to see the eagle over the treetops to the west. Instead he appeared as a tiny speck straight above us, almost lost in the sunshine.

"Yootalee!" Little Deer signaled that he saw him.

Now it was important that neither of us move a muscle. It is hard to believe that Old White Face could see the chicken from that height, but he began to circle. Then he dived.

In this entire world there is nothing faster or more awesome than a diving eagle. One minute he was a spot in the heavens a mile above us. The next minute he was upon us, giant eight-foot wings outspread to brake, wicked talons poised to kill. I was so terrified I could not move. Surely the chicken was dead of heart failure.

At the last second Little Deer grabbed the eagle's claws with his gauntlets of deer hide and the fierce noise of the struggle jolted me into action. Once I got the blanket over his head, putting the vicious beak out of commission, it was an easy matter to cut off two tail feathers. When we released Old White Face there was hatred in his eye as he rose majestically above us.

To this day I still have that eagle feather, and I would not trade it for all the tobacco on Manhattan.

The only thing I remember teaching Little Deer was how to ride. It was against the law even to allow an Indian near a horse so we had to be very careful. I would ride Middernacht to an open field a couple of miles from Vredendale, where Little Deer would join me. Wilden take to horses like beavers to a creek and in no time he could handle the animal as well as I. Sometimes I think Middernacht was fonder of Little Deer than of anyone else.

Horses were no special treat for me, so I used to let him ride off by himself while I fished from a rock overhanging the East River. People say that Indians are born thieves. Middernacht was a very valuable animal and Little Deer could easily have made off with him. The thought never occurred to me. Little Deer was my brother. Sometimes I think he was more my brother than Jesse was.

The problem is that Christians and Wilden do not have the same view of personal property. A Dutchman plants an apple tree in his yard. He thinks the land, the tree and the apples belong to him. To an Indian, the land, the tree and the apples belong equally to all. Papa said that this difference would eventually cause bad blood between the races.

One hot day in August of '41, I was fishing from that rock, musing on this difference, when a Weckquasgeek appeared carrying a pile of beavers. He wore wampum belts, with a long ugly knife hanging down one side. I recognized the Crazy One who was always talking to himself. There was something especially odd in his manner that day, but I never had any reason to be afraid of a Weckquasgeek. In fact I trusted Wilden more than Christians.

He returned my greeting pleasantly enough and asked if I wanted to trade. When I said I had no money and nothing to trade, he offered me wampum for the shirt on my back. The shirt was old and worth much less than the wampum so I agreed. He put down his beavers and climbed up beside me. While I unbuttoned my collar, he started to unfasten the wampum. The shirt was over my head when I suddenly realized that something was wrong.

Moose Foot taught us that every sound had a meaning, and silence was often the loudest of all. Without thinking I had been listening to the faint click of wampum. Now everything was quiet. Why should the Crazy One handle the beads so stealthily? Then, with the shirt still over my eyes, I knew that he had the knife in his hand, not the wampum. For some unknown reason this Weckquasgeek was about to cut my throat.

There was no time even to cry out. Instinctively I threw myself backwards off the rock into the East River. Underwater I managed to disentangle the shirt. Lungs bursting, I swam as far as I could out into the current. When I finally came up for air I was twenty paces from shore. The Crazy One was still on the rock looking more bewildered than vicious, but in his right hand he held the knife, not the wampum.

Moose Foot claimed that you could hear death. Had I been listening to my own? Fortunately I was a strong swimmer and set out steadily for the opposite shore.

When I next looked back I was halfway to Long Island and the Crazy One had disappeared. Was he hiding, waiting for me to return? Why should he want to kill me?

My feet were dragging me down and with some difficulty I removed the shoes and tied them to my belt. Breathing more easily now, I floated on my back and tried to think. Seagulls, temporarily disturbed by the splashing, returned to circle above me, crying out that I had spoiled their fishing. Then in response to some invisible warning they rose and quickly disappeared to the east.

I stared at the sky. Yes, there he was, a tiny speck, so high, yet capable of plunging in seconds to snatch a gull's prey in mid-flight or to grab a newborn lamb from its mother. Old White Face swooped lower to take a better look at this odd fish floating in his territory. I splashed and he soared away.

I wished Little Deer would return. Was I mistaken about the Crazy One? No. Wilden are always shrewd traders. I should have been suspicious when he offered me more than the shirt was worth.

Mother once told me that the Crazy One was a liar. Old Claes said that the Indian's uncle was murdered by Christians back in Governor Minuit's day. When he talked to himself he thought he was carrying on a conversation with the uncle. But he never hurt anyone.

Then, to my great relief, Little Deer appeared riding Middernacht. I shouted and swam gratefully toward them. I even found my shirt snagged on an underwater branch and spread it out on the rock to dry while I related my story.

To my surprise Little Deer did not think that I was krankzinnig. He said that ever since the full moon the Crazy One had been threatening to kill a Swannekin to avenge the death of his uncle, fifteen years before.

"Why me?" I asked, but he had no answer.

We were not far from Turtle Bay and the cottage of Old Claes, who was always generous with cool drinks for thirsty boys. Besides, he knew the Crazy One and should be warned. So Little Deer hopped up behind me on Middernacht and in no time we were tying the horse to the wheelwright's gatepost.

As we approached the cottage, I noticed the door was slightly ajar. I was about to call out a greeting when Little Deer grabbed my arm and pulled me off the path. We crouched in the bushes, listening. I could hear nothing above the chatter of crows in the garden. Warily we made our way around to the rear of the cabin and peered through the one tiny window.

The room was a shambles, ransacked from top to bottom. There was no sign of life, but two half-filled tankards on the table indicated that Old Claes had had a guest. We circled the cottage and entered the open door.

The wheelwright's body lay in a corner on an open chest full of duffle cloth. He had apparently been stooping over the chest when he was struck from behind with his own axe. Blood was everywhere. Only a ribbon of flesh remained to hold head and neck together.

Lost at the Nepperhan

New Amsterdam was in an uproar over the senseless killing of Old Claes. Kieft sent the *Vrede* up the Hudson to Weckquasgeek headquarters to arrest the murderer, but the Crazy One's Sachem refused to hand him over. He said he wished twenty Swannekins had been killed.

Kieft turned purple with apoplexy when he heard, and declared it was time to call out the troops. Sharkface agreed. Papa said it must be better for one guilty Indian to go free than to plunge the whole country into war, but they would not listen. That night Papa was so upset he could not touch his food.

"Starving yourself will solve nothing, mon vieux," said Mother calmly. She was always calm when Papa was agitated. It was only when he was the calm one that she was apt to get herself worked up over things.

"Pour your father some wine, Jan."

"Someone has to stop those two, Rachel." Papa pushed his plate away and began to drum his fingers on the table. I could see the pulse in his throat pounding.

Mother nodded. "Philippe dropped by today, on his way to inspect Isaack's place. He says if Kieft sends an expedition against Weckquasgeeks, we'll all be murdered in our beds."

"Per Deos immortales," whispered Papa.

I poured the wine. "Everyone is talking about the expedition, Papa," I said.

"Vinje-Dam tittle-tattle," he muttered.

Madame Vinje-Dam was the town's leading gossip-monger. The fact that Sharkface was now married to one of her three ugly daughters only made the gossip more official.

"Forget about Sharkface," said Mother. "He has a warped mind and you're wasting your breath trying to change it. Work on the Governor. You are so much wiser than he, mon vieux. Surely you can make him see the light."

"Why not create a diversion, Papa," I said, "like the great generals do?"

He looked at me seriously for a minute, then smiled and took a sip of wine.

The next day Papa created a diversion. Instead of trying to change Kieft's mind, he temporarily went along with the plan to attack the Wilden. However he advised the Governor to cover himself in case anything went wrong. He proposed that the colonists be permitted to elect a board of twelve men to discuss the problem and offer an opinion on the best way to bring the murderer to justice.

"Then if the Company disapproves," he told the Governor, "you can say you were simply carrying out the wishes of the colonists as stated by their chosen representatives."

Kieft swallowed the bait. Even Sharkface did not object too much because he was sure that his Vinje in-laws would be well represented on any board.

"Now all I have to do," Papa told me, "is to make sure that Captain de Vries gets elected."

The election was held at the Fort. It was the first time the people had ever voted for anything or anyone and they took it very seriously. Sharkface was pleased with the result because his father-in-law and his brother-in-law were elected. Papa was pleased because de Vries was not only elected but chosen President.

To Kieft's annoyance the twelve voted to exhaust all peaceful means before resorting to force. So another delegation was dispatched to Weckquasgeek headquarters while the Governor fumed.

In the meantime the Raritans were still brooding over last year's charges of pig-stealing and the armed expedition against them. In September they took their revenge against de Vries's bowery on Staten Island. De Vries himself was absent, but four field hands were killed and the house and tobacco sheds burned to the ground.

"For the second time, the Wilden have destroyed their best friend," said Papa.

Kieft did not consult the board this time. Instead he offered rival tribes a reward of ten fathoms of wampum for every dead Raritan. The lure worked. Haverstraws and Hackensacks brought in Raritan hands hanging from sticks like so many dead fish. The pressure was too great and the Raritans sued for peace. A treaty was quickly concluded leaving Kieft free to concentrate on his pet hatred, the Weckquasgeeks.

Did I really understand the danger? I knew Papa was worried, but he was always worried. With the natural optimism of a twelve-year-old I was sure everything would work out for the best, just as it always had.

Little Deer was two years older than I and much wiser. We were together constantly and he never seemed concerned about any danger. Our private hideout was Slangberg. On a clear day you could see the whole world from the top of Slangberg. Even after ten hours in the fields I would climb the 400-foot rock-face just to sit there for a few minutes and count the ships in the river or watch the autumn fires racing across Long Island. It was here that Little Deer and I had one of our rare political discussions.

We were watching Uncle Isaack build his new house below. The carpenters had finished for the day but he was still sitting on a crossbeam, hammering away, with no one but his gangly bride to hoist planks. With her petticoats tucked up, the homely redhead was as good a worker as any man. It was interesting to watch the hammer swing, then count the seconds before the thud reached us. Papa said you could measure the speed of sound this way if you had a clock that was accurate enough.

"Kieft no good Sachem," Little Deer interrupted my thoughts. He said the Weckquasgeeks wanted to bring back Governor van Twiller.

When I explained that the people had no say in the matter of Governors, he announced "Nehooma kill Kieft!"

The idea of a blind old grandmother murdering the Governor was ridiculous, but I knew better than to say so.

"She never even met Kieft," I told him.

He replied that she had seen him in the flames and was going to put a spell on him.

"Good," I said.

Then he pointed to the sunset behind us. To this day I have never seen anything like it. The sky above the mighty Mahicanittuck was fiery red. Little Deer said it meant blood. I asked if we would still be friends if war broke out. For answer he took his knife, always razor-sharp, and cut a small slash on both our wrists. Then he carefully mixed the blood together and said that we were now brothers and only death could come between us.

The next day Captain de Vries came for dinner. It was the first time I had seen him since the Raritans destroyed his bowery on Staten Island and he was understandably bitter, particularly at Kieft.

"The man is a half-witted flapdrol," he said. "To send an armed expedition against Raritans, over a few pigs they didn't even steal, must rank as one of the greatest blunders in modern history!"

After plenty of wine and roast turkey he mellowed somewhat and began to talk about the new bowery he was building almost directly across the Hudson from us. Then he made me repeat for him every detail of my encounter with the Crazy One. He said the country needed boys like me to be the leaders of tomorrow.

"But if you don't exercise a little more caution, lad, you won't be around tomorrow."

He asked if I had ever been to Weckquasgeek headquarters on foot. I said I had gone once with Little Deer. It was nine miles north of the Wading-Place and I felt sure that I could find it again.

"That might be a piece of information worth forgetting, lad," he said.

I nodded wisely, but had no idea what he meant.

Saint Nicholas Day came and went. By now several delegations had been sent up the Hudson but the Crazy One was still at large. Kieft claimed that the Wilden were losing all respect for the Dutch. Still the board advised patience.

Then in January, the twelve made a few suggestions on other matters and Kieft lost his temper. He said they had instructions to give advice only in relation to the murder of Old Claes. The next day a notice of dismissal was posted, specifically forbidding any further meetings.

With the board out of the way, Kieft and Sharkface secretly made plans for a night attack against Weckquasgeek headquarters. Ensign Van Dyck was to lead eighty men, including ten Company slaves, who would be promised their freedom for bearing arms in the service of the Colony. Willem, now 22, was to be second-in-command and Tobias would be the guide. Willem and Tobias were familiar with the northern end of Manhattan having worked three years at Vredendale. Neither knew a thing about the mainland north of Manhattan which was called the Land of the Tall Birch.

I heard nothing of the plan. Perhaps Sharkface was feeding false information to the gossip-mongers, because even the rumors about an expedition had died. So I was surprised, but not suspicious, when Tobias walked into the barn one chilly morning in March of '42. Tiger welcomed him cheerfully though he could not have seen the man in two years.

Tobias had never been unkind to me and it seemed like old times as he stood there, with his half-purple face, stroking Middernacht and chatting while I milked Rainbow. I was flattered when he said he wished he knew his way around this country as well as I did. He told me that only once had he crossed over the Wading-Place onto the mainland. An Indian guide had taken him to Nipnichen, the small camp on the high hill just north of Manhattan.

"I figures the main camp must be 'bout like Nipnichen," he said.

"Much bigger," I told him, but I don't think he believed me.

"I hear the trail's plain enough till you ford the Nepperhan," he continued. "What comes after the Nepperhan, boy?"

It was at that moment that I began to distrust Tobias. He hated all Wilden. Why should he suddenly want to visit Weckquasgeek headquarters? I remembered de Vries's warning about "a piece of information worth forgetting."

Rather than tell Tobias that I did not know the way, I decided to give him false directions. Five miles north of the Wading Place the trail did cross a Creek called the Nepperhan. On the other side of this the trail disappeared. When I traveled with Little Deer we went downstream about fifty paces, stepping on stones to avoid leaving marks. Opposite a triangular-shaped boulder the trail reappeared leading northwest to Weckquasgeek headquarters.

"Go upsteam a hundred paces, Tobias," I said confidently. "Then due north till you rejoin the trail." Anyone following those directions would be hopelessly lost in no time.

Tobias refused to stay for breakfast. When I reported our conversation to Papa he said I had done well and told me what little he knew about the proposed march. Then he left for town to speak with de Vries and the Dominie. He hoped that the three of them together would be able to persuade Kieft to abandon the expedition.

I helped myself to another bowl of suppawn. Tobias was bound to get himself lost at the Nepperhan so I was not overly concerned about any danger. What did make me angry was the fact that the Giant was not one of those slated to earn his freedom by "bearing arms in the service of the Colony." All the Company slaves had been taught to use a gun except the Giant, who had not been right in the head since the day he was hanged. But if anyone deserved his freedom it was the huge friendly slave.

"They should let the Giant carry a gun," I said to Mother who was already scraping the dishes.

She looked at me as though I were a half-wit.

"Maybe an unloaded gun," I added.

She handed me the pail of breakfast slops, at the same time raising her eyebrows to let me know that I had been demoted to quarter-wit.

"Go feed the pigs," she said.

For weeks now we had four soldiers billeted at Vredendale. Mother complained that they did nothing but eat, sleep and play cards, and she would be much happier without them. Papa said they gave him peace of mind when he was at the Fort.

Papa was at the Fort the night Ensign Van Dyck led his eighty men single file up the Weckquasgeek trail. Tiger's growling woke Jesse, who woke me. From the loft window we peered out into the night but there was nothing to see. All we heard was the eerie rustling sound of men passing in the night. Then silence.

It took the expedition five hours to reach the Nepperhan where they milled around while Tobias searched in vain for the continuation of the trail. Finally Van Dyck got impatient and ordered everyone back to the Fort. In the morning the Weckquasgeeks found the tell-tale marks at the creek and realized all too clearly what had happened. They sued for peace but refused to come to the Fort.

Jonas Bronck offered his home as a suitable site for a treaty and the Governor sent Sharkface to represent him. He claimed that the Secretary had a better command of the language but the truth was that Kieft was a milksop and terrified of stray arrows.

Little Deer and I watched from the roof of Bronck's woodshed as government officials and Weckquasgeek Sachems sat on the ground in a circle discussing terms. The only condition imposed by the Dutch was the surrender of the Crazy One. The Sachems pointed out that the murderer had long since fled, however they agreed to find him and either hand him over or administer justice themselves. Then peace pipes were smoked and finally Bronck's vrouw served refreshments to all. Little Deer and I finished off six olykoeks apiece.

That night Papa was stiff as a board from sitting on the ground, but elated with the result. He said it was a miracle that peace had been restored to Manhattan without one drop of blood being shed.

"When do the slaves get their freedom?" I asked.

He frowned as though he did not know what I was talking about.

"The slaves who marched with Van Dyck," I repeated. "Kieft promised them their freedom for bearing arms in the service of the Colony. They will get it, won't they?"

Papa considered for a long time. "Son," he said carefully, "I am afraid that will require a second miracle."

Old Nehooma

By now the village of Shorakapkok was almost deserted. Little Deer's family remained only because of Old Nehooma. She said she had lived a hundred winters on the island of Manhattan and she intended to die here. If she really planned to kill the Governor, it seemed to me that she had better get started.

The next time I saw Kieft was in May of '42, when Sarie, the Dominie's oldest step-daughter, was married to Dr. Hans Kierstede. The wedding was held at the parsonage on the Strand, and the whole family sailed down in the *Yellow Swan*. This was shortly after the new City Tavern was completed. With three full stories and lofts above, it was now the tallest building on Manhattan.

"It's the biggest in the world!" chirped five-year-old Marie, clutching her pink and white petticoats.

"Silly goose!" said Little Rachel. Then she grabbed her own petticoats as a gust of wind turned both girls into huge pink and white cabbages. I started to laugh but Papa said only those who behaved themselves would get to look out of the top window of the new tavern.

The wedding was held in the parsonage garden, which slopes down to the East River. After the ceremony, drinks were served at the house, while the young people played games by the water's edge. The groom had a little pointed beard and felt he was too dignified for sports, but Sarie tucked up her petticoats and joined in the fun. She and I won the three-legged race. The cheering was so loud that Madame Vinje-Dam hobbled down, glass in hand, and called Sarie a trollop, forgetting that she was the bride.

"Horse piss!" she cackled. "You should be up at the house, drinking like a lady." When we ignored her, she staggered off sloshing gin over the tulips.

After the third round of drinks, Kieft produced a subscription list for a new church, and merry tipplers outdid each other with the size of their pledges. In an effort to avoid contributing, Uncle Isaack joined the spectators watching the games. He did not escape.

"De Forest," cried the Governor, gleefully tracking him down. "You're the last. Look at this list. De Vries has promised 100 guilders! What shall I put you in for?"

Then he saw me. "Come here, young man. Aren't you Montagne's son? How's that dog of yours doing?" He chuckled and massaged his elbow. "Still chasing chickens, eh?"

"You have a lot of Indian friends," he continued in a more serious tone. "I'm told that a Weckquasgeek witch-doctor is trying to cast a spell on me. Of course I don't believe in such things, but you can't be too careful where savages are concerned. Do you know anything about this, young man?"

"No, sir," I said promptly, at the same time inspecting him with great interest to see if Old Nehooma's efforts were having effect. Sadly I could see no sign of any devastating disease.

When the feasting and drinking were over, we sailed home beneath a full moon. Mother was delighted about the church, especially as it was to be named after Saint Nicholas.

"Children, your famous grandfather once touched the finger of Saint Nicholas at the great church in Avesnes." Then she reminded us that it was the lantern of Saint Nicholas at Ilfracombe that guided the *Rensselaerswyck* to safety.

"It is fate," continued Mother. "One day the Weckquasgeek Trail will be a wagon road and we will christen it Saint Nicholas Avenue!"

"The Governor made a good move this evening," said Papa, "but in the sober light of dawn, there are going to be a lot of sorry guests trying to reduce their pledges, especially when they realize that the church is to be built inside the Fort."

"But that's not fair, mon vieux. If the people put up the money, the church must be in the town."

"I agree, my dear, but remember that the church represents progress, and progress always involves injustice somewhere."

"The Governor spoke to me, Papa," I said. "He thinks a Weckquasgeek witch-doctor is trying to kill him."

Papa nodded and muttered something under his breath about "alienation mentale." Was Kieft losing his mind, or was Old Nehooma's spell really taking effect?

In October of '42, twins were born at Otterspoor, grandsons of Old Claes, the murdered wheelwright. Because their grandfather was a town hero, the Governor agreed to be one of four Godfathers, along with Sharkface, Dominie Bogardus, and Jan Dam, who was married to the Witch. Mother was one of the Godmothers and the whole party, even Jesse and I, were invited to the celebration at the new City Tavern.

We were at the dock, just ready to set out for town, when Little Deer appeared from the stand of birches. He said that Old Nehooma wanted to see me.

"Not today," declared Papa hurriedly. "Jan will visit your grandmother tomorrow."

"Tomorrow Nehooma dead," announced Little Deer.

This ended all argument as far as I was concerned. The others left for the christening but I changed my clothes and set off with Little Deer for Shorakapkok.

I could not really be sad about Nehooma. She was 100 years old, certainly a sensible age to die. In fact everything Nehooma did was sensible.

As we ran through the forest the bright colors reminded me of the mischievous spirits that supposedly splash red and orange paint on the leaves after harvest. Little Deer and I had run this trail together a hundred times. I used to think we would go on running it forever. Today, for the first time, I realized that nothing lasts forever.

"How do you know Nehooma's gonna die?" I called as we passed Slangberg.

"Nehooma say."

"What about Kieft? What about the spell?"

"Him dead soon."

"How's she gonna kill him?"

"Drown."

"Holy Jehoshaphat!" I said.

We found the old woman, wrapped in a blanket, squatting by her fire outside the long house. There was a small circle of elders some distance away, and individual Indians took turns sitting with her. Then Tattita ushered us close to the fire and we were alone with Nehooma. All I could see were two yellow eyes flashing inside the blanket.

We squatted in silence for some minutes. Finally Little Deer cleared his throat and said politely that he would miss Nehooma when she was gone. She snorted and began to speak in a hoarse, fierce whisper. She said that she had lived a hundred winters. Her spirit and even her voice were already on their way to the Happy Hunting Grounds. Only this whisper was left. She was like a dried brown leaf of autumn. It was the shape of a green leaf, but it weighed nothing and would soon crumble away to dust.

At that moment a gust of dead leaves rose into the air, swirled about the fire, then vanished with the wind. I looked quickly at the blanket, half expecting it to be empty.

"Tomorrow," she said. "Tomorrow, Nehooma."

Then the old woman pointed one thin, bony finger accusingly at me and began to speak of Happy Squirrel. The wave of guilt swept over me again. I was sure that she knew everything.

Nehooma told us that Wehtah's husband would soon be killed by Mohawks, and when that happened she wanted me to act as uncle to Happy Squirrel. Nothing was mentioned about his being half Swannekin, but this fair-skinned infant was going to need someone to turn to in the Christian world. I might not be as important as the influential Godfathers of the new-born twins, but it was the same idea. Nehooma chose me because I was the only Swannekin she trusted, and I would not let her down. I told her solemnly that I would help Happy Squirrel, even if it meant laying down my own life for him.

Satisfied, Nehooma said she hoped I would always dwell in the sunshine under a blue sky.

The next day Moose Foot reported that Old Nehooma was dead. I was sure she had just disappeared like the leaves and was surprised to discover that the Weckquasgeeks were preparing to bury her body, with much cere-mony, in a grave lined with soft evergreen boughs.

To this day, when autumn leaves swirl about a fire, I can still see the yel-low eyes of Old Nehooma flashing in the flames.

The Snowman

In November Uncle Isaack and Sarah had their first child, a son named Jesse after Grandfather. The midwife said he was a puny pup and not long for this world.

"He is not getting enough air into his lungs," was Papa's verdict. "When he turns blue, take him outdoors and let him swallow the wind."

Mama sent me over every morning to inquire, and the tiny thing held its own for a week. One day I arrived to find Sarah racing around the yard, red hair flying, with the infant in her arms. We went inside together and I helped myself to an apple while she tried to nurse him.

"He was white as death," she said, after catching her breath. "Now his face is all pink again."

He still looked pretty sickly to me but I waited patiently while he made a feeble effort to suck and fell asleep. The sight of his little blue-knit stockings gave me an idea.

"Weckquasgeeks tie leather thongs to a newborn's feet," I told Sarah.

"Humph," she said. "What for?"

"So he won't be lured away from earth by wandering spirits. Thongs fool the spirits into thinking he's tied."

"Hog-wash!" she snorted.

"Maybe, Sarah, but Christian babies die like flies around here. Look at Andries Hudde and Gertrude. Two babies in two years and both dead in a week."

"Domkop!" she snapped. "Don't you dare tell me to tie thongs to this child! That's heathen superstition and you are krankzinnig!"

I could not see that thongs on the feet were any worse than wind down the throat, but I did not push the point.

"Another thing," I said, sensibly, "Weckquasgeeks wrap a sick child in a man's coat to hide it from jealous spirits. Do you have any dead friends who might be jealous?"

She started to hogwash this one too, then changed her mind. "Hand me that red hunting shirt of Isaack's. It can't do any harm. But thongs on a baby's feet? Never if I live to be a hundred!"

The next day Sarah met me at the door empty-handed. She looked even worse than usual.

"He's dead," she said. The square jaw twitched and her eyes were red. "Isaack's gone to fetch the Dominie."

She showed me the cradle where the tiny body was still wrapped in the red hunting shirt with little blue stockings sticking out beneath. Tied to each stocking was a narrow thong of leather. So she had tried to fool the spirits after all.

Papa said it was a blessing because the infant had no chance to make it through the winter. He was buried together with one of the twins from Otterspoor.

In February it snowed for three days without stopping. When the sun finally reappeared, Papa left for town and I made a life-size snowman for Little Rachel and Marie, complete with charcoal eyes and nose of carrot.

In my mind, that snowman represents the end of carefree childhood. I can still see Tiger leaping about us, bounding awkwardly over high drifts as bright red mittens clapped with girlish glee. Even the snowman smiled, his pipe at a jaunty angle and an old black hat of Papa's down over one eye.

That night, Mohawk warriors swooped down the Hudson to the main camp of the Weckquasgeeks, murdering hundreds in their sleep. Survivors fled in desperation to the protection of the Dutch. A handful reached Vredendale, half frozen, having traveled 15 miles barefoot through deep snow.

We had four soldiers billeted here, and the sergeant in charge at first refused to open the gate until Mother pointed out that half a dozen unarmed women and children were scarcely a threat to brave men like himself. We ushered the pathetic group into the cook-house. There was an elderly couple, a young squaw with a papoose, two naked little boys, and a girl about my age, bright eyes peeking out from behind a tangled mass of black hair. I recognized Sunflower, a cousin of Little Deer.

Jesse and I brought blankets and dry clothes while Mama got a fire started and hung the soup kettle. We worked on the children first, soaking each frozen limb in a bucket of cool water until it thawed. They did not howl or whimper like European infants. Even the papoose had an expression of stoic suffering on his wrinkled countenance.

By the time the cookhouse warmed up, Jesse had to leave because the odor was too much for him. Mother and I finished the job with great success if I do say so myself. Everything was saved except for three toes on one of the old man's feet which eventually went black.

The Weckquasgeeks were too numb to tell us much that night, but in the morning I had a long talk with Sunflower, who had somehow managed to get the tangles out of her face into two neat braids down the back. She told me that she had been asleep near Wehtah and Happy Squirrel when the Man-eaters struck. In the flames she saw Tattita being dragged off by the hair of her head, struggling with her captors and at the same time screaming at the girls to run. In the confusion Sunflower raced through the burning camp, stepping over bodies as she fled, and losing contact with Wehtah.

Crossing the icy Nepperhan she overtook the young squaw with the papoose who was alternately dragging and carrying the two naked little boys. Sunflower picked up one boy and they struggled on through the drifts together.

At the Wading Place, Wilden were frantically searching for canoes to take them south to the Fort. Here the elderly couple joined Sunflower, who led her group down the Weckquasgeek trail to Vredendale. When I asked about Little Deer and Moose Foot, she said they had not been at camp but were off with a party of warriors.

After learning all I could from the Wilden, I set out for New Amsterdam to find Papa and to search for Wehtah and Happy Squirrel. At the last minute I stuffed a baby sweater and a pair of little red stockings into my pocket.

The trail was slow going. My boots sank in the deep snow and I marveled how the Wilden could have survived last night in bare feet. As yet the enormity of the disaster had not sunk in. Old Nehooma had predicted that Wehtah's husband would be killed by Mohawks, but she had said nothing about other members of the family so I assumed they were safe. Sunflower said that Tattita had been captured, not killed. Surely Papa could arrange to have her ransomed through his contacts at Fort Orange.

I found Papa in conference with the Governor and other officials. He emerged briefly, looking very weary.

"There are Weckquasgeek fugitives all over town, Son. Search for your friends, then report back here in an hour."

In the background Kieft was shouting, "It's time to wipe the mouths of these savages, men!" I wondered what that meant.

At the old church on the Strand, the Dominie's wife was distributing food to the Wilden, while Dr. Kierstede, her son-in-law, attended to injuries. There was no sign of Little Deer's family, but an old squaw told me that she had come down the East River last night in a canoe with Wehtah.

Everywhere I went villagers were caring for the homeless Wilden. Those who did not have any sleeping in their barns, contributed food and clothing to those who did. Indians had more than once saved the Colony from starvation in the early days and most settlers were happy to repay the debt.

I found Wehtah at the du Trieux home. Happy Squirrel, dressed in European baby clothes, was sitting on Sutje's lap, staring solemnly at her golden curls. With a shock I realized how easily he could pass for a Christian.

Wehtah refused point blank to accompany me to Vredendale. She said they would be returning to the Land of the Tall Birch as soon as the danger was over. I gave her the sweater and little red stockings, and made my way back to the Fort.

This time Papa looked really ill. He was in his room with Captain de Vries and paid no attention to my report at all. However the Captain was interested.

"Mohawks attacked the Tappans too, Jan. My bowery across the Hudson is so full of fugitives that I am not the master in my own home."

"Why doesn't Kieft send troops up-river to punish the bloody murderers?" I cried.

"Son, that is one thing the Governor cannot do. In the first place, the Mohawks are the most powerful tribe in the New World. In the second place, the Company has issued strict orders against interfering in Indian politics."

"What about Tattita," I persisted, "Can she be ransomed?"

He shook his head. "There are a lot of problems to be settled before we can even think about that. First I'm going to take you both to the Wooden Horse for something to eat."

Papa started to object but the Captain overruled him. "You have not had a bite all day, my friend, and this lad needs belly-timber for the journey home."

Only a stone's throw from the Fort, the Wooden Horse was crowded with soldiers drinking and gambling. The landlord gave us a table in a private alcove, and produced a delicious pigeon pie with red wine to wash it down.

I felt quite important in such company and was just beginning to enjoy myself when I thought to ask what Kieft had meant by "Wipe the mouths of the Wilden." Papa hesitated and as usual it was de Vries who answered.

"Kieft claims that God has delivered the Weckquasgeeks into our hands, Jan. He wants to eliminate them."

"Eliminate them?"

"He wants to slaughter helpless women and children who have fled to us for protection. What's more, Secretary van Tienhoven agrees with him."

I could not believe my ears.

"You shouldn't have told the boy," said Papa.

"He's no longer a boy, my friend. Furthermore, we're going to need his help getting the Wilden out of here."

"But the people are doing everything they can to help the Indians!" I protested.

"It's not the people that count, Son. The Governor has eighty soldiers ready to shoot on command." Papa drained his glass and the pulse in his throat was pounding away. "I shall hand in my resignation in the morning," he said.

"Good God! What a gloom-monger you are, Jehan," replied de Vries. "The one thing you must not do is resign. Kieft will only appoint one of the Vinje in-laws as Councillor and then where will we be? At least this way you have a chance to reason with the man, and to counteract the poison that van Tienhoven pours into his other ear."

"Why not create a diversion, Papa," I said, "like the great generals do?"

Both men smiled and immediately started making suggestions.

"I could speak to the Dominie," began Papa.

"Good idea, my friend. He can threaten to excommunicate the Governor and I will poll the defunct board of twelve. Kieft will scarcely fly in the face of elected officials even if they have been dismissed."

By the time the pigeon pie had disappeared, it was agreed that the situation would be under control by tomorrow and it was unnecessary to warn the Wilden. Nevertheless on my way home I spoke to Wehtah again and advised her to get her friends out of New Amsterdam.

"The sooner the better," I said.

It was dusk when I reached Jan Dam's farm which is just north of town and stretches almost the whole width of Manhattan. As I passed the house the old Witch poked her head out and beckoned to me. Inside I found Dam drinking in his undershirt. He had to be 20 years younger than his dried-up vrouw.

"I hear you are a fair hunter, Montagne," he said. "There are three guilders in it for you if you bring me a deer by Monday."

Three guilders is a lot of money and I agreed promptly.

"Not one stuiver if you're late," hissed the Witch, puffing on her pipe. "We are giving a Shrove-tide dinner on Tuesday, young man."

Dam explained that the Indian who regularly supplied them with game, had disappeared in the recent confusion.

"They're all stinking thieves, anyway," screeched the Witch as I let myself out, "and the families who are feeding the varmints are krankzinnig!"

When I reached home, our Weckquasgeek guests had left Vredendale and set up camp on the Creek, a half mile east of us. The next day I was relieved to learn that all the Wilden had left New Amsterdam. Apparently the Mohawk threat was not over, however, and most took shelter near Pavonia, across the Hudson from the Fort. Some set up camp on the East River just north of town, and Wehtah's group joined those already on our Creek. I went over immediately with provisions and extra blankets and was overjoyed to find Little Deer. For some reason he looked much taller than I remembered.

Monday I shot a handsome buck for the Witch. I tied the carcass to Middernacht and led the horse down the Weckquasgeek Trail to the Dam farm where I collected my three guilders. Little did I imagine the villainy that was to take place at that Shrove-tide celebration.

On Ash Wednesday, Mother baked a huge batch of olykoeks for the refugees and I helped her carry the baskets along the frozen creek. When we arrived, some thirty Indians were gathered about half a dozen camp-fires, contentedly smoking their knickaknick. Remains of a deer carcass hung from the spit. Moose Foot escorted Mother from one group to another as she distributed the sugar-coated olykoeks with the fascinating hole in the middle. For Sunflower and others she recognized, there was a special smile and greeting. When she saw Little Deer she was so pleased she put the basket down and gave him a hug, much to his embarrassment and everyone else's delight.

She talked baby talk to Happy Squirrel who was perched on Wehtah's lap, little red stockings peeking out from under a blanket of beaver. He was sucking on a bone which he reluctantly agreed to exchange for an olykoek. Mother pretended to gnaw on the bone which finally produced a brief smile in those big, round eyes. When we departed he gazed after us solemnly again, bone in one hand, half eaten olykoek in the other.

"That child is a Christian!" announced Mother as soon as we were out of earshot. "He must be baptized!"

What could I say? How could I possibly tell her the truth?

After a suitable pause she tried another tack. "Sunflower never took her eyes off you today, Jan. It's one thing to be friendly with Little Deer, but you must never get involved with any Weckquasgeek girl."

"Lots of settlers have Canarsie wives, Mama," I teased.

She was not amused. "No Montagne will ever marry an Indian, Jan!"

"Don't worry," I said. But I did not tell her that I intended to marry Sutje du Trieux.

My devotion to golden-haired Sutje began six years earlier when we stayed at the du Trieux home and Sarah used to be left in charge of us youngsters. The first time I crossed her she whacked me. Sutje, with tears in her eyes, said I was very brave not to cry. Sometimes I crossed Sarah on purpose, just to enjoy Sutje's sympathy. The bossy redhead said I had a butt like a rock and it hurt her hand, so she got a paddle which made more noise but still didn't smart much through heavy breeches. Abram got his share of whacks too, but Jesse escaped, not because he was a cripple but because he was so sickeningly logical.

"Life is much safer, Jan, if you do what she tells you to in the first place."

Then one day Sarah threatened to paddle Sutje, who started to cry and tried to hide behind me. Incensed, I grabbed the paddle from Sarah's hand and swung it. Of course I was no match for the wiry redhead in those days and the end result was that Sutje and I both got paddled and I got an extra whipping from Papa later for striking a girl.

For years I hated Sarah, but it was she who created the lasting bond between Sutje and me.

"Don't worry, Mama. I am not going to marry an Indian."

Icicles

It was the middle of the night and someone was pounding me on the back.

"Hurry!" It was Jesse's voice. "The Man-eaters are attacking the camp of the Wilden. They'll be on us next!"

Now I could hear gunfire coming from the direction of Otterspoor. I pulled on my clothes and rushed outside where Mother stood fully dressed with Papa's long-gun in her hands. For the first time I appreciated the four soldiers anxiously pacing about. It was winter so we had only one field hand in the barracks, a close-mouthed fellow named Wim who was calmly patrolling the stockade as though Indian attacks were an everyday occurrence. Jesse and I got guns and for the next hour all eight of us peered in vain through portholes across moonlit fields. Only the snowman leered back at us.

No one could approach Vredendale without crossing open land, but the shadows were deceptive. Even the snowman seemed to move a little each time I looked. The real difficulty would be to distinguish a Mohawk, bent on murder, from a fleeing Weckquasgeek. Mother had already discussed this with the sergeant.

"A savage is a savage!" he announced loudly. "Anyone crossing that clearing tonight will be a head shorter before he reaches us!"

At this Mother drew herself up to her full height and ordered the sergeant, in the name of Dr. Montagne, Councillor of New Netherland, to instruct his men not to shoot unless fired upon. "I am expecting a messenger from the Fort," she added which was a boldfaced lie.

Gradually the gunfire faded, then stopped entirely. But the silence was worse. Even Tiger appeared to be straining his ears for the slightest sound. I volunteered to steal along the creek to investigate.

"No one leaves this stockade!" barked the sergeant.

Mother and Jesse went indoors to get warm and the men retreated to the barracks where they had a fire of their own. Only one soldier remained on patrol. I stayed by the south gate, Tiger at my heels, my mind tormented by the fate of my friends. Were there no survivors? Surely Little Deer and

Moose Foot would come to Vredendale. Should I slip outside when the opportunity arose? The patrol came up behind me.

"Them trees could hide a savage easy," he said, staring at the birches by the creek. Mother always called them the seven graceful sisters. Then the moon came out from behind a cloud and we could see each separate tree trunk with no sinister figures lurking between. Still something looked strange. Without thinking I counted the trunks twice before realizing that there were eight, not seven. Were we being stealthily surrounded by Man-eaters or was there a wounded Weckquasgeek out there? I racked my brains to think of any natural phenomenon to account for the eighth tree trunk.

All were about the girth of a man but curving gently outward, as if from one central root system. How could a man—if indeed it was a man—remain so still in such an awkward stance? Yet if he moved, my companion would shoot first and ask questions later. To my relief the patrol was not a counter of tree trunks. He soon lost interest and disappeared behind the barracks.

I never took my eye off the birches. Oddly enough it was impossible to determine which one did not belong. Then another cloud passed across the face of the moon turning the graceful sisters temporarily into one solid patch of black. When the moon reappeared there were only seven tree trunks. A lone figure slipped like a shadow across the frozen field until it was completely eclipsed by the snowman. I trained my gun on that round innocent face with its eyes of charcoal.

Still I did not raise the alarm. Tiger, who had been growling under his breath, suddenly began to bark, tail wagging. If Tiger recognized the Indian that was good enough for me. I slid back the bar and opened the gate.

It was Kumtassa, the runner, his left arm severed at the wrist. With his right hand he clutched the stump, vainly trying to staunch the blood. I hurried him into the house. By the light of the fire I could see the remains of a hand dangling as though by a string from the stump. Jesse turned pale while Mother tied strips of linen around the arm, twisting them tight with a wooden spoon to stop the bleeding.

"Bring the medicine chest, Jan, and my needle and thread," she said. "Jesse, fetch the whiskey."

Kumtassa lay on the hearth with his arm resting on the wooden fire stool. He never winced or changed his expression when Mother chopped off the remains of the hand with a meat cleaver. It was too much for Jesse. He handed me the whiskey bottle and limped outdoors, gagging.

"Lay the poker in the red-hot coals," said Mother. Then, to Kumtassa, "You are not going to die on my hearth, young brave! When I am finished, you are going to walk out of here on your own two feet." She had never amputated so much as a finger before but you would not have known it.

"Give him some whiskey, Jan. Now loosen the tourniquet a little." She located the large blood vessels to be tied. As each came in to view it was looped with thread and quickly knotted. "That'll keep you from bleeding to death," she muttered.

When she wasn't talking to the patient, she was snapping orders at me. "Tighten the tourniquet . . . Prop up his head . . . More whiskey . . . Loosen the tourniquet again, Jan."

At one point I asked Kumtassa why no others had reached Vredendale. He said the Man-eaters had attacked from the south, so the survivors fled north. This was strange. Why should Mohawks attack from the south? I reasoned that fugitives would hesitate to approach Otterspoor, where Claes's son was still bitter about the murder of his father. That left Uncle Isaack's place and Kuyter's. Kumtassa said he had doubled back. I looked at Mother and did not need to ask why.

She never did use the poker. When the blood vessels were properly tied, she sewed the flap of skin neatly over the stump. To this day I wonder why God has ordained that chirurgeons be men when women clearly have the more agile fingers.

Finally satisfied, Mother bandaged the stump with fresh linen, and anchored it firmly to Kumtassa's right shoulder with a sling about the neck so he would not injure himself. Then we put another blanket over the patient and left him to sleep while we cleaned up the mess.

In the morning, Kumtassa was still a heap of snoring blankets by the hearth. Outside a thin coat of ice covered the world, and my snowman had lost his nose and one eye. The patrol warned me not to leave Vredendale until orders arrived from the Fort, but I had no intention of waiting. As soon as he disappeared behind the barracks, I was through the gate and halfway to the woods.

The fastest route, just half a mile, was along the frozen creek bed. In the pink light of dawn every icy twig and branch glistened like crystal. Surely this sparkling fairyland could harbor no evil. Then I reached the camp of the Wilden and my world shattered into a thousand pieces.

Most men leave their childhood behind gradually, if at all. Mine vanished forever that morning by the creek. The camping place was a river of blood and butchered Wilden. Too numb to think clearly, I only knew that I had to find Little Deer. As I searched I instinctively counted the bodies.

All my life I have counted things. I remember when I was four years old, being butted by a goat near our home in Leyden. I hollered my head off while Mother checked me over and put a cold compress on the only visible mark. She said if I wanted the hurt to go away, all I had to do was stop yelling and count slowly to thirty-seven. I don't know where she got the number thirty-seven. Her prescriptions varied according to the seriousness of the wound and the arithmetical ability of the patient. By the time we children had reached the proper number, the pain had lessened considerably and it was years before I realized that counting had nothing to do with the cure.

One young girl's head was covered by a tangled mass of black hair. Gently I pushed it aside expecting to find the bright eyes of Sunflower, but there was no face.

I recognized the squaw with the young boys. The papoose had been hacked apart, still tied to his little wooden board.

Seven . . . Eight . . . Nine . . .

There was a roar in my ears. Was it the roar of Hell Gate or the screams of the massacred Wilden still echoing through the valley?

Twelve . . . Thirteen . . . Fourteen . . .

I had seen violent death before. Old Claes's death was bloody enough, but I did not lose my head then. I had to keep my wits, but it was difficult with this noise in my ears. Was the tide racing out or was it the rush of departing souls?

One man lay with his bowels spread out beside him in the snow. He died trying to put them back into his ripped belly. But his scalp lock was intact. Why had his killer failed to collect the scalp lock?

At first I thought Wehtah was still alive. She lay on her back staring calmly upward. In her arms was a headless baby with little red stockings on his feet.

I would have wept if I could. Something told me I would never be able to weep again. Mother had said Happy Squirrel must be baptized. Dimly I remembered that a layman could perform the ceremony in an emergency.

"In the name of the Father, the Son and the Holy Ghost, I baptize thee Cornelis." Without thinking I chose the Christian name of his real father, Sharkface Cornelis van Tienhoven. Was this how I was destined to fulfill my responsibility as uncle to Happy Squirrel?

Then I heard it, a faint whisper floating above the roar in my head. "Water," whispered the voice.

I turned. Propped against a tree, eyes wide open, was the old warrior with the three black toes. I knelt beside him in the snow. But when I touched his face I could tell he had been dead for hours. Was I going mad?

Eighteen . . . Nineteen . . . Twenty.

I tried to look away from the blood, but there was no place to look. Even the icicles hanging from the branches above were tinged with red. Oh God! Blood was dripping down onto me. Now I knew I had gone mad.

In all there were twenty-one dead. Little Deer was not there, nor was Moose Foot.

I was not aware of returning to Vredendale. The next thing I knew the snowman was staring at me, crying tears of ice from his one charcoal eye. Then I was indoors, with the roar still in my ears so I could not hear if anyone spoke, but it did not matter because no one even noticed me.

Papa had returned and was pacing up and down but his face was that of an old, old man. He looked right through me and I did not seem to be able to move. Could I be dead? Why was everyone acting so strangely? Maybe the warmth of the room would thaw my brain so I could think.

Mother sat with her head down on the table sobbing. I had never seen her like this. Oh, she wept occasionally. When Sarah's baby died she sat in that same chair, tears running down her cheeks on to her knitting. But she was always in command. Today she had given up.

Jesse limped around awkwardly, trying to be helpful, but getting in everyone's way. My baby brother, Will, had climbed onto the linen chest and was happily pulling Mother's silver spoons from the rack on the wall. Tiger wagged his tail every time one hit the floor. This was strange too, because Mother did not allow the dog in the house. Had I let him in with me by mistake? Why did no one put him out? Then I noticed Will's feet. He was wearing little red stockings. Suddenly the silver spoons turned to icicles, and blood began to drip down on to my little brother. But it did not matter because he had no head. I shut my eyes.

When I opened them again, someone who looked like Mother was lifting Will off the linen chest. But it was not Mother. It was my sister Rachel who is only nine. I never noticed before how much she looked like Mother. She set the baby on the floor with an olykoek, and directed six-year-old Marie to put Tiger out and pick up the spoons. Then she returned to the hearth where she bustled about exactly like Mother.

There was no sign of Kumtassa. I opened my mouth to ask about the Indian but no sound came out. If only the roar in my ears would stop. Now Jesse was shaking me by the shoulder trying to tell me something, but his voice seemed to come from a great distance. He said it was Dutch soldiers that had raided the camp of the Wilden, not Mohawks. Now I knew why the attack had come from the south and why no scalp locks had been taken, but in my heart I had always known.

Rachel put a shawl about Mother's shoulders. Then she looked directly at me with disgust in her eyes.

"Mille tonnerres! Wash those filthy hands," she said, but her voice came from far away.

Jesse filled the basin for me. When the icy water hit my hands and face something cracked inside my skull. The roar disappeared and I was back in the land of the living.

I stood up straight. "Kieft will burn in Hell until eternity for this night!" I said aloud, but I did not recognize my own voice. It was an octave lower than yesterday.

Papa stopped his pacing. "Son," he said, "this will go down in history as the greatest treachery by civilized man since the massacre of the innocents."

Gradually I learned the whole story, starting with the infamous Shrovetide dinner at the Dam house. I can picture them now, feasting on my venison. Jan Dam and the Witch and her three ugly daughters were there with their husbands, including Sharkface and ver Planck, who like Dam was a member of the defunct board of twelve. Jan Vinje, the older brother, was probably there too, although he did not get along with the others. As a matter of fact none of them got along. It is common knowledge that two of the sisters had a hair-pulling brawl on the Heerenstraat last year. The Secretary's wife was bitten in the arm by her sister and the wound turned septic, which, according to Mother, proved there was bad blood in the whole family.

There was one surprise guest, Maryn Adriaensen, a coarse, violent-tempered fellow who was also one of the defunct board of twelve. This was all part of Sharkface's plot. He had prepared a carefully-worded petition to the Governor purporting to be from the board.

"God having delivered the enemy into our hands, we beseech you to allow us to attack . . ."

Then he persuaded the inebriated Dam, ver Planck and Adriaensen to sign.

The next day, Ash Wednesday, when Papa returned to the Fort at dusk, he was horrified to find an army of eighty soldiers and forty-nine volunteers lined up ready for action. Kieft gleefully showed him the petition from the board of twelve. When Papa pointed out that there were only three signatures, he brushed this aside as of no consequence. Then de Vries dashed into the courtyard where the soldiers were assembled.

"You will be murdering your own countrymen!" he shouted. "There are thousands upon thousands of other Indians in the wilderness, ready to avenge the death of their comrades!"

Sharkface had him removed and assured the men that there was no danger. In the meantime, Papa had sent for Dominie Bogardus who alternately pleaded with Kieft and threatened to excommunicate him, all to no avail. The order had gone forth and was not to be changed.

Eighty soldiers, under van Tienhoven, crossed the Hudson in sloops, to attack the camp of the Wilden near Pavonia. Maryn Adriaensen led the volunteers to the camps on the East River and our creek.

When the troops departed, Kieft retired to his room and Papa and de Vries spent the night in the Governor's kitchen. At midnight they heard gunfire, and ran up to the ramparts where they could see the fires and hear the screams of the butchered Wilden across the water.

Back in the kitchen an hour later, Papa suddenly looked up into a savage face painted with black and white stripes. Speechless, he was unable even to reach for his gun. Fortunately de Vries recognized the Indian who turned out to be a Hackensack neighbor of his. Striped Face's squaw stood in the shadow as he described their escape from Pavonia by canoe. The couple were under the impression they had been attacked by Mohawks.

Bitterly de Vries explained the truth and he and Papa hustled the pair away before they were caught. If nothing else, this incident illustrates how lax was Fort security.

That night of Ash Wednesday, 1643, over 130 Wilden were massacred in their sleep at Pavonia and on Manhattan. By dawn, all the soldiers were safely back at the Fort being congratulated by Kieft for "a deed of Roman valor."

Flight

For seventy-two hours Manhattan held its breath while the Wilden still believed the massacre to be the work of Mohawks. Papa was sure retribution would be swift and bloody when it came, particularly against solitary boweries like Vredendale. He sent the sergeant into town with an urgent request for more soldiers.

While we waited for a reply, the cat produced a litter of nine in the woodshed. Mother fixed a basket for the kittens and transferred them to the barn where they would be warmer. Unfortunately nature had not anticipated so many mouths to feed and the smallest did not do well in spite of Little Rachel's best efforts.

In the meantime Papa dispatched the men to dig a common grave for the massacred Wilden. I was sent on a tour of our neighbors to collect information about survivors. The news was discouraging. Two of the wounded who sought refuge at Otterspoor had their heads blown off by the wheelwright's son. I remembered his father's bloody fate and kept my mouth shut.

One squaw was taken in by Uncle Isaack and Sarah. She died during the night on their hearth. A young Indian made it to Zegendale. Kuyter told me that he left at dawn in good condition. For a brief moment I had hopes that it was Little Deer, but he was too small.

Papa thought that Little Deer and Moose Foot were both dead. I was sure he was wrong.

In the morning we were still waiting for word from the Fort. Little Rachel wept when she discovered the stiff body of the tiniest kitten, astonishing when you consider that she barely shed a tear over yesterday's massacre. I removed the corpse and disposed of it in the forest while my sister lured the mother away with a dish of kidneys. Much to my amazement the cat immediately noticed that her litter was one short. She located the dead kitten and replaced it in the basket. The next time I buried the body. I only mention this incident because it seems to prove that a dumb animal can count to nine.

At noon a corporal finally arrived from the Fort, a big burly fellow with an uneven beard and an uneven gait.

"Where is the sergeant?" inquired Papa.

"Transferred," was the gruff response. "I'm yer replacement. Name's Pia."

"Per Deos immortales! Where are the additional soldiers that I requested, Pia?" asked Papa, trying to remain calm.

"Yer lookin' at the whole platoon, Doktor." And Pia handed him a note from Kieft.

"It would be bad for morale to assign more men to Vredendale at this time, since we anticipate no danger from savages," Papa read aloud. "Kindly report to the Governor's mansion at your earliest convenience."

"Welcome to Vredendale, Corporal Pia," interrupted Mother, Papa being speechless. "Jan will show you to the barracks."

As we departed Papa found his voice. "My earliest convenience is never!" he sputtered.

That night retribution began on the far side of the Hudson. Farmers were murdered and boweries went up in flames. Those that escaped made their way across to the Fort where chaos reigned.

At Vredendale we heard nothing, but a rosy glow hung over the western horizon until morning. The next night Manhattan exploded into flames. Savage war cries intermingled with screams of trapped livestock as the skies blazed with burning homesteads. Blood flowed in rivers and the world became a nightmare of hell on earth.

When Otterspoor went up in flames, Papa made the decision to abandon Vredendale. Guns would be of little avail against blazing arrows on a thatched roof. If any were to survive this night it must be at the Fort. Once the Wilden surrounded Vredendale, it would be too late. The creek had thawed by now but it would be suicide to pass so close to the howling horde at Otterspoor. Our only chance was the Weckquasgeek trail.

"Get the horses ready, Son." Papa's voice was surprisingly calm. "And wrap burlap around each horseshoe."

Only our guns and the clothes on our back would go with us. Mother wanted to save the oak cradle which just shows how illogical a woman can be. All the animals had to be left behind, except for Tiger, a more formidable weapon than any gun, and the horses.

The day before, Uncle Isaack had borrowed Middernacht, leaving in his place a temperamental filly named Poptje. She panicked. When we finally got her under control she refused to budge unless I held her. So we lined up like this: Papa led the first horse carrying Mother and baby Will. Jesse managed the second by himself and I followed, leading Poptje, who carried the two girls.

And so the gate swung open and we set out, Corporal Pia and Wim, our one field hand, in the fore with Tiger on a short lead, then the horses and finally the three soldiers bringing up the rear. For the moment it made no difference how much noise we made as it was drowned out by frenzied war whoops and screaming horses at Otterspoor. Poptje trembled with terror and made a desperate attempt to turn back. In contrast Tiger pulled the line forward, ever eager to decimate the enemy.

When the trail entered the woods everything went black as an underground tunnel and our pace dropped to a slow crawl. We would never reach the Fort at this rate.

"Doucement, Poptje," I whispered in her ear. Then the whole procession came to a halt. Papa's instructions, if this happened, were to stand absolutely still.

"Silence is our strongest safeguard, men."

Father might not be a great general but he had a quiet manner that was good for morale. With one hand I patted Poptje's neck as the tail of Jesse's horse flicked me in the face. Why had we stopped? I estimated our position to be about opposite the waterfall. On my own I would have been halfway to the Fort already.

Now we were moving again. As the howling from Otterspoor gradually receded, the sound of our own caravan seemed to grow. I never noticed before how much noise a horse makes just breathing. The girls fell asleep in the saddle and I had to keep my arm up to be sure they did not slide. Calmer now, Poptje picked her steps carefully as if she understood the problem.

Slowly we stumbled on through the darkness, with only an occasional glimpse of night sky through gaps in the forest roof. Yet I always knew where we were. It was as though I had spent my whole life memorizing every moss-covered rock, every fallen tree-trunk.

Then we stopped again. What was wrong? We had covered only two miles, a quarter of the way. The slow pace was maddening, but standing still was infinitely worse. I kept thinking about Little Deer. He had said only death could come between us.

After what seemed like an eternity a dark figure appeared at my side. It was Wim.

"Yer Pa needs yer up front, boy," he muttered.

Poptje did not object when I handed Wim the bridle. Then I silently squeezed my way past Jesse's horse, which was slightly off line, and Mother's horse, which was even more off line.

"You will have to lead, Son," whispered Papa. "Wim and Pia have no idea which way to go and my eyes are not up to it. Can you manage?"

"Yes," I whispered, taking Tiger's rope. Apparently everyone had been simply following Tiger, and he had decided to head off toward the clearing where I used to teach Little Deer to ride. Fortunately the caravan had not veered far and I soon had us lined up on course again.

"Not too fast, Son. And remember to think ahead."

For myself, I had no difficulty following the trail in the dark but if one of the horses stumbled there could be trouble. I slowed down. The important thing was to make as little noise as possible. We covered another mile. Only five to go.

Papa was always telling me to think ahead. One more mile and we would reach the halfway point, the abandoned cottage of Old Claes on Turtle Bay. It had lain vacant since his murder almost two years earlier. Suppose the cottage had been set to the torch? Indians would still be hanging about and there is no way they could fail to hear our horses. We would be walking straight into an ambush.

I held another whispered conversation with Papa. Reluctantly he agreed that I should go ahead alone to be sure there was no war party near the cottage. Then we would be able to proceed at a more sensible pace. We had been incredibly lucky so far, and with the optimism of youth I was sure our luck would hold.

"For God's sake be careful, Son."

I handed Tiger's rope to Pia. I would have given him my gun too but I had carelessly left that hanging from Poptje's saddle-bag.

By myself there was no need to stick to the trail. We were not far from the big rock where I used to fish and I headed staight for the East River. Sound carries much better over water. If there were Wilden near the cottage I could hear them from the river over a mile away. And if the cottage was on fire I might even see the flames from there. I forced myself to move stealthily, all the while straining my ears. Still nothing but the hum and chirping of insects, the croaking of frogs and the plaintive call of night birds.

Now a pale glow ahead told me I was approaching the river. In front of me was my rock, the same rock where the Crazy One had tried to slit my throat. From there I would be able to hear and see everything.

Then my heart stopped beating. Holy Jesus! There was a figure standing on top of my rock! I froze. But not quickly enough. A little pebble rolled only a few inches from under my foot. It was the tiniest of sounds but the figure turned immediately. Now we were facing each other, only a few paces between us.

With the river behind him I could see the outline of a warrior, tomahawk raised in his outstretched hand. He was six feet tall. Counting the rock he was ten feet tall. I was terrifed. Instinct made me stand motionless, barely breathing. I told myself that he was staring into the dark. If I never moved he could not see me. Lots of things can cause a pebble to roll. I wished I had my gun. Now I could hear the sound of a war party in the distance and far downstream I could see orange flames reflected in the water.

I don't know how long we stood like that. Maybe five minutes. But it was the longest five minutes of my life. In my worst nightmare I can still see that black figure looming above me against the orange glow from the water.

Finally he dropped his hand and turned back to his scrutiny of the river. Cautiously, an inch at a time, I retreated into the woods and made my way back to the Trail and the caravan.

My hands were shaking. I could not seem to control them.

"There's a war party at the cottage, Papa," I whispered frantically.

He put his arm around my shoulder. "We must get the horses off the trail immediately, Son." As always, he spoke calmly. So calmly that my hands stopped shaking.

Somehow we moved the whole caravan through the underbrush an extra two miles to avoid going anywhere near Turtle Bay. We rejoined the Trail near Jan Dam's farm. God be praised, we met no one until we reached the cattle barrier patrolled by Dutch soldiers. The journey from Vredendale had taken six hours.

New Amsterdam was a madhouse. The Fort was jammed and every surrounding house bulged with refugees. My parents and the younger children put up at the Governor's mansion. Jesse and I went to the du Trieux home where we were given a blanket and a patch of floor alongside a dozen snoring bodies. Uncle Isaack and Sarah were already there, having come down by river. I was dead to the world in thirty seconds but Jesse hunched in a chair all night shivering and listening to the commotion outside.

It was still dark when the bossy redhead shook me.

"Wake up, slaapkop!" She whispered.

I turned over and buried my head in the blanket.

"Oh no you don't! Here, smell this." She yanked the blanket and waved a bowl of hot suppawn under my nose."

One whiff was enough to persuade my stomach. I grabbed, but she was too nimble, so I reluctantly groped my way to the table, stepping over bundled sleepers barely visible in the glow from the hearth. Jesse still sat in the same chair wrapped in his blanket. Sarah said he had been vomiting all night.

"Now eat this Jan, and listen carefully," she ordered.

I needed no urging in the matter of the suppawn but I was too sleepy to concentrate on her whispered instructions. Jesse looked terrible. He had spent half his life being ill so I was not surprised.

"Want some water, Jess?" I said.

He shook his head.

"Pay attention, Jan," snapped Sarah. "If you come with us, we'll rescue the cows from Vredendale too."

Gradually it dawned on me that Sarah had access to a flat boat and wanted to take me and Isaack back up the East River after their livestock.

"The Wilden are asleep," she said. "They didn't have time to destroy all the boweries last night. If Boomdale and Vredendale are still standing it would be a crime not to use these next few hours to rescue the animals."

"What do your parents think?" I stalled for time.

"Blikskaters! They'd forbid it. It's not their livestock out there. Do you realize that everything Isaack and I own is tied up in that bowery?

"The way I figure it's this," she went on more sensibly. "There are about forty boweries on Manhattan and the Wilden probably burned four or five of 'em last night. At that rate it'll be over a week before they finish. With any luck we'll have arranged a peace treaty by then and some will be saved. We've always been good to the Indians so ours have the best chance of surviving. But the horses will be dead of panic in twenty-four hours, and think of the torture in store for those cows."

I went out to the privy, convinced that Sarah was krankzinnig. The night air was surprisingly peaceful. It was the thought of Middernacht trapped in Isaack's stable that changed my mind. Besides, I hated to admit that any redhead in petticoats had more guts than I.

We located the barge, and Isaack and I poled while Sarah stood in the bow. It was slow work going upstream but this meant the return journey, fully loaded, would be easy.

As we passed Turtle Bay, the first pale light of dawn appeared over Long Island. On our left were the smoldering remains of the wheelwright's cottage. Almighty God, don't let Vredendale be in ruins. Sarah had removed the man's cap she usually wore and stood with her wild red hair billowing like a figurehead.

"Sit down," I whispered.

"Hog-wash!" she hissed. "Wilden are not pigs like Dutch soldiers. Anyway, they're all asleep."

The last argument was the only one that impressed me as I recalled the bloodthirsty howling of last night. So far, at least, there was no sign of any activity this morning.

It was broad daylight when we tied up to Isaack's dock. Miraculously, Boomdale was untouched and the animals in good condition except that the horses were in a dreadful state of nerves. Middernacht had injured his head and I was quickly covered with blood as he nuzzled his welcome. Fortunately his eyes were all right and there were no broken bones.

Normally good with horses, I succeeded in quieting them, but there was no way these overwrought beasts were going to board any flat boat. I decided to take them overland to Vredendale, while Isaack and Sarah maneuvered the barge into the creek, so I could load our livestock with theirs.

I rinsed Middernacht's head and as soon as I got a saddle on him he was eager to be off. With the other three tied behind, I set out for home.

The shortest route was diagonally through the tobacco fields of Otterspoor but Middernacht refused point blank to go anywhere near the site of broiled horseflesh. Rather than argue with him, I went due west along the branch path to Slangberg, then south on the Weckquasgeek Trail. Soon the way led through open fields. God be praised, I could see Vredendale standing tall in the distance.

Feeling very exposed, I scanned the horizon for signs of life. Nothing. If I gave Middernacht his head he could have done the remaining distance in one minute flat, but I deliberately held him in for fear the others horses would get tangled.

Not until we were inside the stockade did I breathe freely. With plenty of time before the barge was due I considered fixing pack saddles so the rider-less horses could carry some of our possessions, but decided against it. If there was any trouble between here and the Fort, I planned to abandon the other three and make a run for it on Middernacht. Unencumbered by packs, there was a good chance they would gallop along of their own free will.

The cows were complaining noisily so I gave each a brief milking with the cat helping herself to the cream. The kittens were in good condition which would please Little Rachel. I packed three large baskets full of squawking poultry and set them by the gate. Still no sign of the barge. Nervously I checked portholes in every direction. Nothing moved except one lone deer loping gracefully through the empty cornfield.

Then I saw the two figures on the bluff and my blood ran cold. How long had they been watching? From this distance it was hard to distinguish but one of the braves looked familiar. At that moment he raised an arm to point and I could see the other arm was tied to his body. A great wave of relief came over me as I realized it was Kumtassa. When I looked again the figures were gone, but for the time being at least, Vredendale was safe.

Then the flat boat arrived and we loaded her without mishap. Riding perilously low in the water, she began the slow journey downstream. I locked the gate behind me, leaving Vredendale deserted except for the cat playfully tossing a dead field mouse about the yard. How curious that of all domestic animals only the cat can survive without human care.

Holding Middernacht to a careful walk, I set off once more down the Weckquasgeek Trail. Not until the last mile where the road runs through cleared land did I throw caution to the wind and start to canter. At Dam's place I could see farmhands scurrying about trying to rescue livestock. Only half a mile to go.

Suddenly shots rang out from the woods by Kalch Pond. I dropped the connecting rope and dug my heels into Middernacht who began to fly over the ground faster than stampeding deer. More shots. One of the farmhands fell across a fence rail and just hung there like laundry. The others scattered in confusion. Something whizzed by my head and a horse screamed behind me. I knew he was down, but it was all I could do to hang on for dear life as Middernacht thundered down the last hundred yards to safety.

Soldiers helped me catch the two remaining riderless mounts and took them to the stable in the Fort. Then Jan Dam rushed over to ask about his wounded field hand. I told him the man was alive. I had seen his hand move as I flew by. Dam was arranging a rescue party and wanted to know if I thought the fellow could sit a horse.

"Here come the slaves," cried Ensign Van Dyck who was in charge of the rescue operation. "We'll take the Giant. He can carry your man better than any horse."

As Van Dyck was sorting it out with the overseer, the Witch appeared shaking her stick and screeching at Dam.

"Stommeling! Flapdrol! Espèce de canard! Do you know how much it cost to bring one field hand across the Atlantic, and you send him after pigs!"

"Quiet, woman!" yelled Dam. "The big slave'll fetch him out."

"Horse piss! You shoulda sent a slave in the first place."

"Voorwaarts!" barked Van Dyck and the soldiers marched out with the Giant, unarmed, in the middle.

Still holding Middernacht, I joined the group of slaves by the cattle barrier. Newcomers to this country often wonder if the slaves ever sided with the Wilden in an effort to gain their freedom. The answer is no. They were always loyal to us and many fought bravely for the Dutch cause.

Dam and his vrouw interrupted their squabble to watch in silence as the soldiers proceeded in close formation with the Giant's head and shoulders protruding above the others like some huge black doorknob. For 200 yards the countryside was open, with no possibility of ambush. Near Dam's bowery, however, there was a peninsula of forest extending down from the Horseshoe Swamp. If there was danger it was here and the patrol halted just out of range.

"Voorwaarts!" The command was faint from this distance and the soldiers pointed their guns at the woods as the big slave started forward alone.

"That Giant's been living on borrowed time long enough," cried Dam, then he turned to the slaves. "If he brings my man out alive, I'll see to it that you all get your freedom," he lied.

In the distance, the Giant paused, apparently confused. He was never very strong upstairs, even before he was hanged.

"Voorwaarts!" came another faint call from Van Dyck. Still the huge slave hesitated as if he did not know what was expected of him.

"Voorwaarts! Voorwaarts!" shouted the slaves, in unison. Encouraged, the Giant began to march and they chanted until he disappeared from view. The soldiers continued to point their guns and we held our breath.

Five minutes later the big slave reappeared carrying the wounded field hand in his arms like a baby. Even the slaves knew they would not really get their freedom. Still they sang with joy and clapped to the beat as the soldiers escorted the mighty Giant home.

I rode over to join the crowd gathered along the Strand. All eyes were on the flat boat slowly coming down the East River. She had been an easy target for eight miles and it was a miracle that no one fired at her. Now as she approached safety, the spectators cheered wildly.

What a sight she was, a biblical ark bulging with cows, pigs and goats. Seagulls circled overhead and in the bow stood Mrs. Noah with her red hair flying in the March wind.

The Big Fish

The situation continued to grow more and more desperate. By night, skies blazed as the labors of a lifetime went up in flames. By day, anyone who ventured more than a few hundred yards from the Fort was lucky to escape with his scalp.

The cannon from two ocean-going vessels offered some protection. One, in the East River, was laden to the gunnels with terrified colonists abandoning the New World. The other was anchored out in the harbor. Her Captain refused to take any new passengers but agreed to stay for a few days as a threat.

Old Nehooma used to say the Wilden would one day disappear from Manhattan. She was wrong. It was the Swannekins who were disappearing.

At first the Canarsies on Long Island remained neutral. Then they joined the other river Indians until eleven tribes were united in an effort to wipe us from the face of the earth. All able-bodied men were conscripted into a civilian militia. Counting the regular army this gave us a force of a little over 200 against thousands and thousands of warriors. Our only chance was to arrange a peace treaty, and the problem was how to do it. In the meantime we were all prisoners in the shadow of the Fort.

Much to my chagrin Papa would not allow me to join the militia, although at thirteen I was better than most with a gun. Food supplies being low, I was persuaded to go into the fishing business with two other boys, Abram du Trieux and my English friend, Sacky Allerton.

We could not set nets or go too far from shore because of the danger of attack. Every morning we launched an old battered rowboat from Weepers' Point, and by afternoon had transferred the catch to a wheelbarrow for door-to-door distribution.

The boat was too difficult for Jesse, so he was in charge of keeping the books, a task more complicated than it sounds because customers rarely paid in coin or wampum. Most were on credit, and he would eventually collect a gallon of vinegar here and a firkin of butter there.

New Amsterdam housewives always cleaned their fish in the road, leaving the entrails for the pigs. We did such a thriving business that the whole town soon stank. Mother said it was a disgrace. Papa said it was just like a woman to yammer about garbage when we were all in danger of losing our scalps.

Of course Governor Kieft was responsible for our predicament, but he tried to pin the blame on Maryn Adriaensen, one of the leaders of the Ash Wednesday massacre. Adriaensen had a bad temper to begin with. Having his home burned to the ground and his livestock destroyed did not help. When he learned that Kieft was blaming the war on him he exploded.

I was delivering fish to the Wooden Horse when Adriaensen strode past, pistol in one hand, sword in the other, and a face like a thunder cloud. He disappeared into the Fort as his vrouw came tearing along after him, shrieking,

"Stop him! God allemachtig, stop him! He's out to murder the Governor!"

I dropped the wheelbarrow and began to run. Others joined me, but I noticed nobody breaking any speed records. Then I remembered that Papa was almost surely alone with Kieft at this very moment. I dashed through the gate and sprinted across the cobblestones, shouting at the top of my lungs. The front door was wide open and soldiers scurried up the stairwell. I bounded up three steps at a time as a wild voice from above cried,

"You are a liar from the bottom of your belly to the root of your tongue!"

Then we burst into the room and the soldiers grappled with the assassin. Papa was quite calm. He said Adriaensen was temporarily insane and ordered him locked up. Kieft was badly shaken.

"Young man, your father just saved my life," he said, massaging his elbow. "That traitor had his pistol pointed at my head. I was looking down the barrel at eternity when your father struck the flintlock. I could hear the hammer snap against the murderer's thumb."

According to Papa, Adriaensen was so intent on shooting the Governor that he never realized anyone else was in the room. Mother said later that it might have been better for all concerned if Papa had not been so quick off the mark.

"The Governor is my commanding officer, Rachel," he replied stiffly.

Word quickly spread that Adriaensen was in jail, and by the time I left to recover my wheelbarrow, a crowd had gathered outside. The ringleader was a servant of Adriaensen, named Stangh, who was loudly demanding the release of his master. Papa and the Governor came out onto the doorstep to try to calm people down. Suddenly Stangh leaped forward and two shots rang out. The guards returned fire and everyone ran for cover.

Stangh's bullets had slammed harmlessly into the brick wall. Stangh himself lay dead, killed instantly by a shot through the eye.

Kieft wanted to have Adriaensen tried and executed on the spot, which almost produced a riot. Finally he agreed to ship the prisoner back to the Fatherland to stand trial. As for Stangh, Kieft ordered his head stuck up on a pole as a warning to others. When Mother saw it she told the Governor to his face that it was barbaric to keep that grinning skull leering down at people. I thought he would be furious but he only bowed slightly and remarked, "I learned long ago, Madame, to pay no attention to the opinions of the gentler sex."

In the midst of this chaos, New Amsterdam had an important visitor, Governor Roger Williams of Rhode Island, who was on his way to England to obtain a charter for his new colony. Banished from Massachusetts for his liberal views, he was unable to embark from Boston and had booked passage on the Dutch ship now anchored in the harbor. Because of the Indian uprising he arranged to sleep on board where he was able to watch the countryside burn from a position of relative safety.

Isaac Allerton, Sacky's father, gave a small private dinner for Williams at the City Tavern. My parents were there as well as the Governor, and half the regular army was on duty outside. We boys were not invited which was just as well, as it would have taken a week to get rid of the fish smell.

It was the next day that we had the accident. For some reason Abram was not with us, and Sacky and I decided to try our luck among the Capsies, tiny islands of rock off the tip of Manhattan, like boulders dropped by some prehistoric giant. Gradually we drifted farther and farther away from Weepers' Point out into the harbor, which was empty except for the one vessel a mile to the south. Her cannon actually represented more protection to us than the Fort.

For a long time the fish refused to bite and Sacky whispered continuously which annoyed me. Furthermore he whispered in English. Fishermen are supposed to be quiet. When Little Deer and I went fishing we never said a word. I wondered if we would ever go fishing together again.

By concentrating on the monotonous sound of waves slapping against the boat I was able to shut out Sacky. Suddenly something big hit the line and I was wide-awake.

"It's a whopper!" whispered Sacky.

From the way it struck I was sure it was a striped bass, maybe six or eight pounds. We used line of plaited horsehair, barely strong enough for a four-pounder. If I'd had any sense I would have cut the line and given up on this fellow, but I accepted the challenge and gave him all the footage I had.

I must have fought that fish for a good fifteen minutes, continually working him back and forth until he began to tire. Now we could see him, and Sacky held the net ready. It was definitely a striped bass well over two feet.

Then the incredible happened! From the depths of the harbor a huge gray monster shot up, swallowed the bass whole, as if it were a minnow, and leaped out of the water almost on top of us.

One minute I had a pole in my hand with an eight-foot monster on the end of the line. Then pole and line were whisked away, but the monster remained suspended in mid-air for several horrible seconds which have been stamped forever in my memory. One ugly fish eye stared at me as I seemed to be falling helplessly toward those evil jaws. Beside me Sacky grabbed an oar for a weapon but he was falling too. The whole boat was going over.

The next thing I knew, Sacky was dragging me out of the drink, and the monster had vanished as suddenly as it appeared. The boat was swamped to the gunnels and we had lost our catch. Worse yet we were missing an oar.

"Holy Jehoshaphat!" I gasped, coughing up a gallon of sea-water. "What was that?"

Sacky was bailing furiously. He handed me one of the buckets hooked beneath the thwarts.

"God knows! But you'd better get to work or we'll have to swim home, that is, if we don't freeze to death first."

When the water level was under control, I took our one oar and tried using it as a paddle. The wind was from the northeast however, and I could make no progress toward Manhattan, so we decided to head for the Dutch vessel where I was sure we could borrow an oar.

Oddly enough, with the elements pushing us southwest, it was comparatively easy to row with one oar and head directly south. As we approached the ship, I noticed a scholarly-looking gentleman standing by himself in the bow, holding a long spyglass. When we got closer he called out in English.

"I see you let that big fellow get away, young man."

I laughed in spite of the cold. "Oh he didn't get away, sir. We threw him back!"

"Manhattan housewives prefer shad, sir," added Sacky.

"Well, well," chuckled the gentleman. "I must find out how two Dutch lads can row with one oar, catch whales on a fishing pole, and speak perfect English to boot."

Five minutes later we were dressed in dry clothes and given a new oar. Then before setting off we were served ale and cold mutton in the private cabin of Governor Roger Williams of Rhode Island.

The next morning I arrived at Weepers' Point at dawn. A white mist was rising and at first I did not see the tall figure of Captain de Vries by the water's edge. I stowed my gear and joined him. He finally broke the silence.

"This is the third time, Jan," he said.

I nodded. In the space of ten years he had established three great boweries, all in ruins through no fault of his own. The remarkable thing was that he was alive to tell the tale.

"I'm too old to pick up the pieces again," he said.

"My father says you are the best man we have, Captain."

"That is generous of him, lad. How is your mother weathering this? Surely she is ready to abandon the New World."

I shook my head. "Mother believes Vredendale will be spared. It is the one little corner of this earth that belongs to us, and come what may we must protect it."

He seemed to stand a little taller. "She is a remarkable woman, Jan."

"Everyone wishes you were the Governor," I said. "They say you're the only one who can get us out of this mess."

"God knows I tried to be Governor. The Directors in Amsterdam were aware that I was by far the best qualified. Do you know why they chose Willem Kieft instead of me? Because his grandfather was a magistrate! Even van Twiller, besotted domkop that he was, would never have gotten us into this mess, lad."

"Suppose you were the Governor now, Captain. What would you do?"

"I'd swallow my pride and make peace on any terms."

"But how? How can you make peace with eleven tribes?"

"That's easy," he laughed wryly. "The answer is one at a time."

"But how can you make peace with even one tribe when any man who leaves these few acres is a dead man?"

By this time Abram and Sacky had arrived and I was needed to help drag the boat into the water. As we shoved off I heard the Captain's voice.

"An opportunity will come, Jan. And when it does we must be ready to grab it."

The opportunity came sooner than expected. Later that very day I had stationed the wheelbarrow on the Heerenstraat where I was surrounded by buzzing flies and haggling housewives. Marie du Trieux was buying bass for the tavern. She was Abram's half-sister and gave us free beer so I had just agreed to give her half price if she took perch instead of bass, when the commotion began.

Three braves, carrying a white flag, beached a canoe on the Strand and came trotting across town, past gaping housewives, to disappear into the Fort. I did not recognize them, but Marie knew every Indian for miles around and claimed that they were Canarsies.

They were sent by the one-eyed Chief Penhawitz to invite the Governor to a powwow at a place called Coney Island. Kieft naturally refused to leave the Fort and other officials were equally reluctant. De Vries said that this was the opportunity we had been waiting for and volunteered to go alone if necessary.

"He's the only man here with any iron in his balls," screamed the Witch as he set out with the Canarsies. But New Amsterdam was sure it had seen the last of Captain David de Vries.

New Amsterdam was wrong. Not only was de Vries back in 24 hours, he brought the famous Penhawitz and a few lesser Chiefs with him to attend a powwow at the Fort. At the last minute, one of the younger braves warned the Chiefs that they were walking into a trap and would all be killed by Dutch soldiers, but Penhawitz said he trusted de Vries and would come on the strength of his word alone.

For once Kieft received the Canarsies cordially. A meeting of all officials was convened, and the Captain sent me to fetch the Dominie's step-daughter to act as interpreter. Even Little Deer admitted that Sarie Kierstede spoke the language as well as any native. When I reported that she was in bed with fever, de Vries decided to act as interpreter himself and asked me to sit behind him.

"Van Tienhoven is fluent enough, lad, but I hate to depend on that hoerenloper for anything."

And so I got to hear one of the greatest political speeches of all time.

Everyone sat on the ground in a large circle and de Vries spoke first. He welcomed the Chiefs and thanked them for accompanying him to the Fort so that Penhawitz's words could be heard, not by himself alone, but by the Governor of New Netherland and all his ministers. Kieft only nodded and massaged his elbow.

Then Penhawitz began to speak, his mutilated eye uncovered, empty socket displayed proudly as a badge of courage won in battle. In contrast, his one good eye, which was twice as big as life, held the audience spell-bound.

Wilden greatly admire powerful oratory and the youth are carefully trained in the art. Chiefs are often chosen as much for their silver tongue as for their bravery in war. But if Penhawitz spoke with a silver tongue I was not aware of it. He never smiled or frowned or raised his voice, and yet we were all transfixed by that one magnetic eye which seemed to penetrate the very soul.

De Vries did not attempt any translation. Even those who could not understand the words, were motionless prisoners, impaled by the eye.

Penhawitz's topic was the white man's debt to the Wilden. He started with the wreck of the Tiger, ten years before the Colony even began. Captain Block and his crew survived because Canarsies brought them food throughout the long winter, and in the spring they provided timber for a new ship.

In his hand Penhawitz held a bundle of small sticks. At the conclusion of each point he detached one stick and placed it deliberately on the ground before him. Sometimes a single sentence sufficed.

"We taught our guests to grow maize."

How astonishing that Europe knew nothing of this delicious staple. Acres of tall green corn flashed before my eyes as he put down another stick. Sometimes one word was enough:

"Maple syrup."

The Wilden had introduced us to the miracle of the sugar maple. I remembered my delight as a small child when Tatitta gave us cups of birch bark, filled with fresh snow and topped with hot syrup.

Penhawitz always referred to the Dutch as "guests." He used few words but somehow the effect of the eye, together with the placing of the stick, produced a clearer picture in the mind than would a thousand adjectives.

Finally only one stick remained in his hand. Penhawitz paused and looked down, temporarily releasing his audience who stared at that last dreadful stick.

"We gave our daughters to the guests." Once more the eye transfixed us. "Now the guests have murdered their own children."

I closed my eyes, but I could not shut out the picture of Happy Squirrel lying headless in the snow, with little red stockings on his feet. If Penhawitz had called the Dutch monsters it would not have been so effective. Slowly, in total silence, he placed the final stick upon the ground.

The Whippoorwill

Thanks to the eloquence of Penhawitz, a treaty with the Canarsies was quickly arranged and sealed with an exchange of gifts. De Vries insisted that generosity here was the glue that held a treaty together, and Kieft dipped liberally into the treasury. Penhawitz, in turn, used his influence with the other Chiefs, so that within two weeks a general peace was declared with all the local tribes. Unfortunately the Dutch gifts were far from lavish this time.

"The savages want peace to plant their crops," gloated Kieft. "Why pay them for something they want as much as we do?"

Papa worried about long-term prospects, but Papa always worried. The rest of the family rejoiced that Vredendale had been spared. Little Rachel was ecstatic to find eight healthy kittens frolicking about the stockade.

The terms of the treaty prohibited armed Wilden from approaching within so many paces of a European home and we had a near disaster when a nervous patrol fired at the first Indian to visit Vredendale. Papa had the soldier replaced immediately, and gave strict orders against any further shooting, but we had no more visitors. Even Kumtassa stayed away. As for Little Deer and Moose Foot, Papa said we had to assume that they were dead but I was sure he was wrong.

I forced myself to return to the site of the massacre. The nightmare of blood and ice and death had vanished in a burst of green springtime. Pink dogwood blossomed, and the ugly scar that was the grave of the Wilden was covered with wildflowers. Only the restless shadow of the wind in the tall grass reminded me of rushing souls.

Sometimes I met Indians in the woods but they rarely returned my greeting. I went to Shorakapkok to find it deserted except for one very old Weckquasgeek, laboriously knotting a fishing net. When I asked about Little Deer and Moose Foot, he just shook his head.

We had been home nearly a week when Jesse and I heard the whippoor-will. It was a warm summer night and we took off our boots in the dark, to avoid attracting the tiny insects that pass so effortlessly through the finest netting. Then the whippoorwill began to call. Instinctively I counted as he sang his name over and over again in three long throaty notes. Once, a year earlier, I counted sixty-five. This fellow only did seven.

"Little Deer can imitate any bird call," I said. "How do we know that isn't he out there?"

"We don't, but it sounds like the first whippoorwill of the season to me," said Jesse. "I wonder why they only sing in the dark. There he is again."

Eight more calls cut through the night air. Then silence. I threw myself onto the bed and was just drifting off when he began again. How comfortable to fall asleep to the music of the whippoorwill. . . .NINE! . . . Holy Jehoshaphat! . . . Suddenly I was wide awake.

"Jess! It *is* Little Deer! Don't you see? First he called seven times, then eight, then nine. Birds can't count. Next time it'll be ten. I'm going out there!" I whistled the notes of the whippoorwill as I pulled on my boots.

Jesse had not been counting and was skeptical, especially as a moment later the whippoorwill called seven times not ten. But I was undeterred.

"He's starting over," I insisted. "He's been doing seven-eight-nine, and we were so late going to bed we almost missed him."

I knew better than to ask permission to leave the stockade. I simply waited for the patrol to pass behind the barracks, then slipped through the gate. Jesse agreed to notify him in a few minutes so I would not be shot coming back.

Once outside I headed for the woods. Waywahtassee flashed by in the darkness, reminding me of bygone summer evenings when Little Deer and I used to chase these tiny flies of fire.

At the edge of the clearing I paused. A lone owl hooted and from the direction of the creek came the deep croaking of a bullfrog, but no whippoorwill. Was I walking into a trap? I tried whistling the notes myself. No answer. Could it have been a real whippoorwill after all? I had never seen one myself. Little Deer said they were small brown birds that nest on the floor of the forest and only sing at night. No! Seven-eight-nine-seven was too much of a coincidence. Little Deer was alive and I would find him tomorrow.

At dawn I climbed Slangberg. If Little Deer were to leave a message, it would be here, where no deer flee and no hunters follow. I scaled the east face with Uncle Isaack's bowery spread out neatly below. A thin curl of smoke rose lazily from his chimney and I heard the distant music of copper cow bells. To the south lay the silent ruins of Otterspoor. Cornelis Claes and his family, including the one surviving twin, had escaped. Their livestock had been roasted alive.

When I climbed higher I could see the smoke from Bronck's bowery on the mainland. Jonas Bronck had dropped dead a month earlier from the shock of the war. I wondered whom the wealthy widow would marry.

I half hoped to find Little Deer waiting on the summit, but Slangberg was deserted. On the ledge where we used to sit, someone had placed a flat stone the size of a pancake. On it were arranged three small oval stones like robin's eggs. No one else ever climbed this mountain of rock so it had to be a message from Little Deer. I sat down and tried to think.

Suppose I were an Indian and was warned that I would be shot if I approached Vredendale. The Whippoorwill plan was perfect and seven-eight-nine were ideal numbers. Anything smaller would arouse the suspicion of even the dullest patrol. Anything larger would take too long.

So much for the whippoorwill. Now for the stones. Most Christians think they are more intelligent than Wilden because they can read and write. Sometimes I think it is the other way around. Because we have been taught to write, we are unable to read anything that is not written.

I remember one day we had been running when Little Deer suddenly darted off the trail after some invisible tracks, then pointed with great interest at the forest floor. I could see nothing but a few scuffed up leaves and a bit of blood. He explained that his cousin and a friend had just killed a mountain lion, and the friend had been bitten in the leg. We hurried up to Shorakapkok in time to watch the cousin skin the beast while a squaw tended the wounded friend. How much was guesswork and how much had Little Deer read from those leaves?

Another time we were out in the swamp, in the flat-bottomed weyshute, gathering salt grass for the cattle. Moose Foot passed by on his way to Shorakapkok to consult Old Nehooma about something. He told us to meet him afterwards at the Wading Place.

By the time we had paddled the weyshute back to Vredendale, we were a half hour behind Moose Foot on the trail. At the branch path which leads to Uncle Isaack's dock, Little Deer stopped abruptly and pointed to a broken twig. He said Moose Foot had turned off to catch a fish as a gift for Old Nehooma and we were to wait there. At the time I did not question this, particularly as Moose Foot arrived shortly with a good-sized bass hanging from a stick. It was only later that I wondered how a bent twig, two inches long, could mean so much.

Little Deer knew that I had difficulty even noticing a twig, let alone reading it. Besides, nothing much grew on the rocky summit except for one scrubby pine springing from a crevice. I went back to examine this, and there before my eyes, was a recently broken branch that I had missed.

I compared the color of the live wood with the broken twig dangling from its strip of bark. Moose Foot would have known the exact hour that it had been damaged. My guess was yesterday. I snapped a branch myself, and returned to the problem of the stones.

Sitting on the ledge, I stared at the mighty Mohicanituck as I pondered. Along the far shore are high cliffs which the Wilden call weehawken because they resemble huge palisades. The day Moose Foot launched his dugout, we crossed the Mohicanituck and glided along in the shadow of these towering cliffs. Moose Foot said the Great Spirit placed the giant weehawken there to make men aware of their own insignificance. Once he told us the same thing about the dangerous rocks in Hell Gate and I asked why the Great Spirit would repeat the same message.

"Men no listen first time," he said.

Then the meaning of the stones came to me. Little Deer had broken the branch to let me know he had been here and when. Fearing that I might not listen to this first message he had spelled out the same thing in capital letters on the ledge. The round flat stone stood for the full moon. The three small egg-shaped ones stood for days. Today was the fourth day after the full moon which meant Little Deer had been here yesterday. I added one stone and went home for breakfast.

Because of the war we were late with the planting this year. We were also shorthanded. Even Mother and the girls pitched in. In town there were so many women helping that the fields looked like flower-beds of colored petticoats.

Council meetings were suspended and Papa worked side by side with the men. Needless to say I was in the fields from dawn till dusk. I kept an eye out for Little Deer, but there were always soldiers posted nearby and no Wilden appeared.

The next morning I climbed Slangberg again, certain this time that Little Deer would be waiting. Our friendship was the most important thing in my life. Could it survive so much bloodshed? It was as though unseen forces over which we had no control were forcing us apart.

Again this morning the summit was bare, but a third twig had been broken on the scrubby pine, and five egg-shaped stones rested on the ledge. Someone had been here today, though it was barely dawn and I had passed no one on the way up. The only explanation was that someone was on the summit with me. I turned around.

Twenty paces away stood Little Deer. He was taller and straighter than I remembered. For one perilous moment a gulf yawned between us, a gaping chasm twenty paces wide and five thousand years deep. Then we stepped across the gulf and it vanished in the morning sun.

Nightmare

Our last month at Vredendale started well. After my reunion with Little Deer, he came back to the house and Mother insisted that he join us for breakfast. Everything was just like old times except that Little Deer, who never used to say a word in Dutch, now answered all questions competently if briefly. And Little Rachel, who used to chatter like a magpie, had suddenly turned into a shy young lady waiting on table with downcast eyes.

Word of the visit spread fast and the next day Moose Foot arrived with Kumtassa, who now called himself Kumtassa-One-Wing. He proudly showed us his stump and Papa inspected the results of Mother's surgery with astonishment.

"My dear, this is as clean as a whistle," he said. "The finest doctor in Europe could not have done better."

Mother beamed.

Moose Foot brought up the subject of the treaty settlement. He said that if Kieft had been sufficiently generous, no Weckquasgeek would ever again speak of the massacre. As it was, even the smallest papoose on the board would remember for the rest of his life. He particularly warned us not to wander in the woods alone. Weckquasgeeks would never harm anyone from Vredendale, but Hackensacks and Siwanoys and many others roamed these woods today. He said the younger braves hated all Swannekins, and the Sachems were having great difficulty controlling them.

That night Jesse had a nightmare and woke me up with his screaming. He dreamt that he saw Moose Foot coming toward him, carrying Mother's dead body. At breakfast he was still shaking. Mother said he had eaten too much spiced cabbage for supper last night, but Papa said Moose Foot's warning was the cause.

"Nevertheless, my dear, perhaps you should postpone your visit to Mistress Hutchinson until another day, especially as it means passing through Hell Gate."

Mother laughed. "Mon vieux, you are not superstitious about a dream! Besides, the pilot is already here. Come in, Egbert, and have some breakfast before we sail."

Egbert van Borsum with his bushy red beard, was a familiar figure on the waterways around Manhattan. "Bezorgd zich niet, Heer Doktor," he said gruffly. "I know them rocks like the back of m' hand."

As usual Papa gave in, but he insisted that Corporal Pia accompany us and that Pia, Egbert and I all carry guns.

Mother sniffed. "Jan is coming along because he speaks English. Why do I need a Dutch corporal to pay a call on an English neighbor?" But she agreed.

And so the four of us set out. I took the tiller in the creek and gave it over to Egbert when we reached Hell Gate Bay. I could have handled the yawl easily without a pilot, since we passed through Hell Gate at slack water when there is no whirlpool and no roar. But in half an hour the water would race through, crushing even the strongest hull on the jagged rocks below.

Anne Hutchinson was known throughout New Netherland long before her arrival. From a distance we had followed reports of her collision with the Boston authorities and her trial for heresy. She was well-educated, unusual for an Englishwoman. A mother of fourteen, she was also a skilled nurse and midwife, and outspoken in her efforts to improve the short, sad lives of women in Massachusetts.

The highlight of the week up there was Sunday, when everyone dressed up in black and attended two church services plus a prayer meeting. At this last, men were permitted to discuss religious doctrine. Women were not. So Anne, herself the daughter of an English minister, organized a Monday prayer meeting for women at her own home. Pretty dull if you ask me but the housewives loved it.

Puritan doctrine held that certain persons were selected at birth to go to Heaven. The rest were destined to burn in Hell. In contrast, Anne believed in a God of love and mercy. The clergy were outraged and she was tried for heresy.

Sacky's father told me that Anne defended herself eloquently and every right-thinking person was on her side, but with the clergy against her she did not stand a chance. After she was declared "a person unfit to live in Massachusetts society," Anne, her ailing husband, and most of the children, fled to Rhode Island where they were welcomed by Governor Roger Williams, himself an outcast from Massachusetts. When her husband died, Anne wrote Governor Kieft for permission to settle in the Dutch Colony. This was granted providing she took the oath of allegiance, which she did.

The Hutchinson homestead was on the north shore of Long Island Sound, about ten miles from Vredendale. It took us two hours to reach the mouth of the Aque-an-ounck on a point of land called Anne's Hook. From there it was a short sail upstream to her dock. Frenzied barking directed us to the stockade just as a small, blond girl in green gingham darted through the gate.

"Mama is tying up the dogs," she shouted in English, bouncing up and down like a chipmunk as she ran. "Everyone else is off in the fields except me 'cause I've got the pox. Look!" She pointed proudly to her splotchy face. By the time I had translated, her mother appeared and assured us in excellent French that eight-year-old Susan was no longer contagious.

Mistress Hutchinson had faded gray hair, a faded blue dress, and a beautiful face. I don't remember ever before thinking that a woman in her forties could be beautiful, but she was. Delighted to have guests, she produced refreshments for everyone including Egbert and Pia. She and Mother sat on the stoop, knitting as they gossiped, while Susan and I drank apple juice and played backgammon in the shade of a leaning willow. One black piece was missing and had been replaced by a black pawn, a detail which would one day prove significant.

Backgammon is the same as our tric-trac, so I expected to beat the girl easily, but she was surprisingly sharp as well as lucky. I was only a few points ahead when Egbert said that we had to leave to be sure of reaching Hell Gate by slack water.

All in all it was a successful visit, and Mistress Hutchinson promised to return the call soon and bring Susan with her.

"I had no idea that an Englishwoman could be so gracious," Mother told Papa when we got back. "Just the thought of having such a charming neighbor makes me happy." For the first time in months, she sang as she prepared supper.

The next day as I was working in the cornfield my mind returned to Jesse's nightmare. Indians put great stock in such things. I wondered if I should mention it to Moose Foot. At that moment, my train of thought was interrupted by the peculiar sound of a whippoorwill calling in broad daylight. I glanced at the nearest field hand, a dozen rows away with his back to me. Then I put down my hoe and walked nonchalantly into the woods, past the patrol snoozing against a stump.

I found Little Deer immediately, but neither of us spoke until we were out of earshot. When I asked why he had imitated a night bird in the middle of the day, he told me that he had tried ten other bird calls first.

"Jan has mud in ears," he said.

Then he asked if I remembered a young Siwanoy named Wampage who had entered the snow-snake competition at the Weckquasgeek winter festival a few years before.

I remembered him immediately because he was such a bad loser. Twenty-five boys had competed that year, mostly Weckquasgeeks, but there were a handful of outsiders including myself and Wampage who was a Siwanoy from the north shore not far from Anne Hutchinson's place.

The wooden snow-snake was thrown like a javelin, and each boy got two turns with only the better distance counting. The first boy remained champion until his distance was beaten. As the contestants competed in order of size with the smallest going first, the lead changed often and the winner was bound to be one of the last to throw.

My turn came early and my first attempt was far short of the previous champion. But my second throw was a beauty, gliding over the snow far beyond the others. In fact it was so good that none of the next few competitors, including Little Deer, came anywhere near it. I was still champion when it was Wampage's turn to throw. He was much older than I and would almost surely beat me.

Wampage's first shot caught a bad bounce and finished short. His second throw was good and went about the same distance as mine. After much measuring it was called an exact tie. Weckquasgeek custom was to break ties in favor of the earlier contestant, but Wampage claimed the tie should be broken by comparing our other throws, which would easily make him the new champion. An argument followed and he became quite angry when the Weckquasgkeeks insisted that I was still champion. It was a short-lived victory because the next player beat us both handily but I had no trouble recalling Wampage.

"Is he still such a poor loser?" I asked.

"Wampage talk big," said Little Deer. He told me that the Siwanoy was a warrior now, and claimed that he was going to kill an important Swannekin like the Governor, and become a Chief.

"What about the treaty?" I asked. "If you kill someone during peacetime you are a common murderer like the Crazy One. They didn't make him a Chief for killing Old Claes."

Little Deer said that no Siwanoy would give an inch of white wampum for the peace treaty. He was surprised to see Wampage this morning in the woods near Vredendale, and he warned me that the Siwanoy might be planning to kill my father.

This made some sense. Papa was the second most important person in the government. It would certainly be a lot easier to kill him than Kieft who never left the Fort.

Little Deer was on his way to join the Weckquasgeek warriors in the Land of the Tall Birch. He warned me to be careful myself. If Wampage failed to kill my father he might take a shot at me.

The idea of Wampage trying to kill me was ridiculous, but as I returned to the cornfield and picked up my hoe, I remembered Jesse's dream. Could Wampage be planning to kill my father, and kill Mother instead? Impossible! Warriors do not murder women. But that was before the massacre. Maybe everything was different now.

Mother and the girls were bleaching linen that morning. In my mind's eye I pictured dozens of snow-white napkins spread out to dry on the grassy slope by the creek. In the center lay Mother, in a pool of blood, with a Siwanoy arrow through her skull.

This gruesome vision quickly vanished at the sight of Mother approaching in the wagon with the midday meal. Pia walked on one side and Moose Foot on the other. As the men set up the long trestle-table for the food, I told Moose Foot about Wampage and also about Jesse's nightmare. He nodded but did not answer.

It was a few days later that Father broached the subject of our leaving Vredendale. A Dutchman named Bout Fransen was anxious to lease the bowery and farm it for us on shares.

"It would be pleasant to live in town for a while, my dear," he went on quickly before Mother could object. "There are a dozen empty houses since the war. We can buy any one of them today for a song."

"Mon vieux," said Mother firmly, "Vredendale is not only our home. It is the children's inheritance. What else have we to leave them? And I do not plan to entrust it to any tenant-farmer. This is the finest piece of land in the Colony and I will not be chased away by a silly dream."

"But it's so lonely for you out here, my dear. With Otterspoor in ruins and Bronck's widow leaving for Fort Orange, there isn't another woman in miles, except that impossible redhead of Isaack's, and Vrouw Kuyter, who doesn't speak anything but Danish."

Mother laughed. "Sarah is good for Isaack and I like her," she said. "And I'm not lonely. Hendrick used to say 'When you can see the smoke from your neighbor's chimney, the countryside is too crowded'. How I wish he could see this place now. No, mon vieux. We have been forced to leave Vredendale twice. Please God let me stay now forever."

And so ended all discussion of living in town, much to my relief. There was one person, however, who did not forget about Jesse's nightmare. That was Moose Foot. Since the day I first mentioned it, he had paid us a short morning visit to check on Mother. Occasionally I noticed an Indian standing on the bluff in the distance just watching the house. I was certain he was a lookout set by Moose Foot.

Wampage never appeared and I eventually discovered why. Moose Foot had sent a message to his good friend Toteneke, Sachem of the Siwanoy, warning him that the spirits foretold a fatal accident for Wampage on the island of Manhattan. No wonder the coward stayed away.

On Sundays, the whole family would sail down the East River to church. Afterwards Mother and the younger children called on Madame du Trieux or the Dominie's wife, while Jesse and I visited our own friends. Papa sometimes had a drink with Dominie Bogardus. More often he spent the time at the Fort with Kieft and Captain de Vries.

Then Papa and the Dominie had a falling out. What happened was this. After the massacre, Bogardus became more and more outspoken in his criticism of the Governor, who naturally refused to attend service.

"The man only gives two different sermons, one when he's drunk and the other when he's dead drunk."

The next Sunday troops were ordered to march outside and beat drums during the sermon. This drowned out some of the abuse but added greatly to the fun. Secretly I admired the Dominie for daring to say what he did from the pulpit, but there is no doubt that his sermons went beyond the bounds of decency. I quote from one of the worst.

"In Africa," he began, "owing to the intense heat, different animals copulate together to create various monsters. But in such a temperate climate as ours I know not how such monsters of men are produced who . . ." and as usual he went on to accuse the Governor of everything under the sun. Even in his cups, Bogardus spoke in loud resounding tones with much pounding of the fist for emphasis.

This time the Dominie was thrown into jail, making him a hero in the eyes of his congregation. With difficulty Papa was able to arrange his release but the feud between Governor and Dominie continued until its tragic end a few years later.

In the meantime Papa sided with Kieft. He tried to reason with the Dominie but they quarreled. Papa said Bogardus had let drink become his master and Bogardus said Papa had the liver of a lily and the guts of a mouse.

"The family will not be attending service this morning," announced Papa stiffly, the next Sunday.

Mother had just dressed little Will, and was getting herself ready for church. "The girls can stay home," she said, calmly. "I don't like them listening to some of the Dominie's language, anyway. And the men of the family may do as they please. But I am going to church." Unruffled, she continued to get ready.

Papa was never able to say no to Mother when she had made up her mind. So it was arranged that the field hand, Wim, would accompany her in the *Yellow Swan* and wait while she visited her friends after church.

I was on the dock as Wim prepared to cast off. Mother was sitting in the stern with baby Will on her lap. At the last minute, Little Rachel ran down to the creek and Will held up his arms to her. She reached out and grabbed him just as the yawl pulled away from the dock. On such a slender whim hung the life of a babe.

There was a strong west wind as the *Yellow Swan* moved briskly downstream. Wim was at the tiller with his back to us. Mother sat toward us, with the wind in her face, smiling and waving "au revoir" in the bright sunshine.

That was the last time I saw my mother alive.

It was mid-afternoon before we suspected anything was wrong. I had taken a letter from Papa to Heer Kuyter at Zegendale. The Dane insisted I have a drink while he wrote a brief answer. Vrouw Kuyter brought beer and koekjes and I did my best to make small talk with her in Danish. Then as I was taking my leave, Kuyter said I had missed an interesting sermon this morning. I told him Mother was at church and I would no doubt hear all about it at supper.

"Madame Montagne did not attend church this morning," he corrected me. "I looked for her, particularly." Then he went on to relate a few of the Dominie's more outrageous remarks.

On the way home I began to wonder how Heer Kuyter could have missed Mother. When I went to church the first thing I did was scan the women's section to see if Sutje was there. It was easy to spot her because she had dozens of golden curls peeking out from under her little white cap. In fact most of the men studied the women's section, some more discreetly than others, but it would be difficult to miss anyone.

At this point I decided to run the rest of the way. I had been gone two hours and the *Yellow Swan* would surely have returned by now. But the creek was empty.

Indoors everything was normal. Jesse and Papa were engrossed in a game of chess, and Little Rachel had just gotten Will up from his nap. He sat on her lap, still in his long white nightgown, looking like an angel with sleep in his eyes.

I forced myself to speak calmly.

"Where's Mother?"

Papa looked up with his usual worried frown.

"She is not very late. No doubt she is having such a pleasant visit she has forgotten the time." Then he added, more to himself than me, "I am glad Wim is with her."

"Heer Kuyter says Mother was not at church today," I said.

Father stood up. "I expect Heer Kuyter is mistaken. Nevertheless I shall take the rowboat and start for town myself. I will probably meet the yawl halfway."

"I'll row," I said.

Papa nodded and took his long gun down from the wall. I headed for the woodshed to pick up a pair of oars. At the gate I suddenly thought to look up at the bluff. As usual there was an Indian watching the house. When I took off my shirt and waved it back and forth he disappeared.

Papa and I righted the rowboat and slid it into the water as Jesse came limping down the path, his bad leg dragging behind like a wet mop.

"What should I do, Papa?" He sounded frightened but Papa did not even notice him.

"Moose Foot will be here shortly, Jess," I answered with a show of confidence. "Tell him everything, then do exactly what he says." I pushed off and began to row.

When we emerged from the creek, there was no sign of the *Yellow Swan* in Hell Gate Bay or the East River. Papa sat in the stern scanning the shoreline with his telescope. By unspoken agreement I went around the far side of Tenkenas Island. Years ago the yawl had come loose from her moorings during a storm and was eventually found, badly damaged, in a cove of Tenkenas. Today the cove was empty.

As we approached New Amsterdam, boats of various sizes came into view. Father studied every sail intently through the glass. The yawl was not on the river, nor was she riding at anchor by the Strand. A few old men were gossiping on the pier. I called out to them but none had noticed the *Yellow Swan*.

We beached the rowboat and went straight to the parsonage. When the Dominie's wife said she had not seen Mother since last Sunday, Papa's face looked as gray as yesterday's ashes.

"Did you try the du Trieux home?" asked Anneke.

He shook his head. "What we need now is a sturdy ship," he said calmly. "Jan, you check with the du Trieux, then meet me at the Fort. De Vries will lend me his yawl if it's there. If not we will take the *Vrede.*"

Hell Gate was never mentioned but we all knew what had to be done.

"You'll need a pilot," said Anneke. "I'll get Egbert." She hurried off.

There was no news at the du Trieux household. When I reached the Fort, Papa was on the ramparts scanning the harbor. De Vries's yawl was anchored some way off shore, and along the water's edge a small crowd buzzed with speculation. The buzzing died as I approached.

I remember Kieft putting his arm around my shoulder. He handed me the Company telescope. "This is the finest glass in the Colony, Son." It was the first time I ever felt kindly toward the Governor.

Then Egbert arrived and somebody rowed us out to the yawl. In addition to myself and Papa, there was Captain de Vries and the pilot and two of de Vries's men who were already on board ready to weigh anchor.

As we rounded Weepers' Point and headed up the East River, half of New Amsterdam was on the Strand to watch us set out. Most stood silently, but there was an occasional cry of "God go with you," and I was sure I heard Sutje's voice calling, "Bonne chance, Jan!"

At one point I overheard Egbert tell Captain de Vries that he had seen the *Yellow Swan* after it was damaged, years ago.

"Blikskaters! I'd a scrapped her in a minute," he said, tugging at his wild, red beard. "She'd always have a weakness in her after that bashing. But the flapdrol shipwright weren't about to turn down good money for repairs."

The Captain muttered something that I could not understand.

"Rudderhead broke, I reckon," replied Egbert.

Could that be the answer? Suppose the rudderhead had broken just as Wim was preparing to come about in Hell Gate Bay. The yawl was not carrying much sail in the creek, but with a strong wind behind her, there would be a tremendous strain on the rudder. If the rudderhead broke at that moment, there would be no way to control the yawl and the wind would carry her into Hell Gate. At slack water it would not matter, but she left this morning during ebb tide, the most dangerous. Every year there were one or two accidents, mostly by unwary fishermen, and always when the tide was racing out.

We were approaching Hell Gate Bay now, and it was decided to call in at Vredendale first, to see if there were any news. Halfway up the creek I noticed smoke coming from the chimney, which was odd as the fire is never lit on Sunday. Uncle Isaack met us at the dock. I knew from his expression that it was all over.

After Papa and I had set out in the rowboat, Jesse began to shake so badly that he had to sit down on the dock for a while. Then, to his relief, Moose Foot arrived. After hearing the full story, the Indian told him to go up to the house, light the fire, and put on the largest kettle of water. He, Moose Foot, would return by the time the water had boiled. I suspect he was just trying to give my brother something to do. In fact Jesse pulled himself together immediately and did as he was told.

The kettle was barely on the boil when Jesse saw Moose Foot coming up the path with Mother's body. It had been caught on one of the rocks in Hell Gate. Jesse said it was exactly like his nightmare.

"Her skin was gray like putty, Jan."

Moose Foot sent for Uncle Isaack and Sarah, who was now in the bed-chamber preparing the body.

"You can't go in, Papa." Little Rachel was rolling dough with tears streaming down her face. "Sarah says Marie and I have to bake."

"Open up, Sarah!" Father pounded on the door but he was no match for the stubborn redhead.

Captain de Vries left to search for Wim and the *Yellow Swan,* but no trace of either was ever found. Uncle Isaack poured himself a drink, while Papa paced back and forth. Will sat on the floor howling. Jesse limped over to the basin to vomit and I smashed my fist against the wall.

Sarah stuck her head out. "Jesse, stop that vomiting! Jan, take Will out-doors for a run, right away!"

It was better to be angry with Sarah than to think, and it was easier to obey than to argue. I hoisted the knaap onto my shoulders. As we went out Sarah was telling Papa to sit down immediately and make a list for the aanspreker. With Sarah, everything had to be done immediately. I pictured the aanspreker with long black streamers on his hat, making his rounds to invite the funeral guests.

When Will and I returned, the chaos had disappeared and Sarah was teaching the girls to bake doodkoeken.

"Take your clothes off this minute, Will," she said. "Marie is going to give you a nice hot bath. Jan, you may go see your mother now."

I clenched my fists until they hurt and walked slowly into the bedchamber. All my life people had told me how beautiful my mother was, but until that moment I never noticed it for myself. She lay on the big feather-bed, dressed in her best blue dress, her hair loose in waves on the pillow like a young girl. Somehow Sarah had brought the color back into her face. Only her little folded hands were white as porcelain.

At midnight, Tiger began to bark as a lone figure rowed up Montagne's Creek in the moonlight. Dominie Bogardus had come to watch through the night with us. He and Father embraced like brothers, all quarrels forgotten.

The next day it rained for the funeral. Uncle Isaack wanted Mother to lie next to Uncle Hendrick in the cemetery on the Heerenstraat, but Papa said she would choose to remain forever at Vredendale. The heavens wept quietly and the last tulips bowed their heads as we buried Mother in the garden she loved.

The Race

After Mother's death, Uncle Isaack and Papa tried to run Vredendale and Boomdale together as one bowery. Sarah bossed everyone around and did all the cooking with Little Rachel to help. Six-year-old Marie was forced to mind little Will. Jesse was Sarah's favorite so he got the easy chores like shelling peas. I did ten hours in the fields and when supper was over I still got the blackest pot to scour.

For weeks Papa did nothing but pace the floor. He rarely spoke or tasted his food, not that it was worth tasting. No one dared mention Mother. Moose Foot said the silver birds of sorrow were flying over Father's head and there was nothing we could do but wait until they passed. It was Sarah who finally jolted Papa out of it.

"We have a special treat today," she announced, after the remains of the hutspot were cleared away. "Little Rachel has made huckleberry cobbler." She dished some blue mush into bowls and handed them round.

Papa was sipping his wine but not eating and not listening. She put a bowl directly in front of him.

"Eat this," she said, with an edge to her voice that we all knew meant, "Eat this or else!" That is, we all knew except Papa who shook his head and pushed it away.

Uncle Isaack broke in quickly. "This is very fine cobbler, my dear," he told Little Rachel.

"Yes, very fine," agreed Jesse, always eager to make everyone happy. Little Rachel turned pink with pleasure.

"Tastes like blue mush to me," I muttered under my breath.

"What did you say, young man?" snapped Sarah.

"It tastes like blue mush," I repeated loudly, swallowing the last mouthful in a hurry. One thing I always had was a good appetite. I held out my empty bowl, adding innocently, "Please, may I have another helping?"

"Humph!" The redhead turned her back on me and warned Papa once more to eat his cobbler. Again he ignored her. This time she exploded.

"God Allemachtig!" she shouted. "The gypsy told Rachel she was going to drown. If she was meant to drown, nobody could save her, not even you,

Jehan!" For a minute I thought she was going to haul off and whack him, but she only pounded her fist on the table and went on shouting. "Maybe you can't stop the birds of sorrow from flying over your head. But you can stop them from building a nest in your brain!"

For a long time Papa stared at her coldly. Then he ate his cobbler.

The next day he made the decision to leave Vredendale. He bought a house in town by the sheep meadow, and leased the bowery out on shares to Bout Fransen. Uncle Isaack also leased Boomdale and bought a tiny house along the Fort wall.

In September Bout Franson claimed that he was threatened by savages and he got permission of the court to break the lease. Then he brought all the livestock and furniture down river by barge.

Leaving Vredendale empty was potentially very dangerous but Papa was more upset about a missing piece of paper.

"Rembrandt's sketch of your grandfather has disappeared, Son. I remember seeing the broken frame on a box in the attic beside the rolled up picture. You will have to go back for it." Then he added, "Better take a gun. The Wilden are very restless."

I set out, angry and without a gun. I was angry with Papa for leasing the bowery. I was angry with Bout for breaking the lease. I was angry with Sarah for bossing everyone around. I was angry with Kieft and Sharkface for causing the war. I think I was even angry with Mother for dying.

My mind slid back to the massacre of the Wilden and I began to run to escape the roar in my ears. Faster and faster I pushed myself until the pain in my chest was unbearable. By torturing my body I was somehow fighting the anguish in my brain.

Then it happened, just as Kumtassa always said it would. My feet were no longer pounding the ground. They were no longer even touching the ground. The roar had vanished. All pain had been replaced by a state of effortless elation. At last, like Kumtassa, I was running on the wind.

Rows of tall birches raced by me. Now it appeared that I was not actually moving at all. It was the ground that was rushing past me. Moss-covered rocks surrounded by little red berries vanished beneath my feet, but I dared not look down or even blink for fear of crashing. The wind stung my eyeballs and penetrated my skull, sweeping away the roar and with it my anger.

Not until I reached Vredendale did the elation disappear and my leg bones turn to boiled cabbage. I had to lean against the fence until they slowly hardened. Then I unlocked the gate.

Today there were no frolicking kittens to greet me, only brown sparrows busy in the garden and a little chipmunk perched on Mother's gravestone. As I approached, the birds rose like leaves in the wind, but the chipmunk stood his ground, head cocked to one side, bright eyes carefully watching. Mother would have fed him. If there was any food in the house I would bring him something.

But there was nothing in the house. Nothing but cobwebs and long shadows and empty rooms, echoing with voices from the past. The place already smelled deserted. On the hearth Mother's kettle lay on its side, black and forgotten.

"Stop filling the boy's head with that nonsense, mon vieux," whispered the chimney.

I hurried up to the loft. From the window a single shaft of dusty sunlight pointed to the broken picture frame just where it was supposed to be. But there was no picture rolled up beside it. I searched high and low, then gave up in renewed bad temper.

When I emerged from the gate a familiar canoe lay beached at the landing place and Little Deer was fishing from the dock. I did not ask how he knew I was there. Instead I found an old pole in the woodshed and joined him.

Weckquasgeeks say the Great Spirit gave man tobacco to bring him peace of mind. For me it is fishing that brings peace of mind. All morning we sat on that dock without exchanging a word.

Nearby a giant bullfrog kept one glassy eye upon us, and one upon the blue dragonflies skimming over the lily pads. Across the creek a doe with her fawn came down to drink and, high above, Old White Face circled. Gradually the years slipped away and all was right with the world.

When we had a dozen bullheads, we made a fire and roasted them whole. I had not realized how hungry I was and nothing ever tasted more delicious. We gave one to a Siwanoy runner who came by to investigate our fire. As he was leaving he told us that Wampage and a gang of young Siwanoys were on their way to burn out Anne Hutchinson.

What a coward! Wampage had failed to kill the Governor. He had failed to kill my father or an important official. Now he was trying to murder a widow living miles from civilization.

"She has grown sons," I said. "And enough dogs to scare any Siwanoy. They can hold out against Wampage and his gang."

Little Deer shook his head. "Wampage act friend. Tell tie up dogs. Then kill."

He was right. If Mistress Hutchinson tied up those dogs it would be all over. And Susan had said that her mother was always inviting Wilden in for refreshments.

I stood up. "We have to warn them."

Little Deer did not argue. In one smooth motion we launched the canoe and leapt in. It is amazing how fast a canoe will go with two paddling. We flew down the creek in seconds.

Now we were skimming across Hell Gate Bay. I could tell from the roar that it was well past slackwater. We would have to go ashore on the mainland south of Bronck's bowery. The canoe would be easy to carry but the portage would waste an hour.

Little Deer had the stern which meant he did the steering and I just pulled with all my strength. I don't know when I realized that we were not headed for the mainland. I glanced behind. It was no mistake. Little Deer intended to go through Hell Gate. I shouted and lifted my paddle pointing toward the mainland, but he just shook his head and kept going.

Now we were in the white water. With salt spray in my eyes I could see nothing, but there was no way for me to help anyhow. I stowed my paddle and held on so hard I thought my hands were welded to the gunnels. Mother's death flashed through my mind. Was I meant to die the same way? What for? Trying to warn a woman I had only met once. Little Deer had never even seen her. He was risking this for me.

Moose Foot once told me that he had been through Hell Gate at ebb tide and knew every stone by heart. God Almighty! The noise was like thunder. Rocks rose from nowhere, then disappeared in an instant as we sped along blindly at a ninety-degree angle.

At last we shot out into open water, drenched but safe. God be praised! I took a deep breath and retrieved my paddle. Little Deer never missed a stroke.

Soon we were racing along the north shore. Ahead rose two columns of smoke. There were three families living on the north shore of Long Island Sound, all recently arrived from New England: the Cornells, the Throckmortons and, most remote, Mistress Hutchinson. The smoke had to be from the Cornell and Throckmorton stockades and it was not the thin, disciplined curl of smoke from a chimney. Flames appeared. Was this the handiwork of Wampage and his gang? With the roar of Hell Gate receding in the distance, I could hear horses screaming as we flew past Cornell's place.

Little Deer pointed toward the south shore where a ship was heading our way. Thank God someone had seen the smoke. Now we were approaching the neck of land belonging to Throckmorton. Beneath the smoke, flames burst from the stockade as insane war whoops drowned out the screaming livestock. On the beach a handful of Christians were making a last stand against the howling Indians. A blast from the ship's gun gave them courage.

The Cornell and Throckmorton families were temporarily staying in town. We could do nothing to help these men on the beach. If they could hold out for another half hour they would be rescued by the ship.

On we sped around Throckmorton's Neck, keeping a good distance from shore. Now we could see Anne's Hook. The mouth of the Aque-an-ounck is this side of the Hook and I searched the horizon as we skimmed along. There was no sign of smoke. Were we in time? The ship would surely follow us after rescuing the men on the beach. It would take her an hour to cover what we did in fifteen minutes.

Something about Anne Hutchinson reminded me of Mother. Maybe it was the light in her eyes. My arms ached as I tried not to miss a stroke. They should not ache. I was used to swinging an axe or a scythe all day. Little Deer was tireless.

As we neared the Aque-an-ounck we heard a shot and redoubled our efforts. Now we were in the river and I knew it was too late. Human screams rose above wild barking and gunfire.

We beached the canoe well below the Hutchinson landing place. Little Deer led the way cautiously inland to a giant rock not far from the homestead. By now the gunfire had ceased. Barking and screaming had given way to bloodcurdling war whoops. We lay on our stomachs on top of the rock and peered down at a frightful sight. Painted warriors, carrying torches and emitting earsplitting shrieks, ran madly about setting fire to everything.

In the open gateway lay the scalped bodies of two women. Inside, still straining at his chain, was a bull mastiff with so many arrows through his body that he looked like some monstrous porcupine.

There was nothing we could do now except try to save our own skins. I signaled to Little Deer that it was time to go but he shook his head and pointed to the bushes directly below us.

At first I could see nothing. Then it wriggled, a tiny thing in a blue dress some twenty feet below me. Nearby was an upside-down berry-basket. It was too small to be Susan. It must be the younger sister. Then a few yards to the left, I saw Susan, in her green gingham, huddled head down under a bush.

Holy God! Was everyone murdered except these two little girls? If they could only stay hidden until the Siwanoy left.

Just then little Blue Dress poked her blond curls above the bushes. Instantly a Siwanoy grabbed her by the hair and sliced off the head all in one motion. I steeled myself not to move a muscle until he returned to his insane war-dance. Little Deer grimly fingered his knife. I wished I had brought my gun.

Soon the murderer returned to search the bushes for more stragglers. At the same time Susan, who had seen nothing, was cautiously raising her head to look for her sister.

"Stay down, Susan!" I cried.

The Siwanoy looked up immediately. I know he saw me. In a flash Little Deer hurled the knife. One minute the Siwanoy had his mouth open to call out. The next minute he was dead, without a sound, and a knife in his throat.

By now the whole stockade was a roaring bonfire and the heat was appalling, even up here. Naked bodies glistened in the flames as the warriors grew wilder. Were they drunk with whiskey or with blood?

The wind shifted and we were temporarily protected from view by a cloud of smoke. I leaned far out over the edge. Susan was still down there with her head buried deeper than ever.

"Do not move, Susan!" I called in English. The Siwanoys were making such a racket they could not possibly hear me. "I will come for you when it is safe. Stay exactly where you are."

Could the child hear me? She was as still as death. Was it possible to die from terror? Her green dress was almost the color of the bush. If it were not for an inch of white petticoat I would hardly be able to find her.

"Susan," I called. "Try to pull your dress so the petticoat does not show."

For a long time she did not move. Then a tiny hand reached back to tug at the green skirt. The patch of white disappeared.

Once more the wind shifted and our smoke cover was gone. We crouched motionless. I remembered how clever Susan had been at trictrac. Could she keep her wits now? Surely the ship must be here soon. If only I had a weapon. I slid my hand along the surface until my fingers closed on a jagged piece of loose rock. Better than nothing.

At last the frenzied war dance came to an end. For the first time I recognized Wampage as he led the Siwanoys away from the fire through the bushes below us.

They found the dead warrior first. Wampage himself lifted the body, almost stepping on Susan as he passed within a few feet of what looked more like a green stone beneath the bush than a child. Half a dozen Siwanoys followed him and Susan never breathed. Now there was only one left, the rear guard.

He spotted her immediately. As he leaned down, my fingers tightened on the makeshift weapon. At the same time Little Deer gripped my wrist in a vise of iron. He was right. If either of us moved we were both dead.

To my surprise, the warrior picked the child up gently. Was she dead or asleep? I could not tell. He ran off after the others with Susan in his arms.

I sat up. "We must follow them."

Little Deer shook his head. "Siwanoy no more crazy. No hurt child." He said two of the warriors were Weckquasgeeks. Through them he would be able to contact Susan, but not today. Then he jumped down and retrieved his knife from the bushes.

We found the canoe and headed home. Our race to warn Mistress Hutchinson had been useless, the mad dash through Hell Gate in vain. No, not in vain. If Susan survived, it would not be in vain.

At the mouth of the Aque-an-ounck we met the ship which belonged to a colonist named Opdike. He had saved the field hands at Throckmorton's Neck. No one was alive at Cornell's place. After listening to my report, Opdike continued up-river to check for possible survivors at the Hutchinson home. There were none.

Tomorrow I would find a way to rescue little Susan Hutchinson.

The Year of the Blood

But there was no tomorrow. The Siwanoy raid was the spark that set tribe after tribe back on the warpath. April's treaty was brushed aside like so many cobwebs. Once again the countryside exploded, this time into a bloody war that was to last two years.

Our house by the sheep-meadow was much too exposed. Uncle Isaack and Sarah had a home along the Fort wall and took in the younger children. Papa and Jesse shared a bed at the Governor's mansion, leaving me to sleep on the floor at the du Trieux house.

The previous spring Papa had said that I was too young to bear arms. If Mother were still alive he would have said the same now. As it was he made no objection when I joined the civilian militia. I was thirteen years old.

During the day the regular soldiers put on a good show, parading the ramparts in full uniform and patrolling the town limits. We civilians were employed patching up the Fort walls that would not keep a pig out. Mostly we did guard duty after dark.

My memory of the next two years is like one long confused night. Individual scenes flash out bright as orange flames against a black sky. I remember the day Ensign Van Dyck led the first expedition up the Weckquasgeek Trail to Zegendale. He asked me to go along as guide. The soldiers made more noise than a herd of buffalo, so every Indian from here to Shorakapkok knew we were coming. Still none molested us.

After we passed the blackened ruins at Dam's place and Old Claes's cottage, I steeled myself for the prospect of Vredendale. Deep down inside of me there was still a little soft spot that prayed for a miracle. I should not have prayed. Only the brick chimney stood tall amid charred rubble. The men stared at me out of curiosity, or maybe pity. I never changed my expression and the soft spot disappeared.

We continued north past Slangberg and the ruins of Boomdale. Across on the mainland were the remains of Bronck's beautiful Emaus. The only bowery still intact on Manhattan, except for a few at the southern end, was Kuyter's Zegendale. The Dane and his family were at the Fort, but he had some two dozen men here. So far they had not been attacked. Van Dyck delivered a letter to the sergeant in charge and we returned to the Fort without so much as a glimpse of an Indian.

The worst part of night patrol duty was trying not to let your mind wander. My friend, Corporal Pia, said it was a sure way to go mad.

"Fix yer wits on one thing, boy. Don't pay no heed to nothing else."

Pia had just lost his wife in childbirth and the baby lived only a few hours. I did not ask what he concentrated on but he told me anyway.

"You know what I think about, boy? I think about how much I hate them Indians, and how good it's gonna to feel to tear their guts out."

I could never hate Weckquasgeeks. Every time I imagined myself in battle, it was Little Deer I was shooting. For months I held on to my sanity by clinging to one idea. I was determined to rescue eight-year-old Susan Hutchinson from the Siwanoy.

The Long Island tribes had not yet gone on the warpath. Using Canarsies as intermediaries, an effort had already been made to ransom Susan. It failed. On Kieft's behalf, Papa wrote to Boston with details of the massacre. Deputy Governor Winthrop responded that Mistress Hutchinson's death was the judgment of God upon this misguided woman. Nevertheless, her relatives were most anxious to have little Susan returned, and they guaranteed the ransom money. Another attempt was made, again through Canarsies. Word came back that Susan was alive, but not to be traded for any amount.

Still she was alive. That was the important thing. If she could not be ransomed she must be rescued, and I spent my hours on the watch working on a plan. Late at night as I climbed over snoring bodies on the du Trieux floor, looking for a spot to lay my head, my last thought was of that frightened little girl, sleeping on the bare ground at the camp of the Siwanoy.

Why should Wampage want to keep an eight-year-old child? If it killed me I would rescue the little girl in the green gingham. The next day I spoke with de Vries about my plan.

"Forget it, Son. It's 20 miles to the camp of the Siwanoy. You'll be dead before you get 20 yards. And don't expect your Weckquasgeek friends to spare you. Oh, they might if they recognized you. Today Wilden shoot first, recognize later."

It is hard to imagine that anything funny could occur in the midst of all this horror. Yet in my entire life I never laughed harder than I did that September morning. Ensign Van Dyck first spotted what seemed to be war canoes and sounded the alarm. Women with babies and screaming kinderen crowded into the Fort. Every able-bodied man ran for his station. No one knew exactly what was coming down the East River beneath the rising mist, but there were no Christian boats up there and something was certainly moving. I loaded my gun.

"Hold your fire, men, until I give the order." Father was in command of the army but his voice was that of a stranger.

For days we had been expecting an all-out attack. There were thousands upon thousands of Indians out there, easily able to overrun the Fort. With luck, we could drive off the first wave. Out of the corner of my eye, I could see Jan Dam trying to button his pants with one hand and balance his gun with the other. There was a knot in the pit of my stomach. This was it.

Then, out of the mist, sailed an old herring boat with a crazy Dutchman madly waving his cap and shouting,

"Madeira for sale!"

Every gun in town was trained, not on a fleet of Indian war canoes, but on a hundred barrels of Madeira. Mouths fell open. Then New Amsterdam collapsed with laughter. Jan Dam roared so loud his pants fell off.

The crazy Dutchman turned out to be a fellow named Jacob Blenck from Rotterdam. He had bought a hundred barrels of Madeira in the Canary Islands and decided to make his fortune by sailing across the Atlantic and selling it to thirsty Virginians.

Being a fisherman, not a navigator, he missed Virginia and landed in Boston, clearly the wrong market. Nothing daunted, he headed down the coast for Manhattan. With no charts to guide him, he naturally came into Long Island Sound instead of the harbor. The herring boat, appropriately named the *Fortune,* reached Hell Gate at slack water and Blenck sailed through, unaware of the dangerous tide, and knowing nothing about any Indian war. His luck held. Wilden never fired a shot as he sailed down the East River to his most unusual welcome.

After the astonished Blenck and his ragged crew were suitably wined and dined, and New Amsterdam had finally stopped laughing, it was time to bid on the Madeira. You might think that it did not matter too much what you paid for Madeira today when you were likely to be scalped tomorrow. Not so. A Dutchman looks for a bargain with his dying breath and Blenck eventually sold to Isaac Allerton, the Englishman. Sharkface reminded Blenck that he had to pay duty on the Madeira before sailing and so matters stood for one week.

On October 8th, I was not due on the ramparts until midnight. Black clouds covered moon and stars, but I knew every shadow on the water by heart. It was I who reported the *Fortune* missing. Somehow she had slipped out into the harbor, under the very nose of the patrol, meeting up with Allerton's bark near Staten Island. The Company yacht filled with soldiers arrived too late to stop the exchange, not too late, however, to seize the *Fortune*, haul her up before the Fort and charge Jacob Blenck with smuggling.

Sometime later, de Vries joined me on the Fort wall. Together we stared at the dark water.

"You must have the eyes of a cat, Son," he said. "I can't distinguish a thing out there." Then he added, "Kieft should have removed the *Fortune*'s rudder."

"She'd never make the Narrows in the dark without a pilot," I said.

He nodded. "Nevertheless I am going out there. If you see a rowboat, don't sound the alarm, lad. It's only me." He shook my hand. "If you were my son, Jan, . . ."

He did not finish. I heard him climb down the steep path to the Hudson and a few minutes later a small black shadow crept silently over the water.

In the morning the *Fortune* was gone and Captain de Vries with her. He left a letter for Papa.

> . . . God knows I am not afraid to die, my friend. I have given my heart and soul to this country. Three times I have been burned to the ground through the stupidity of the Company and her employees. Three times my life has been spared. Now I am leaving the New World forever . . .
>
> You must get out also, before it is too late. Ah! I know what you will answer. You are second in command here, after the Governor, and it is your duty to remain until the end. You are a good man, Jehan. However, it is not my duty to remain until I am finally scalped . . .
>
> I have arranged to pilot the Fortune this night through the Narrows and around Sandy Hook in exchange for my passage to Virginia. From there I shall return to Europe and my paternal home at Hoorne.
>
> God's blessing upon you and your children,
>
> David Pieterse de Vries
>
> Postscript. Kieft should have removed the rudder!

The loss of de Vries was a bitter blow. Everyone knew that he had single-handedly extricated us from the last war. I never heard any call him coward for leaving. The question was, who would save us this time?

As for Jacob Blenck of the *Fortune*, the court sentenced him, in absentia, to pay 300 guilders for smuggling. They never collected.

Deep gloom settled over New Amsterdam. A ten-page petition for help was sent, not to the Company, but to the States General of the Netherlands.

> ... *We wretched people must skulk with our wives and little ones that still survive in poverty together, in and around the Fort, where we are not safe for an hour, whilst savages daily threaten to overwhelm us. Little can be planted, so those of us who may yet save our lives must perish next year of hunger and sorrow ...*

I was never so foolish as to think that I could rescue Susan Hutchinson by myself. Nor would Dutch soldiers be any use. To have a chance I needed Weckquasgeek help, and the first step was to contact Little Deer. For this I worked out a plan which I was forced to keep secret. I trusted Little Deer, but nobody else would.

Once a week Kuyter continued to send a squad of men up to Zegendale. Sometimes he went himself. More often Ensign Van Dyck led the men. So far the Wilden had not interfered with this weekly exchange between outposts, but Van Dyck considered it prudent never to travel on the same day twice. Thus if one week's expedition was on Wednesday, the next would either be Thursday or Tuesday, never Wednesday. A silly precaution in my opinion, as a seven-day week means nothing to an Indian. Still Van Dyck felt he reduced the chance of ambush by not making up his mind until the last minute.

For my plan to work, I needed to know the exact day a week ahead. I solved this by waiting for Van Dyck to choose a Monday. Except for emergencies the men consider Sunday a day of rest. So next week was bound to be Tuesday.

Corporal Pia was a regular member of Van Dyck's squad. His knee had been giving him trouble lately, and he was only too pleased when I offered to take his place. Kuyter led the men this Monday. He was easier to talk to than Van Dyck. As we approached Slangberg I mentioned the view from the summit and how advantageous it would be to check on the number of Weckquasgeek camps in the area.

"Too dangerous, boy. Can't take a chance on ambush to say nothing of snakebite."

When I volunteered to go myself he reconsidered. He agreed that the men would cover me from the foot while I climbed. I took off quickly before he changed his mind. Twenty minutes, I told him. There was no time to spare.

The woods had eyes, Weckquasgeek eyes. I could feel them on my back. Did they recognize me? I hoped so. Even if they did not, word would spread that a Swannekin had climbed Slangberg. Little Deer would know it was me.

Once on the rocky slope I was out of firing range. Now I was relatively safe unless there were Wilden on the mountain itself, which I doubted. As I approached the top I called out a greeting in Algonkian. No answer. The summit was deserted and I scanned the countryside for signs of life.

On the creek were six wigwams, one only half-built, and all abandoned. Far to the north, columns of smoke marked the campfires of Shorakapkok. On the bluff to the south I thought I caught a glimpse of a scout. Captain de Vries used to say, "When you see an Indian scout, it's because he wants to be seen." There was no trace of any warriors.

I deliberately broke three twigs from the scraggly pine for sharp Weckquasgeek eyes to puzzle over. This was camouflage. Little Deer knew I was inept with branches and would ignore them and go straight for the ledge. Here it was easy enough to leave word that I would return in eight days. I used small pebbles, so casually arranged as to look meaningless to any one else.

Kuyter was concerned with my report of wigwams on the creek. I told him I would check again next week. "If the unfinished wigwam is still untouched," I said, "you can rest assured the camp is abandoned."

The Dane had a considerable amount of business to attend to at Zegendale and it was dusk before we returned. I could feel the eyes following us again, but we reached the Fort without incident. Now I had to go on duty without any supper.

Winter nights are no joke, particularly on the west wall with the wind coming in off the water. I tried to forget about my empty stomach and concentrate on the plan for next week. Would Little Deer be waiting for me? Would he agree to help? Just when I could think of nothing but hunger pains, there was a rustle in the bushes below.

"Psst, Jan! I brought you something."

Sutje's golden curls bounced in the moonlight as she climbed halfway up the wall to hand me a slab of bread and cheese.

"I'll keep the hutspot warm for you," she whispered.

Then she was gone before I could even thank her, which may have been just as well. Sentries were under strict orders not to "dally." It was also forbidden to eat on duty. I wolfed the food down quickly and went on pacing and scanning the river. Nothing moved but clouds across the face of the moon. I estimated another hundred lengths before my late-night hutspot.

When I eventually came off duty, the du Trieux house was dark, and a chorus of uneven snores greeted me. At first I thought Sutje had forgotten. Then in the faint glow from the embers I saw her squatting on the low cooking bench inside the fireplace. An over-sized body, wrapped in a striped blanket, blocked the hearth, and a dozen more lay in less advantageous spots. I stepped gingerly over sleeping obstacles and crouched down to join her. There was no fire, just a few live coals under the back bar where the hutspot kettle hung.

"I kept it hot for you, Jan," she whispered, dishing out a bowlful of the delicious smelling mixture.

To prolong the pleasure I forced myself to eat slowly. Sitting with Sutje reminded me of school days, years ago, when we sat on the same bench and I used to help her with her numbers. Sutje was never bossy like Sarah. How odd that two sisters could be so opposite in disposition.

Then Striped Blanket let out a booming snort and turned over. I recognized Evert Wendell, from the militia, who was always hanging around Sutje. For a brief moment the general snoring subsided as other blankets readjusted themselves. Soon the rumble swelled again until the chimney was a small cozy nook, surrounded by blackness and raucous breathing. The louder the snores, the more Sutje and I seemed to be alone.

"Why did you volunteer for Zegendale today?" she whispered. "Is it to do with that poor little English girl?" Her face was invisible but one curl twinkled in response to the dying embers.

"Will you swear not to breathe a word, Sutje?"

"I swear." She squeezed my hand.

I told her about the day's expedition and my plan to contact Little Deer. "Next Tuesday when we reach Slangberg, I will hand Kuyter a sealed envelope and joke about it's being my last will and testament, to be opened only if I am not back in twenty minutes. In case Little Deer is not on the mountain I will reclaim the envelope and no harm done. But if I don't return,

Kuyter will read my instructions telling him to proceed without me, and to notify Papa and the night watch that I will be coming down the East River with Susan Hutchinson about midnight."

"Blessed Jesus!" she whispered. "They'll kill you before you get off the mountain!"

"Be patient, Sutje!" I had spent many hours constructing this plan and did not like my masterpiece interrupted in mid-air, so to speak. "I will have a knapsack containing whisky and Indian clothes, also blacking, scissors and bear grease for my hair. After dusk I will look and smell just like a Weckquasgeek."

"What's the whiskey for?"

"You'll see in a minute. Now, just before slack water, Little Deer will bring his canoe to Isaack's dock."

"How do you get to the dock from Slangberg without being scalped? Sarah says Wilden are always lurking about that fishing path."

"Sutje, I know every inch of those woods like the back of my hand. I won't go near the path. Once on the river we will be safe enough. We pass through Hell Gate at slack water and no one can touch a canoe flying across Long Island Sound. Then on Throckmorton's Neck we beach her and walk north to the camp of the Siwanoy. Little Deer knows the way."

"You've forgotten the dogs," she whispered.

"No I haven't. Long before they bark we pour whisky over ourselves. Then Little Deer shouts. He knows half the Siwanoy by name anyway. At the last minute he throws me over his shoulder as though I were dead drunk and staggers into camp. Once there he dumps me in a dark corner, face away from the fire, and proceeds to share the rest of the whisky with his friends. By the time it runs out he will have discovered the whereabouts of Susan. Then when everyone is asleep I pick up the child, speaking to her in English so she won't be frightened, and we make our escape through a sea of snoring Siwanoy."

It was a well-thought-out plan, if I do say so myself, but I waited in vain for any praise from Sutje.

"Please don't go, Jan." She squeezed my hand again. "I can't bear for you to be killed. Why not let Little Deer go alone? He could travel by day which would be much safer."

"Little Deer has no chance alone," I said patiently. "The child doesn't speak Dutch. Why would she trust a strange Weckquasgeek who doesn't know a word of English?"

"Then give him a token to carry, something that belongs to you."

"Sutje, I only met Susan once for a few hours. We played tric-trac and drank cider." The effort to whisper was making me hoarse.

"So give him a tric-trac piece."

Holy Jehoshaphat! There had been a piece missing from the Hutchinson tric-trac set and Susan and I joked about having to use a black pawn. A black pawn would make a perfect token! At least it was worth a try. If it failed, nothing was lost and my plan could follow.

Sutje said there were chess pieces set up on a table in Kieft's office. "I'll steal a black pawn for you in the morning," she whispered. "Now you must get some sleep."

She covered the embers, gave me a quick kiss on the cheek and vanished in the dark. When I heard the chamber door close softly, I found a blanket and curled up on a patch of floor as far away from Striped Blanket as possible.

The next day, armed with nothing but a feather duster, Sutje managed to pluck a black pawn from under the nose of the Governor himself, her quick little fingers rearranging the other seven so cleverly that it was days before the theft was discovered. By that time the token was well on its way to its destination.

On Tuesday, Little Deer was waiting for me on top of Slangberg. I never had any doubt that he would agree to help. When you ask a Christian for a favor he can offer a hundred different excuses. With Wilden it is a point of honor to help a friend without question and regardless of danger.

In addition to the black pawn, I had brought a letter for Susan, written in simple English by Sacky. It referred to Little Deer only as "Jan's friend," one of several phrases that I insisted he memorize carefully.

"Don't forget the white flag," I said, handing him a handkerchief. If Little Deer succeeded, he would bring Susan to Zegendale. Regardless of outcome, we agreed to meet on Slangberg next Wednesday.

Alas, the best-laid plans misfire in an Indian War. That Friday, Zegendale burned to the ground, surrounded by screaming warriors. It was a miracle that Kuyter's men made it safely to the Fort. None had seen any sign of a young Weckquasgeek with a white flag or a little girl in green gingham.

There was nothing to be done until Wednesday, when I would persuade Papa to send a posse up to Slangberg so I could keep my rendezvous. Would Little Deer bring Susan with him? Was she even now safe at Shorakapkok or perhaps Nipnichen? Surely that was better than being a slave of Wampage at the camp of the Siwanoy.

The next day a heavy fog rolled in over the harbor. By the time I came on duty at night, the world was covered by a blanket of ink so thick you could not see your own lantern at arm's length. I had to feel my way along the wall with my feet.

With Zegendale in ruins, we expected an attack on the Fort any minute, so the guard had been doubled. Pia and I were on patrol together. My job was to watch for anything moving on the water, but if a thousand war canoes were on our very doorstep no one could see them tonight. I decided to concentrate on listening, but all sounds were half smothered by fog, and those that did get through seemed to shift direction for no apparent reason. Pia was behind me, yet I could hear him cursing off to the left.

As I approached the west bastion, I braced myself. There was an owl in the abandoned windmill that made a terrible screech when anyone mounted this bastion at night. Sometimes he caught me off guard and I almost jumped out of my skin. This was not a good night for jumping.

But brace as I would the owl never screeched. Could someone have scared him away? Suppose Indians were hiding in the mill only yards from the Fort. Impossible! There were soldiers with dogs patrolling the cattle barrier, now no longer just branches, but whole tree trunks stretching in a line from river to river. No Wilden could pass the cattle barrier without alarming the dogs.

But they could beach a canoe at the foot of the steep path leading up to the mill. I began to imagine that I smelled bear grease. Poppycock! Wilden would never choose a night like this to attack. I strained my ears for signals, normally the sound of ground birds or even crickets. Then I heard it. Through the thick blanket of fog came three faint notes—the call of the whippoorwill!

There are no whippoorwills this late in the season, so Wilden would never use such a signal among themselves. It had to be Little Deer. Silently I climbed down the wall and stood stock still, waiting. Again the quiet whistle, this time from the direction of the mill.

As I explained to Sutje later, I felt no fear. It was Little Deer who was in mortal danger. The fate of the few prisoners captured by the Dutch was not pretty.

The next signal seemed to come from the river below. I made my way cautiously down the steep bank, through black fog laced with the fishy smell of low tide. Now I was below the high water mark and could feel patches of slime on the rocks.

Little Deer's low, disembodied voice startled me. "Susan no come," he said.

Invisible waves slapped against black rocks beneath our feet as we greeted each other and he told me about his visit to the Siwanoy. He had no difficulty locating the little blond child who was part of a group removing field stones under the watchful eye of a middle-aged squaw. Wampage was nowhere to be seen, but a handful of young braves were helping to dislodge the bigger rocks, at the same time joking with the older girls.

Little Deer decided to tackle a stone near Susan, who was working alone at some distance from the others. His plan was to arrange a rendezvous at a later date at which time it would appear that she had simply wandered off into the woods.

No one objected to his speaking with the child and he was pleased to find that she understood simple Algonkian. To his surprise, however, she did not recognize any of the English words he had memorized. She also insisted that she had never heard of anyone named Jan.

In some way he was able to pass her my letter which she turned over and over in a bewildered manner before handing it back.

"Susan no read. No speak English," he said.

After six months in the wilderness, Susan might well have forgotten how to read. Perhaps she never knew. I was certain that she had not forgotten how to speak English, but I knew better than to contradict him.

"Did she recognize the black pawn?" I whispered.

He said that she had no idea of its purpose but was pleased by the neatly carved toy, and actually smiled when he said she could keep it. Finally, in desperation, he asked Susan if she remembered her mother. Far from being distressed by the question, she simply pointed to the middle-aged squaw. Apparently she thought this was her mother.

"Susan no remember bad. She belong with Siwanoy," he said firmly.

At first I was irritated. Then I realized that he was right. For six months I had been wasting my time trying to return Susan to some distant relatives in Boston whom she had never laid eyes on. Wilden are much kinder to children than Christians, to say nothing of holier than thou Puritans from New England. Susan was not a slave of Wampage. She was just a child with a Siwanoy mother. I would make no more plans to rescue the little girl in green gingham.

At that moment Pia began to shout. "Godverdoemme, boy! Where's you at?"

I grasped Little Deer's hand. "Goodbye," I whispered.

"Good hunting, my friend," he replied.

They were the last words we would ever exchange.

As I scrambled up the rocky bank I heard the swoosh of a canoe being launched behind me.

"Only the call of nature, Pia," I shouted, mounting the ramparts in record time.

"Next time piss off the wall, Domkop!"

The Long Ring
of Silence

During the early campaigns, Papa saw to it that I remained behind on guard duty. The first was against a Raritan camp on Staten Island. When the army got there, the Wilden had vanished. One very old Indian was captured and agreed to lead our army to Weckquasgeek strongholds in the Land of the Tall Birch. This time they found three stockades, amazingly well-built, but all deserted.

"Thirty Weckquasgeeks at any one of 'em coulda held off our whole bloody army," reported Corporal Pia.

By now even Penhawitz and his Canarsies had turned against us. Our men went on an expedition to Cow Bay on Long Island, near the new settlement of Hempstead. This time they took the Wilden by surprise, killing 120 at the cost of only one Christian. They also captured four Canarsies, two of whom drowned while being towed home with ropes about the neck.

From the Fort wall I watched the troops celebrate their first victory around a huge bonfire on the Marketfield. They butchered the two remaining prisoners. One died doing his dance of death as bloodthirsty swords gradually hacked him to bits. When the head rolled on the ground, Madame Vinje kicked it around like a football, while Kieft stood there gleefully massaging his elbow.

Loockermans sliced off the testicles of the other prisoner and stuffed them into the brave's mouth. I clenched my fists till they hurt and tried to remain hard as a rock inside. To think was to go mad. I told myself that every dead Canarsie must bring us that much closer to the end of this nightmare.

Then the door to Isaack's house swung open. As God is my witness, the bossy redhead leaped from the stoop, petticoats flying, and raced into the crowd waving her broom. Before anyone could stop her she whacked Loockermans over the head until he fell to the ground. For some reason this brought Kieft to his senses and he ordered the bodies removed, but the revelry continued far into the night.

A few days later word came that hundreds of Wappingers were celebrating a festival near Greenwich. This time I was one of 130 men selected to set out in three ships. Pia and I were in the lead ship, under command of Captain Underhill. He was an experienced professional soldier who had served well in New England, but had left after some trouble with the Puritan clergy. (He was convicted of "mental adultery.")

We sailed through Hell Gate at slack water, around Throckmorton's Neck, past Ann Hutchinson's River, finally making land at Greenwich during a heavy snow. In the morning we proceeded on foot over stony ground, fording two streams, and climbing sometimes on hands and knees over ice-covered hills.

It was ten o'clock at night by the time we surrounded the Indian village, but the full moon against the snow gave as much light as many a winter's day. Taken by surprise, wave after wave of warriors rushed out to defend the camp, and were cut down to a man by our swords and muskets. Then Underhill ordered the whole place set to the torch. When escape proved impossible, the survivors returned to their long houses, preferring death by flames to the sword.

Now the heat forced us to pull back into a wider circle. We listened for screams of the dying but there were no screams, nothing but the sound of the fire. In awe we realized that hundreds of men, women and children were perishing within, without uttering a single cry. Even in death, the Wilden defied their enemy with a valor none could match. The ring of silence must haunt us all unto eternity.

Ice-covered fields shone red from the fire, and a hundred bodies strewn on the ground seemed to waver like flames. I thought I recognized one, but on closer inspection I could not be sure. Then another looked familiar, and another. For the first time I began to suspect that there were Weckquasgeeks here, not just Wappingers.

Slowly I picked my way across flame-colored ice, nearer and nearer to the blazing camp. My face was on fire and the roaring was in my ears so I could not hear Pia shouting at me. Sometimes I think I was born with the roar of Hell Gate locked inside my brain, ever threatening to drive me insane.

Then one last brave burst forth from the flames, clothes burning like wings of fire. His knife flashed as he raced toward me. I raised my gun. The thunder in my ears reached a crescendo and I knew that this was how life was meant to end. The face, blazing with hatred, was the face of a stranger, but I was sure that it was Little Deer. I lowered the gun. He lunged. Then his head exploded into a thousand pieces.

"Blikskaters, boy! I thought you was coffin-fodder for sure," yelled Pia. He had shot the brave, now he dragged me away from the heat.

"Here's a memento from the Indian devil." He handed me the brave's knife and the roaring was so loud I could hear nothing more. It was Little Deer's knife.

I don't remember too much after that. At some point Underhill ordered everyone back to Greenwich and I found that running through the snow, difficult though it might be, actually eased the tumult inside my brain. If I fell, I have forgotten. Soon I was far ahead of the others.

At dawn when I forded the second river, the troops must have been two hours behind me. Soaking wet, I sat down on a slab of rock, wishing I could fall asleep and freeze to death. Somewhere I had lost my gun, so I was an easy target for roving Wilden. I scanned the distance for signs of life. There was nothing but white snow and winding stream.

Little Deer's knife was still welded to my right hand. Clean things, like weapons, are always carried in the right hand. Carefully I passed the razor-sharp blade across my cheek and the roaring in my head grew louder. With one stroke I could end the terrible noise forever. First I removed my left glove and ran bare fingers across the stray hairs on my chin. Moose Foot used to say that the only reason Christians grow beards is because they are too cowardly to pull the hairs out by the roots.

My left hand slid along the rock until it located two thin slivers of slate. Alternately I contemplated the slate and the knife until I suddenly realized that I was no longer alone. A young Indian boy was squatting on the ground only twenty yards from me. How he got there without my noticing was a mystery. He must have been the same age as Little Deer was when I first knew him.

The knife would have to wait until the boy was gone. Carefully I polished the blade with my handkerchief and sheathed it in my belt. Then I began the torturous process of extracting the hairs with the slate, one by one, forcing myself not to wince, while the boy sat there impassively. Without a mirror, I made a bloody mess of my face and had to keep washing it with snow. For some reason the pain reduced the roar in my ears. How could little children burn to death without crying out? Maybe the squaws suffocated them. God, I hope so.

Occasionally I glanced at the boy. It was strange how much he looked like Little Deer used to look. Perhaps the real Little Deer was already running through the green forests of the Happy Hunting Ground.

Pia found me there, still sitting on that slab of rock.

"Blikskaters!" he shouted. "You coulda lost yer scalp out here alone, Son. Underhill'd have yer hide for runnin' off, 'cept he's been wounded."

"Don't hurt the boy," was all I said.

"Boy? What boy? Yer mad, Son. There ain't no boy here."

In the Presence
of the Sun and
the Mighty Waters

In July, Company mismanagement in South America resulted in a stroke of good fortune for New Amsterdam. The *Blue Cock* reached Manhattan with 170 Dutch soldiers chased out of Brazil by the Portuguese. Kieft promptly billeted them around town.

"You can't sleep here anymore, Jan," said Sutje. "With five soldiers and a corporal on her hands Ma says she's at her wit's end."

After Greenwich, Papa had seen to it that I was retired from the civilian militia. I was now working for Uncle Isaack's new brewery, and he and Sarah said I was welcome to sleep on their hearth. But I missed Sutje. Even when we never got to exchange a word, it was a comfort to know that my golden-haired Sutje was safely asleep in the next room and not being chased about by that lout, Evert Wendell, the heavy snorer with the striped blanket.

"Can we go for a walk occasionally?" I asked her.

"Ma says I'm not to see you for one month."

"Why? What have I done?"

"Nothing. Ma says it's the way of the world." She began to cry. "Please, Jan. A month is not so long." She kissed me and ran into the house.

It was one week later to the day that Sarah broke the news. As usual she did not mince words.

"Sutje and Evert Wendell will be married Sunday."

I did not answer and I did not change my expression.

Of course I had always known that there was no such thing as marrying a childhood sweetheart. In this country, girls are wed at sixteen, boys not until twenty-five if at all. And Sutje was sixteen, a year older than I.

"Evert's a good man, Jan. He'll take care of her. What with soldiers everywhere, Ma says she will never rest easy in her bed until that child is safely married to a full-grown man."

"I wish Sutje had told me herself," I said.

There were two soldiers and a corporal sleeping in Sarah's kitchen.

"Did you sail here directly from Brazil?" I asked the corporal.

"No, young fellow. We was told to report to Governor Stuyvesant at Curaçao."

"He sent you up here?"

"Bastard's a bonehead! He made us attack St. Martins and got hisself hit by a cannon ball. We had to drag him out and hightail it back empty-handed to Curaçao. Then he says we ain't good enough to fight Portuguese and he sends us up here to fight savages."

"Did he live?"

"They chopped off one leg and shipped him back to the Fatherland. Man's a goner if you ask me."

The arrival of troops from Brazil meant the end of Underhill's involvement in the war. Kieft sacked him to save money.

Since the Battle of Greenwich, there had been only a few outbreaks and some tribes had agreed to a truce. Our immediate neighbors, however, remained on the warpath. By night they stole into the city, murdering innocent citizens less than a hundred yards from the Fort. And in broad daylight, a man still could not go beyond the cattle barrier without risking his scalp.

"There has to be some way to get them to the peace table," said Uncle. He and Papa and I were sitting on the de Forest's stoop in the cool of the evening. Sarah was in the kitchen, but the top half of the door was open so she could hear every word.

Uncle sucked on his pipe till it glowed. "Weckquasgeeks'll never forget Greenwich," he said. "Only way is to kill 'em all."

I wanted to shout "NO! There must be a better way," but I couldn't think of one on the spur of the moment.

Then Sarah leaned her skinny elbows on the bottom half of the door. "If I was Governor," she announced, "I'd bring the Weckquasgees to the peace table fast enough."

"And just how would you do that, woman," asked Uncle?

"I'd go up to Fort Orange and hire Man-Eaters."

"Per Deos immortales!" exclaimed Papa. "The Mohawks are the most vicious savages in the world, Sarah. It would be suicide to involve them."

"Weckquasgeeks are not afraid of us," she continued. "And they are not afraid of dying. But they are terrified of Man-Eaters. Pay Mohawks to attack 'em and they'll sue for peace before you can say 'Potverdriedubbeltjes.'"

For one whole minute nobody said a word. Sarah might be homely but she had a good head on her shoulders. I watched the little pinpoints of light across the Marketfield where clay pipes waved and neighbors gossiped on their stoops. The August moon began to rise above the treetops and I wondered if Wilden were even now concealed in the shadows, waiting for dusk to turn to night.

"Enlist the enemy's enemy," muttered Papa, knocking his pipe against the marigold pot.

"It's playing with fire!" said Uncle. "Suppose the Mohawks turn on us?"

"Why should they?" asked Papa, wryly. "We supply them with the guns they need for their raids against the Hurons and the French. Of course they'd make us pay through the nose."

"Kieft wouldn't touch it with a ten-foot poker," declared Uncle.

"He would if it was his own idea," I said.

Two days later the Governor announced his new policy, "Enlist the enemy's enemy." He and Papa, together with almost half the army, sailed up to Fort Orange. This was the first time Governor Kieft had so much as spent a night outside Fort Amsterdam in the seven years he had been in this country. The project was costly but successful. In August of 1645, after two years of bloody warfare, a treaty was signed outside the Fort with Mohawks acting as intermediaries.

I stood with the crowd surrounding the parade ground. Indian Chiefs, wrapped in blue and red duffel blankets, sat silent and grave in a semicircle on the ground. Opposite them, also on the ground, were the Dutch officials in gloomy black. Squatting beside Papa, in her lace cap and Sunday dress, was the official interpreter, Sarie, the Dominie's step-daughter.

There was a hush as Director General Willem Kieft arrived, surrounded by his guard of honor in breastplates and helmets. Even he sat on the ground, but on a black pillow. Oratamy of the Hackensacks was the most important Chief. I saw Penhawitz, the one-eyed Sachem of the Canarsies, but Rechnewac, the Weckquasgeek Chief, was not there. I wondered if he had been killed at Greenwich. In all, eleven great nations were represented by seven Chieftains. Then, in the presence of "the Sun and the Mighty Waters," the treaty was signed, pipes were smoked, and peace was restored to our world.

A thousand lay dead, yet there was only one live prisoner still in enemy hands, the little English girl, Susan Hutchinson. The treaty provided that she be turned over to her Boston relatives and the Siwanoy agreed to bring the child to the Fort, Monday. Papa was to handle the transfer and Sarie would be there to interpret with the Siwanoy.

Monday dawned fresh and clear. I was splitting kindling in the road when the Siwanoy procession passed by. In the lead was Chief Toteneke. Two important-looking braves came next followed by a squaw, her back bent under a load of beavers. Bringing up the rear was little Susan, ragged and filthy enough to be a Siwanoy herself except for the blond hair. I would never have recognized her.

They had no sooner disappeared through the Fort gate when a soldier dashed out with a message from Papa. Sarie was in bed sick and I was needed at the Governor's office immediately as interpreter. I was also to bring Sarah. As Isaack and Sarah's house was directly against the Fort wall, it would be convenient for the girl to go home for the night with Sarah.

"Tell them I'll be along as soon as I finish feeding this infant," snapped the redhead.

When I arrived at the Governor's office there were six soldiers guarding the open door. Inside, Papa was attempting to speak English to ten-year-old Susan, who clung desperately to the squaw. Chief Toteneke and the two braves stood motionless by the window, faces carved of stone. The lace curtains swaying in the summer breeze looked more alive.

Frustrated by the lack of progress, Kieft sputtered advice alternately in Dutch and French. "God Allemachtig! We aren't going to hurt the girl. Tell her we're sending her to live with her nice auntie in Boston." This in Dutch for the benefit of the Wilden who do not approve of striking a child. Then in French, which they don't understand, "Sacrebleu! Drag her away, Montagne. Throttle her if you have to, but let's be done with it." He pounded his fist on the mahogany game-table where a chessboard was set up at the ready.

"I don't believe she understands a word of English," muttered Papa. I could see the pulse in his throat hammering away. He tried a few more halting words but the girl only buried her face deeper in the beaver skins and locked her arms about the squaw's neck.

"Of course she understands English!" shouted Kieft as the soldiers fingered their guns restlessly. "She *is* English! Send for Allerton. You don't speak it correctly."

The chessmen danced as the Governor stamped his foot and I noticed that a black pawn was still missing.

"She has forgotten how to speak English," I said.

"Don't talk nonsense, Son."

"She's bound to know a little Algonkian," I continued.

"Then you come over here and try to reason with the child."

But I had no more success than Papa. It was clear that she understood some Algonkian but she refused even to lift her head.

"Look at me, Susan. Don't you remember when I came to your house and your mother gave us apple juice to drink and we played backgammon beneath that leaning willow tree?" She would not look.

Frustrated, I tried to unclench her grip on the squaw, which was a mistake. Chief Toteneke gave a disapproving grunt causing the soldiers to glower and finger their guns again as I quickly put my hands behind my back.

At this moment Sarah marched in. Of all stupid things she had an infant in each arm. One was hers, the other was little Pieter Bogardus from next door.

"Well, you took your time getting here," growled the Governor, eyeing the infants with distaste. "Now see if you can persuade that girl to go home with you so we can dismiss these Siwanoy. Then we will ship her off to Boston in the morning."

Sarah looked around as if searching for a friendly lap. No one offered to hold an infant. They were all too important to bother with an infant. I am not very good with babies but somebody had to volunteer so I held out my arms. Sarah ignored me and marched over to the girl. I think she would have whacked her if she had had a free hand. Instead she announced loudly, in Algonkian,

"Men are as useless as tits on a bull!"

Chief Toteneke and the braves pretended not to hear and the Dutch soldiers did not understand the language. There was a moment of silence broken only by a giant bluebottle fly buzzing angrily back and forth behind the lace curtains. Then I caught a twinkle in the squaw's eye and the girl relaxed her grip long enough to glance at Sarah, who quickly handed her a baby and continued speaking in Algonkian.

"Hold this one, Susan. His name is Pieter."

The girl cuddled the infant like a doll, then pressed her filthy face against his clean one. What Pieter's mother did not know would not hurt her.

"You carry Pieter," said Sarah, "and I'll carry this one. Her name is Susan just like yours. Now walk fast, follow me and don't look back."

Out they marched, full stride, past the Siwanoy, past the soldiers, past the Governor whose mouth hung open in astonishment.

Crossing the cobblestone courtyard the child continued to nuzzle little Pieter as she hurried to keep up with Sarah.

Neighbors were generous. One brought a petticoat another a pair of shoes.

"It was no easy task getting her into the tub," Sarah told me later. "You would have thought I was trying to drown the child. Good thing Little Rachel was here and volunteered to bathe first. When she survived the ordeal the child finally submerged herself in the suds and I was able to burn the filthy rags she came in. All except this. Have a look at it, Jan."

It was a leather pouch on a strap. Wilden often wear a carved wooden Manitou around the neck for protection, sort of a guardian angel. I chuckled at the picture of her Boston relatives throwing up their hands in horror at the heathen relic.

But when I untied the strap I found, not a wooden Manitou, but Governor Kieft's black pawn! I laughed out loud. Of course I had to tell Sarah the whole story. Then we both laughed.

"I can easily put the pawn back where it belongs," I said.

"You will do no such thing. The child likes this and she's going to wear it." Sarah carefully retied the pouch. "Let those pious Puritans figure this one out!"

Malala

The war was over by the time the Board of Directors finally got around to recalling Governor Kieft for incompetence. He was to remain in charge, however, until his replacement should arrive. Predictably furious, Kieft devoted the remaining months to punishing his enemies. Many settlers pulled up roots and took the next ship back to the Fatherland. With the government in chaos, and the countryside dotted with charred ruins, the population of New Amsterdam dwindled to a few hundred souls.

My one ambition in those days was to rebuild Vredendale, but Kieft refused to grant permission for any construction outside of town. He claimed that it was the existence of isolated boweries that had caused the war in the first place.

Papa said I must be patient. "Wait until the new Governor arrives, Son. We have just learned that it is to be Pieter Stuyvesant, former Governor of Curaçao. He's the one who lost a leg to a Spanish cannon ball. A new man, even with one leg, is bound to be sympathetic toward rebuilding."

In the meantime I still worked for Isaack six days a week, mostly at the brewery. But I was expected to help Sarah with heavy tasks around the house too, like fetching water and splitting wood. I was not really needed at home, because Papa, being Councillor to the Governor, had soldiers at all times to do the heavy work. Furthermore I did not like our neighbor, the Widow Agnietje, who thought it was her duty to look after a widower with five motherless children. So I usually slept on the de Forest's hearth. I did not tell Papa, but every Sunday Tiger and I would run the eight miles to Vredendale. There I spent my time shoveling, dragging away burnt timbers, and drawing plans in my head.

Kieft did manage to do one good thing before he was given the sack: He freed the slaves. Not all the slaves, but the eleven survivors of the original twelve plus their wives. He praised them for their loyalty and courage and gave each of the eleven a parcel of land near the Kalch, which is the largest lake on Manhattan, half a mile north of town. It would be one of the best sites on Manhattan if it were not so close to a large horseshoe-shaped swamp.

One Sunday morning in 1647, Tiger and I were on our way up to Vredendale when I decided to go by way of the Kalch to see the new Free Town and maybe say hello to my friend, the Giant. I heard that he had a son born two years after the hanging.

However, I was not anxious to run into Jan t'Fort Orange. I had long ago come to the conclusion that Sarah had been right and Fort Orange was the one who murdered his fellow slave, Premero, after an argument over the latter's wife, Maria Grande. The authorities tried to hang the Giant for the crime. Later, when the hue and cry died down, Fort Orange up and married La Grande.

"G'morgen, Mista Jan."

Speak of the Devil. Here was La Grande, herself, on her way to town, head held high and three large bundles balanced effortlessly on top. Even more astonishing was her immense bosom which rode straight out front, defying all the laws of nature.

"Goedemorgen, Maria."

The woman had a mouth like an oversized beaver trap but the rest of her was so spectacular that I could not help staring. Her ample rear end seemed to be in perpetual motion, grinding up, down and around beneath a thin, yellow skirt.

Fort Orange's first wife had been a frail-looking black woman with soulful eyes, named Magdalena. They say he beat her, and she died in childbirth shortly before Premero was murdered. The baby girl survived, and was passed around among the other Angolan women who took turns nursing her. The foster-mothers said nothing when Fort Orange chased after Maria Grande, but when he had the infant baptized Maria instead of Magdalena, they rebelled and called the child Malala. I wondered if she could still be alive.

Now the sound of joyous singing reached me from the fields near the Kalch. After eighteen years of slavery they were at last sowing their own crops, but their only beast of burden was the Giant, yoked to a plow. He paused at the end of each furrow to lift up his own voice in a marvelous bass. The plowman was Jan t'Fort Orange, so I did not stop.

The village homes were slipshod lean-tos along the lake, half a wall here, half a roof there. Youngsters romped gaily among the weeds and rubble, with an occasional shy smile for me and timid delight with Tiger who was always good with children. Their happiness was catching. Then I remembered that the Directors had approved Kieft's freeing the parents, but insisted that all children, born or unborn, remain Company property. Greedy klaplopers, all of them!

I recognized Michael, the Giant's son. A sturdy four-year-old with a big grin, he was already as large as the average eight-year-old. The youngsters were all coal-black except for one brown-skinned girl with large solemn eyes who wore nothing but a ragged shift of duffel. About seven years old, she stood apart from the others and something about the eyes prompted me to speak to her.

"Who's your mother, little girl?"

"Dead, Mista."

"And your father?"

"Jan t'Fort Orange."

I was right. Magdalena's soul was in this child's face.

"Is your name Malala?" I asked.

She nodded, solemn eyes fixed steadily on mine. Then I noticed the black and blue marks on her arms which she tried to hide behind her back. I did not have to ask if her father beat her. What kind of a life could Magdalena's child lead with that bruiser for a father? Yet her hair was neatly braided in six little pigtails, each tied with pink string. Somehow I could not picture La Grande plaiting pigtails.

"Does your step-mother fix your hair, Malala?"

"No, Mista. My aunties does." She meant the Angolan women.

That evening I told Sarah about Malala.

"You should have brought her here," scolded the redhead, who was very pregnant and having trouble walking. "I could use her to run after Susan."

Sarah had given birth to three children, but so far two-year-old Susan was the only one to survive.

"What did you want the boy to do, woman? Kidnap the child?" interrupted Isaack.

"Men!" She scoffed.

Monday morning Sarah "borrowed" Abram's fish wagon and the broken-down nag that pulled it. (Gone were the days when a wheelbarrow was sufficient to deliver fish.) Being that Abram was her younger brother, Sarah naturally omitted the formality of asking permission, as I discovered when I was given the task of returning the horse and wagon.

In the meantime Sarah had driven up to the Kalch, found Malala and promised her a necklace of pink beads if she would come to the house every morning for the next month to chase after two-year-old Susan.

Shortly after dawn Tuesday morning, Malala appeared at the door in bare feet and ragged shift. Sarah put her in a patched hand-me-down of faded calico, too large but at least clean, and tossed the duffel in the ragbag.

At breakfast the child was very shy with Uncle and me. She sat at the far end of the table next to Susan, who watched, fascinated, as Malala wolfed down her suppawn like a hungry pup.

"Not so fast, Malala," corrected Sarah, refilling the bowl. "Susan's not eating. You must help her."

This time the child alternated, a spoonful for Susan then one for herself. The two-year-old thought it was a game and smiled happily. Finally, when no one appeared to be watching, Malala smiled back at her. Even with one front tooth missing it was a beautiful smile.

The houses in this row had no yards to speak of so the children all played in the road. Malala spent the morning dragging Susan away from pigs and goats to say nothing of horses' hooves and wagon wheels. At eleven, Uncle and I returned for the midday meal, and afterwards, while Susan napped, Malala helped Sarah with the dishes before being sent home.

"That child belongs to the Company, woman," warned Uncle when Malala had gone. "You need permission from the Governor."

"Poppycock! Kieft won't grant permission for anyone to do anything. And he doesn't give a hoot."

Malala had been to the house exactly twice when Madame Vinje-Dam reported Sarah for stealing Company property. Fortunately the Governor ignored the report, and Sharkface told his mother-in-law to mind her own business.

Malala had nimble fingers. If she stayed on after the baby was born, Sarah planned to teach her to sew. A slave who is handy with a needle has a much easier lot in this world. In the meantime Sarah cut up an old pink skirt and made the child a proper dress for church. It would go well with the beads which I was sent to purchase from the Company store.

The pink frock got its first airing on May 11th when the new Governor and his fleet of four sailed into harbor. Everyone donned his best bib and tucker and assembled along the shore to welcome Lord General Pieter Stuyvesant, the new Commander of all Dutch possessions in North America and the Caribbean. Malala stood up front beside Susan. I stood just behind with Uncle and Sarah.

The cannon boomed a festive salute until the powder ran out. Then the crowd cheered madly as Stuyvesant was rowed to the quayside where Governor Kieft and other officials, including Papa, waited to greet him.

The Honor Guard in breastplates and helmets stood rigidly at attention as the tall imposing figure, carefully dressed in the usual black, stepped on to the quay. His good left leg had striped hose with a rainbow-colored scarf at the knee and a red rosette on the shoe. We all craned our necks to see his wooden right leg, which had a silver band glistening in the sun.

"Man's a pompous peacock!" muttered Isaack in my ear.

"With a big nose," whispered Sarah in the other ear.

Now Vrouw Judith Stuyvesant was being helped ashore. She was expecting and looked very tired, which was no surprise. Eighteen passengers had not survived the voyage.

After the formal introduction of officials there was a hush as Stuyvesant turned to the people and made a short speech promising to act as a father to all his subjects. Then Kieft said a few words of welcome and ended up thanking the citizens for their loyalty, which provoked grumbling from the crowd.

"What'd the klaploper ever give us?" complained someone.

"Nothing but a pile of ashes!" came the loud reply in Kuyter's unmistakable Danish accent.

Stuyvesant raised his hands for silence. "Bygones will be bygones," he announced in words of steel. Then he accompanied Kieft across town to the Fort, stomping along with vigorous speed as though to demonstrate that a wooden leg was actually an advantage. Vrouw Judith followed more sedately. As she passed us she smiled at little Susan who clung tightly to Malala's hand.

Stuyvesant styled himself "Lord General" and it was soon clear that he intended to rule with an iron hand. To make matters worse, he asked the lecherous Sharkface to continue as Secretary, infuriating just about everyone. New Netherlanders have always been obstinate as mules and a clash was inevitable.

The first confrontation involved two of our most important colonists, Kuyter and Melyn, who planned to visit the Fatherland in order to raise money to rebuild their ruined boweries. Before leaving, they drew up a report of Kieft's mismanagement and presented it to Stuyvesant who promptly threw them out, repeating his "bygones be bygones" dictum.

The matter might have ended there if Kieft had not countered with charges of treason against Kuyter and Melyn. This time Stuyvesant said nothing about bygones but gave the pair 48 hours to answer the charges. In court the new Governor acted as both prosecutor and judge, and New Amsterdam shivered at the verdict: permanent exile for Kuyter and the death sentence for Melyn who was the more outspoken. This was worse than anything Kieft had done in nine years!

Papa had been appointed to Stuyvesant's Council and thanks largely to his influence, the sentences were reduced to three and seven years exile plus heavy fines, but horns had been locked. The Lord General would get no cooperation from the citizens of New Amsterdam.

Sarah had her own personal run-in with Peg-Leg over Malala. When the Witch saw that nothing was too small for the new Governor's attention she again reported that Sarah had stolen Company property, this time even going so far as to accuse her of beating the child, which was a lie. The scars on Malala's back were put there by Fort Orange, not Sarah.

It turned out that the charges of beating did not apply as Malala was a slave, not a servant, and the fine was waived because of Sarah's condition. But the court ruled that Malala could no longer go to the de Forest home for any purpose whatsoever. In desperation Sarah offered to buy her from the Company. This was refused, and I heard later from Papa that Vrouw Stuyvesant wanted the "neat little child in the pink dress," for herself. Greedy klaplopers, all of them. Still, I would rather she belonged to the Stuyvesants than to Fort Orange.

That night Sarah finished stringing the pink beads. It was a few days shy of a month but Malala had earned them well. The next morning Sarah planned to tell the child about the court's decision and send her home after breakfast with her new necklace. But, for the first time, Malala did not arrive for breakfast. And she did not arrive after breakfast.

"I'm worried," said Sarah.

"Someone must have told her about the ruling," said Isaack, sensibly.

"Suppose she's hurt. Maybe her father beat her up," continued Sarah. "Go fetch Abram's horse and wagon, Jan. I'm going up there to give Malala her necklace and see for myself that she's all right."

"Abram's angry," I argued. "He won't lend it to you. Give me the necklace. I can run up there in no time."

"I said go fetch that horse and wagon!" snapped Sarah.

"Better do what she says, Jan," warned Isaack, accompanying me to the door. "When a woman is nine months along it's best to do what she says."

So I hurried over to Beaver Street and caught Abram just as he was leaving to check his nets. At first he was adamant that he would never lend Sarah anything again. But he finally came around, as I knew he would.

"All right. You can have them on one condition. You do the driving. That bossy sister of mine is a terrible driver. She'll kill poor old Nelly, and I can't afford a younger horse. You'll find the harness hanging by the stall."

Ten minutes later Sarah was sitting beside me on the wagon seat, trying to tuck that wild mop of red hair under her cap. The trouble with Sarah is that she takes after her father, Phillippe du Trieux—the same square jaw and broken-looking nose. It is all right on a man, but downright homely on a woman.

The old horse was even more decrepit than usual today. She hung her head and shuffled slowly forward, one foot at a time.

"Well at least there is no danger of harming the baby at this speed," I said, trying to make polite conversation.

"It makes no matter. The baby's dead. It hasn't kicked in weeks. Isaack thinks I'm mistaken but I know it's dead."

There did not seem to be any answer to this so I got down and led Nelly which improved our progress slightly.

Today the road leading from the Heerenstraat to the lake was deserted. Even the fields were empty but we could hear distant shouting from the direction of the Horseshoe Swamp. Now I was aware of someone running behind us. It was Isabella, one of the Angolans.

"Where is everyone, Isabella?" cried Sarah.

"In the swamp, Miss. They's looking for Malala."

"Why should Malala be in the swamp?"

"Her Pa done send her to check his traps."

"He must be crazy to send a seven-year-old into that swamp. When was this?"

"Yesterday, Miss."

"Good God! Has Malala been missing all night?"

"Yes, Miss. I thought she was to her Pa's. He thought she was to me."

If I had Tiger I was sure that I could find Malala. But first I had to get Sarah home. Carefully I led Nelly so as to turn the wagon around.

Now there was a commotion from the direction of the rescue operation and that brute, Fort Orange, emerged from the swamp. He yelled something but the distance was too great.

I threw the reins onto the wagon seat, jumped on to a nearby rock and cupped my hands. "Did you find Malala?" I shouted.

He shook his head and yelled something unintelligible.

"He say the Swamp Devil done sucked her down," wailed Isabella.

"God Almighty!" exclaimed Sarah. "We need soldiers here with dogs."

"I jes done speak to th' overseer," said Isabella. "He say NO soldiers is goin' in NO swamp for NO black child!"

"Oh he did, did he! We'll see about that," snapped the redhead. "Tell the men to keep searching. I'll have soldiers with dogs up here in no time." She grabbed the reins and gave Nelly a flick with the crop.

I leaped for the wagon, but too late. The old horse bolted like a spooked filly. Down the road she charged, wagon rattling from side to side, and me running behind yelling like a madman.

Sarah leaned on the reins in vain. Nelly had the bit firmly in her teeth. Now we were past the cattle barrier and still racing. Out of the corner of my eye I saw housewives snatch infants from the road as every dog on the Heerenstraat joined in the chase, yelping its head off. The first pothole was bound to cause a terrible crash.

Miraculously Sarah managed to avoid the potholes. Finally she succeeded in jerking Nelly's head up, and the wagon lurched to a halt by the Fort where the horse immediately slumped into her former decrepit self.

Bystanders cheered as Sarah dismounted with as much dignity as possible. Then she marched through the Fort gate announcing loudly, "Important message for his Lordship!"

I led Nelly back to Beaver Street at this point, and then went to fetch Tiger so I did not actually see what happened next, but I heard the story from Papa as well as Sarah.

It seems Sarah received unexpected support at the Governor's mansion. As two soldiers tried to stop her from bursting into the office, Vrouw Judith Stuyvesant came downstairs to investigate the disturbance. Sarah appealed to her.

"Malala is lost in the swamp, Mevrouw. She's been missing since yesterday. We need soldiers with dogs up there immediately."

Vrouw Stuyvesant nodded and without a word opened the door to the office. Sarah entered to find the Governor and his entire Council in serious deliberation over what to make the minimum legal weight for a loaf of rye bread.

Stuyvesant cleared his throat. "To what do we owe this rude interruption, Madame?" he demanded as everyone stared.

For a moment Sarah was taken aback by the hostile expressions and Papa rose to his feet in an awkward attempt to help matters.

"This is Madame de Forest, your Lordship, my late wife's sister-in-law. In her condition she has perhaps been distressed by . . ."

"I can speak for myself, Jehan," Sarah broke in, marching over to the desk. "Your Lordship, the little slave girl, Malala, has been missing in the swamp since yesterday. Soldiers and dogs must be sent at once."

Sarah may be no beauty but she has more guts than ten men put together.

"And pray, Madame de Forest, who gave you permission to enter this office?" asked the Governor. Then he suddenly became aware of his own wife, with her hand still on the doorknob. He turned away quickly. "Ensign Van Dyck, you will see that a platoon is dispatched to the swamp immediately."

"With dogs," added Sarah as the former ensign got reluctantly to his feet. He lost an arm in the war and had not shaved since. In consequence his black beard was almost as long as the missing arm.

"With dogs," repeated Peg-Leg. "Now Councillor Montagne, will you kindly remove your late wife's sister-in-law from this office."

By the time I had taken care of Nelly, fetched Tiger, and returned to the Kalch, soldiers had arrived and roped off the area this side of the swamp. Even the residents were forbidden to go beyond the ropes.

Isabella told me in tears that she had provided Malala's blanket for the dogs to sniff. Then the corporal in charge blew his whistle. "Release the dogs," he yelled! "Forward, men!"

A half dozen yelping bloodhounds dashed eagerly into the overgrowth, followed more cautiously by twice that number of soldiers.

"They'll have your girl out within the hour," the corporal told the weeping Isabella. Then he saw me with Tiger on a lead.

"Get that mastiff out of here immediately!" he shouted. "I don't want him distracting the bloodhounds."

Temporarily I returned to the de Forest home where I found Sarah sitting at the table with her bare feet up on a stool. Her ankles were almost as big around as her stomach.

"Did they find Malala?" she asked immediately.

"Soldiers with bloodhounds have just entered the swamp." I said. "The corporal claims they will have Malala out within the hour. What's the matter with your ankles?"

"I don't know, but my pains have started. Isaack's gone for the midwife."

"Holy Jehoshaphat! What can I do? Do you want me to take Susan up to Little Rachel?" (My sister was thirteen now but the family still called her Little Rachel.)

"Little Rachel was here already and took Susan. What you *can* do though is keep me posted on the search for Malala. Dear God, I know the baby's dead but I can't bear for Malala to be dead, too."

"Don't worry, Sarah. It's only during spring floodwaters that there is any real danger. And I have Tiger with me. If the soldiers fail, Tiger will find her."

"I wish I had something of Malala's for Tiger to sniff," she said. "I know! Take that filthy duffel that I threw in the ragbag."

For the rest of the day Tiger and I went back and forth between the swamp and the de Forest house, with one stop at home to feed Tiger and incidentally have a short discussion with Papa about the swamp.

"According to Old Nehooma," I said, "when the first Weckquasgeeks reached Manhattan it was two islands separated by a narrow strait which has gradually filled in with silt. The Horseshoe Swamp and the Lake are remnants of that strait."

"She could be right, Son. Every report of digging on Manhattan has resulted in finding bedrock almost immediately, except for those on the east–west line through the Kalch and the swamp, where there appears to be no rock at all. This would be the ideal place to dig a canal some day. But the swamp is dangerous, Jan. For God's sake, be careful!"

I was at the de Forest home when Tryntje, the midwife, stuck her head out of the bedroom to announce that Sarah had given birth to a stillborn baby boy with deformed limbs. She said it was a blessing that the infant was dead. Tears ran down Uncle's cheeks as he tried to enter the bedroom.

"Not so fast, Isaack de Forest," Tryntje blocked his way. "I'll tell you when you can come in." She shut the door firmly.

"Did they find Malala?" came Sarah's voice from within.

"No word yet," called Isaack, wiping his eyes.

"You're lying!" screamed Sarah. They found her body and you're not telling me."

"As God is my witness, Sarah," I shouted through the closed door, "the soldiers are still searching."

A few minutes later the midwife reappeared, with the dead infant wrapped up like a small parcel.

"Get this baptized right away," she told Isaack, handing him the parcel. "And while you're next door chasing up the Dominie, ask Anneke to lend me a hand with these sheets."

I left for the Kalch, where no progress had been made. In fact there was a rumor that one of the bloodhounds was missing, which meant that any further efforts would be toward finding the missing bloodhound, not the missing Malala. Then at sundown the search was called off. The dog had reappeared, soaking wet and covered with slime, but Malala was declared to be missing and presumed dead.

As far as I could see, Isabella was the only one in tears. Malala's step-mother, Maria Grande, was unconcerned. Malala's father, Jan t'Fort Orange, was more angry at wasting a day's work than at losing a daughter. I suspect he was always embarrassed by Malala's light color. Two coal-black parents are not supposed to produce a chocolate-colored offspring.

When the soldiers finally departed I showed Tiger Malala's duffel. Then I took him into the swamp. Nose to the ground he raced back and forth trying to pick up the scent, to no avail.

Soon we were ankle-deep in seething water, listening to the gurgle which some claim is made by the Swamp Devil. Unfortunately the water covers up the scent.

Years earlier, Little Deer had shown me a path of tree trunks laid end to end over the worst ground. The wood had rotted by now, but we crossed over safely. Without the tree trunks we could easily have fallen into one of the watery fissures on every side, which is probably what happened to the bloodhound. That he had been able to pull himself out was remarkable.

Perhaps Malala never went into the swamp. Could she have drowned in the Kalch? It would be better to drown in the Kalch than to be sucked down into the swamp.

It was dusk by the time I took Tiger home and returned to the de Forests. Anneke, the Dominie's wife, had brought a pot of turkey soup. She and Uncle were at the table having bread and soup. I joined them.

"Any luck?" asked Anneke.

"No," I said gloomily. "Tiger never even found the scent."

"Sarah is finally asleep," said Uncle. "I gave her brandy."

"Ensign Van Dyck was just here," said Anneke, "with a message from his Lordship. He says the soldiers did everything humanly possible, and the death of the little slave girl is much to be regretted. Of course he took pains to mention that it was the Company's loss, not Sarah's, since Malala was Company property."

"Hah!" I said.

When Anneke left I took my blanket, lay down by the hearth and was asleep almost before my head hit the floor. What happened next is difficult to understand.

It must have been about four in the morning that I was awakened out of a sound sleep by something poking me in the back. I opened one eye. Sarah was sitting on the hearth stool with the long-handled hearth brush in her hand.

"Go back to bed," I said and shut my eye again.

"Jan, listen to me! I just saw Malala! She's alive!"

"No, you were dreaming, Sarah. Malala's dead. They called off the search." I turned over and tried to bury my head, but she hit me with the brush.

"Do you remember Jesse's dream before your mother drowned? Nobody believed him either." Now she was stirring the fire with the poker. "Do you know why Malala is brown instead of black, Jan? Because she's Sharkface's bastard! That makes her Happy Squirrel's half-sister."

She had my attention now. I sat up.

"How do you know?" I whispered.

"Isabella told me. What did you ever do for Happy Squirrel, Jan?"

"I baptized him," was my miserable reply.

"You promised Old Nehooma to protect him with your life, and the only thing you ever did was to baptize his little headless body. Now Happy Squirrel's sister is lost in the dark and dying, and you and I are the only two people in the world who know she's still alive. What are you going to do about it?"

"I'll get her if it kills me, Sarah." Now I was on my feet. "Tell me where she is."

"In the forest."

"Do you mean the swamp?"

"It was more like forest. In the dream I was looking down from above at Malala's body lying on the forest floor. It was night but somehow I could see her, even a little pink ribbon on one pigtail. At first I thought she was dead. As I watched, cunning animal eyes peered out from the darkness and stole cautiously toward the body. Then her hand moved and the eyes shrank back. It was the sound of Malala moaning that woke me up."

"Did you notice any landmarks?"

"Nothing."

"That's not much to go on, Sarah. You say you were looking down from above. Were you looking through shrubs or branches of a tree?"

"A big tree. Maybe an oak."

"There are no oaks in the swamp." I took the brush and began to sketch on the sand floor with the handle. I drew the Horseshoe Swamp, then the Kalch and the adjacent streams. "The really bad ground is here," I pointed.

"Put a log on the fire, so we can see better," she said. "Is it possible that Malala crossed over the bad part? She weighs hardly anything."

"There must be more details," I said. If you could see the body, you must have been able to see other things. Think, Sarah."

"Well, there were the animal eyes. And there was an owl. I couldn't see the owl—just two big, round, yellow eyes, staring."

"Where was the owl? On a branch?"

"No, it was in the hole of the tree opposite. In fact there were two holes in that tree, one on top of the other, like a figure eight."

"My God!" I said. "That's it, Sarah! I know that tree!" I grabbed my jacket and ran out into the night.

As I hurried along, I thought about the day Happy Squirrel was conceived. I had stuffed the bag of spoons into a hollow tree so they would not jangle while I investigated the commotion in the clearing. I remember thinking at the time that the tree was very unusual, with two holes, one on top of the other, like a figure eight. Could there be other trees like that?

By the time I reached our house on the sheep meadow, I was beginning to have doubts about Sarah's dream. Why should it be different than any other dream?

Tiger as usual was shut up in the barn for the night. Of course he was eager to resume the search, and I was glad I still had Malala's duffel in my pocket. The barking probably woke Papa, but there was no time to stop and explain. Besides, Papa would not understand. I did not understand myself.

I kept Tiger leashed as I followed the Weckquasgeek Trail which veers far to the East to avoid any bad ground. Could Malala really be miles from the swamp?

When at last I thought we must be parallel with the clearing, I let Tiger sniff the duffel again and unleashed him, which was a mistake. Nose to the ground he raced up the trail ahead. Then suddenly he bounded left, off the trail into the woods, yelping, with me following as best I could.

Dawn was breaking and a few streaks of light were beginning to sift through the forest canopy onto the trail. But here in the woods it was still midnight. I could hear Tiger in the distance. Something must have gone wrong because the hollow tree was only a few paces from the trail. I wished I had had the sense to keep the dog leashed.

Now Tiger was barking excitedly. He had found something, even if it was only a dead squirrel.

"I'm coming, Tiger!" I yelled.

I wasn't fast enough for him and he dashed back to see why I was dragging my feet. This was a good sign. Tiger would never dash back to tell me about a dead squirrel. This time I put on the leash and Tiger literally pulled me to the far edge of the clearing.

There lay Malala. She was alive but unconscious. One foot was caught in the iron jaws of an old bear trap. Her bloody hands were witness to her desperate efforts to free herself. Quickly I released the iron jaws. She moaned when I removed the crushed foot, but remained unconscious. Gently, I picked her up. She weighed nothing.

"Good work, Tiger," I said, and together we brought Malala home to Sarah.

By noon the child was able to sit up and drink some turkey broth. Sarah had already bathed her and put ointment on a thousand insect bites. Then Papa and Doctor Kierstede both examined the injured foot and debated at length about whether it would have to be amputated. In the end they decided to bind it up with splints and wait two weeks.

"But if it turns septic, that foot comes off!" was the verdict.

Malala had absolutely no memory of how she had come to be two miles from the swamp. What I still cannot understand is how she happened to be 100 yards from that hollow tree.

"What are you going to do, woman, when his Lordship sends for his slave?" asked Isaack after the doctors had departed.

Sarah pointed to the gun over the fireplace. "I'll use that," she said. But she need not have worried about the Governor. The next morning an official document arrived signed by Lord General Pieter Stuyvesant himself:

Acting in accordance with the manifest will of God, we do hereby transfer ownership of the slave girl known as Malala, to Madame Sarah de Forest.

And so little Malala came into the de Forest family. The foot did not have to be amputated, but for the rest of her life one leg was always shorter than the other.

The Front Stoop
Conspiracy

In late spring my brother, Jesse, then eighteen, was appointed bookkeeper. Every morning Papa drove him to the Company store before taking himself to the Governor's mansion to undertake the endless duties of Councillor to Lord Peg-Leg. As the store closed at 4 o'clock and the council rarely finished its business before five or six, Jesse waited at Isaack and Sarah's place, directly across the road from the store. In good weather he would sit out on the front stoop reading *Horace*. I had not seen him so happy in years.

The trouble started during the cicada plague. For a time it seemed as though the whole world was covered in grasshopper-like insects with red eyes and squashy white bodies. Fortunately they only appear every seventeen years. On this particular day, I returned from the brewery to find Jesse studying, not the familiar brown leather *Horace*, but a tattered old notebook. On the bench beside him was a pile of four more old notebooks.

"What happened to *Horace*, Jess?" I had to raise my voice to be heard over the monotonous din of cicadas and the raucous cries of feasting birds.

At this point Sarah came out to sweep the stoop. "Move your other foot, Jesse," she shouted.

Jesse put down his notebook and used both hands to lift his useless leg, while she swept under the bench. The whole stoop was covered with discarded cicada skins and the marigolds in the earthenware pot were crawling with live ones.

"I mean to be the finest bookkeeper ever," said Jesse, "which means understanding all the accounts right from the beginning. These five are from the days when Secretary van Tienhoven was bookkeeper. I found them hidden away on a dusty shelf in the warehouse."

"Hah!" snapped Sarah, "that Sharkface is crookeder than a toad's elbow, and so was his bookkeeping."

"That's where you're wrong, Sarah," said Jesse. "His figures are the best, and every page balances. Have a look."

"Where would I get time to add up all those numbers?" she snorted. "Besides, I have enough on my mind. Isaack came home today, wheezing like a pot on the boil with a stuck lid. He says cicada eggs in the air are worse than ragweed. I will never understand why that man can't breathe through his nose like the rest of the world."

She glanced at Malala and Susan who were busy making mud pies in the road. "Malala! Bring Susan in now and get washed."

The little slave girl still walked with a crutch, but unlike Jesse she hopped about nimbly enough, easily managing Susan with her one free hand.

"As for you," Sarah turned to me, "I need two extra buckets of water today. Try the well on the Strand this time, the lid's better. Cicada eggs are falling right out of the sky."

When I returned, Jesse announced in a surprised voice that he had just found a zero in the wrong place.

"Never mind that zero," snapped Sarah. "Supper is on the table. You may as well eat with us, Jesse, unless of course you prefer Agnietje's cooking."

Sarah's suppers were always very plain; suppawn, bread and beer. Still, it was better than watching Agnietje simper at Papa.

"What do you mean by a zero in the wrong place, Jesse?" Sarah asked when everyone had been served.

"A credit of 1010 guilders was carried forward as 1001 guilders. I know it's easy to reverse digits, but the strange thing is that the totals still balance. If it was a mistake, the credits and debits should be off by 9 guilders."

"Whose credit?"

"It belonged to old Guillaume Vinje."

"Goede Hemel! exclaimed Sarah, "He died when I was a child. What happened to the money?"

"Madame Vinje received 1001 in trust for the children and the monthly total balances which means the 9 guilders must have been credited somewhere.

I thought nothing of this conversation but Uncle Isaack was apparently disturbed. "Better keep your nose out of van Tienhoven's accounts, lad. Sharkface is hand in glove with his Lordship and with the Directors in Amsterdam. You'll only ruin your career if you pry into those accounts. Stick to Latin."

Speaking of Latin, there is a strange camaraderie between Latin scholars which seems to exist regardless of difference in age or temperament. According to Sarah, Dominie Bogardus had nursed his Madeira on the stoop next door for three years, conveniently ignoring his neighbors except when he needed a favor. With Jesse here, it was a different matter. For the last few days there had been a constant flow of *Horace* back and forth over the railing.

"Parturient montes, nascetur ridiculus mus," intoned the Dominie. "What a marvelous concept, lad! A huge mountain in labor giving birth to one ridiculous mouse."

Now there was also much that had nothing to do with Latin.

"Another zero misplaced, Jesse? I think I shall have a look at these cryptic ciphers of yours."

The Dominie never staggered. He swayed majestically down his steps to the road where Malala was helping Susan and little Pieter Bogardus to build a fort, then up the de Forest path, glass still in hand. For the first time in three years he settled his corpulent but still handsome self on the high-backed bench next to Jesse, just as Sarah came out with a bucket of mop-water.

"Ah, good morning Madame de Forest," he said, starting gallantly to rise, until Sarah waved him down again. "I am delighted that your slave's leg is so improved. Have you noticed that she has the same eyes as her mother? Magdalena, I believe the name was."

Sarah nodded and poured half the mop-water into the marigold pot.

"Remarkable woman, Magdalena," he continued. "When she knew she was dying she made me promise to baptize her baby. The church does not approve of baptizing slave babies, you know."

"I thought the church wanted to baptize everyone," I said.

"Ah, there's a ticklish problem, lad. The Church holds that it is acceptable to enslave heathens, but not Christians. Once you start baptizing little slave babies, they become Christians and then where are you? Anyway I did baptize Malala, and I have made myself extremely unpopular with the Amsterdam Chapter by baptizing every little slave baby born since."

"Why do you do it?" asked Jesse.

"Because I am a nonconformist, Son." He waved his glass grandly and turned to Sarah. "A man can barely hear himself think above the orchestra of cicadas today, Madame. I believe they are celebrating the imminent departure of Governor Kieft in all his corruption." He drained the Madeira. "You don't believe that do you, Sarah?"

"Hogwash!" Sarah tossed the remaining mop-water over the railing and went inside, closing the bottom half of the door after herself.

"Alas, boys," said the Dominie, raising his voice for Sarah's benefit. "Women are not free to let their imaginations soar, being forever tied to this earth by an endless web of umbilical cords."

Sarah slammed the top half shut.

Jesse should not have discussed Sharkface's accounts with the Dominie. If Papa had not gotten himself tangled up with Agnietje, this would not have happened. As it was, Jesse obviously found it easier to confide in the Dominie. Fortunately the budding front-stoop conspiracy could not last long. The Dominie was due to return to the Netherlands on the *Princess Amalia* with former Governor, Willem Kieft, to answer charges about his own behavior.

The next day the two sleuths found another example of reversed digits, again with the totals balancing. They were as excited as hounds after a hare.

"The first thing is to make a copy of these records, lad."

Bogardus produced a fat blue notebook and in 48 hours Jesse had neatly duplicated the accounts of all five years. Now the hounds were able to sniff at the hare without budging from their respective stoops.

A few days later, I was on my knees helping Sarah to weed the vegetable patch, when Madame Vinje-Dam paused in her daily trek to lean against one gatepost while Gimpy lifted his missing leg against the other.

"What's that crazy preacher gossiping about with the boy?" she hissed.

"*Horace*," snapped Sarah, attacking a bit of cow grass in with the beans.

"And just who is Horace?"

"Some dead Roman who thinks mice come from pregnant mountains."

"Tchah!" snorted the Witch. "What fools men are!"

Sarah yanked the cow grass out by the roots, murdering a perfectly good bean plant in the process.

"Don't break your back over weeds, girl," cackled Madame Vinje-Dam. "Cicadas'll get us all before the season's out." She glanced suspiciously at the two sleuths with their notebooks, then raised her voice. "How is your mother-in-law, Dominie?"

"Poorly thank you, Madame Vinje-Dam. Madame Bogardus is with her now, but I am afraid the years are finally taking their toll."

"Horse piss!" screeched the Witch. "It's cicada dust that's choking Tryntje, not age!" She whacked the gatepost with her stick and hobbled off with three-legged Gimpy in close pursuit.

"Is van Tienhoven aware that these notebooks are in your possession, Jesse?" asked the Dominie when our visitor was out of earshot.

"I don't know."

"I am sure that he is not aware of these reversed digits," continued the Dominie. "They must be genuine mistakes."

Jesse stared blankly and Sarah dropped her trowel in astonishment.

"Aha! So you were eavesdropping, Sarah." The Dominie waved his glass triumphantly.

"Humph!" she said, ignoring the Madeira. "Are you trying to tell me that Sharkface is not crooked?"

"No. I am simply stating that he is too clever to leave this evidence. With half the colonists illiterate, and beavers being credited left and right at different rates for Europeans and Wilden, there are a dozen ways for a bookkeeper to cheat without reversing digits. However, it is these simple errors that will lead to his downfall."

"But if they're genuine mistakes," faltered Jesse.

"If you reversed a pair of digits like this," said the Dominie, "you would discover it immediately when the totals failed to balance. Van Tienhoven was always fiddling so he never expected the debits and credits to add up. He balanced the books by sweeping the surplus into his own account, probably claiming extra beavers for himself into the bargain."

"The skins are counted every week," said Jesse.

"By whom?"

"I do it."

"That means van Tienhoven did the counting in his day, and was able to borrow against future beavers when necessary. The reversed digits are only clues along the trail, Son," Bogardus announced grandly. "The real proof is buried in these records and together we will dig it out."

"Uphill work to follow a ten-year-old trail," Sarah muttered, dumping the weed-pile into the road. "And Jesse is going to be in the hutspot up to his ears if Sharkface gets wind of it. Here he comes now."

The Secretary emerged from the Fort, deep in conversation with his father-in-law, Jan Dam. Fortunately they were not as nosy as the Witch, and barely glanced at the hounds panting over their notebooks.

The cicadas soon disappeared, but the front-stoop conspiracy continued until August 16th, the day the *Princess Amalia* sailed for the Fatherland. The hounds claimed to have made great progress, although I was too busy to pay much attention to their growing "List of Discrepancies." Then came a scare.

After work the last afternoon, Jesse settled on the stoop with the fifth black notebook. The Dominie had been sorting papers all day, much of it evidence against former Governor Kieft for the upcoming hearings. Anneke was packing his clothes.

"Don't let me leave this behind, my dear." He appeared on his stoop waving the blue notebook in one hand and his Madeira in the other. "Now Jesse, where were we?"

I left to fetch water. When I returned with a full pail in each hand, I was horrified to see Sharkface at the gate and the two naive hounds completely unaware of his existence.

"Good afternoon, Mynheer van Tienhoven," I said loudly.

He ignored me and addressed the others in a voice of ice. "What are these notebooks that you find so engrossing, gentlemen?"

"Good afternoon, Cornelis," cried the Dominie, springing to his feet with surprising agility. "I have spent the entire day sorting evidence for my appearance in Amsterdam. Now I must finish packing." Blue notebook safely under his arm, he stepped nimbly through his front door.

But there was no escape for crippled Jesse and no place to hide the black notebook. Van Tienhoven opened the gate and started up the path, jaws wide-open in that shark-like smile. If I could get ahead of him I might be able to create a diversion. But the only way to pass him was to put down the buckets, which I was loath to do. Spilling a full pail of water was the only diversion I could think of.

At that moment Sarah swept out on to the stoop, waving the hutspot ladle in the air like someone demented, and shouting, "Stop it! Stop it, I say!"

I did not dare look at Jesse. Somehow he had managed to stuff the "List of Discrepancies" into the marigold pot, but the tell-tale black notebook lay conspicuously on the bench. As the Secretary mounted the steps Sarah sat down squarely on top of the evidence.

"What were you and the Dominie discussing, boy?" repeated Sharkface, his voice now slippery as silk.

Jesse was not a good liar and he just stared helplessly.

"I'll tell you what they were discussing," shouted Sarah. "They were discussing *Horace,* and mountains in labor, giving birth to a ridiculous mouse!" She shook the hutspot ladle at Jesse. "Here's your ridiculous book. I'm sitting on it."

With difficulty she searched beneath her skirt as Jesse looked on, terrified. When she finally extracted *Horace,* the relief on his face was so obvious that she had to whack him with the ladle to change his expression.

"Let me see that please, Sarah." Sharkface reached forward, careful not to jostle the crutches leaning against the rail only inches from her knee.

Giving Jesse a final whack, she swiveled at the waist, brandishing ladle and *Horace,* and doing her best not to look like someone being goosed by a notebook spine. Sharkface grabbed. Sarah dropped *Horace,* at the same time swinging her foot so the crutches clattered to the floor. As he scrambled to catch things I added to the confusion by dropping a bucket, splashing water over everyone, while Sarah whipped the black notebook under her apron and slipped through the door to return with a mop.

"Clumsy knaap!" She handed me the mop and went back inside.

Out of the corner of my eye I watched Sharkface replace the crutches and examine *Horace* with suspicion.

"I'm sorry about the water, sir," I said.

He ignored me and handed the book back to Jesse. "Very high-spirited, that Aunt of yours." He then raised his voice for Sarah's benefit. "I am afraid she has broken the binding."

The next day the whole town turned out to watch the *Princess Amalia* set sail for the Netherlands. She was carrying 6500 beaver skins and a for-midable list of passengers, half of them not speaking to the other half. All morning rowboats plied back and forth between ship and Strand as dozens of colonists headed home, many abandoning the New World for-ever. Then came the two exiles, Kuyter and Melyn, who were secretly carry-ing a chest full of documents incriminating the former Governor. The most elaborate departure was that of Willem Kieft himself, with trumpets and drum to mark the official farewell between Governors. He carried with him evidence to justify his administration, as well as proof of treason against the exiles and charges of drunken misconduct against the Dominie. He also took all his pretty watercolors.

The last to board was Dominie Bogardus. He insisted that the East River was not large enough for himself and Kieft together, and made everything twice as difficult by departing from the shore of the Hudson. Abram and I carried the Dominie's chests down the steep path behind the windmill, and the family said their farewells by the water's edge. The footing was too treacherous for Jesse, but Sarah was there helping Anneke with the young-sters. For once the Dominie was almost sober.

"Careful of those boxes, boys. They contain Madeira for the journey. Sarah, my dear, tell Jesse that after I clear my own name, and see to it that Kieft receives his just deserts, I intend to enter charges of fraud against

Secretary van Tienhoven." He patted the blue notebook in his pocket. "This is Jesse's insurance policy. As long as I am alive that shifty petticoat-chaser can do nothing to the boy."

Then he hugged his little sons and all the stepchildren and finally Anneke.

"Don't worry, my pretty one. I shall be back in six months, a year at the most."

While the Dominie was being rowed around the tip of Manhattan the rest of us trudged back up the bank to join the crowd on Weepers' Point. There was wild cheering when Bogardus came into view. Besotted or sober he was always a favorite.

Annie Melyn stood on an overturned rowboat, tears streaming down her cheeks as she waved farewell to husband and son. For some reason Cornelis Melyn had decided to take their six-year-old with him. Annie had a twitch. Her mouth jerked even when she was happy. When she wept, her face was a fright. Vrouw Kuyter and Anneke climbed up to join her, standing one on each side.

Long after the ship had disappeared and the crowd dispersed, the three women remained standing on that overturned rowboat, peering out into the gathering dusk.

Banquet
for Balthasar

It was the evening after the *Princess* sailed that Papa asked me to go for a stroll on the Heerenstraat with him. I knew what was coming.

"Agnietje and I are going to be married, Son."

I wanted to shout, "No! How can you replace Mother with that woman." But I held my tongue.

"Your mother has been dead four long years now, Jan. No one can ever replace her," he said quietly as if he could read my mind. "It is very difficult for a widower to care for five children. Yes, I know you and Jesse are grown. But I can't leave Little Rachel in charge of the house with soldiers coming and going all day. She's only thirteen, and you know what soldiers are like. It wasn't so bad under Governor Kieft, where I had much more free time. But his Lordship requires six full days a week."

In all fairness, I had not thought of that angle. Jesse did say that the house ran more smoothly with Agnietje in charge. I had to say something. Papa was waiting for me to say something.

"Jesse told me that Agnietje is very kind to Will and the girls," I said.

Papa breathed a sigh of relief. "Agnietje is a good woman, Son."

The rest of New Amsterdam had no trouble accepting the new Madame Montagne. In fact at the festivities for the Christening of little Balthasar Stuyvesant, she and Papa sat at the head table with his Lordship.

It was late October and a lavish banquet had been laid on in the Great Hall adjoining the Governor's mansion. Half the town was invited, even Jesse and I. Jesse had one of his bad spells that day and was unable to go. Sarah made him lie down in their bed cupboard where he soon fell asleep. Papa and Agnietje stopped by on their way to the party and Papa took a quick look at the patient.

"Nothing a good night's sleep won't cure," he announced with his usual worried frown.

So we left Jesse there with Malala in charge.

Festivities began at five o'clock and the first hour was mainly drinking and swallowing oysters and finding your assigned seat. There must have been at least 75 guests in the room plus two dozen black slaves in livery waiting on table.

Papa, being the baby's Godfather, made the first toast to the newborn. No one paid much attention, however, because word was circulating that a ship had just entered the Narrows.

"I could get a letter from Everardus," whispered Anneke, still a great beauty even in her forties. As Godmother, she also sat at the head table, as did Sharkface and his wife and the new Dominie Backerus. Anneke had a lapful of Balthasar, with his long gown trimmed in Brussels lace and his blanket crocheted in loyal orange, white and blue.

"A mite soon for news of the *Princess*," hissed Madame Vinje-Dam who was not pleased with her assigned seat and preferred hobbling from table to table. "Tchah! What do I smell around here?" She poked one bony finger into the baby's bottom and sniffed hopefully.

"He's clean as a whistle," said Anneke, indignantly straightening the Brussels lace as the Witch tried a new tack.

"Too bad your Ma didn't live long enough to bring this knaap into the world," she cackled. "A Governor's son would be quite a feather in Tryntje's cap."

"Mother lived a long and full life," snapped Anneke.

"Long and full life, horse piss! She was choked to death by cicada eggs if you ask me!"

"Nobody asked you," retorted Anneke, but Madame Vinje-Dam was already badgering someone else.

By now we knew that the incoming ship was flying English colors which meant little chance of mail. Still everyone was always eager for news from England, particularly the next episode in the never-ending battle between King Charles and his Roundhead Parliament.

When last heard, the King was a prisoner locked up in Hampton Court, and the country was being run by that wart-nosed Cromwell. As I saw it, the King's Cavaliers wore their hair in long curls and believed that only the King had the divine right to chop off heads, while Cromwell's Roundhead Puritans cut their hair short and believed Parliament should have equal right to chop off heads. I am not much for politics but if Cromwell's Puritans were anything like those in New England, I was for the King.

When the venison arrived, Anneke passed Balthasar to Agnietje and it was time for Sharkface to speak. With fresh rumors racing round and round the room like lumps of butter whirling in the whey, nobody planned to listen to him either. The English ship had not even entered the East River yet but there were always small boats in the harbor shouting at each other. Of course the language barrier made it unlikely that anyone would get anything straight. Dock hands scurried back and forth to the Fort, and the latest news reached the least important guests by the door first. I was seated with Isaack and Sarah and Doctor Hans Kierstede and his wife Sarie, Anneke's eldest daughter. We were in the center of the room near the head-table where we were last to hear anything. The only believable tidbit was that the ship was out of Bristol and bound for Boston.

Sharkface had barely opened his mouth, when Annie Melyn, near the door, suddenly staggered to her feet, face twitching, gave a thin cry and crumpled to the floor. At the same time the Witch screeched into my ear: "*Princess Amalia!* Gone to the bottom with all hands!"

For the next few minutes there was chaos in the hall as guests began to excuse themselves amid a dozen equally implausible rumors. The most persistent was that the ship's Captain was carrying a letter addressed to someone in New Amsterdam. With festivities on the verge of collapse, Peg-Leg stood up and raised his hands for silence.

"Citizens and friends," he hammered the floor with his wooden leg for emphasis, "I have dispatched Mister Newton, our new Councillor of English affairs, to intercept the incoming ship. He will speak personally with her Captain and bring all tidings directly here, so that my guests in this hall will receive them before any persons gathered at the shore. If there is a letter to one of my subjects it will be delivered here also. So please remain in your seats, continue to enjoy your meal and do not concern yourselves with unfounded rumors."

Vrouw Melyn had already been revived and escorted home, but the Governor insisted on making room for Vrouw Kuyter next to Anneke at the head table. Then he ordered pipes and more wine to be passed and the band played merry tunes to liven things up.

At last Mister Newton returned. The music faltered as he held a whispered consultation with the Governor and handed him a letter. Once more Peg-Leg pulled himself to his feet and the music died with one last, tuneless sigh.

"Citizens and friends," Peg-Leg sounded very tired this time. "Mister Newton has been informed that on the 27th of last month the *Princess Amalia* was wrecked on the coast of Wales some 80 miles from the port of Bristol. As to loss of life, it is believed to be considerable. Vrouw Kuyter may be able to enlighten us after reading this."

He passed her the letter but her hands shook so that Papa had to open it for her. There was not a sound in the hall as she read to herself, slowly, with no change of expression. My eye caught something flashing and swinging back and forth under the head tablecloth. It was the silver band on the Governor's wooden leg. Then Vrouw Kuyter cleared her throat and began to read aloud with many pauses to translate from the Danish into her awkward Dutch. I stared at the flashing silver band.

This 28th day of September, 1647,
At Swansea on the coast of Wales

My dearly beloved helpmate,

The greatest of all disasters has befallen and it is only through the incredible mercy of Almighty God that I am alive to tell it. Yesterday the Princess Amalia *was destroyed and a hundred souls drowned with her. As of this writing I know of only two passengers to survive, Cornelis Melyn and myself.*

For three days we were driven before a violent storm until we lost all bearings and crashed onto the rocky coast of Wales. When the ship broke up, the port quarter became grounded on a sandbar some distance from shore. Here I found myself clinging in the dark, almost by the fingernails, until God directed my hand to an iron deck-cleat. With a firmer hold I was now able to raise my head and became aware of six or eight others sharing this temporary refuge. To my left I recognized the portly figure of Dominie Bogardus. I shouted but the words vanished on the wind before I could hear them myself. To my right was a wiry seaman named Urbane who was holding the wee Melyn lad. I had noticed him several times on the journey, teaching the boy to tie knots. Now, before my eyes, he lost his grip and the two of them began sliding away. I grabbed the boy's sleeve but the cloth ripped in my hands. Then at the last minute my fingers closed on the length of rope he always wore knotted at the waist. I tied him to the belaying cleat just as the next wave crashed over us. Urbane was gone.

When I lifted my head again the Dominie had disappeared. God rest his valiant soul. Beside myself and the lad, only two figures remained. I learned later that they were sailors from Zeeland.

And so the night passed with the sea threatening to pull my arms from their sockets as I tried to support the boy so the rope would not crush his lungs. Again and again I set those agile little fingers onto the cleat horns but there was no strength in them. Always the next wave left him dangling. In the morning the lad's body was still tied to the cleat, but the Lord had taken his soul unto His bosom.

When the wind subsided, the two Zeelanders and I built a raft and were able to reach shore. We found the local Welshmen more interested in looting shipwrecked cargo than saving lives. Someone directed me to the tavern at nearby Swansea where I was overjoyed to be reunited with Cornelis Melyn. He also had a remarkable escape, having been washed ashore together with a heavy cannon. He is well, although exceedingly distressed about the boy.

As to the cause of this terrible disaster, I can only speculate that it was divine judgment upon the sins of Willem Kieft. Please convey my condolences to Vrouw Melyn on the loss of her son, and to the widow Bogardus. Tell her the Dominie will face his God with head held high.

A small boat sails from here within the hour for the port of Bristol where many ocean-going vessels are to be found. I trust this letter finds you and the children in good health.

Your affectionate husband,

Jochem Pieterse Kuyter

When Vrouw Kuyter finished reading there was a moment of silence.

"Old Nehooma did it," I said aloud. "She said she would drown Kieft and she has."

"Don't be daft, boy," said Doctor Kierstede, his little pointed beard pretending to add authority to his words. "Divine judgment upon the sins of Willem Kieft is the logical cause." Then he turned to Sarie. "Come, my dear. We had better get your mother home.

Throughout, Anneke had remained composed as though she had known all along. With every eye upon her she graciously thanked the Governor and Vrouw Judith Stuyvesant for their hospitality before departing with a train of daughters and sons-in-law in her wake. Only the second daughter, Tryn, was hysterical and she had never liked her Dominie step-father.

"Houd op, Tryn," said Anneke, calmly.

Again Peg-Leg rose, this time with difficulty.

"Citizens and friends," he said slowly. "I have requested Dominie Backerus to lead us in prayer for the Honorable Willem Kieft, Governor of this Colony nine years, for the Reverend Everardus Bogardus, Dominie of this parish fourteen years, and for all our friends and relatives aboard the ill-fated *Princess Amalia.*"

Between prayers I noticed that the Witch had grabbed Sharkface's place at the head table. Sharkface had disappeared. Of course, he could have given his seat to his mother-in-law, but that was not like him. For some reason it made me uneasy.

Dominie Backerus was quoting from the Book of Job when Papa suddenly excused himself and left the hall. One of the slaves had handed him a note and I remember thinking it must be very important to cause him to depart at this solemn moment.

"I wonder if Jesse is all right," muttered Sarah.

Dominie Bogardus had said, "As long as I am alive van Tienhoven can do nothing to the boy."

Again I looked around for Sharkface but there was no sign of him. As inconspicuously as possible I made my way to the door. Once in the courtyard, I raced across the cobblestones and through the Fort gate to the de Forest home.

Inside, Doctor Hans Kierstede and Papa were leaning over the bed-cupboard trying to force air into Jesse's lungs while little Malala rubbed the soles of his feet, tears running down her chocolate cheeks.

"It's no use. He's gone," said the Doctor at last, gently pulling my father away. "He suffered a great deal in this world, Jehan. At long last, God has ended his ordeal." He covered Jesse's face with the sheet.

"God did not end his ordeal," I said. "He was murdered! Sharkface killed him!"

They both stared at me as though I were someone who fed bones to his horse and straw to his dog.

"Why should van Tienhoven wish to kill the boy?" inquired Hans, skeptically.

"Because he knew Jesse and the Dominie had evidence against him and he couldn't touch Jesse as long as the Dominie was alive but with the *Princess* gone to the bottom he saw his chance and killed him before . . ." The words tumbled over each other without making much sense.

"What evidence are you talking about, Son?" asked Papa, bewildered.

"Evidence of fraud in the accounts from the days when van Tienhoven was bookkeeper," I said more slowly. "You would have known about it if you hadn't been so busy getting married." I picked up a pillow from the floor. "Here! Look at this! Sharkface must have used it to suffocate Jesse!"

Papa frowned and shook his head. "Secretary van Tienhoven was at the head-table with me. He's still at the banquet."

"No. I looked for him. He had disappeared."

"Who else knows about this so-called evidence?" interrupted Hans, sarcastically.

"Sarah knows. But I can prove it to you with Jesse's "List of Discrepancies." The Dominie had a copy and he said it contained enough evidence to hang your average bookkeeper."

"Van Tienhoven was a long way from your average bookkeeper," muttered Hans under his breath.

Papa sat at the table with his head in his hands, but Kierstede never took his eyes off me as I removed the bookshelf from the wall. After Sharkface's unexpected visit, Jesse had kept the "List of Discrepancies" well hidden in an open slot behind the shelf. I had seen it earlier in the week. Now to my horror the slot was empty. Frustrated, I turned to Hans: "How did you get here so fast?" I asked.

"We were escorting Anneke home when Malala came out shouting for help. She had been asleep with little Susan in the other room when she thought she heard Jesse falling out of bed. It was I who sent for your father." He grabbed me by the shoulders. "Listen very carefully, Jan. Jesse was a sick boy and suffered, among other things, from consumption in both lungs. He died in his sleep and if you know what's good for you, you will forget all about that "List of Discrepancies.""

Furious, I shook him off. I think I would have punched him one on that fancy little black beard if Papa had not been there looking so miserable.

At that moment Sarah came in. She apparently had heard about Jesse.

"Ah, Sarah," said the Doctor. "Jan tells me that you know about some "List of Discrepancies" compiled by Jesse and Dominie Bogardus."

"I don't know what you are talking about. Jan must be dreaming," she lied. At the same time she gave me a look that said in no uncertain terms: "Keep your mouth shut, Idiot!"

She was right. If Sharkface had indeed killed Jesse for knowing too much, what was to stop him from killing me and Sarah?

"Maybe I was dreaming," I said abjectly. But to myself I vowed to avenge my brother if it took my whole life. Killing was too good for Sharkface. Instead I would topple him from his pedestal as number two man in the

Colony. I would push him to the bottom of the ladder where he would be scorned by everyone down to the lowliest slave.

By now people had begun to gather out front. Sharkface was there with his ugly wife and uglier mother-in-law. Doctor Kierstede stepped out on to the stoop and addressed the growing crowd.

"Consumption, horse piss!" screamed the Witch when he had finished speaking. "The boy was choked to death by cicada eggs growing in his lungs!"

The next day Jesse was laid to rest in the little cemetery on the Heerenstraat. Among the mourners was Lord-General Pieter Stuyvesant, Commander of all the Netherlands' forces in North America and the Caribbean. Beside him stood his number two man, Secretary van Tienhoven, with his hand on his heart, and his shark-like soul concealed behind a mask of bereavement.

It would be eight years before Jesse was avenged.

Slooterdyk

In 1652, war broke out between England and the Netherlands. While the two fleets battled it out on the other side of the Atlantic, Peg-Leg decided to protect New Amsterdam by building a wall across Manhattan along the line of the cattle barrier. In a matter of months a palisade was constructed of twelve-foot posts, sharpened to a point at the top, and extending one half mile from river to river. There were two gates: the Land Gate on the Heerenstraat and the Water Gate by the East River.

People here were not so worried about the English. They just hoped the Wall would protect them from Indians. Unfortunately, a run, leap and a scramble was enough to get any young brave over the top.

In the winter of '53 Tiger died in my arms. I buried him by the ruins of Vredendale.

In '54 the war with England was over. When Uncle Isaack mentioned that he was looking for a reliable young man to take a consignment of tobacco to the Fatherland, I volunteered. I would not have gone if Tiger were still alive.

"You will have to bargain to get the best price, Jan. Then you must reinvest the proceeds for resale here. Good wines and spirits, and bolts of high-grade, durable fabric sell best."

To my surprise, Papa raised no objection to the trip. I now think he had learned about my visits to Vredendale and was relieved to have me out of harm's way for a time.

"Of course you will visit Leyden, Son. There are several small business matters that I want you to attend to in Leyden. And you must call on Cousin Crispin de Forest and his wife Margariet, who was your mother's dearest friend. It would be nice to take her a little gift. As I remember she loved hats. She once asked your mother to send her some bright colored feathers from the New World to decorate a hat. They don't have all the beautiful birds in Europe that we have here."

By the time I sailed on the *King Solomon* I had a dozen commissions, mostly tobacco, some beavers and several small gifts or letters to be delivered. For my cousin Margariet I had purchased half a dozen brightly colored feathers from a friendly Canarsie.

It was no longer illegal for a private citizen to ship furs out of the Colony, but the duty was exorbitant and officials were apt to make trouble. This did not worry me. I was twenty-three and eager to see the world. As soon as I completed my commissions I would be off, first to Paris, then who knows?

The sea voyage itself was remarkably uneventful. I shared a cabin with Vincent Pikes, a decent fellow who had only been in the Colony for a couple of years. He had been hired by Govert Lookermans to do much the same thing that I was doing for my uncle. The difference was that Lookermans had an agent in Amsterdam ready to sell the goods. I would have to fend for myself.

Vincent had a full, if somewhat unkempt, beard, which made him look older. In fact we were the same age and whiled away many hours together playing cards or backgammon or even mumble-ty-peg. He invited me to come with him to visit his family in the village of Slooterdyk.

"Mother's a good cook, Jan. And Slooterdyk is only a hop, skip and a jump from Amsterdam. Besides, I have a little sister, a real beauty. People used to say we looked alike."

One glance at Vincent's hairy face ruined that picture. I thanked him, but refused on the grounds that I had promised to visit Leyden first. I did not tell him that I planned to see the world, not the tiny hamlet of Slooterdyk.

On September first, in the English Channel, we overtook a convoy of four Dutch ships returning to Amsterdam from Virginia. They invited us to join them, but I was pleased when our Skipper refused the offer. It may be safer to travel in convoy but it slows you down. At 23, speed outweighs safety any day.

"Probably loaded with Virginia tobacco," groaned Vincent, as we gradually drew abreast of the lead ship. "Why should Virginia tobacco fetch a better price than Manhattan tobacco, anyway? What terrible fortune! "

"Good fortune, you mean," I said. "When that convoy unloads at Amsterdam, the market for tobacco will be temporarily glutted. But until then there is likely to be a shortage. We will dock a good 24 hours before the convoy. This means we should get a fine price, possibly an excellent price, if we sell instantly."

"You're right!" he exclaimed. "I'll slip the cargo officer a florin to unload our tobacco first. Then the minute we land, I'll hire a cart and take it to

Lookerman's agent. He'll dispose of it quickly before word of the convoy gets around. This means you will have to attend to the business of the duty on all the beavers. We'll settle up later."

Everything went as planned. We reached Amsterdam early on a Thursday morning and Vincent set out promptly for the Kalverstraat, where Jud, Loockerman's agent, did business. He was happy to sell for both of us, and did so at lightning speed. Even after he had taken his commission I found I had realized almost 2000 florins, much more than anticipated. As Loockerman had more tobacco, Vincent's share was even greater. Fortunately we both had pockets for banknotes, sewn inside our shirts to foil the light-fingered.

In the meantime I had experienced no trouble with the customs inspector over the beavers and was delighted when Vincent told me that Jud had volunteered to sell my skins as well as his. So we loaded the lot onto the cart and pushed it down crowded, noisy alleys to the little hole in the wall that was the agent's office.

Jud was a small, ugly man, but very sharp and well-organized. He said that rumors of the convoy were all over town now and he had sold our tobacco in the nick of time. As to the beavers, however, there was no hurry. He instructed us to return Monday afternoon, by which time he would have sold all at the best possible price. Of course we agreed.

"Now you have no excuse not to come to Slooterdyk," Vincent told me cheerfully. "There is no way to visit Leyden and be back here by Monday. Besides, it will save you lodging, to say nothing of food."

This time I accepted and Vincent led us away from the bustling dock area to the more attractive part of the city. I must admit I was impressed by the beautifully-paved avenues and the elegant municipal buildings decorated with statues of marble.

Vincent's uncle ran a tavern just off the Heiligeweg where we celebrated our new business partnership with wine and pork pie. Then we went back to the *King Solomon* and each put our belongings into a large sack. With this over a shoulder, we trudged a hundred paces to where the northbound canal boats lay. Two horses were already harnessed to the foremost, which had several vacant seats, and Vincent arranged with the boatman to carry us as far as the branch canal to Slooterdyk for a few stuivers. From there we had to walk. It was less than a mile, but with all my belongings on my back it felt like twenty.

"Which way now?" I asked as I paused to wait for Vincent to catch up. Maybe his sack was heavier than mine.

"Straight ahead," he gasped. "The cottage is just around that copse of trees."

When I reached the trees I set my bag down to wait for Vincent again. It was his home and he should be the first to reach it, but curiosity got the better of me. I peeked around the trees and nearly fell over with the shock.

There, with her back to me was Sutje, her golden curls sparkling in the September sun. She was sweeping the front steps to the cottage and dancing as she swept. Beneath a bright blue skirt, white ruffled petticoats swirled above dainty ankles. For a moment I was dumbstruck.

Then Vincent dropped his heavy sack beside me and shouted "Peternella!"

"Vinnie!" she cried and raced into her brother's arms.

Of course it was not Sutje. I had always thought of Sutje as having a sweet face. This girl was indescribably beautiful.

"Jan, this is my sister, Peternella. Peternella, I want you to meet my new business partner, Jan Montagne."

"I'm happy to meet you, Jan."

She smiled. It was a joyous smile and a feeling of great happiness came over me. But my voice was still paralyzed. I had to say something. They were waiting for me to say something.

"You are much prettier than Vincent," I stammered finally and everyone laughed.

My visit to Slooterdyk seemed to pass in a flash. Vincent's mother was indeed a good cook. The first evening she served only fish soup with fresh bread, but I never tasted anything so delicious.

Vincent's father used to be a schoolmaster and was a man of substance in the village. In Slooterdyk, someone with half an acre to his name was a man of substance, and the family could scarcely believe it when Vincent insisted I tell them the size of Vredendale.

"Two hundred acres! Imagine that," exclaimed Mother. "How did Vredendale fare during the dreadful Indian uprising?"

Vincent had warned me to understate the danger from Indians so his mother would not worry about him.

"Not well," I said. This was an understatement if I ever heard one. "I plan to use my earnings from this trip to make the bowery better than ever."

In four days I was not once alone with Peternella, nor did we have any real conversation. The nearest was at the village church where I sat between Peternella and Vincent at Sunday service. Conversation was not to be considered but at least I could enjoy listening to her sing. She had the voice of an angel.

"Why aren't you singing," she whispered?

"I prefer listening to you," I whispered back and I could swear that she blushed.

After church the parents stayed to chat with neighbors, leaving the three of us to walk home together. I had some hope that Vincent would find a friend, or at least walk on ahead, but it was not to be.

"Do you know any Indians, Jan?" asked Peternella.

"Many." I answered. "My best friend was a Weckquasgeek. We were like brothers."

What happened to him?"

"He was killed at the battle of Greenwich."

This was the first time in ten years that I had been able to speak about Little Deer. Something in my voice however, must have warned her to change the subject.

"Tell me about Vredendale," she said.

I happily described the bowery as it was at its peak, concentrating mainly on the geographical aspects that were still there, like the creek and the waterfall and the acres of rich black soil.

"It is the finest piece of land in the Colony," I told her and that was the truth.

When we reached the house I gave Peternella the two prettiest red feathers in my collection.

"They are beautiful, Jan. I will make a red hat and set these around the brim."

Then it was Monday, and time to leave for Amsterdam and on to Leyden, then the world. But I no longer wanted to see the world. Paris was a silly idea. All I wanted was to spend the rest of my life with a girl named Peternella.

"Is your sister going out with anyone in particular?" I asked casually, as Vincent and I retraced our steps to Jud's place in the Kalverstraat.

"Not that I know about, but I've been away for two years. Why don't you come back to Slooterdyk when you finish your business in Leyden? Mother says you are welcome anytime."

"Thanks. I would like that."

Jud had again done a good piece of selling and we were both happy with the proceeds from the beavers. Some would say the agent's cut was too high but in my opinion he was worth every stuiver.

"Now," said Jud, "is either of you gentlemen interested in purchasing Madeira? I bought six cases this morning from a former client who was in a desperate hurry for ready cash. I offered him less than half what the Madeira was worth and he took it."

Who could resist such an offer? We took three cases a piece and even after Jud had taken his commission we had an unbelievable bargain. Fortunately Jud was happy to store things for a small fee.

Before we parted company Vincent showed me where to find the canal boat for Leyden. It would not leave until morning, but for an extra stuiver, the boatman agreed to stow my bag overnight. Having the afternoon free I decided to carry out Papa's one Amsterdam commission, to deliver a gift to his old schoolmate, Rembrandt Harmenzoon, in the Jodenbreestraat.

It was an imposing house on an elegant street and I felt rather awed just lifting the heavy brass knocker. The door was eventually opened by what I took to be the housekeeper, a pleasant woman of indeterminate age.

"Come right in, young man," she said when I had explained my errand. "I know the Master will want to talk to you about your father."

She ushered me in to a rather formal entrance hall crowded with portraits, many of the same buxom young woman.

"Wait here, please, while I tell him who is calling."

I had barely begun to examine the first portrait when Rembrandt burst into the hall. He was a large man of about fifty, with a menacing mustache, happily offset by a twinkle in the eye.

"So you are Jehan Montagne's son." He shook my hand enthusiastically. "Jan, is it? Come in to the sitting room, Jan. Hendrickje will bring us some wine."

The sitting room walls were also lined with paintings. A tiny coal fire burned in the grate, so different from the magnificent wood fires we are accustomed to in the New World. A pair of heavy mahogany chairs stood on either side of the fireplace and nearby was a small table covered by an oriental carpet. Hendrickje spread a white linen cloth over this and set out two glasses and a fancy decanter of red wine.

"Now tell me how is your father, Jan? I have not heard from him in over a year."

I said that Papa was in good health but very busy as a member of Governor Stuyvesant's Council. Then I gave him the gift which I knew to be a copy of Papa's 1639 map of Manhattan. To my surprise Rembrandt appeared genuinely pleased with it.

"Island of Manhattan," he read. "Ah! Here is the Fort. So way up here must be Montagne's Creek. Now which of these two boweries is Vredendale? Why are they not marked by name?"

"There wasn't room to label all the plantations," I explained. "The only bowery to be named on the map itself is Zegendale and that is because it belongs to the wealthy Jochem Pieterse Kuyter, who put up the money for the map."

Rembrandt laughed. "Isn't that the way of the world everywhere?"

The housekeeper returned with a dish of sweet cakes.

"Can you find an empty frame for this, Hendrickje?" said Rembrandt. "Maps are very stylish today in all the best houses. We will put it in that vacant spot to the left of the mantle."

He turned to me. "Now tell me, young man. When did you arrive in Amsterdam and how long do you expect to stay?"

I gave him a brief account of my movements to date. When I said I was leaving in the morning for Leyden, he immediately offered me a bite of supper and a bed for the night, which I was happy to accept. I was certainly doing well on expenses.

Supper was very plain; porridge with hot bread and cheese and more wine. We were joined by Rembrandt's twelve-year-old son, Titus, who was mentally alert but struck me as being frail physically. When Hendrickje was not busy serving, she ate with us in the formal, but somewhat chilly, dining hall.

Afterwards Titus showed me around the house. It seems that the pretty woman in so many of the pictures was his mother, who died when he was born. Rembrandt was broken-hearted and never remarried. The boy was brought up by Hendrickje.

According to Titus, Rembrandt was being threatened by bankruptcy proceedings. I did not see any sign of this, although I did think it odd that there was no servant to help Hendrickje cope with such a large house.

Rembrandt himself was exceedingly hospitable and obviously devoted to my father. At the University of Leyden Papa had apparently been the only one to appreciate his art. After Titus went to bed Rembrandt told me how Papa had helped him.

"It was the summer of 1620, Jan. I was fourteen, and had just completed my seven years at the Leyden Latin school. My parents were determined that I become a student at the University and as a command of Latin was the only entrance requirement, I was accepted. But I hated it. Every class was conducted in Latin. Students were required to speak Latin to each other at all times. They wanted us to THINK in Latin! But I wasn't interested in studying astronomy or Greek or geometry. All I wanted was to draw faces, especially older faces with character lines. Instead of attending class I used to wander around Leyden, sketching. Needless to say I was decidedly unpopular with my professors. My fellow students teased me because I had no time to join in their pranks. My parents continually scolded me for not appreciating my opportunities. As for my art, I was certain that I could never learn to paint in Latin. All in all I was thoroughly miserable.

"Then along came Jehan Montagne. He was a student of medicine and much older than I, but a fellow-student nevertheless. It was he who volunteered to speak to my father. He told him that I had a special gift and was destined to be a great artist. But I needed help. He suggested that I be apprenticed to a Master, which would involve twelve hours work a day, far more than the University.

"If Rembrandt remains at University," Jehan told him, "he has the ability to become a fine scholar. But if he is allowed to follow his destiny, he has the ability to become the greatest artist Europe has ever known."

"To everyone's astonishment, my father agreed. So after only a few months as a student I resigned from the University and began to study art under a Master. I never looked back."

"Titus showed me some of your portraits, sir. I don't know anything about art but they are marvelously lifelike, particularly those of Titus's mother. She was beautiful. And that sketch you did of my grandfather saving the little Puritan girl from drowning was wonderful."

"Thank you, Jan. Would you believe that the little girl's name was Remember? Is that not poetic? Your father wrote me that the sketch was destroyed when Vredendale burned to the ground."

I did not contradict him, although I was personally convinced that the sketch had not been in the empty house when I searched it.

Early the next morning I crept down the stairs so as not to wake the household, but Hendrickje was before me.

"This is for you, Jan."

She handed me a package of bread and cheese for the canal journey.

"Thank you, Hendrickje, and please thank the Master again for his hospitality."

The Netherlands is laced with canals, and the horse-drawn boats make the journey easy and predictable, though far from swift. Amsterdam to Leyden took the better part of a day and I was grateful for that bread and cheese.

Most of the trip I spent dreaming of Peternella. What a beautiful name! I never knew anyone before named Peternella. It rolls off the tongue . . . Peternella . . . Peternella . . . How remarkable that the most beautiful name in the world should belong to the most beautiful girl in the world. And to think that I nearly passed up the chance to visit Slooterdyk. The very thought was frightening.

Leyden I remembered from my childhood. But as a five-year-old, I had not appreciated the rows of handsome brick houses, the graceful church spires stretching skyward, or the blue-green canals spanned by a hundred bridges of hammered stone. However I did remember the friendly windmills sitting atop the city walls to catch the wind.

My first stop was to visit Mother's cousin, Crispin, whose wife, Margariet, had been Mother's best friend. They welcomed me with open arms and insisted I stay with them, which I was happy to do. It was during this visit that Cousin Margariet told me she had saved all of Mother's letters. She could not bear to part with them yet but she promised to see that they were sent to me eventually. (That is, all but one or two which she said were very personal and would have to be destroyed.) I must confess that I was too busy with my own thoughts to pay much attention to a collection of old letters.

Crispin was exceedingly helpful with my business problems, the most important being the final settlement of Mother's estate. As she had been dead eleven years this struck me as somewhat snail-like. The good news is that there was much more money than we anticipated. In fact there was enough to pay off the entire mortgage on Vredendale, if Papa chose.

Crispin had inherited his father's dye business and knew everything about wool. With his help, I purchased bolts of different colored wools for Uncle Isaack at a substantial discount. I also bought, with my own money, several yards of very expensive, red plaid from Scotland for Peternella. I was assured that it was more than enough for a skirt. For her mother I bought the equivalent amount in plain lavender. Some bottles of good wine would be perfect for Vincent and his father.

I had told Vincent that I would be in Leyden about three weeks. What with one delay after another, it was December before I returned to Slooterdyk. My gifts of wool were a big success. In fact Peternella sat down immediately to start work on her skirt.

"Oh it is beautiful, Jan! And it will go so well with my new hat."

She had already shown me the red felt hat she had made with my feathers on it. Very clever, but personally I would rather look at those golden curls.

"There is enough material here to make pleats," exclaimed Peternella.

"If it's pleats you're after, I had better help," said Mother. "Now don't lay a hand on those scissors until we have everything pinned down."

With the kitchen table covered in red plaid, it looked as though supper would be a long time coming. I took my bag up to the loft which I shared with Vincent. When I came down the father opened a bottle and we started on the wine.

"Lucky you got here this afternoon, young man," he said. "Dominie Meursius says a cold spell is setting in tonight. Canals will be frozen solid tomorrow."

Peternella laughed. "Good! I'll wear my new skirt to skate in."

"You will do no such thing," said Mother. "This material is much too beautiful. Now we will fold up here and get supper on the table before the men starve to death."

"Does the Dominie get his weather information directly from God," asked Vincent, "or from his own creaky bones?"

"Don't be blasphemous," admonished Mother.

I never did learn where the forecast came from, but it was certainly sound. We woke up the following morning to a different world, a world lightly covered in white powdered snow but cold enough to freeze the milk inside the cow. The Slooterdyk Canal was frozen solid and boys were already sweeping the snow from its glass-like surface.

Ice skating on the canals is said to be a national pastime in the Netherlands. It certainly is in Slooterdyk. Until this moment I had never seen Peternella when she was not involved with housework. Today, without a care in the world, she was ready for skating as soon as breakfast was cleared away. Vincent had an extra pair of skates for me and the three of us joined a throng of others all skating happily in a large circle. In the afternoon her parents joined in, skating gracefully in tandem, as did a few other couples.

I always thought of myself as a good skater but Peternella was better. She wore a blue skirt with a white knitted pullover and a long blue scarf that flew out behind as she raced along. Sometimes she twirled in the center of the circling skaters, so fast that you could barely see her face, just those beautiful golden curls flying.

For five days all Slooterdyk skated. Then it was Sunday and Dominie Meursius announced from the pulpit that the cold spell would be over tomorrow. Accordingly he said he was cutting short his sermon so that his parishioners could have one last full day on the ice. I wondered how many put something extra in the plate that Sunday. I know I did.

It was a lovely day, brisk but sunny. We rushed home from church to get our skates but left our Sunday clothes on. Peternella wore the new plaid skirt with pleats and the new red hat with feathers covered all but a few of those golden curls.

"Would you teach me to skate together like the couples do?" I asked Peternella as we were fastening our skates at the almost empty canal. The others were still changing from their Sunday best.

She laughed. "It's easy, Jan. You stand here, beside me, with your arm around my waist, like this, and we hold hands, like this. Now the important part is that we both start with the same foot and stay in step. Otherwise we will crash."

We set off tentatively. It was much easier than I thought and soon we were flying over the ice. I never had such a wonderful feeling. When I looked at Peternella I could tell that she felt the same way.

"We are going too fast," I said, reluctantly, as more and more skaters took to the ice.

She nodded and we slowed down to a more sensible speed. Then it happened. A little boy got turned around and started skating in the wrong direction. Peternella had to veer to avoid a collision and suddenly we were out of step. I tried to correct. At the same time she tried to correct and our skates caught. The next thing we knew we were both flat on the ice and still sliding.

"Are you all right?" I asked as we entered into a final gentle spin.

"Fine," she said, "but I've lost my hat." Vainly she tried to push back those golden curls.

I pointed to the hat, which was sailing along the ice on a tangent course, red feathers proudly aloft. We both started to laugh. We laughed so hard the tears came. Now her face was only inches away from mine. We stopped laughing.

"God, I love you, Peternella."

She looked so happy that I was filled with courage. Out of the corner of my eye I could see Vincent skating over to check on us. It was now or never.

"Will you marry me, Peternella?"

"I will," she whispered.

Angel

Peternella and I were married in the New Year of 1655, at the little country church in Slooterdyk. Then we had a glorious two weeks together in Amsterdam before the *King Solomon* was due to sail. The arrangement was that Vincent and I would depart as planned. Peternella would follow in three months. Her parents had agreed to the wedding, on condition that she remain in Slooterdyk until I had a roof to put over her head. They figured three months would give me time to restore Vredendale. I only hoped that I would get permission to rebuild.

Yes, I hated being separated from Peternella, but I was far from miserable. She brought so much joy into my life that on balance I was a very happy man. I told myself that three months was not forever.

I had written home that I was about to be married to the most wonderful wife a man could ever hope for and that "she just happens to be the most beautiful girl on either side of the Atlantic!" When the *King Solomon* dropped anchor at Manhattan the whole town was on hand, supposedly to welcome Peternella but really to decide for themselves whether she was or was not the most beautiful girl on either side of the Atlantic. You can imagine the jeering when I failed to produce any bride at all.

I was worried about Papa's reaction to the marriage but I need not have been.

"Vincent Pikes has a good reputation here, Son. I am sure we will all be happy to welcome his sister into the family."

When I broached the subject of rebuilding Vredendale, however, he was firm. He said that violence on the part of individual Indians had increased sharply during my absence. Sarah's father, old Phillipe du Trieux, was found dead only 100 yards from the Wall with an arrow through his neck. Then Jochem Pietersen Kuyter, our Danish neighbor, having survived the shipwreck of the *Princess,* had returned to Manhattan and rebuilt Zegendale, only to have his skull split by a tomahawk on his own front stoop. In response the Governor had prohibited all construction north of the Wall.

"On no account go anywhere near Vredendale, Son. You do not want Peternella to arrive in this country to find herself already a widow. Buy yourself a place in town. Perhaps your Uncle Isaack will sell you the little house where he and Sarah used to live."

Uncle was so delighted with all my financial transactions abroad that he decided to give me the little house on the Marketfield as a wedding gift.

"It is not in very good shape, Jan, and being only two rooms with no loft, it has not sold. Still, with a new roof and a little repair-work, it would be perfect for a young couple just starting out."

He also suggested that I work for the Brewery only half days for now. "This will give you time to fix up the house before Peternella arrives."

So with Vincent to help me I began work on the little house on the Marketfield. As long as we needed a new roof I was determined to raise it a few feet and give ourselves a proper loft with a window. Vincent claimed to know how to make a circular staircase, which took up not much more room than a ladder but was much more elegant.

In the meantime I had many long, wonderful letters from Peternella, usually including a funny story about life in Slooterdyk. She was a much better correspondent than I. All I could think about to tell her was how much I loved her and how much I missed her. I wrote nothing about troubles with the Wilden for fear that her parents might forbid her to sail at all. I simply told her that Peg-Leg had put a temporary ban on any construction north of the Wall, and until this was lifted we would live in a cozy little white house on the Marketfield and did she prefer blue shutters or green?

Peternella's next letter brought amazing news. She was expecting! I was going to be a father!

This was followed by a disappointing letter. Her parents wanted the baby to be born in Slooterdyk:

"It is much safer, Jan dear, but I told them I would sail as planned if you insisted. Please do not insist."

How could I insist after that? I told myself that nine months was not forever.

A few days later Sarah stopped in to see how the work was progressing.

"By the way, Jan, there is a ship coming in this morning. The signal on Staten Island is up."

My heart leapt. There might be another letter from Peternella.

"I was very sorry to hear about your father, Sarah."

She coughed. "Stop by for supper if you want, and bring Vincent. I'm roasting a side of venison."

"Thanks, Sarah," shouted Vincent from the roof. "We'd love to."

At that moment Madame Vinje-Dam came up the Marketfield at full hobble. Gimpy had not made it through the winter but the Witch still paused at each gatepost where he used to lift his missing leg. She had the latest report on the incoming ship.

"It's a slaver," she screeched. "Straight from Africa with 300 naked souls chained below decks!"

"Don't upset yourself, Madame Vinje-Dam," I said. "They won't let her unload here. She must be on her way to Virginia."

"Tchah! It's a disgrace." The Witch shook her stick at me. "They should outlaw the whole slave-trade if you ask me. Come along, Gimpy." She waited another few seconds for the invisible Gimpy to finish his business.

By afternoon the *White Horse* was anchored in the East River and the stink along the Strand was appalling. I was wrong about her destination. For the first time in the history of New Amsterdam, an African slaver was unloading her cargo at Manhattan.

"Tomorrow they'll be selling slaves on the parade-ground," announced Uncle Isaack at supper. He poured out two glasses of red wine.

"Pass these to the young men, Malala."

Then he poured one for himself. As usual Sarah preferred beer. Susan and Malala drank buttermilk. The three little ones were already in bed.

"May Malala and I go watch the slave market, Papa?" asked Susan, the apple of her father's eye. It has always amazed me that anyone as homely as Sarah could have given birth to such a beautiful child.

"You may not!" snapped Sarah. "Furthermore we are not buying any slave, Isaack de Forest. Get that notion right out of your head. How dare the Company unload here? Why not take them to Curaçao like they always do?"

Every year the Company shipped thousands of slaves from African Angola to the West Indies. There they were "seasoned" on the vast sugar-plantations and resold at a huge profit, many to Virginia. In New Amsterdam we received an occasional small parcel of 20 or so, most of whom belonged to the Company. To unload 300 unseasoned Angolans here was unthinkable.

"The venison is delicious, Madame de Forest," said Vincent.

He reminded me of Jesse, always trying to smooth ruffled tempers.

"If slavery's illegal in the Netherlands," asked Sarah, "why isn't it illegal here, too?"

"Fact of life, woman. Too much money in it. Why is there no bread on the table? Besides, international law justifies slavery if the slaves are heathens."

"Hog-wash!" retorted Sarah. "If this world were run by women, slavery would be illegal. Pass your Pa the bread, Susan."

"If this world were run by women, we would all go deaf from the babble," said Uncle. "Where's the butter?"

"There is no butter. Have cheese. How much do they cost, anyway?"

"About 300 guilders for an able-bodied man, not much more than a year's wage these days. What's the use of owning a cow, if I can't have butter with my bread?"

"The Company can't force people to buy slaves," persisted Sarah.

"That's where you're wrong, woman. The Company wants New Amsterdam to become a slave port, so this first shipload is being sold at a discount." Isaack extracted a clean white handkerchief from his coat pocket and blew his nose loudly. "You know a Dutchman can never resist a bargain."

"Nobody from this house is going anywhere near that parade-ground tomorrow," announced Sarah, flatly.

The next morning was unusually hot, and Vincent decided to take the day off. I was eating my mid-day bread and cheese out on the stoop where Jesse used to sit. The railings were broken, but the honeysuckle vines still flourished and I was determined to save them if possible for Peternella.

One gets used to the smells of New Amsterdam: the sour smell of boiling mash, the earthy smell of manure baking in the sun, the rancid smell of yesterday's garbage, all mellowed by the sweet fragrance of yellow honeysuckle. Today there was an ominous new odor drifting in above the others, the foul stink of the *White Horse* and her sinister cargo.

They say that half the slaves die crossing the Atlantic. Were the dead left chained to the living? It was an appalling thought. Packed together in the dark hold, how did they avoid shitting on each other?

There are so many terrible things in this world that it is human nature to ignore those thousands of miles away in Africa, Curaçao, even Virginia. But it was impossible to ignore the *White Horse*. All morning I listened to shouts from the crowded slave market. The town dogs were excited by the unusual smell, and waves of frantic barking periodically drowned out the auctioneer's voice.

As I watched, two figures came around the corner of the Fort on to the Marketfield. It was Uncle Isaack leading a scrawny, naked slave with a rope around his neck. A vicious-looking dog, snapping at the slave's unprotected backside, impeded progress as Uncle tried to guard his new property without becoming entangled in the rope. Then a second mongrel entered the fray and things became serious.

When dogs join forces, the wolf pack instinct is quick to surface. I grabbed a section of broken railing and ran out into the road waving it and shouting at the beasts. When I succeeded in striking one of them it ran off yelping. The other immediately pretended to be an innocent bystander, interested only in sniffing at a gatepost.

Now for the first time I had a good look at the slave. He was not much more than a boy and a poor specimen at that, with head hanging down, ugly saddle sores all over his body and ribs that stuck out like a starved calf in a drought.

"Good work, Jan," said Uncle. "You won't believe it but I bought this fellow for 75 guilders. Couldn't help myself. He will be worth 300 in a couple of years when he is full grown."

"Isaack de Forest!" shouted Sarah, striding down Brewer Street, angry as a she-bear with a bull mastiff on her tail.

"Now just a minute, woman. Loockermans is shipping a parcel of twenty down to Virginia tomorrow, for a quick profit," said Isaack. "If I say the word he'll take this fellow, too."

"He will not!" She snapped. "This boy is going nowhere tomorrow. He'll be lucky if he lives until tomorrow." She took a closer look. "My God! He hasn't eaten in months!"

"Only water gruel. That's what the dealer told me."

" And take that rope off his neck," continued Sarah.

Uncle removed the rope hesitantly as though he expected the prisoner to bolt.

"What else did this dealer tell you?" persisted Sarah.

"Only that he is 15 years old and is registered by the name of Angel."

"Angel!" she snorted. "What a ridiculous name to give a black slave." She turned to the boy. "Is your name Angel?"

For one moment the slave looked up. His eyes, sunk deep into their sockets, were full of misery without hope.

"Angel," he repeated and hung his head again.

"There are some old clothes of Jesse's that will fit him easily," said Sarah. "He needs a bath and plenty of Kierstede's ointment on those sores. Then I'm going to give him a good breakfast. He can sleep in the hayloft. Come along, Angel."

Head hanging almost to the waist, Angel slowly followed them up Brewer Street.

A few days later I happened to be on Brewer Street and noticed a commotion behind the de Forest home. Popje's Girl was harnessed to the wagon, and Sarah and Malala were struggling in vain to load four beer barrels by rolling them up a wobbly plank leaning against a wobbly tailboard. Angel stood nearby, in Jesse's shirt and pants, with head still hanging. Sarah was shouting instructions at him but he obviously had no idea what he was supposed to do.

"He won't work until you whip him," cried Goosie van Cortlandt over the back fence. The van Cortlands had four slaves so Goosie considered herself an authority.

"Here, let me help," I said. "Malala, you hold Popje's head."

"This is Popje's filly, Mister Jan. Popje is long dead."

"I know, Malala, but she looks just like her mother."

I braced the plank firmly against a rock and carefully rolled a barrel up into the wagon bed.

"Where is Uncle Isaack?" I asked, as I started on the second barrel.

"Left yesterday for Fort Orange," said Sarah. "He must have forgotten that he promised to deliver these barrels to Madame Vinje-Dam, today, without fail."

"I'll do it," I said. "Why didn't you ask me in the first place?"

"I didn't know the damn barrels were so heavy. Do you mind taking Angel along to help you. I know he is not much help but a change of scenery might do him good. Doctor Kierstede says there is nothing wrong with his neck but it has been hanging like that for three days."

Of course I was happy to take Angel. I invited him to sit on the driver's bench with me but he preferred to slouch against the tailboard, eyes on the ground.

At the last minute, Malala decided to ride part way with us. She wanted to deliver some blue stockings that she had knitted for her step-mother, Maria La Grande, and the Angolan Aunties. We dropped her at the fork to Kalch Pond and Free Town.

"We'll pick you up on the way back," I called after her.

She waved, then strode off, her strong but slightly lopsided gait always a sad reminder of the bear trap.

At Dam's place, the Witch directed proceedings as usual by screeching and threatening Angel with her stick. He kept his distance. I wondered if they had any bad-tempered old women in Angola.

On the way home we turned north at the fork in order to pick up Malala. Free Town had more than tripled in the last ten years, thanks to our peculiar custom of "half freedom." Here a slave can look forward to his liberty eventually, but there is usually a string attached. He may be required to pay his former master one fat pig a year or, in the case of a female, she may have to return one day a month to do housework. It is not total freedom. But few colonists come here totally free.

Free Town was always a mess. At least in summer it was a colorful mess and every ramshackle lean-to supported its own rainbow of tall holly-hocks. Today a parade of little children with bright-ribboned pigtails skipped down the road to greet us. Chickens scurried out from under the wagon wheels as we drew up before a sagging front porch. Here Malala sat gossiping with her friends, and the Aunties proudly pranced about in their new blue stockings.

The children made Popje's Girl nervous, so I did not dare leave the wagon. Isabella came over to show off her stockings, which drooped because her legs were so skinny. Being from Angola she was able to talk with Angel while I waited impatiently for Malala to say her goodbyes.

Then, like a battleship in full sail, La Grande swooped out on to the porch. Her stern and prow were both so spectacular that I had never noticed her legs before. Now she raised her skirts and kicked up one mag-nificent, blue-clad limb. The crowd cheered. She turned sideways and kicked up the other leg, this time as high as her shoulder, an astonishing performance. I applauded with the others. When I glanced at Angel he was standing up straight with a big grin on his face.

I don't know whether it was La Grande, or Free Town, or something Isabella told him. But from that day forward, Angel the slave held his head as high as any man.

Peaches

In August a Dutch ship, the *Waegh*, arrived at Manhattan, carrying thirty-six cannon and two hundred soldiers. This, combined with our standing army of about a hundred, gave us more than enough force to rid the Colony of the illegal Swedish settlement on the Delaware. The trespassers would either have to swear allegiance to the Netherlands or get out.

Vincent and I both volunteered for the expedition but were turned down. Peg-Leg wanted only regulars. He did need older men as officers, however, and Uncle Isaack was conscripted, much against his will.

"Keep an eye on Sarah and the children for me, Jan. You know she is expecting again. By the way, when is your Peternella due?"

"Not until October," I said. "I think I made a mistake in not insisting that she have the baby here. Her mother told her that it was safer to give birth in the Fatherland."

"My boy, you did the right thing," he said. "My experience is that half the babies born into this world are either dead or die within a few weeks. It doesn't matter where they are born. If you insisted on the baby being born here, and it just happened to die, believe me, you would never hear the end of it."

He had a point there.

"Don't worry about Sarah and the children," I told him. "First thing in the morning I will go over to check on them and if they need me any other time I'll be right here."

On Sunday, September fifth, a fleet of small local vessels, led by the mighty *Waegh*, set sail for the South River. Peg-Leg was personally in charge and everyone anticipated a bloodless coup, lasting no more than a week. How long could it take for three hundred soldiers with thirty-six cannon to persuade a few dozen farmers and a handful of Swedish soldiers to switch allegiance?

Here in New Amsterdam everything went smoothly at first. Without Peg-Leg stumping around, the town seemed to relax. The fact that he had left Sharkface in charge was barely noticed, except by my step-mother, Agnietje.

This was one of the rare occasions when I was home for dinner. Just the three of us: Papa, Agnietje and me, with two soldiers serving the food and two more in the kitchen. I found it rather awkward, but Agnietje obviously enjoyed being waited on.

"Your father is now the number two man in the Colony," she told me proudly. "He is about to be named Vice-Governor of New Netherland." Then under her breath and with much bitterness, "When the Governor is away he should leave your father in charge."

"Please do not make a fuss, my dear," said Papa, mildly. "Let us just hope that no problems arise in the next few weeks." He turned to me. "Tell us how the house is progressing, Son."

"The roof is finished and by next week I expect to be sleeping there permanently."

Agnietje's eyes lit up at the prospect of having one step-child permanently out of her hair. My two sisters, Little Rachel and Marie, were both betrothed now, busy leading their own lives and soon to be out of the nest for good. That left only Will, who like any other fourteen-year-old spent very little time at home anyway.

Most evenings after work, Vincent and I had supper at Marie's Tavern on the Heerenstraat, which was normally chock-full of soldiers. Now with the army away, we were able to get the best table out on the high stoop overlooking the Hudson. This particular evening we were joined by Marie and her new husband, a fur-trader named Peeck. We were waited on by Marie's son Aernoudt.

"Best view in town's from this here stoop," said Peeck. Then to his wife, "Sit yersel down, woman. Aernoudt can handle things. There's hardly nobody here anyways." He raised his voice. "Beer and hutspot for four, Aernoudt!"

"The only thing wrong with this view," laughed Marie, "is that one-armed Black Beard." She pointed to a bushy face in the window across the Heerenstraat. "Look at him sitting there just waiting to report me for something."

After losing an arm during the war, Ensign Van Dyck served on Peg-Leg's council until he was sacked for being drunk all the time. Now he did nothing but grow his beard, nurse the bottle, and report Marie for breaking regulations. She had already been fined 13 times, mostly for serving liquor to Wilden.

As the sun began to set we were treated to the remarkable spectacle of a fleet of 64 Indian dugouts speeding down the Hudson, each carrying some

20 to 30 Wilden. Peeck said they were Mohicans, Esopus and Hackensacks on their way to a corn festival on Long Island.

When they reached New Amsterdam, two or three from each canoe were put ashore in search of food, and a few Hackensacks made their way to Marie's Tavern. She welcomed them hospitably and sold out the whole larder before they ran out of wampum. Then as they were leaving she called out: "Aernoudt, bring beer for my friends."

"God Allemachtig!" cried Peeck, "Black Beard's watchin' yer every move, woman."

"Then I'll serve 'em myself out back. No friend of mine leaves here thirsty." Marie wedged her broad beam gracefully between tables, giggling like a silly goose when a customer pinched her well-padded behind.

"Ain't she somethin'!" Peeck nudged me in the ribs. "Breaks her back to be friendly even to Indians. Wintertime she runs this place on her own, you know."

"You should stay home more," said Vincent.

Peeck laughed. "Can't give up the beaver trade, young man. Too much money in it. I got my own kill—flows into the Hudson 'bout fifty miles upriver. I just sits there and Wilden bring in the beavers."

While Vincent listened to the merits of Peeck's kill, I watched two young squaws filling their baskets from the orchards along the Hudson. Dark, graceful silhouettes, they appeared to be dancing against a background of bright red sunset. Suddenly Van Dyck stormed out of his house, gun waving wildly in his one good arm.

"Thievin' scoundrels!" he yelled, blasting away at point-blank range. "Get your hands off my peaches!"

One squaw fled to the boats as the other crumpled to the ground. Three peaches slowly rolled from her basket into the long grass.

"Crazy blockhead!" shouted Peeck, as Black Beard returned to his house and slammed the door.

Hackensacks brought the wounded squaw over to the tavern, but the life had already spilled out of her. Gently they carried the body back to her own canoe.

Instead of continuing to Long Island, the Wilden camped for the night north of the Wall, near the wreck of the old *Tiger*. For the time being all was quiet, but it was not a good moment for Peg-Leg and the army to be chasing Swedes on the Delaware.

In the morning I was on Brewer Street by sunrise as usual. Sarah was making suppawn. Malala was milking Bieltje, and Angel had already filled the woodbin and gone to fetch the day's water. The boy had settled in well. His ribs had disappeared, and the misery in his eyes had been replaced by a willingness to help and a respectful worship of Malala.

The jingle-jangle of copper bells soon announced Gabriel, the cowherd, driving his morning parade of cows through the streets. Like most burghers, the de Forests had no room to swing a cat, much less pasture a cow, so they depended on Gabriel. Sarah claimed he was a half-wit because his eyes swiveled around in different directions and he never said a word. But how could a half-wit handle 30 cows all day long with nothing but a stick and a small dog? What's more, he always brought each cow safely back to her own door in time for the evening milking.

Today, as Bieltje patiently took her place in line, Gabriel opened his mouth for the first time.

"They's killt Black Beard," he gasped.

"God Almighty!" cried Sarah. "Who killed him, Gabriel?"

But the cowherd's eyes wandered off in their sockets and he had run out of words. Sarah called out to Goosie who was hastily prodding her own cow to the gate next door.

"Gabriel says Van Dyck's been murdered."

"Grote genade!" cried Goosie. "What happened, Gabriel? Not that he didn't deserve it."

The cowherd only honked his horn.

Van Dyck had indeed been murdered, and there was worse to come. With the army away, our twelve-foot Wall was more of a challenge than an obstacle to agile Indians. By breakfast-time hundreds raced through town destroying property and demanding drink.

Papa helped Sharkface to organize a civilian militia, and we marched up one street and down the next putting on a show of strength, only to have the rioting break out anew in our wake. Even the slaves were enlisted. Of course Angel was not armed, but he marched with the others.

Housewives were told to bolt their doors and windows, and assured that the civilian militia would protect them. Nobody believed this, and in any event, a brewer's home was hardly the best place to defend. Somehow I had to get Sarah and the children to the Fort. There was no chance that Sharkface would give me a half-hour break from militia duty. I would have to make my own break.

The next time we marched down Brewer Street I calmly stepped out of line just as we passed the big horse-chestnut tree in the de Forest's front yard. I stayed there until Sharkface and the militia had turned the corner. While I was hiding, the de Forest front door opened and Sarah emerged with the children.

"Quick, follow the militia," she ordered. "You take the boys, Malala. Susan can carry the blankets. Get them settled inside the church and I'll join you when I finish up here."

At fourteen, Malala was wiry and strong as a boy despite the misshapen foot. I watched as she loped unevenly down Brewer Street, the baby in one arm, two-year-old Philly slung over the other shoulder and five-year-old Johnny clinging to her skirt. She had the same determined set to her jaw as Sarah. In spite of her dark skin and stiff black pigtails Malala was more Sarah's child than doll-like Susan, who tripped daintily along behind, blankets trailing in the mud.

Once the militia had turned the corner, I leapt up on to the stoop before Sarah could close the door.

"Why aren't you marching," she snapped?

"I'm on a half-hour break," I said, stepping quickly inside. "Tell me what needs to be done and I'll finish up. You go tend to the children."

"I'm not leaving till I finish," she said, bolting the door, "but as long as you're here you may as well help. All that stuff goes below."

She pointed to an open trap door in the middle of the kitchen floor and beside it a huge pile of "valuables" to be hidden.

"I didn't know this house had a cellar, Sarah."

"Few houses do. I just hope the Indians won't know it either. This used to be a brewery. When you finish dragging everything down, I'll sweep sand over the trap door and it will disappear."

I carried Isaack's whisky supply, bottles of wine, Sarah's good dishes, candlesticks and I don't know how many bags and boxes, down into that dark cellar where I placed them carefully between rows of empty beer casks. The last thing down was the old oak cradle that had rocked four generations of de Forest infants. After Mother died Papa gave it to Uncle Isaack, who was Mother's brother. He and Sarah had certainly made good use of it. When I finally closed the trapdoor, the last thing to catch the light was a brass candlestick, still rocking gently back and forth on top of the old cradle.

Sarah was ready with a bucket of sand to throw over the trapdoor, which became invisible as soon as the floor was raked smooth. With any luck the Wilden would never discover it, but they would notice all the footprints in the rest of the house and the drag marks leading to the kitchen. Indians are far smarter than Europeans at reading footprints.

Now the church bells began to ring out urgently, over and over again. Through a crack in the shutter I saw housewives herding children between gangs of marauding Wilden.

"We will have to plant new footprints," I said.

Sarah was racing from room to room, grabbing small things like a silver thimble and a silver spoon, then stuffing them up onto a hidden ledge inside the chimney.

"I know," she said.

We both deliberately tramped about adding footprints. To my horror, when I looked at the trap door again, the sand had settled into the cracks leaving the outline of a door as plain as the snout on a pig.

Desperately I looked about for something to stuff the cracks.

"Have you any paper, Sarah?"

She shook her head. Then she pulled from a drawer the thin brown volume of *Horace* that Jesse had always loved.

"It's the only book we have," she said, "but nobody in this house reads any Latin."

Papa would be appalled, but a few pages would have to be sacrificed. When I opened the book however, some folded sheets of loose paper fell out.

"Jesse's notes on *Horace*," said Sarah. "In Latin," she added.

"Perfect!"

I glanced only briefly at the first page. The notes were in Latin and the handwriting was indeed Jesse's. The heading was "Discrepare." I had no idea what that meant and I could not care less. It was a relief not to have to destroy *Horace.*

Quickly Sarah swept the sand away while I lined up the sheets of paper to cover the cracks. Then we gently replaced the sand. Finally I put the table over the area to protect it and act as a smoke screen.

When everything was raked smooth again and new footprints planted, we stood back to admire our handiwork. The trap door had disappeared, and the eye went straight along the rows of footprints to the far wall, where two full kegs sat on a sideboard ready for tapping.

"That should keep the devils busy," said Sarah.

By mistake I had left *Horace* sitting all by itself on the table, but I was certainly not going to add any footprints in that direction. I grabbed my gun and we fled just as drunken Indians broke into van Cortlandt's place next door.

For fifteen years people had condemned Governor Kieft for building the Church of Saint Nicholas inside the Fort. Today they forgave him. The place was packed with screaming children gone wild, and exhausted mothers tearing their hair out. Malala had cleverly penned in the boys with two benches forming a V against the wall near the vestry door. She and Susan sat on one, Philly and the baby were asleep on the other and Johnny was crawling about under a blanket pretending to be a beaver.

I told Sarah that I would be back when I could get away again. Carefully I opened the vestry door an inch and peered out. Only a few yards away my father and Sharkface were arguing.

"For God's sake, Cornelis," Papa's voice was agitated. "At all cost we must pacify the Wilden until the army returns. Order your men to hold their fire!"

"May I remind you, Councillor Montagne, that the Governor left me in charge during his absence," the other replied coldly. "I have no intention of allowing the stinking devils to get away with murdering Van Dyck. Besides only one of these Indians in fifty has a gun. As soon as the civilians are off the streets we open fire."

"And what happens to the outlying farmers?"

"That's not my concern," said Sharkface, stalking off.

"Has anyone been sent to the Delaware?" I asked Papa, when Sharkface was out of sight.

"Yes, Kumtassa-One-Wing, but it will be days before the army gets here. God almighty! It will be fatal to open fire!" Papa hurried off after Sharkface and I quickly rejoined the rear of the militia.

A few hours later I was assigned to procure food and water for the women and children in the church. I could select two men to help me and I chose Vincent and Abram. First we brought buckets of water from the well on the Strand. There was no trouble here because the Wilden were not interested in water, and the few nearby loiterers quickly vanished at the sight of our guns. Then we helped ourselves to loaves from the bakery. Papa gave me a written authorization to obtain two whole cheeses from the pantry of the Governor's mansion which was inside the Fort and heavily guarded. I got the cheeses all right but when I asked for cups for the water I was told that I needed another authorization. Finally the guard let me "borrow" two cups which I was required to sign for.

So we set up two water stations inside the church, and thirsty housewives and children quickly formed lines. Abram and Vincent each had knives and were in charge of cutting bread and cheese for the hungry. I used the collection plate to pass some to those who were nursing infants and could not stand in line.

My last piece of bread and cheese I saved for Sarah, but Malala had already over supplied the de Forest brood so I gave it to Liesbeth, who was nursing a scrawny newborn on the next bench. Liesbeth was perhaps the only person to hate Sharkface more than I did. Daughter of an Amsterdam basket-maker, she had met the Secretary when he was in the Fatherland on official business. Against her parents' wishes she agreed to elope to New Netherland with him.

"I did think he had a lot of money to throw around, Jan, but as God is my witness I never dreamt he was a married man."

Not until they disembarked at Manhattan did she learn that he had a wife and three children. In tears, Liesbeth took her case to the Council, but of course nothing was ever done. So she dried her tears and married the good-looking Jacob van Curler whose infant she was now suckling.

"Did you know that the new Councillor, Nicasius de Sille, is collecting evidence of fraud against Sharkface?" said Liesbeth. "He says my testimony will be very valuable."

"My poor crippled brother had enough evidence to hang the man," I told her. "Only it disappeared when Jesse died."

Still the significance of the sheets of paper from *Horace* had not struck me. Although I did not know it, all Sarah and Uncle Isaack's possessions plus Jesse's evidence were riding on the same trap door.

Housewives were continually passing rumors from bench to bench. One said that Papa had organized a powwow with the Sachems and the rioting would soon stop. It did not. Another had it that Marie was still at her tavern merrily handing out beer to the rioters. This I believed.

In the late afternoon firing broke out and what started as a riot became a full-fledged battle, though a brief one. Outgunned, the Wilden soon took to the canoes and sped off in two directions, some toward Staten Island and some to the north. God have mercy on the farmers.

We trudged back to Brewer Street to find the de Forest house littered with broken window glass and smelling of spilt beer. But the Wilden had not found the cellar.

The first thing I did was to retrieve Jesse's Latin notes, carefully blow off the sand and replace them inside *Horace*, which I put on the mantle. Again I noticed the heading "Discrepare." Could it be a Latin infinitive? As I was dragging Sarah's bags and boxes up from the cellar I wondered why the word sounded familiar. In another minute I think the solution would have hit me, but all thought was suddenly interrupted by a loud honking. It was Gabriel driving his parade of cows across Brewers Bridge. Bieltje was home for the evening milking.

The Wedding Gift

In the week following the theft of Van Dyck's peaches, enraged Wilden destroyed 28 farms, murdered 40 men and took more than 100 prisoners, mostly women and children. Peg-Leg's return with the army restored the peace, but negotiations over hostages proved interminable. The Indians wanted guns, not wampum, and although we were now well into November only about half the prisoners had been ransomed.

Uncle Isaack was appointed Orphan-Master, which involved assigning guardians for a growing multitude of orphans. He and Sarah themselves took in six-year-old Apollonia Switzer. After the war, the Switzers had bought what used to be Uncle Isaack's bowery so we knew the family well. Mother had been Godmother to one of Apollonia's brothers.

Although the girl was unharmed, her clothes were badly bloodstained and it took Malala days to get the little apron white again. I wondered if it was her father's blood. The bewildered child believed that her mother and four brothers were still alive.

One week after Apollonia was released, it was rumored that a few prisoners were to be exchanged at noon. Apollonia was certain her mother would be among them. Uncle Isaack and I took her down to the beach to watch the proceedings.

We stood with the crowd on the damp sand, peering out at a gloomy gray East River. On the pier a black tarpaulin covered the stacks of muskets, and officials huddled around like black crows waiting for the Hackensacks.

"I don't much like this arms-for-hostages plan," muttered Uncle in my ear. "Hackensacks'll end up shooting us with our own guns."

"Here they come," shouted someone and I grabbed Apollonia's hand as the crowd surged forward.

"Mama! Mama!" cried the child, fighting to break my grip.

"Stand back, everyone! Stand back!" ordered Peg-Leg as two canoes swooped around Weepers' Point and veered swiftly in to shore.

Soldiers held the crowd in check while the Governor greeted the Hackensacks and escorted them to view the stacks of muskets beneath the tarpaulin. Apparently satisfied, the Wilden regained their canoes and sped away. The crowd began to disperse as soldiers transferred the guns onto wagons to be returned to the Fort. Word circulated that some prisoners would be released at noon the next day, but few believed it.

In the excitement over hostages we barely noticed a small skiff coming down-river, until she was almost beached. As the lone occupant leapt ashore, Apollonia slipped from my grasp and raced toward the newcomer. At the last minute she tripped over her own petticoats and tumbled ass over kop at his feet.

"Medius fidius!" He cried, picking her up. "I didn't expect such a hearty welcome."

It was Sacky Allerton, my English friend, who had left here eight years before to study at Harvard. I recognized him fast enough, although he had thinned out a bit and grown a fancy English moustache. His father had moved to New Haven a few years earlier, and we had not seen hide nor hair of either since.

"Sacky! What a welcome sight you are," I cried, helping to drag the skiff above the high-water mark. "Where on earth did you come from, my friend?"

Sacky had come all the way from New Haven with a wedding gift for me and Peternella, although how the news of our marriage reached New Haven is baffling. He also knew all about Peg-Leg's successful expedition to the Delaware and the terrible uprising of the Wilden in the absence of the army. What he did not know, and was horrified to learn, is that we were trading arms for hostages.

"Do you know where my Mama is?" asked Apollonia timidly. She appeared to connect Sacky with the recently departed Hackensacks.

"No, I don't, young lady. What is your name?"

"This is Apollonia Switzer of Boomdale," I told him, as Uncle brushed the sand and dry seaweed out of the girl's hair. "Boomdale was destroyed in the uprising and until last week Apollonia was a hostage. We were hoping that her mother would be released today."

"Bring your belongings, Sacky," interrupted Uncle. "You can stop with us."

Sacky threw his knapsack over one shoulder and we started back toward Brewer Street. It was beginning to rain, so Uncle ran ahead with Apollonia.

"Switzer," muttered Sacky. "She must be the granddaughter of Old Claes who was killed by the Crazy One at Turtle Bay."

I nodded. "Ironic isn't it? Her grandfather was murdered by a Weckquasgeek and her father by a Hackensack."

"Did they destroy Vredendale, too?"

"Vredendale is still in ruins from the war, but they finished off Zegendale and murdered Kuyter's widow. And they scalped Tobias Teunissen, who worked for us in the early days."

"Good God! What about Staten Island?"

"Wiped out. Melyn and his wife were captured, but have been ransomed. Do you see that old woman standing by the pier? That's Annie Melyn. Her mouth used to twitch even before the younger son was drowned on the *Princess*. Now the older son was scalped right before her eyes and her whole face twitches all day long. She does nothing but stand by the water's edge twitching and waiting, for what I don't know."

News of our guest spread quickly and friends dropped in throughout the day. First to arrive was Abram, who greeted Sacky like a long-lost brother and promptly began to joke about our fishing exploits during the war when the three of us used to take that old leaky rowboat out every day.

"You smelled like dead fish," remarked Sarah, with a sniff, "and your hair was so long and dirty it was hard to tell you apart."

Now there was little resemblance. Sacky wore his fancy English moustache, Abram had a full-grown beard that badly needed scissors, and I had the smooth face of an Indian.

Then Papa appeared, dignified as ever with neatly-trimmed gray side whiskers and the silver buttons of his coat freshly polished. He used to help Sacky with his Latin and was anxious to hear all about Harvard. One of Papa's pet complaints these days was the fact that New Amsterdam still did not have a proper Latin school, much less a university. At least we had a free school here for all children, something they did not have in Boston.

"I trust that your worthy father is well, young man," began Papa.

"As well as can be expected for three score and ten, sir, but his memory has failed and he's no longer able to cope. I have been at the house trying to organize his papers which is how I happened to come across a most extraordinary item."

Sacky opened the knapsack and took out a long roll wrapped in oilskin which he handed to me.

"Congratulations on finding yourself a wife, my good friend!"

Everyone gathered round while I removed the oilskin and there, to my astonishment, was Rembrandt's sketch of Jesse de Forest.

"Holy sacrament!" I cried. "I told you it wasn't in that attic, Papa. Where did your old man get this, Sacky?"

"He doesn't recognize the picture or remember anything about it. On the reverse is written 'Jesse de Forest, 1576–1624,' which is how I was able to identify it."

"Mirabile dictu!" cried Papa with tears in his eyes. "I was sure this had gone up in flames with Vredendale." He put on his spectacles and carefully held the picture up to the window. "Look at the expression on your grandfather's face, Jan. He was a great man, the greatest I ever met. Do you know who the child is, Sacky, with her wet hair covering her face? That is your half-sister, Remember. It was the day the Puritans left Leyden by barge on their way to join the *Mayflower*. Little Remember fell into the Rapenburg, and Jesse jumped off that bridge and pulled her out. Deo gratia!"

Sacky said he had barely known Remember, who was twenty years older than he and now long dead. "Besides, this is a picture of Jesse de Forest, not Remember Allerton, and it rightfully belongs to Jesse's grandson." He peered over Papa's shoulder. "Do you know who the artist was, sir?"

"I certainly do, young man. My good friend, Rembrandt, the miller's son, drew this at the age of fourteen. We were at the University of Leyden together and he is now the greatest artist in Europe. Open another bottle, Isaack. I would like to make a toast."

In the morning Sacky was up at first light, determined to reach New Haven by nightfall. Sarah gave him a good breakfast of ham, suppawn, and eggs cooked in beer, and wrapped bread and cheese for the journey.

"The whole family is very grateful to you, Sacky," I told him. "If there's some way we can repay you, you have only to name it."

Sacky finished off a second bowl of suppawn while he thought this over. "I'd really like to borrow Jesse's *Horace*," he said at last, pointing to the thin brown volume, which was still on the mantelpiece. "The thing is, I don't know when I will be able to return it."

"Help yourself," Uncle said heartily.

As Sacky transferred the book to his knapsack, the loose sheets of notes fell to the floor.

"Whoops! What are these sandy pieces of paper?"

"Jesse's Latin notes on *Horace*," I told him. "We used them during the rioting to cover the cracks in the trapdoor. Take them if you want."

He scanned the sheets briefly, put them back on the mantel and gave Sarah a parting hug. I carried his knapsack down to the beach where I helped drag the skiff into the water. It was nothing but a rowboat with a centerboard and a slip of a sail. Today there was no wind to speak of so he rowed.

"By the way, Jan," he called out, resting on the oars for a moment. "Those Latin notes of Jesse's have nothing to do with *Horace.* They are bookkeeping notes. Something about discrepancies."

What a domkop I was! I waved a last goodbye and dashed back to Brewer Street, terrified that the papers might have disappeared, but they were still on the mantel. Gently I blew off the few remaining grains of sand. Here was the evidence that I had been searching for, right under my nose, only I did not suspect because it was in Latin.

The Dominie used to say there was enough evidence here to hang your average bookkeeper. Well, the slippery Sharkface was far from average. He was the second most powerful man in the Colony and everyone but the Governor knew he was as crooked as a whole nest of rattlesnakes. Why old Peg-Leg continued to protect him was hard to understand.

My first instinct was to hand everything over to Papa but I decided against it. New Amsterdam now had a four-man Council: Peg-Leg, Sharkface, Papa and the new man, Nicasius de Sille, recently sent by the Amsterdam Board of Directors, ostensibly to augment the Governor's Council, but secretly to verify evidence against Sharkface. Papa was too honorable to go behind anyone's back. If I wanted Jesse's evidence to go directly to de Sille, I would have to give it to him myself.

Long before noon people began to gather on the Strand again. Uncle was away on business so I took Apollonia. Today the water was a sparkling blue, seagulls soared above the fishing boats and children built castles in the sand. Even the sight of poor, twitching Annie Melyn by the water's edge could not dim the mood of optimism. To add to the excitement, the flag on Staten Island was up. This meant that an ocean vessel had just rounded Sandy Hook and there would soon be mail from Europe. With any luck there would be a letter from Peternella.

I gave Apollonia's hand an encouraging squeeze as she stood beside me, freshly scrubbed, hair tied back neatly with a yellow ribbon.

"Here they come!"

There was a sudden hush as canoes swept around Weepers' Point and raced the last few hundred yards to the landing place. However one may dislike Hackensacks, it is impossible not to admire the breathtaking speed with which they maneuver these canoes. There were three today, with one hostage in the stern of each; a woman, and two boys, aged twelve or thirteen. I picked up Appollonia and put her on my shoulders so she could see but the crowd was too thick.

At first I thought that the woman might be Apollonia's mother, but it turned out to be Jannetje, widow of the purple-faced Tobias. I put Apollonia down and held her hand. One boy was a nephew of the Melyns, so poor twitching Annie would have something to celebrate after all.

Officials counted out the proper number of guns per hostage and the Wilden promised more releases in three days. At first nobody recognized the second boy, who was ill and had to be carried ashore. Then someone yelled:

"Hey! It's one of the Switzer boys!"

It was Apollonia's brother, Izzy. I carried him back to Brewer Street with his sister running along side crying, "Here I am, Izzy! It's me, Apollonia!"

In the meantime we learned that the ship in the lower bay was the *Fire of Troy* out of Amsterdam. A pilot was dispatched to guide her through the Narrows and the crowd began to settle down again to wait for news from the Fatherland.

Izzy was delirious with a high fever, and as soon as I got him settled on a trundle, Sarah looked at his chest and announced that it was measles.

"Did you ever have measles?" she asked Apollonia, who was anxiously squeezing her brother's hand.

The child did not know, which meant of course that she never had.

"Malala, bring me two towels and a basin of cold water," Sarah shouted. "Then go fetch Doctor Kierstede."

"I'll get the Doctor for you, Sarah," I told her. "I'm going right by the house."

Papa used to say that few grow up in this world without surviving measles and the sooner they got it over with the better. Jesse and I and Little Rachel and Marie all came down with measles in the epidemic of 1638, the year after we arrived in this country. Measles is not kind to adults. Look at my friend, Sarie, who is now married to Doctor Kierstede. She managed to avoid measles till she was married, then she caught it from her own children and almost died.

Doctor Hans Kierstede was visibly upset by my news.

"God! I hope Sarah is wrong about measles, Jan. We can't afford an epidemic right now on top of everything else. The sister is bound to catch it. I'll have to quarantine the whole house.

"Believe me," he continued, "It will be a different story for those Hackensacks in about eleven days. I don't know why diseases strike the

Wilden so violently. Last year Fort Orange lost three Christians in the smallpox epidemic and two nearby Indian villages were wholly wiped out, with nobody left even to bury the dead."

With these cheerful words he grabbed his black bag and set off for Brewer Street. I thanked my lucky stars not to be included in the quarantine and went back to the Strand where Nicasius de Sille was among those waiting for mail.

"The papers which I told you about have been found, Sir," I said quietly. Then I handed him Jesse's notes, which he quickly pocketed.

"Keep moving, Jan. It would be better if we were not seen together."

I kept moving and soon spotted Vincent coming toward me with a letter in each hand and a big grin on his face.

"I got a letter from my father with the good news!" he said. "Here's one for you from Peternella."

I ripped open the envelope, read the first paragraph, then read it aloud with excitement:

> *This 20th day of October,*
> *In the Year of Our Lord 1655,*
> *At Slooterdyk, the Netherlands*
>
> *Our son was born this morning just before cockcrow. He is a big, strong, beautiful baby boy and tomorrow he will be christened John, after his father and both his grandfathers.*
> *I am well and full of happiness.*

At this point Vincent started to whoop and dance around. I joined him and we both were acting like drunken Canarsies at a corn festival. At least a hundred people came over to congratulate me.

"Let's go celebrate!" cried Vincent. "After all, it's not every day that one gets to be an uncle!"

I said I had to let Papa know first. "It's not every day that one gets to be a grandfather."

"Here he comes now," said Vincent, pointing behind me.

I turned around to see Papa smiling broadly.

"I have just heard the wonderful news, Son."

I laughed. "I haven't even finished reading my letter and the whole town knows what's in it already."

The next two months passed quickly. Miraculously we recovered all the hostages, including Apollonia's mother and the three other brothers.

In the meantime, Uncle's various businesses were flourishing to such an extent that he needed a full time secretary-bookkeeper. He always refused to have anything to do with numbers himself, so I was promoted to private secretary. Once I got things organized I began to appreciate his shrewdness.

"When you make money, Jan, you can't just let it pile up under the bed. You must invest it. My policy is to buy real estate."

The little house on the Marketfield was now finished, and painted white with green shutters and green window boxes. Vincent had constructed a handsome circular staircase of oak leading up to the spacious new loft with its big airy window. Papa and Isaack gave me a few pieces of furniture and I bought a few more second hand.

When Peternella wrote that she was taking passage on the next ship to Manhattan, I gave my rowboat a fresh coat of paint and put the name *PETERNELLA* in large green letters across the stern.

Whenever the signal flag announced an incoming vessel, I would tie my rowboat to the little pier on the Strand and wheel my freshly-scrubbed cart down to Weepers' Point. Then I would stand on the cart, spyglass in hand, and wait for the ship to come through the Narrows. If she was not a Dutchman I gave up at this point. But if she was sailing under the orange, blue and white, my heart would start to pump with excitement. For five months and fifteen false starts this went on and still no Peternella, although there was usually a letter with a perfectly reasonable explanation.

Finally, on a beautiful April morning, a Dutch ship came through the Narrows and something told me this was it. I was glad that Peternella's first glimpse of New Amsterdam would find the city at its best with all the tulips in bloom.

"She's a Dutchman all right, I can see her colors," shouted Abram, who had his own telescope and was standing on top of his fish wagon. He had to shout to be heard over the gathering crowd.

"It looks to me like the *King Solomon*," said Vincent, joining me on the cart."

"It *is* the *King Solomon!*" I shouted. I was certain that this was a good omen.

With the wind from the north, the *King Solomon* had to tack back and forth across the harbor to make any headway.

"I can see people lined up along the rail," yelled Abram. His telescope was clearly better than mine. "Do you know what Peternella is wearing?" "She promised to wear the red hat. Look for a red dot by the rail."

By now the southern tip of Manhattan was teaming with men, women and children. It was as though the whole town had come out to welcome Peternella.

"No red dots," called Abram a few minute later, with a shake of his head. "Maybe she forgot."

I refused to be discouraged. "You can only see half the ship from this angle," I said with my eye glued to the spyglass. "Wait until she comes on to the starboard tack."

We waited impatiently for the *King Solomon* to come about. By now I could see the heads for myself but no red dot. Finally the ship turned. Lo and behold, there, midships, was a tiny red dot!

By the time the *King Solomon* had anchored in the East River, I was alongside in my freshly painted rowboat, bursting with happiness and pride as I waited to collect my wife and son.

Peternella's trunks and boxes actually reached the pier before we did and my friends had already piled them onto the cart. We put Peternella on top. There she sat, prettier than any could imagine, waving at everyone and laughing, with the baby in her arms and her golden curls spilling out from beneath the red hat. The crowd cheered as we pushed my new family across town to the little white cottage on the Marketfield.

Harlem

Not long after Peternella's arrival, Governor Stuyvesant received orders from the Amsterdam Board to dismiss Cornelis van Tienhoven "from any and all offices he may hold on charges of gross misconduct." I had been waiting eight years for this day, but it brought little satisfaction. Nothing could ever bring Jesse back, but at least a measure of justice was being done.

In a last-ditch effort to save his favorite, the Governor ordered a hearing to be held at which Sharkface would answer the charges. In the meantime no one, other than Councillor Nicasius de Sille, knew exactly what the evidence consisted of. All Papa could tell me is that it was "blatant fraud and corruption in high office."

It was a beautiful Sunday morning and needless to say the churchyard buzzed with rumors about the upcoming hearing. Sharkface himself rarely attended service and was not there today. We were walking home after church with Little Johnny riding happily on my shoulders, when Peternella remarked, "I'm beginning to feel sorry for the man."

"Well don't feel sorry for him," I said, curtly.

I had never told Peternella that I suspected Sharkface of murdering Jesse and now was not the time.

"Are you going fishing?" she asked, neatly changing the subject.

I usually went fishing after Sunday service. Peternella was particularly fond of striped bass, which she claimed did not exist in the Fatherland.

"Of course I am going fishing and this youngster will be coming with me in a couple of years." I put Johnny down on the front stoop. "How many do you want?"

"Kinderen or fish?"

"Fish," I laughed. It was impossible to remain curt with Peternella.

"I'll take a half dozen of each, please," she said handing me my box of night crawlers from under the stoop. Peternella sternly objected to worms in the house.

Ten minutes later I had stowed my fishing gear in the rowboat and was heading up the East River. As always, the closer I got to Hell Gate the better I felt.

After all these years, Hell Gate is still God's country to me. When I hear that roar I always feel that I have come home. Even in the midst of the darkest forest I never lose my sense of direction, thanks to Hell Gate. And I always know the time. Even when there is no roar, my body knows just how long it has to wait. In the city it has to wait forever.

It was my habit to row briskly up-river without fishing. For the benefit of any possible spectators, I braced my rod in the stern as though trolling, with hook, line and sink-stone but no bait. Fish seldom interrupt the thoughts of a fisherman with no bait.

Then after relaxing for a while in God's country I would drift gently down-river, fishing when and where I chose, usually in places that Little Deer and I had fished together, years ago. Fish were plentiful around Manhattan. There was no such thing as not catching any.

Today I was still inhaling the fresh air of God's country, and musing on the chance that I might soon get permission to rebuild Vredendale, when something gave a gentle tug on my still unbaited line. My first thought was that the hook had become tangled in weeds. Then it looked as though I had somehow snagged the corpse of a small animal, maybe a squirrel. On closer inspection my catch proved to be a man's beaver hat, well soaked but otherwise in good condition. Sharkface had a hat just like this, but so did half the men in New Amsterdam. There was no identifying mark.

A minute later I spotted a gentleman's cane floating near the shore. On it were the initials C.v.T.—Cornelis van Tienhoven!

Fishing was now out of the question. I spent a few more minutes searching, unproductively, for additional evidence. Then after fixing the location firmly in my mind, I headed South and bent my back to the oars.

Before I had even beached the rowboat, I heard the news. Sharkface had disappeared this morning while everyone was at church. Pinned to a piling on the van Tienhoven dock was a paper on which was written only one word: "Farewell."

When his wife identified the hat and cane, it appeared that Sharkface had indeed taken his own life. The Governor ordered a search for the body while old Dominie Megapolensis did his best for the salvation of the soul.

During the afternoon friends continually came to our house to discuss the latest details and naturally to stare at Peternella, the prettiest girl on either side of the Atlantic.

About Sharkface there was much arguing. Some viewed the whole thing as an unfortunate accident, some insisted that Sharkface had skipped town to avoid the hearing and some were convinced that it was a case of suicide. Personally, I was sure that Sharkface was too self-centered to kill himself.

Then there was the Vinje clan. Led by his mother-in-law, Madame Vinje-Dam, the family maintained that van Tienhoven was the victim of foul play by his enemies, Councillor Nicasius de Sille and Jan Montagne in particular. Fortunately no Vinjes were present and the discussion here was surprisingly good-natured.

All this changed about three o'clock when Goosie van Courtlandt burst in with the latest development.

"It's not his handwriting!" she gasped, breathlessly. "The farewell note . . . His wife swears it was not written by him! So does his mother-in-law! Peg-Leg says . . . Blikskaters, I need a drink!"

"Sit down, Goosie," I handed her a beer while she caught her breath. "Now tell us what the Governor says."

"He says it may be murder. He says van Tienhoven made a lot of enemies in the course of his official duties, and now each of these enemies will be investigated. I expect we'll all have to write the word 'Farewell' for him to inspect."

The room fell strangely silent. Everyone here hated Sharkface except maybe Peternella, who had not even met him. And I hated him more than anyone.

"Of course Oloff and I never had any reason to dislike Secretary van Tienhoven," lied Goosie through her teeth.

"Well I did," I said grimly. "And if Peg-Leg plans to investigate everyone who had cause to hate Sharkface, life is not going to be worth living around here for a very long time."

Then everyone began to talk at once.

"Odd that Jan should be the one to find the hat and cane," muttered someone behind me.

"He claims to have been fishing," whispered another. "But he was gone over two hours and never caught one fish!"

"I heard that he was seen on the Strand, passing some suspicious-looking papers to Nicasius," confided yet another.

Anger welled up inside of me. With difficulty I held my tongue. Then Peternella walked over to the long table where bread and cheese were laid out for the guests. She turned, facing the crowd and announced with her usual enchanting smile,

"Back in Slooterdyk, there was a man who pretended to drown himself."

As if by magic the room was quiet.

"He was very rich," she laughed. "But he had a battle-axe for a wife." She laughed again, the laugh of a happy child. "So he disappeared with all the money and left the battle-axe behind. Years later it was discovered that he had changed his name and started life over again in the West Indies. Is Sharkface rich?"

What a perfect solution!

"Of course he's rich!" cried the audience. "He's been cheating and stealing for years."

"And he has a shrew for a wife," added Goosie, "and a battle-axe for a mother-in-law."

"Don't forget his two sisters-in-law," called another.

The next day the Governor ordered the van Tienhoven strong-box broken open. It contained only worthless paper. No corpse was ever recovered, and Peternella's "Slooterdyk solution" gradually became the accepted version of the facts.

In the wake of Sharkface's exit there were several changes in our lives, the only sad one being Papa's reluctant removal to Fort Orange where he was to be Director-in-Charge. Papa protested that he and Agnietje were too old to survive a winter up North, but Stuyvesant insisted that Papa was the only one he could trust to deal with the growing Indian problems there.

With Papa and Agnietje gone, my brother Will, now in his teens, moved in with us. This could have been awkward, but actually proved a great blessing. Like every other male in town, he was enchanted by Peternella and anxious to do any chores she might assign.

The best news was that Peternella was delighted with the idea of rebuilding Vredendale. It was a beautiful day in mid-May that I first took her to see the place. Mother always said Vredendale was at its best in May when the dogwood and crabapple were in bloom.

I had long ago removed some of the more unsightly rubble, and what remained was now happily covered with ivy or honeysuckle vines. Over the last fifteen years I had been unable to do any construction, but at least I had succeeded in keeping the forest at bay. The brick chimney still stood tall and proud against a background of pink blossoms, and three bright red tulips stood guard by Mother's gravestone.

"Oh it is beautiful, Jan! Why won't the Governor give you permission to rebuild?"

"He thinks that isolated boweries are at too great a risk from the Wilden."

"But dearest, we can't possibly use 200 acres. Why not get a few other would-be householders and form a village? Then we wouldn't be isolated."

And that is what we did.

I had no trouble finding six couples eager to join in the venture and Peg-Leg gave his permission to found a village, but not at Vredendale. The house lots were to be side by side on my Uncle Isaack's old bowery, where part of his original stockade still stood to serve as a temporary protection. In addition, each householder would get 20 acres for tilling from the cleared portion of Zegendale. A charge of 4 guilders per acre would go toward paying off the debts of the former owners, and each householder was to receive fifteen years exemption from all taxes.

The village was bound to expand and in a year or two Vredendale would no longer be isolated. We would build only a small house this time. When the village outskirts reached Vredendale we would build the house of our dreams and sell the first one.

As long as we were founding a village, I was determined to avoid the mistakes of New Amsterdam. For one thing the city streets were narrow, crooked, and full of potholes and garbage. With a little forethought this could be avoided.

I drew up a plan for the village main street along the line of Uncle Isaack's old cowpath, only much wider and straighter. This new street would eventually extend from the East River toward Slangberg, where it would join the Weckquasgeek trail. Then I put a score of square house lots on either side of the street, all the same size. The lot nearest the river was reserved for a church. I numbered the other lots, put my name on the first lot, next to the church, and invited the others to choose their own sites. Each was required to sign a paper agreeing to the following: Brick or stone chimneys, not wood or clay; No privies to be built within ten feet of property line; No garbage to be thrown in the street; No livestock allowed to roam free (cowherd to be provided).

Will and Vincent both helped me with construction, and our home was the first to be completed. In 1659 I sold the house on the Marketfield and moved my growing family up to God's country.

By this time Peternella and I had three sons: John, Vincent, and newborn Nicasius, named after his Godfather, Councillor Nicasius de Sille.

In 1660 the village had a dozen occupied homes, another dozen under construction, and yet another dozen in the negotiating stage. But still no church. So we decided to hold a festival to raise funds. Isaack generously volunteered to provide free beer for everyone. A Dutchman never can resist an offer of free beer. It was a beautiful August day and a whole flotilla of small boats, decorated with colored streamers, sailed up to our new village dock.

On the site of the future church, a long table was set up for tapping and another sagged under the weight of hearty dishes contributed by the village housewives. Peternella spent hours preparing one of her special peach cobblers as a prize for the person pledging the largest amount for the church. Not surprisingly, the winner was the guest of honor, Governor Pieter Stuyvesant, although he probably used Company funds.

After the feast, Peg-Leg made a fancy speech congratulating the village on its good start and promising to provide slaves to widen the Weckquasgeek Trail into a wagon-road all the way from New Amsterdam. Then he asked us what we wanted to name the village, and as usual there was great dissension on the matter. Each wanted to call it after his own hometown in the Fatherland. One said New Delft, another New Dordrecht. I wanted to call it New Avesnes after the birthplace of Grandfather, leader of the Walloons, but nobody agreed with me. In fact, no two persons could even agree with each other.

Finally Stuyvesant cut the discussion short, stamped his wooden leg and demanded: "Is there any householder from Harlem?" There was not.

"Very well," he announced. "I hereby christen this village New Harlem!"

And New Harlem it became.

Back to Vredendale

Everything went as planned. In no time New Harlem had reached the borders of Vredendale and we were able to select the perfect site—twenty acres along the creek. Construction began. In the summer of '61 I sold the small house on the main street of New Harlem and moved my family to a wondrous land called Vredendale.

I worked hard and was determined to make New Harlem the finest village in the Colony. At one time or another, I was town clerk, firewarden, deacon, magistrate, sheriff, schoolmaster and comforter of the sick—sometimes three or four positions simultaneously. .

While our first citizens traveled just the few miles from lower Manhattan, it was not long before they began to come directly from the Fatherland. Many were Walloons, counting on a helping hand from the grandson of Jesse de Forest. I would not let them down.

When I asked the first group of settlers to choose a spokesman from amongst themselves they unanimously elected Isa Vermilye, from Leyden, a military man, now in his sixties, who was to become New Harlem's oldest resident. This meant that instead of chasing after me all day, the newcomers took their problems to Spokesman Vermilye, who solved those he could, culled out the trivial and brought the remainder to me.

The immediate problem was money. Most had spent their life's savings to bringing their families across the Atlantic. There was nothing left to pay the agreed four guilders per acre.

"It was a misunderstanding, Master Jan," explained Vermilye at our first meeting. I was schoolmaster at the time, which accounts for the Master.

"In Leyden," he went on, "we were assured that the customary medium of exchange here was wampum. We would never have come if we had thought to be burdened with a debt of eighty guilders in coin for our promised twenty acres."

The exchange rate at this time was about three-to-one. In other words a guilder in wampum was worth only a third as much as a guilder in coin. Something clearly had to be done and I volunteered to appeal to the Governor on the group's behalf.

As usual Peg-Leg was in one of his high and mighty moods.

"And how is the grand metropolis of New Harlem doing, young man?"

We were sitting in what used to be Governor Kieft's office. It looked much the same, except that the walls were bare, Kieft's pretty water colors being at the bottom of the Bristol Channel.

"Growing fast, your Honor. We now have a volunteer militia and will soon be able to serve as northern outpost for New Amsterdam."

He liked the outpost idea, but when I mentioned the immigrants' money problems, he erupted.

"Like it or not they will pay the agreed amount," he shouted. "If you have come to plead for these ingrates, young man, you can get out NOW!"

It was obvious that my appeal was lost before it had begun. I had to think fast. But my mind was whirling in circles. Suddenly the solution popped out of nowhere like the cork from an exploding champagne bottle.

"Your honor, I have an idea which would insure that the Company receives the full, four guilders per acre and probably more. At the same time it would be affordable to the immigrants."

Peg-Leg grunted sarcastically.

"Your Honor, several of these men have military experience." I was stalling, at the same time juggling figures in my head.

"Get to the point, man," he growled, but there was a light in his eye at the mention of "military experience."

"Your Honor, the immigrants have been promised fifteen years exemption from taxes. If you cut this to eight years, instead of fifteen, the extra seven years of collected taxes will more than compensate for the whole purchase price of the land."

I quickly jotted the figures down for him, using the current tax rate. "Who is to say, Your Honor, that the tax rate may not go up after eight years?"

He smiled, knowing full well "who is to say."

"Very well, Master Jan. Write this up and I will sign it."

My immigrants were convinced that I could walk on water and makeshift tents quickly gave way to dirt-floor log cabins. It might be years before they could afford a proper house.

"At my age there are not that many years left, Master Jan," said Vermilye. "I promised the wife we'd build a real home this time."

With three full-grown sons, labor was no problem. Money for the sawmill was. I offered to loan him the money but he refused. Instead he proposed a deal. I would pay his sawmill charges. In exchange, Ursula, the oldest Vermilye girl, would come in once a week to help Peternella with the housework. I didn't think much of Ursula. She was a big, strong, homely woman, partially gray, with little education and absolutely nothing to say. But for some reason Peternella liked her, so I agreed. Anything that made Peternella happy was all right with me.

Speaking of "happy," I don't believe I have ever been happier. A cheerful, loving wife (slightly thinner but still the most beautiful), three strapping sons, the home of my dreams, and now neighbors who thought I walked on water. What more can a man ask for?

I should have known it could not last. Why did I not suspect something was wrong when Ursula began to come in more than once a week. But I was gone all day and hardly noticed. By this time I had persuaded my younger brother, Will, to take over as schoolmaster, but I still had much too much to do. When I wasn't trying to solve the growing problems of a rapidly expanding New Harlem, I was working side by side with my own field hands. Rarely did I get home before dusk and by that time the children were in bed, supper was on the table, Ursula had disappeared, and Peternella and I discussed village politics as we ate. In my eyes all was well with the world.

Then one Tuesday I arrived home early just as Ursula was leaving, her homely face even more miserable than usual.

"I thought you came on Mondays, Ursula?"

She looked like someone about to burst into tears. "Your lady is very sick, Master Jan."

This surely must be the longest sentence she had ever uttered and the effort set the tears flowing as she groped her way out.

At first I thought Ursula must be mad. There was nothing wrong with Peternella. Then it hit me. God! How could I have been so blind? Everything had been running smoothly because of Ursula. I went in to the other room where Peternella lay on the bed.

"You're home early today," she said with her usual bright smile. "I was just finishing a quick beauty nap."

"Why didn't you tell me that you were ill, Peternella?"

The bright smile faded. "I thought it would pass in a week or two and I didn't want to worry you. I love seeing you so happy, Jan. Please don't be angry."

"I'm not angry, dear, but I have to know the truth. Exactly what is wrong?"

"I'm just tired all the time."

"Is that all?"

"I don't seem to be able to lift anything. I can't even pick up little Nicasius wthout getting a pain here." She pointed to her stomach. "I think something is growing inside of me, Jan, and it's not a baby."

I sent for Doctor Kierstede immediately. He took his time arriving, only to confirm Peternella's suspicions.

"She has a tumor," he announced, stroking his silly little pointed beard. "If it grows any larger I shall have to remove it. In the meantime give her one spoonful of this twice a day." He handed me a bottle of thick, brown liquid, labeled "Kierstede's Tonic." Then he turned to Peternella. "Rest as much as you can, my dear, and do not pick up anything. I will be back in a few days."

I was terrified by the word "remove," which I knew meant "the knife." I had seen the Doctor's collection of razor-sharp knives and hacksaws. God, I hoped Peternella did not understand. She looked quite calm.

The first thing I did was to write a long letter to Papa, giving him Kierstede's diagnosis and asking for advice. It would take at least a week to reach Fort Orange by water, so I sent it by runner, regardless of cost. Wilden take great pride in doing the 150 miles to Fort Orange in less than 24 hours, with only about eight runner-changes. In 48 hours I had a reply.

> *At Fort Orange*
> *This 14th day of March, 1663*

My Dear Son,

    I have just received yours of March 13, and hasten to write this brief reply for the return-runners.

    I am distraught by the news of Peternella's condition. The one encouraging aspect is that she is under the care of Hans Kierstede, whom I believe to be the best man in the Colony today.

    Thank you for the compliment, but I have not really practiced medicine in many years. Hans is much younger, and more familiar with all the modern techniques.

    As it happens, it would be almost impossible for me to leave Fort Orange at this moment anyway. The Esopus Indians have been causing considerable trouble in the vicinity of Wiltwick, about which I shall write more later. I wish to God that Little Rachel did not live in

Wiltwick. I have asked her and Guisbert to stay with us until the danger has passed.

May the Lord be generous to our lovely Peternella.

Yours affectionately,

Papa

On his next visit Doctor Kierstede announced that an operation was indeed necessary.

"Every day that we delay, the tumor grows larger and more difficult to remove."

Peternella took the news much better than I.

"We must be practical, Jan," she said when we were alone. "If I should die I want you to promise to do something for me."

"I promise. I'll do anything you ask, dearest, but you are not going to die. Papa says Hans Kierstede is the best in the Colony."

"I'm serious, Jan. In case I don't survive the operation I want you to marry Ursula."

"Good God!" was all I could say.

"I don't mean right away. Wait a month or two."

"I'm never going to get married again to anyone, Peternella!"

"You have just promised."

"Then you must release me from the promise."

"Of course I release you, you but how are you going to raise three boys by yourself?"

"I'll hire Ursula."

"That won't work. You know there are ten bachelors in this country for every eligible female. Ursula may have been a confirmed spinster in the Fatherland, but not here. Did you know that she has had three proposals of marriage just in the short while she has been with us? Mind you, they haven't been very good ones. Every woman wants to raise her own family, Jan. Ursula will take the first good offer and you'll have seen the last of her."

"She's too old to start a family."

"She looks older because she's partly gray, but she is thirty-five, only a tiny bit older than you."

"Then I'll hire someone else."

"There is no one else. Besides, the children love Ursula and she loves them. I am glad she is homely because it means I won't have to be jealous.

One day you will have a baby girl, dear. It would make me very happy if you named her Peternella."

The operation was performed early Monday morning, here at Vredendale, and Dr. Kierstede proclaimed it a great success. Alas, my sweet wife lived only three more days. Thursday at sundown, Peternella died in my arms.

Little Rachel

For a long time after Peternella's death I had great trouble sleeping. I fell into the habit of rising well before dawn and climbing Slangberg at first light. It was good to look down upon the village as it slowly emerged from night. There was no need to worry about leaving the boys. Ursula was always with them.

Being so high above the earth made me feel closer to Peternella, and as there was never anyone else on the mountain, I found myself talking to her aloud. She answered silently as I listened with my heart.

One morning when Peternella had been dead about two months, I was telling her about my conversation the day before with Ursula's father.

"He says it is bad for Ursula's reputation to be living in, now that I am a widower."

"He's right, Jan."

Did she really say that or did my imagination put words into her mouth?

"What should I do about it?"

"Marry Ursula."

"I wish I could hear your voice again, just once, Peternella."

At that moment a gust of wind hit the mountain-top. Above the swoosh of rushing air I was sure I could hear Peternella's unique, lilting laughter. It was enough for me. That very afternoon I asked Ursula to marry me. She agreed. The church granted dispensation of the banns, and a few days later we were duly wed.

In the beginning, life married to Ursula was very much like life not married to Ursula. She continued to sleep with the children and I continued to sleep by myself. I suggested that she would be more comfortable sleeping with me and I even promised not to touch her if she did not want me to, but she refused. When I asked her why, she just shook her head.

Before we were married I had worried about the wedding night. Would I be able to perform with someone so homely? Now I was completely frustrated. Did Ursula want me to force myself on her? I did not think so. Besides, I found it difficult to imagine myself raping anyone, especially my own wife. Perhaps she really was a confirmed spinster. Well, I had married her for the children's sake and for Peternella's peace of mind, and I had got what I deserved, a good nanny, but a wife who would hardly speak to me, much less sleep with me.

Then on Saturday night, exactly one week after the wedding, I was lying in bed, irritated and frustrated beyond belief, when I thought I heard a gentle tap at the bedroom door.

"Come in," I said automatically, although I was sure it was a branch tapping against the windowpane.

To my astonishment, the door opened and in came Ursula, completely naked. In her hand was a candle, which gave enough wavering light for me to enjoy a brief glimpse of heaven. I had no idea that such a large, strong woman could have such an enchanting body. She blew out the candle and slipped into bed.

Love-making with Ursula was much like wrestling with a wild filly; very exciting but exhausting. When I woke up hours later, she was gone.

At breakfast everything was back to normal. After the children had left the table I tried to introduce a little polite conversation.

"That was very pleasant last night," I ventured.

No answer, but I thought I detected a tiny smile.

"I hope you will return this evening, Ursula."

She shook her head.

"Tomorrow?" I persisted.

"No."

"When then?"

"Only on Saturday."

Argue as I might, Ursula was firm. "only on Saturday" it would be. As I look back now I realize that it was the "Only on Saturday" policy that helped keep our improbable marriage alive all these years.

On the whole, Ursula turned out to be a good wife and mother. Her homely face no longer bothered me. In fact I thought of it now as a kindly face. It is true that she still did not talk much, but I know many men who would give their eyeteeth for a wife that did not talk much. And when we had domestic quarrels, as all married couples do, I could always remind myself that Saturday was not far away.

Since the founding of New Harlem four years earlier, relations with our Indian neighbors had been good. Alas, at dawn on the eighth day of June, 1663, Kumtassa-One-Wing brought terrible news. The Esopus had destroyed Wiltwyck and were planning to descend upon New Harlem next. Even as we spoke, a letter from a Wiltwyck survivor was being delivered by runner to Governor Stuyvesant.

Oh God! Little Rachel lived in Wiltwyck. I had been so preoccupied with events here that I had forgotten the danger to my own sister. What had Papa said in his letter? He had asked Little Rachel and her husband, Gysbert, to stay at Fort Orange with him until the Esopus threat was over. But did they accept?

Wiltwyck, which later was to be renamed Kingston, was ninety miles north of Manhattan on the other side of the Hudson. There was nothing I could do from here. Anyway, my first duty was to protect New Harlem and my own family. Please God, let Little Rachel be safely at Fort Orange with Papa.

Peg-Leg had already provided us with half a dozen regular soldiers. Together with New Harlem's volunteer militia, temporarily under command of Sergeant Isa Vermilye, my new father-in-law, this gave us twelve somewhat experienced men. In addition we had seventeen able-bodied householders with no military experience whatever. Isa was doing so well with the volunteer militia that I put him in charge of our whole force of twenty-nine strong. I could not have made a better choice.

A good part of my Uncle Isaack's stockade was still standing. We had intended to rebuild the remainder, but something always came up that seemed more important at the time. Now it was vital that the stockade be repaired immediately. It was also essential that I appeal to Peg-Leg at once for weapons, ammunition and if possible more soldiers. When I told Isa that he would have to be in charge of repairs, all he said was: "How long do I have?"

"Sundown, tonight," I answered, but I feared the job would take a week.

"Sundown tonight it is," he said and promptly organized the men into three groups: the first to fell trees, the second to trim branches and drag tree trunks, and the third to do the actual construction.

As I was leaving for town, members of the first party were already setting out, gun in one hand, axe in the other. Surprisingly, Isa had chosen no recent immigrants for this group, even passing over his own three stalwart sons.

"No great forests, to speak of in the Fatherland," he explained, "so nobody gets any practice felling trees."

Would I have thought of that myself?

I reached the Fort about nine in the morning only to find a long line of people outside the gate waiting to speak to the Governor. The line was not moving and I was told that Peg-Leg was tied up in a Council meeting. As soon as the meeting finished he would address the people from the Fort wall and read out a letter from an eyewitness to the attack. Rumor had it that the eyewitness was the gloomy Dominie Blom of Wiltwyck. I wondered how he had escaped.

"Jan! What are you doing here?"

It was my younger sister, Marie, now married to Jacob Kip.

"Is Little Rachel at Fort Orange with Papa?" I cut in abruptly, at the same time thinking how odd that someone thirty years old should still be called "Little Rachel."

Marie shook her head sadly. "Oh Jan! I had a letter from her just last week. She said Gysbert is the only doctor in Wiltwyck, and he refused to abandon his patients so she refused to abandon her husband."

"Is there a list of the dead?"

"I don't know. Jacob is at the Council meeting. He'll know. Why are you in line?"

"I need guns and ammunition for New Harlem. How long do you think this meeting will go on?"

It seemed like hours but eventually Peg-Leg appeared as promised. First he gave a brief account of the treacherous attack on Wiltwyck, in mid-morning when our men were at work in the fields. By the time they realized what was happening it was too late. Half the town was ablaze, and the ground strewn with the bodies of murdered women and children. Altogether some eighty persons, including men who were unable to reach their guns in time, were either known dead, captured, or just plain missing. Then he read the letter from Domimie Blom, one sentence of which still sticks in my mind:

"The bodies lie like dung heaps on the field, and the burnt and roasted corpses like sheaves behind the mower."

Next came a list of 24 known dead. Praise be to God, Little Rachel was not on that list. Then he read the names of the captured or missing. The last entry was "Rachel Montagne, wife of Doctor Gysbert van Imbrogh."

Finally the Governor announced his plan to send an army up to Wiltwyck to free the prisoners and wipe out the whole Esopus tribe. Enlistment conditions were favorable: unlimited plunder, six years exemption from chimney tax, and generous compensation ranging up to 800 guilders for the loss of the right arm or both legs. Well, I had no intention of tying my hands by volunteering for Peg-Leg's army.

Eventually I got in to see the Governor, but it was clear that the only interest he took in New Harlem was as a northern outpost for New Amsterdam. So I exaggerated a little.

"Your Honor, the old stockade has been completely restored but we are badly in need of cannon and soldiers."

"Hell's teeth, Son, I have only 24 cannon and I cannot spare a single one."

"What about those three in the courtyard that are not in use, Your Honor?"

"Those are steenstucken for firing stones," he laughed. "By all means take them, but on no account use them! They are lethal. The stones go in all directions and are much more likely to kill your gunner than to harm the enemy."

He wrote me an authorization to collect three steenstucken, two dozen muskets, plus powder, flints and fifteen bars of lead for running bullets. Better yet, he gave me three more soldiers and the loan of a flat boat.

Thanks to the soldiers, the trip up the East River was fairly painless and I spent the time working on a plan to rescue Little Rachel. Of course the first thing to try was ransom. If all efforts in this direction failed, then it must be right to "enlist the enemy's enemy."

Esopus, like all River Indians, are terrified of the powerful Mohawks or Man-Eaters. Once, when I was at Shorakapkok with Little Deer, a single unarmed Mohawk arrived by canoe to collect the annual corn tax. To my surprise, Weckquasgeeks quickly gave him all he asked for and food for the journey as well. Little Deer explained later that if that one Mohawk did not return safely to his headquarters, every last Weckquasgeek would be slain or captured. The lucky ones would be slain. The others would be tortured and forced to die some horrible death such as being slowly cooked while still alive.

Well, if one unarmed Mohawk could inspire such fear, why could he not insist on the release of a captive? But it must be done in a timely manner. If Stuyvesant's army attacked, the prisoners would be the first to die.

It was barely sundown when we reached New Harlem, where to my great surprise and delight, we found the stockade completely repaired.

"Tomorrow I'll have a watchtower put up," said Isa, after I had expressed my appreciation. "What the devil are those?" He pointed to the steenstucken beng dragged up to the stockade.

I explained that they were for show only and much too dangerous to use.

"No matter," he said. "Just the sight of 'em is enough to scare the shit out of any savage."

The next day, Captain Martin Cregier was sworn in to lead Peg-Leg's army of eighty-some Company mercenaries plus a handful of civilian volunteers, some Canarsies and seven slaves. They sailed up the Hudson to Wiltwyck, but of course the enemy was long gone.

All ships coming down from Fort Orange were ordered to stop at Wiltwyck so Manhattan got news almost daily, but usually a week late unless it was important enough to send by runner.

Because our men could not tell the difference between Esopus and other Indians, it was necessary to warn all neighboring tribes to stay out of the way. At the same time, they were asked how they stood in the Dutch-Esopus conflict. Sarie Kierstede, the official interpreter, was indisposed the day the Hackensack delegation arrived and I was asked to fill in.

"Chief Oratamy claims he has not a bad spark in his heart toward the Dutch," I translated literally.

"What a liar," muttered Peg-Leg out of the corner of his mouth. "Should I believe him?"

"Who could prove such an answer to be either true or false, Your Honor?"

"Humph," he growled. "Sometimes you sound just like your father."

When all the River Tribes had been contacted, only the Wappingers allied with the Esopus. All others promised "to stay out of the way of the Dutch army."

So far official efforts to recover prisoners had failed. Through the Wappingers came word that the enemy had refused all offers of ransom. Prisoners would be killed immediately if the Dutch attacked. But our army had not yet even located the Esopus stronghold, much less attacked anyone. After several unproductive sorties in different directions, Captain Cregier wrote Stuyvesant that the whole Esopus tribe seemed to have disappeared from the face of the earth.

In my opinion the other River Indians, who were staying obediently out of the way, knew perfectly well the whereabouts of the enemy and were laughing themselves sick at our incompetence. In all events the Esopus were much too busy to descend upon New Harlem at this point, which was a relief.

I had written Papa suggesting the plan to "enlist the enemy's enemy." He replied that he had already contacted a Mohawk Chief with the improbable name of Smits-Jan, and promised him a king's ransom to rescue Little Rachel. Papa added that he had word from Wiltwyck that Gysbert was in a terrible state and had to be restrained from running off into the woods to search for his wife.

In July came wonderful news. After 31 days in captivity, Little Rachel had escaped with the aid of Smits-Jan, the Mohawk. Not only was she able to give Cregier detailed directions to the enemy stronghold, she also agreed to accompany the army as a guide. I could not believe that Gysbert let her go.

"I promised the others that I would return and bring the army with me," she told her husband, "and that is what I am going to do."

Led by Little Rachel, soldiers dragged wagons and cannon over mountains, and built bridges to cross creeks swollen by summer rains. After two days when they finally reached the enemy Fort, it was deserted. The Esopus had fled taking with them the prisoners. Cregier sent search parties in every direction with no success. He then ordered the fort destroyed as well as the harvest in the fields. The army returned to Wiltwyck loaded with plunder, but no Esopus and no prisoners.

Still, the campaign was a major success. With their crops destroyed and no Fort in which to defend themselves, the fate of the Esopus was sealed. When they started to build another Fort our soldiers were able to surprise them, killing more than thirty warriors, including the Chief, and rescuing the remaining twenty-one survivors from Wiltwyck. All this at a cost of only three soldiers.

No longer was my sister called "Little Rachel." As the heroine of Wiltwyck she was invariably referred to as simply "Rachel," and always in a tone of great respect.

Treachery

In July of 1664, Uncle Isaack bought himself a new yawl, the *Roseboom,* and was anxious to try her out on a trading expedition to Virginia. For crew he took Sarah's brother, Abram, and Angel, the slave, who was now married to Malala. As usual, Uncle asked me to look in on Sarah and the family while he was gone.

"Women are good with children and housework, Jan, but for important matters they need a man's advice. Not that anything important is likely to come up. We will only be away a couple of weeks."

I could not remember a single occasion on which Sarah had ever taken my advice on anything. Nevertheless I promised to look in as often as possible. I was in the city for one thing or another almost every day, anyway.

The *Roseboom* had barely disappeared into the Narrows when the *King Solomon* arrived with alarming news. Four British ships of war had been sighted off Newfoundland. The Netherlands and England were not at war. Nevertheless, Governor Stuyvesant ordered the city walls repaired and wrote the Amsterdam Board with an emergency request for more soldiers. For weeks the whole town could talk of nothing but the English fleet and what was it doing on this side of the Atlantic.

"You can never trust the English," announced Goosie. "They're all mad."

It was my first visit to Sarah, the day after the *Roseboom* sailed. She and Goosie van Cortlandt from next door were drinking beer on the front stoop. Each was bouncing an infant on her lap, at the same time keeping an eye on the gang of noisy children racing up and down Brewer Street with their bats and balls.

"Malala," Sarah raised her voice. "Bring beer for Jan."

The brown slave appeared promptly with the beer, her gait strong, but still lopsided.

"Good morning, Master Jan."

"It's good to see you, Malala."

The scatter-brained Goosie persisted. "Did you hear about the first King Charles and his extra undershirt?" She paused to shout at a pint-sized youngster in the road. "Jacob! Stay away from the big boys or you'll get hurt. Go play with your sister."

"What extra undershirt?" I asked, curiously.

"The day he was beheaded was very cold and the King asked for an extra undershirt so the people wouldn't see him shiver and think he was afraid to die."

"Are you trying to prove how brave Charles I was?" interrupted Sarah.

"No, I'm trying to prove how mad the English are. They chop off the King's head and a few years later they want him back. Of course, I hear that Charles II is even handsomer than his father."

"Bah! He's nothing but a petticoat-chaser," said Sarah. "I don't know why the Netherlands bothered to save his life."

"There you are!" continued Goosie. "The English King has to be grateful to the Dutch for protecting him for so many years. So why the fuss over a few frigates?"

"Don't forget the King's little brother," I said.

James, Duke of York, had spent the exile in France with his mother, and hated everything to do with the Netherlands. At the Restoration he was made Lord High Admiral of the Navy. Maybe he was anxious to get his fleet into action.

"Little brothers don't count," exclaimed Goosie, triumphantly. "Only a King can declare war!"

In August the fleet put in at Boston. Word reached us, through the most trustworthy sources, that the fleet's Commander, Colonel Nicolls, had simply been commissioned to make a new determination of New England's boundaries. Reassured, everyone relaxed. Peg-Leg took the army up the Hudson to help Papa with another Indian outbreak and the *Roseboom* still had not returned from Virginia.

The English ships did not remain in Boston. They were soon streaming southward and we discovered, too late, that we had been duped. Even the Dutch ambassador in London, with all his agents, had failed to uncover the treachery. The King had secretly given his brother a charter to the territory between New England and Virginia and the fleet was here to seize it.

Stuyvesant rushed back from Fort Orange, reaching Manhattan just as the first English sail was sighted off the coast of Long Island. The next day I stood with the crowd on Weepers' Point as the four warships entered the harbor. The Flagship, *Guinea,* anchored by Nut Island, her decks lined with soldiers in bright red coats. The other three ships stationed themselves so as to seal off the Narrows.

Stuyvesant dispatched a delegation to the *Guinea* requesting an explanation for this intrusion. In return he received a demand for the unconditional surrender of all Dutch towns, forts, and strongholds in the name of his Majesty, King Charles II of England. The paper was unsigned, so Stuyvesant played for time by returning it for signature. Then he prepared for war. Every man, bound or free, was put to work with shovel and pick.

The Governor summoned me to his office.

"Over and over again I have begged the Amsterdam Board for a few warships to be stationed here and another 200 mercenaries," he growled. "I might as well not have wasted the paper and ink." He tapped his wooden leg against the desk for emphasis.

"I have ordered the garrison at Fort Orange sent down," he continued, "and I have dispatched an urgent request for volunteers from all the Long Island towns. From New Harlem I need my nine soldiers returned, plus every able-bodied man you can lay your hands on. Those four English ships, together, carry at most a total of 400 Redcoats. We have a standing army of 150. If we enlist every able-bodied civilian in town we will be almost up to 400. Report here first thing tomorrow."

The next morning I considered riding Prince, my black stallion, but it felt more natural to walk beside my volunteers, particularly as there were only eight. The nine soldiers had been sent on ahead.

As the Long Island towns had failed to provide a single volunteer, Peg-Leg could scarcely complain that New Harlem had produced only eight. In fact he made me an officer and gave me two pieces of advice.

"Get yourself a good-looking horse, Lieutenant Montagne, and always keep your eye on your men."

My men were assigned to construct new breastworks for Weepers' Point. As they shoveled, Stuyvesant stomped up and down the ramparts, bellowing encouragement to some hundred workers within range of his gravelly voice.

"Remember that righteousness shall prevail over duplicity, men. The English have committed an act of unparalleled treachery, while we are fighting for our homes and our families. God is on the side of the just. With His help we shall drive the Redcoats into the sea!"

At that moment a Dutch sloop, manned by slaves, appeared from behind Nut Island. The *Guinea* discharged one shot across her bow and ordered her to heave to, but she ran. Instantly the ship's cutter gave chase, firing in cold blood at the terrified slaves who quickly abandoned the sloop on Nut Island, escaping unharmed into the woods. God Almighty! The *Roseboom* was long overdue. Uncle must be warned.

Wednesday morning I arrived on horseback, this time with nine volunteers. I carried a gun as befitting an officer and at the last minute, for no good reason, I stuck Little Deer's knife into my belt.

The enemy had already been joined by several New England merchant ships, greedy vultures waiting to get in on the kill. Still no volunteers from Long Island. Word came that they did not dare leave their wives and children unprotected. No answer yet from Fort Orange.

At noon Stuyvesant received a 48-hour ultimatum from Nicolls. If we did not surrender by noon, Friday, the British would open fire and New Amsterdam would be razed to the ground. If we surrendered, Nicolls claimed that his Majesty's terms would be generous. In a fury, Peg-Leg tore the document to shreds so no one could read the terms.

Late afternoon a small craft flying Dutch colors was spotted coming through the narrows. Sarah came racing down Brewer Street, her hair not so red as it used to be but just as wild.

"It must be the *Roseboom!*" she shouted, pushing her way to the front of the crowd on Weepers' point.

Of course, all work stopped. I joined Sarah, just as the *Roseboom*, in full sail, emerged from the Narrows. Unaware of the danger, she swept toward Manhattan with seagulls skimming. Now I could see Isaack at the tiller, and Abram and Angel at the ropes. Then the *Guinea* fired a volley of grapeshot and the gulls scattered with surprise as the *Roseboom* obediently hove to.

With six men at the oars and an officer shouting instructions, the *Guinea's* cutter sped over to the yawl. When Uncle stood up to protest he was struck in the head by the butt of a musket, then thrown into the cutter.

"My God! The bloody Redcoats have killed him," yelled Sarah, shaking her fist at the *Guinea*.

"It takes more than one bump to kill a de Forest," I tried to reassure her.

After a brief conversation with Abram and Angel, the officer shouted more instructions and the cutter raced back to the *Guinea*. Across half a mile of water I watched my uncle being slowly lowered into the bowels of the enemy Flagship. From this distance it was impossible to tell if he was dead or alive.

To everyone's surprise, the *Roseboom* was released with cargo intact. Quickly raising the lugsail, she limped home.

I dismissed my men early and hurried over to the pier to question Abram and Angel. Sarah was there before me.

"They say Isaack is alive," she said. "The Redcoats have thrown him into the powder hold."

Abram explained that the officer of the cutter spoke some Dutch. It was he who informed them that the prisoner would be left to rot in the powder hold. Angel, still shaken by the experience, had nothing to add.

"If that blow on the head didn't kill him, the dust from the powder certainly will," continued Sarah. "One night in a powder hold is a death sentence to a man who can choke himself unconscious over a bit of ragweed."

Neither Abram nor Angel had any idea why Isaack had been captured or why they themselves had been released. The only question Abram could remember being asked was "What is your name?"

"What did you say?"

"Abram du Trieux, of course."

"Did they ask Isaack for his name?"

"No. He was unconscious. They asked me who he was and I told them."

I tried Angel again. "Did they ask for your name, Angel?"

He nodded. "I say ONE WORD: Angel."

Why had he put the emphasis on ONE WORD. I must remember to ask. There was no time for further conversation at the moment. Two Dutch soldiers had arrived to escort Abram and Angel to the Governor's office for interrogation. I followed Sarah back to Brewer Street, where I had left Prince in the tiny paddock behind their stable.

"We have to get Isaack out of there," she said. "Do you remember that time he almost died from cicada skins in his lungs? And he was much younger then."

I sat down on the top step, gun between my knees. Sarah sat down beside me.

"Peg-Leg is mad," she said. "How can we fight the bloody English? The Fort has only 24 cannon and none of them can even change direction without destroying our own homes. Those four English warships together have 89 cannon."

"No choice, Sarah. Stuyvesant is the commanding officer. When he says "FIRE," the soldiers fire. Don't think about numbers. It's strategy that counts, not numbers."

"You are as mad as Peg-Leg," she snorted. "Why are men driven to clash swords like bulls driven to ram horns?"

I laughed.

"Seriously, Sarah, what have you done to prepare for a siege?"

"We will hole up in the old cellar. Malala has already stocked it with a three-day supply of drinking water, and the boys have filled the rain barrels with canal water in case of fire."

"Please, Sarah, take the whole family up to New Harlem," I begged. "Stay at Vredendale with us until the fighting is over. You'll be safe there."

"Thank you," she said after a long pause." I'll send the boys up tomorrow with Susan to help Ursula. Not that Susan is much help to anyone. Isaack and Malala have always spoiled her. Now she is betrothed to that de Riemer boy and he spoils her too."

Then she added in a tone of voice that was not to be contradicted, "Malala and Angel and the baby stay right here with me in the old cellar. I will not leave without Isaack. God! What am I going to do about Isaack?"

For an instant my fingers brushed against the handle of Little Deer's knife. What would my Weckquasgeek blood-brother have done in my shoes?

That was easy. If Moose Foot had been captured, Little Deer would not be sitting here weighing his chances of success. He would be off rescuing his uncle.

I stood up. "I'll get him, Sarah," I said, heading for the stable.

Obviously the first step was to get myself out to the *Guinea*. The second step was to board her, and the third step was to find Uncle. Step four naturally depended on Isaack's situation. Was he conscious? Was he locked in somewhere? Was he tied up? If so, Little Deer's knife would come in handy. I did not believe in the powder-hold theory. Perhaps Abram misunderstood the officer's Dutch.

Nothing could be done until almost midnight. With time on my hands I found myself riding slowly up the Herrenstraat, past the cemetery and the little house where we first lived. Now I was opposite Marie's tavern. Just on the odd chance I took a quick look inside and there, to my surprise, was one of my volunteers, Ursula's brother, Jacobus. I joined him in a pint of beer and a dish of boiled tongue.

Jacobus was a good man, not as sharp as his father, but just as dependable. He gladly agreed to warn Ursula that four little de Forest boys plus an older sister would be descending on Vredendale some time tomorrow. He also promised to lead the New Harlem volunteers in the morning if I was not home in time.

As we left the tavern together, it occurred to me that Prince would soon be more of a liability than an asset. Jacobus was good with horses. Why not let him ride Prince home? Of course Jacobus was delighted and promised to take good care of the stallion.

By this time it was dark and the roads were almost deserted. Many families had already left the city to take refuge with friends elsewhere. Only a few lights showed in tavern windows.

My first task was to find a canoe. There were usually a few elderly rowboats beached on the Strand. If I could not find a canoe I would have to settle for the least noisy of these. Luck was with me. There was a perfectly sound canoe, with paddle, sitting on the pier as though waiting for me. I launched her without delay.

Originally I had planned to swim the half mile from Weepers' Point out to the *Guinea*. Fortunately I had the sense to realize that it would be much easier to take a canoe as far as Nut Island. From there it would be only a short swim of a hundred yards or so to the Flagship.

I hid the canoe on the far side of Nut Island, leaving my gun and shoes inside. Armed only with Little Deer's knife and a small wedge, I stepped cautiously into the water and swam leisurely around the tiny island until I was facing the *Guinea*. Here I waited for about an hour until the ship was completely dark except for two lamps, one fore, one aft, which I suspected would stay lit all night. Standing still in water up to one's neck sounds uncomfortable, but it was not. In fact the water was warmer than the air.

There was no moon but I could just see the watch standing on the *Guinea*'s bridge, outlined against the night sky. He could not see me because I was in the dark shadow of Nut Island. But there would be a long stretch of water before I reached the shadow of the ship. Slowly, with measured underwater strokes, I began to swim toward the Flagship.

The watch was paying more attention to Manhattan than to anything else, although every few minutes he would do a circle, scanning all horizons. My instinct was to take advantage of this and swim faster when he was facing Manhattan. But there could be others awake. I did not dare take the risk of even one splash.

At last I was in the black shadow of the *Guinea*, with waves slapping gently against her hull, and my fingers exploring her barnacles. She lay heavy in the water and the lower gun-ports were only a few yards above my head. I found a break in the caulking and drove my wedge into the seam for a toehold. The ship began to swing with the changing tide, and the grinding anchor-chain covered the noise of my scrambling up her side and through an empty gun-port.

I waited motionless until my eyes adjusted to a new degree of darkness. All around me the deck was covered with snoring bodies. Little Deer used to say that a Weckquasgeek could slide "like shadow," when necessary. In bare feet I slid "like shadow" between sleeping Redcoats.

After a few false starts I found the hatchway leading down into the *Guinea*'s hold. Here I located a compartment containing powder kegs, some lashed down as for a sea voyage, others unlashed, ready for battle. There was also a supply of planks and posts, apparently for shelving. Could Uncle be in here, lying in the dark, bound and gagged and maybe unconscious? I did not think so but I had to make sure. I placed Little Deer's knife safely on top of the pile of planks before crawling on hands and knees between rows of powder kegs.

Three times I whispered, "Uncle, are you there?"

There was no sign of Uncle, but I counted 50 kegs of powder and they were 30-pound kegs. This gave the *Guinea* 1500 pounds of powder and the four British warships together, probably 6000 pounds. Stuyvesant must be told.

Up until this moment luck had been with me. Now it appeared to be running out. When I tried to retrieve the knife it was not there. In the dark I ran my fingers from one end of the top plank to the other. The knife had simply vanished. At that moment I heard footsteps above, heading this way.

"What bloody fool left this hatch open?"

It was a gruff, threatening voice and, worse yet, its owner was swinging a lantern. I stepped back, into the darkest corner, as he tried unsuccessfully to peer down the hatchway. He began to descend, holding the ladder with one hand and the lantern in the other. I caught a glimpse of a pistol beneath his red coat.

Yes, I was scared. I was terrified. It was him or me. I lifted one of the posts. When the Redcoat reached the bottom rung, I swung hard. Without so much as a murmur, he crumpled, unconscious, into a heap at my feet.

After dragging the man into a corner, I "borrowed" his coat. It was much too large, but in the dark I could now easily be mistaken for a British soldier. Thanks to the lantern I found the missing knife. I simply had not realized that there were two different stacks of planks. Before continuing my search for Uncle, I extinguished the light. This time I remembered to close the hatch.

The first thing was to find myself a good hiding place. I chose the sail-cupboard on the main deck. It seemed unlikely that anyone was going to be looking for sails in the next few hours.

Relatively safe inside the cupboard, I sat down on a pile of canvas and tried to work out my next move. I had not really expected to find Uncle in the powder-hold. No Captain would let a prisoner anywhere near any powder. Either the officer on the cutter was making an idle threat or there was a misunderstanding caused by his limited Dutch.

The most likely place to keep a prisoner must be the ship's brig. Cautiously I set out to find it. A Redcoat on his way to take a piss, hurried past. He paid no attention to me.

The brig was a failure. Not only was it empty, it was unlocked and there was no guard, and no evidence of any recent occupancy. Disappointed I returned to my sail-cupboard.

It was very warm inside but I did not dare take off the red coat. Seated on my relatively comfortable pile of canvas, I am ashamed to say that I dozed off for a few minutes.

The sound of voices woke me. Two men were speaking English but the accent was so dreadful I could not understand a word. Then in the midst of the gibberish, I caught the phrase "cheese-head's cabin." The other voice answered something like "Twice, Gorblimey" before they passed out of range.

Cheese-head is English slang for Dutchman! They had to be talking about Uncle. How many Dutchmen could there be on this ship? What did "twice" refer to?

Thanks to the short nap my mind was clearer and I made a mental list of questions that needed answers:

    I. *Why did the English capture Uncle?*
    II. *Why did they hit him on the head?*
    III. *Why did they release Abram and Angel and a valuable cargo?*
    IV. *Why had Angel put the stress on "ONE WORD"?*
    V. *Assuming "cheese-head" referred to Uncle, why were the Redcoats so friendly as to put him in a cabin when there were very few cabins to be had on these ships? What did "twice" refer to?*

Now all I had to do was find a scenario that fitted reasonable answers to all the questions. It was hard to reconcile numbers II and V. If one planned to treat the prisoner to a cabin, one would hardly start by almost killing him.

Number III was equally puzzling. Abram reported a large cargo of excellent tobacco. What enemy ever turned down free tobacco?

It was not until I thought about number IV, that I began to get somewhere. Angel's emphasis on "ONE WORD" sounded like a suggestion that someone else had been overly talkative. That someone else could only be

Abram. When asked for the name of his unconscious companion, it would be just like Abram to say "Isaack de Forest, son of Jesse de Forest, famous leader of the Walloons, who would have been New Netherland's first Governor if he had lived."

This would also account for the discrepancy between II and V. Suppose Colonel Nicolls was, for some purpose, looking for a reliable, influential, long-time citizen of New Amsterdam. He could scarcely do better than my Uncle Isaack. The officer did not know anything about Uncle when he was struck and tossed into the cutter. At sea Uncle wore the same scruffy clothes as Abram and Angel. In the eyes of the meticulously uniformed Redcoats, this made all three of them equally deserving of a blow on the head. After hearing from Abram, however, Uncle was transferred more gently to the Flagship, where he was treated to a cabin.

Number III then became easy. Abram, Angel and cargo were all small fry compared to Uncle, who was the big catch. When you have the big catch within your grasp, you do not let yourself be distracted by small fry.

Now all I had to do was figure out why Nicolls wanted to capture an influential, local citizen in the first place. I was sure the motive was to persuade Governor Stuyvesant to surrender. He must have planned to tell Uncle something which Uncle would of course repeat to Stuyvesant. No, that would not work. Who would believe anything the enemy said? Nicolls must be planning to *show* Uncle something. Then Peg-Leg would be almost forced to believe. Show him what?

I was within an inch of the solution when someone shouted that a soldier had been attacked near the powder hold. There was a cry of "Action stations!" and in no time the commotion was unbelievable. The ship's bell rang again and again, while soldiers and seamen rushed about in every direction.

I realized now that whatever the solution, it was to Nicolls' advantage to treat Uncle well, which meant that it was high time for me to get out of there. I slipped from the sail-cupboard and followed the crowd. In the dark with the red coat on, no one noticed my bare feet. At the first opportunity I discarded the coat and dived overboard.

Unfortunately I miscalculated slightly and scraped my side against the ship's hull. It was painful but not serious, or so I thought. I was more upset by the fact that Little Deer's knife had come loose and was now at the bottom of the harbor.

It was not until I reached Nut Island and tried to launch my canoe, that I realized how weak I had become from loss of blood. I simply could not lift that canoe. Finally, after much pushing and pulling, I was afloat and headed for the pier. Best of all, thanks to Angel, I had solved the mystery behind the kidnapping of Uncle Isaack.

It was still dark when I stumbled up the de Forest front steps. Sarah was already awake.

"God Almighty! What's happened to you?"

"Nothing," I gasped but my head was spinning. "Must see Peg-Leg," I whispered. "Uncle home soon." With this I collapsed to the floor, completely unable to move or speak.

I felt nothing when Sarah applied Kierstede's ointment to my left arm and leg and wrapped them with strips of linen. At one point Malala appeared and tried to spoon some chicken broth into me. Someone put a pillow under my head and covered me with a blanket.

"You are going nowhere, young man," said Sarah. "Sleep a while now. When you wake you can tell me everything and I will take a message to Peg-Leg for you." She forced some Dutch gin down my throat and that was the last thing I remember.

I slept 24 hours. It was Sarah's voice that woke me.

"The ultimatum expires in six hours, Jan. If you want me to take a message to Peg-Leg you have to wake up."

"It's only Thursday morning," I murmured.

"No. It's Friday morning. You have been out like a light for 24 hours. Isaack's back, unharmed except for the bump on his head. He spent most of yesterday at the Fort arguing with Peg-Leg and the Council. Now what is this message you want me to deliver?

"Thank you, Sarah, but I can deliver it myself, now."

"You cannot! In the first place you have no clothes on except a pair of drawers. Angel dried your wet things by the fire but they are all torn. Looks like they were slashed by a knife. Malala has gone to Vredendale to get your Sunday clothes. She will be back in an hour. Until then just wrap yourself in that blanket. Now tell me what's happened.

I told Sarah the whole story. For once she did not interrupt except occasionally to slap her forehead and mutter, "The man is mad." When I finished, all she said was, "What do I tell Peg-Leg?"

"There are actually two messages. First and most important, tell him that the *Guinea* is carrying 50 kegs of gunpowder. They are 30-pound kegs. Write it down. This means that the *Guinea* has 1500 pounds and the four warships together probably have 6000."

With difficulty she found a scrap of paper and wrote doom the figures and I initialed them.

"What about the second message?"

"Isaack was duped, Sarah. "Nicolls badly wants Stuyvesant to surrender. So he kidnaps a highly respected citizen, and shows him something that makes surrender almost mandatory."

"Such as?"

"Such as apparent proof that the British have 800 men, not 400."

"Apparent proof?"

"Suppose Nicolls arranged for Uncle to be locked in a cabin where the porthole has been boarded over. Only a small crack remains, an obvious oversight. When the bosun pipes the call to assembly, Nicolls knows that the prisoner will be trying to count Redcoats through the crack, so he has ordered every soldier to pass by that boarded-up port-hole 'twice' on his way to assembly."

"You could be right," Sarah admitted, grudgingly. "Isaack says that, unbeknownst to the enemy, he was able to count 200 redcoats on the *Guinea* alone, which means 800 for the four ships. Peg-Leg says Isaack was duped. The rest of the Council believe Isaack has the right of it and the result was a real brouhaha. Peg-Leg adjourned the meeting and tabled the matter until sunrise this morning, which is just about now. Isaack left for the Fort half an hour ago."

On a second scrap of paper she scribbled, "Isaack duped. 100 Redcoats on *Guinea*. Not 200."

Again I initialed it and she stuffed both scraps into her pocket as Angel came in with beer and a huge bowl of suppawn for me.

"Help Jan with his breakfast, Angel. Then take your shovel and go join your work group." The bossy one paused slightly before giving me my instructions. "Jan, you are in charge of baby David." She pointed to the old oak cradle with its tiny occupant. "He's fed and he's dry, and with any luck he'll still be asleep when I get back." She tied her best cap down on top of that wild hair and set off for the Fort.

"How you feeling this morning, Master Jan?" Angel helped me over to the table.

"Much better, thank you, Angel." I took a swig of the beer. "By the way, I wonder if you can remember something for me. When the officer on that cutter asked for my uncle's name, did Abram say simply 'Isaack de Forest', or did he add details?"

"He add many, many words. Too many I don't understand."

"Thank you, Angel. You have been very helpful."

He gave me a friendly smile, picked up his shovel and was gone.

I knew it would happen. The minute I was alone with baby David, he began to cry. As a father of three, one would assume that I had long ago mastered the art of pacifying a crying baby, but I never had. I tried pulling the cradle closer to the table, a difficult procedure with nothing but a blanket wrapped around oneself. This way I could rock the cradle with my good foot and eat the suppawn with my good hand. David did not approve. So I gave up eating and tried singing the songs my mother used to sing to us. He cried louder. I was soon reduced to pacing the floor, rocking the baby in my arms, holding on to my blanket and singing, all at the same time and to no avail.

Help finally arrived in the form of Malala, who quickly took the hysterical infant from my arms. Almost immediately the screaming stopped and after a couple of happy, little burps, baby David was back in his cradle and fast asleep.

Malala had brought everything I needed to wear, and I felt much better fully dressed. My arm and leg were still very stiff but did not hurt much unless I bumped into something.

Sarah returned as I was finishing off the suppawn. Somewhat out of breath she sat down opposite me.

"Did you get to see Stuyvesant? I asked quickly.

"Of course I did. I told the sentry that I had a private message for the Governor from Monsieur Jehan de la Montagne." She laughed. "I may have forgotten to add the 'Junior.' Can I help it if he thought I meant your father? Anyway, Peg-Leg left the meeting and saw me in his office."

" Well, what did he say?"

"He said only a mad man would board an enemy warship, and it is a miracle that you are still alive. He claims that the gunpowder figures are very important and he is going to see to it that you get a promotion."

"What did he say about Isaack being duped?" I asked.

"I didn't give him the second message," was the curt reply.

"Why ever not, Sarah?

"Peg-Leg is much more likely to surrender if he thinks there are 800 Redcoats, not 400."

"Then I'll tell him myself," I said angrily. "I have to tell him, Sarah. It would be dishonorable not to tell him. And believe me it will make no difference. Stuyvesant is a soldier right down to the bottom of that wooden stump. He is not going to surrender whatever happens."

"Well I hate the English," she said, "but I would rather live under an English King than die for that greedy Board of Directors back in

Amsterdam. It is surely more important to save lives than to obey a commanding officer who is mad."

Goosie van Cortlandt barged in at this point, without bothering to knock. "Have you heard the news, Sarah?" she cried. "Oh, I didn't see you, Jan. I hope I'm not interrupting anything."

Out of the corner of my eye I could see Sarah frantically signaling me to keep my mouth shut. I stood up slowly. "Hello Goosie. I'm just leaving," I said but she blocked my way.

"Did you hear about the big excitement on the *Guinea*, night before last? Someone boarded her and seriously wounded a British sergeant. Nicolls has sent word that the culprit will be hanged from the yardarm when they find him."

"It must have been an Indian," said Sarah. "No Christian would be crazy enough to board an enemy ship of war."

"Another thing," said Goosie. "My Oloff is circulating a surrender petition for people to sign. It will be presented to Stuyvesant by old Dominie Megapolensis, just before the deadline. If we get enough signatures Peg-Leg is bound to surrender." Goosie's voice was becoming shriller. "Even Stuyvesant's own son, Balthasar, has signed."

"Balthasar is only seventeen," muttered Sarah as I deftly bypassed Goosie and set out for the Fort.

She called after me, "Why are you limping, Jan?" I pretended not to hear. Let Sarah think up an explanation for that one. A few minutes later I heard someone running behind me. It was Goosie again.

"Wait for me, Jan."

I had no choice. If I tried to go faster it would only exaggerate my limp. It would also be extremely rude. So I waited, and we walked on together.

"Sarah says you have an important secret message for Peg-Leg, Jan. Will you tell me if I cross my heart not to tell a soul?"

I shook my head. "No."

"Did you know that Nicasius de Sille has pasted together the ultimatum that Peg-Leg tore into a hundred pieces? Nicolls' terms really are generous. If we surrender before noon today we get to keep our own houses, our own religion, and even our own government officials, except for Governor. Nicolls would replace Stuyvesant as Governor."

"Yes, I did know that."

"Do you know who Goldie is, Jan?" Goosie had a disconcerting habit of jumping from one subject to another. "Goldie is sweet on the artillery officer and he told her that New Amsterdam has only 600 pounds of usable gunpowder left. Now, what do you think of that, Jan Montagne?"

I said nothing but if Goosie had the facts right, this was a disaster. Six hundred pounds would not last a whole day.

Now we were passing Weepers' Point. Over the heads of breastwork-diggers I could see the *Guinea* rocking gently with the morning swell. Nearby, Nut Island lay green and silent, deserted except for birds.

It looked as though half the inhabitants of New Amsterdam were milling around outside the Fort. Hoping to disentangle myself from Goosie I plunged into the crowd, only to find myself face to face with Doctor Hans Kierstede and his silly little pointed beard. I had barely spoken to him since Peternella's death.

"Three hours left to the deadline, Jan," he announced. "Dominie Megapolensis should be here any minute with the surrender petition. It is a good thing your Uncle discovered we were up against 800 Redcoats. Stuyvesant would never surrender to a mere 400."

"Would we have a chance against 400?" I asked quickly.

"No chance! If we do not surrender by noon today, New Amsterdam will be one mass of burning debris by tomorrow."

I had been trying to work out a winning strategy for Peg-Leg. We were outmanned 400 to 150. We were outgunned 89 to 24. And we were out-powdered, if there is such a word, 6000 to 600. This did not leave much room for strategy.

Out in the harbor the *Guinea* began to raise some canvas. At first I thought she was just moving away from Nut Island to discourage any more midnight visitors. Then I realized that all four warships were under sail bristling with cannon and heading this way. As if in response the Fort gate swung open and Peg-Leg himself marched out followed by five platoons. He charged up the Heerenstraat posting men at vantage points in case of an attempted landing.

"Jan has an important message for the Governor," announced Goosie to no one in particular.

"Here comes the petition," cried the Doctor as the ancient Dominie Megapolensis shuffled slowly along the Marketfield, supported on either side by his two sons.

Having distributed the men to his satisfaction, Peg-Leg stomped energetically back toward the Fort.

"Here's your chance to speak to him, Jan," cried Goosie.

Sarah was right. It must be better to surrender than to fight to the last man for that mercenary Board of Directors back in Amsterdam.

"I've changed my mind," I said. All I wanted was to get home to my family and my beloved Vredendale.

Peg-Leg reentered the Fort and swung himself vigorously up on to the bastion where gunners stood ready.

"My God! He's going to fire!" shouted the Doctor. "He's not going to wait for the ultimatum! Megapolensis won't make it in time!" He dashed toward the black-robed figure, still mincing along on tiptoe, skirts dragging in the mud.

"Lift him up, men!"

They lifted. With an air of benign surprise the Dominie glided through the gate, toes a few inches off the ground and still paddling. I slipped through in his wake.

Inside, officials in their long black coats waited anxiously. Uncle stood in the front row, silver buttons straining against middle-aged waistline. The walls were alive with soldiers and above one could just see the English topsails against a blue September sky. But every eye was upon the tall, commanding figure on the west bastion, and the eager gunner beside him with lighted match.

"Petrus! Wait, Petrus!" cried Megapolensis from the foot of the bastion. "I have an important document." He held aloft the scroll.

Peg-Leg turned at the word "document" and paused while the old man was boosted up a ladder. "If that is another letter urging surrender, you can save your breath, my friend," he rasped. "I'd rather be carried out of here in my coffin!" The silver band on his stump flashed impatiently as he took the scroll and began to read.

There were 93 signatures on the petition which began, "We, your sorrowful community and subjects, . . ." Peg-Leg read only as far as the eighth name, "Balthasar Stuyvesant." Then his head slumped and the ancient Dominie led him away.

I watched the tears run down Uncle's cheeks as the white flag rose above Fort Amsterdam. Only the seagulls overhead cried out in protest.

Unusual Words

Aanspreker   Funeral inviter

Algonkian   Group of related tribes along the Atlantic coast

Blikskaters   Thunder and lightning (Dutch)

Bone-ace   Card game, probably from (French) good ace

Bowery   Plantation or farm

Canarsie   Long Island tribe

Deo gratia   By the grace of God (Latin)

Domkop   Blockhead (Dutch)

Doucement   Softly (French)

Flapdrol   Milksop (Dutch)

Hoerenloper   Whore-chaser (Dutch)

Hutspot   Stew (Dutch)

Jesuits' bark   Quinine

Huron   Iriquois tribe, near Lake Huron

Kinderen   Children (Dutch)

Knaap   Boy (Dutch)

Krankzinnig   Crazy (Dutch)

Mekane   Indian dogs

Milles tonnerres   A thousand thunders (French)

Mirabile dictu   Wonderful to say (Latin)

Mohawk   Meaning man-eater in Algonkian, fierce Iriquois tribe with headquarters in the Mohawk Valley

Mon vieux   My old one (French term of affection)

Olykoek   Doughnut (Dutch)

Per deos immortales   By the immortal gods (Latin)

Potverdikki   Mild exclamation (Dutch)

Raritan   Algonkian tribe west of Staten Island

Rensselaerswyck   Ship on which the family cross the Atlantic

Sachem   Tribal chief or wise man

Samp   Corn

Sang de Dieu   God's blood (French)

Siwanoy   Algonkian tribe in modern Westchester county

Slampamper   Good-for-nothing (Dutch)

Suppawn   Corn porridge

Swannekin   Algonkian word for European

Swannendale   De Vries's failed plantation on the Delaware

Wampum   Money in the form of shells

Waywahtassee   Fireflies

Weckquasgeek   Algonkian tribe with headquarters at Dobbs Ferry

Wilden   Native Americans (Dutch)

Yockey   Apple treat

People

Allerton, Isaac Merchant; *Mayflower* passenger, later in Manhattan

Allerton, Sacky Son of Isaac

Andriessen, Albert Norwegian farmer, with wife Annetje and brother Lanky

Block, Captain Captain of ship, the *Tiger*, wrecked on Manhattan

Bogardus, Everardus Minister in Manhattan

Bornstra, Gertrude Married to Hendrick de Forest

Bornstra, Margariet Cousin of Rachel, and her correspondent

Bronck, Jonas The first settler on the mainland, which became the Bronx; his bowery, named Emmaus, located at Southern Boulevard and Willis Avenue

Crazy One Deranged Weckquasgeek

Dam, Jan Slave overseer, married to Mme. Vinje-Dam

De Forest, Hendrick Son of Jesse, sister of Rachel

De Forest, Isaack Son of Jesse; brewer (for sister Rachel, see Montagne)

De Forest, Jesse (1570 to 1624) Leader of the Walloon refugees, who died of malaria before reaching Manhattan

De Vries, Captain David Bowery owner

Du Trieux, Marie Tavern-keeper; daughter of Philippe by first wife

Du Trieux, Philippe and Susannah Children Sarah, Sutje, and Abram

Grietje Leading Manhattan whore, married to Antony Jansen, the Turk

Hans Blacksmith's apprentice

Happy Squirrel Bastard son of van Tienhoven and Wehtah

Hudde, Andries Head of Governor van Twiller's Council

Jans, Anneke   Widow with five children

Jansen, Antony   The Turk, married to Grietje

Jonas, Tryntje   Midwife; mother of Anneke Jans

Kieft, Willem   Governor of New Netherland, 1638–1647

Kierstede, Dr. Hans   Doctor in Manhattan

Kumtassa   Indian runner

Kuyter, Jochem Pieterse   Danish colonist at Zegendale

Little Deer   Jan's Indian friend

Loockermans, Govert   Business partner of Isaac Allerton

Melyn, Cornelis   Danish colonist

Minuit, Peter   Governor of New Amsterdam, 1626–1631

Montagne, Jehan   Medical doctor and adviser to two governors of New Netherland

Montagne, Rachel de Forest   Wife of Jehan, daughter of Jesse de Forest, mother of Jesse, Jan, Little Rachel, Marie, and Will

Moose Foot   Indian friend of Montagne family, uncle of Little Deer

Pikes, Vincent and *Peternella*   Brother and sister from Slooterdijk, Netherlands

Rechnewac   Weckquasgeek chief, brother of Moose Foot

Rembrandt   Famous artist; sketcher of Jesse de Forest

Schellinger   Captain of *Rensselaerswyck*

Stam   Cargo officer of *Rensselaerswyck*

Stieffy   Hog dealer

Switzer, Apollonia   Granddaughter of Claes, the wheelwright

Switzer, Claes   Wheelwright, tenant; at Otterspoor, then Turtle Bay

Tattita   Little Deer's mother

Thomas, Cornelius   Blacksmith from Rotterdam, married to the Muis

Tobias   Indentured to Hendrick de Forest

Van Cortland, Goosie   Neighbor of Sarah, married to Oloff

Van Curler, Jacob   Neighbor of Montagne family at Otterspoor

Van Rensselaer, Kiliean   Amsterdam diamond merchant and patroon;

absentee owner of large tracts
of New Netherland

Van Tienhoven, Cornelis
Company bookkeeper, later
Secretary ("Sharkface")

Van Twiller, Wouter Governor
of New Amsterdam,
1632–1638

Vermilye, Isa New Harlem settler;
father of Ursula

Vinje-Dam, Madame The
town's leading gossip-monger,
known as "the Witch";
wife of Jan Dam

Wehtah Little Deer's sister

Willem Indentured to Hendrick
de Forest

Note 1   The first 12 African slaves, who arrived 1625–1626, were Jan Premero, who
married Maria Grande and was murdered; Manuel de Gerrit de Reus ("The
Giant"), hanged; Jan t'Fort Orange, married Maria Grande; Simon Congo;
Anthony Portugies; Paulo d'Angola; Gracia d'Angola; Little Anthony; Little
Manuel; Big Manuel; Pieter Santomee; and Jan Francisco.

Note 2   All the characters in the book are part of the historical record except for Little
Deer and his family. A few names have been modified to avoid confusion.

Places

Aque-an-Ounck   Now the Hutchinson River

Anneke Jans Farm   Buried beneath the World Trade Center site

Claes the Wheelwright's Cabin   At Turtle Bay; beneath the United Nations building

Fort Orange   Now Albany

Heerenstratt   Early name for Broadway

Hell Gate   Treacherous passage between East River and Long Island Sound (danger largely removed by blasting in the 19th century)

Hutchinson House   Site on the west side of Hutchinson River Parkway, south of Cross Country Parkway

Manhattan   Island of hills

Montagne's Creek   Later Harlem Creek; from East River about 109th Street, navigable as far as Fifth Avenue; filled in during the 19th century

Nepperhan, The   Later known as the Sawmill River; entered Hudson where Yonkers Railroad Station is today.

Nipnischen   Small Weckquasgeek stronghold located at Henry Hudson Parkway about 233rd Street

Nut Island   Governor's Island

Otterspoor   On Montagne's Creek; built by Jacob van Curler

Shorakapkok   Indian village, north of Dyckman Street at Payson Avenue

Slangberg   Snake Mountain, later modern Mount Morris; stub of mountain is still there, which is why there is no Fifth Avenue between 120th Street and 125th Street

Vredendale   De Montagne's bowery, extending from about 105th Street to 120th Street, close to Saint Nicholas Avenue

Wading Place, The   Site of original Kingsbridge, built in 1693; north end of Manhattan altered in 20th century by construction of Harlem Ship Canal; site of bridge located on 230th Street at Kingsbridge Avenue

Waterfall, The   The remnants can still seen from the

Northbound Park Drive at
about 105th Street

Weckquasgeek Headquarters
Located on Wickers Creek,
which enters the Hudson at
Dobbs Ferry

Weepers' Point   South tip of
Manhattan; named after
Weepers' Tower in Amsterdam,
where loved ones waved their
last farewells

Tiger, The   Ship, the remains of
which subway workers found
in 1916 at Dey Street and
Greenwich Street, which was
the Hudson River shoreline

Zegendale   Kuyter's bowery;
house located about 128th
Street and East River

Afterword

Nicolls proved a benevolent Governor, permitting the Dutch to keep their homes and their religion and to elect their own officials.

Peter Stuyvesant was summoned to the Fatherland to answer charges in connection with the surrender of New Netherland. He took Jehan Montagne with him as adviser. The hearings lasted three years, but Stuyvesant was fully exonerated. He returned to his family and his Manhattan bowery which, to this day, is referred to as "The Bowery."

Now in his seventies, Jehan remained in the Fatherland until his death a few years later.

Jan stayed active in Harlem affairs. He and Ursula had five children, including a girl named Peternella. He died soon after his father.

Isaack died in 1674 and was one of the last to be buried in the little cemetery on the Heerenstraat, now called Broadway. Sarah remained in the house on Stone Street, formerly Brewer Street, until her death in 1692. She was survived by 7 of her 14 children. All 7 remained in the city until after her death.

Little Rachel, who was the heroine of Wiltwyck after her escape from the Esopus, died in childbirth in October of '64, one month after the surrender. She was 30 years old.

Marie de Trieux, after many arrests, mostly for serving alcohol to Indians, was eventually banned from New Amsterdam. She went only as far as Fort Orange and seems to have returned within a few years. Her second husband, Jan Peeck, was a fur trader who anchored so often on the same kill that it was named for him. The city that grew up on the banks of that kill is called Peekskill.

Storm, the Norwegian boy born on board the *Rensselaerwyck,* adopted the surname Van der Zee and became the ancestor of the Van der Zee family of Albany.

Kiliaen van Rensselaer never did visit the New World, but after his death his son, Jeremias van Rensselaer, married Maria, the daughter of Oloff and Anna ("Goosie") van Cortlandt.

Susan Hutchinson had forgotten how to speak English after her two years with the Siwanoy. When she was 17 she married John Cole and is now the ancestor of about 100,000 Americans. The Aque-an-ounck became known as the Hutchinson River, and today thousands commute daily along the Hutchinson River Parkway with scarcely a thought for the brave woman its name commemorates.

It was customary for an Indian to take the name of an important person he had killed. Wampage, the young Siwanoy who led the raid on Anne Hutchinson, took the name "Ann Hook." His signature appears on land deeds farther and farther away as the Siwanoy migrated. The final deed was in the Highland Mountains where, with the trembling hand of a very old man, he signed away the last domain of his people.

Nine years after the surrender a Dutch fleet recaptured New York and renamed it New Orange. the Dutch held it for 14 months before the States General of the Netherlands traded it back to the English, calling it "a place of no importance."

Sarah and Isaack had a grandson named Jesse de Forest, whose spoon I now own.

The Spoon

As a girl I was fascinated by a battered old family spoon that my father had inherited through his grandmother, Blanche Wendell. On the back was inscribed "N & I D F" and nobody had any idea whose initials these were. "You can have it if you can figure out who it belonged to," said Dad.

It was not until I went off to Smith College in Northampton, Massachusetts, with instructions to pay a call on great-cousin Anna Waterbury, that I had any success.

"Aha!" exclaimed the nonagenarian. "So Blanche got one of those spoons too. They are historically important. I gave mine to the Albany Museum and you must too."

I privately determined to hang on to my spoon.

Cousin Anna told me that the spoons had belonged to her (and Blanche's) great-great-great-grandparents who were married in Albany in 1718. Their names were Neeltje Quackenbush and Jesse de Forest. ("I" apparently stood for "J.") She also wrote down for me exactly how I was descended from these two, but she knew nothing about them or their ancestors except that the family was one of the first to settle in New Netherland.

"Probably outcasts," said my history professor. "Holland was the most comfortable place in Europe in those days. Nobody left Holland but fools and outcasts." Anyhow, I had my names and the spoon was mine.

When I was 20 I got married and went off to the Midwest, with spoon, to raise my own family. Every time I looked at that spoon I would wonder about my outcasts. When friends spoke of the terrible trials their grandparents weathered on their way to this country, I wished I knew how my outcasts had fared.

In the meantime, my parents' house was broken into and all their silver stolen. If I had not taken my spoon it would long ago have been melted down into a few dollars worth of silver.

It was not until the children were grown and I returned to New York that I began to dig into the early history of New Netherland. I learned that the first 30 families to settle here were not Dutch at all. They were Walloon refugees who had fled to Holland from what is today Belgium, but was then under Spanish control. The leader of these refugees turned out to be the great-grandfather of my spoon. Also named Jesse de Forest, he did not live to reach Manhattan but three of his children did. They became the first to settle in what is today called Harlem. This is their story. It is also the story of the fierce Weckquasgeeks whose hunting grounds surrounded the family. And, perhaps even more important, it is the story of the first twelve African slaves to be sent to New Netherland in 1626.

All persons of European origin and all the African slaves are real people. Most of the Indians are real, including Chief Rechnewac who lived in a small village near what would today be 102nd Street and Park Avenue. Little Deer and members of his family are imaginary.

—Dorothy Hayden Truscott